CUBA IN REVOLUTION

NOTES ON CONTRIBUTORS

ROLANDO E. BONACHEA and NELSON P. VALDÉS are Ph.D. candidates in history, Bonachea at Georgetown University in Washington, D.C., and Valdés at the University of New Mexico in Albuquerque. Together they have edited *Che: Selected Works of Ernesto Guevara* (MIT Press, 1969) and *The Selected Works of Fidel Castro* (three volumes, forthcoming from MIT Press).

LUIS AGUILAR is Associate Professor of History at Georgetown University and was a professor at the University of Oriente in Cuba. He is the editor of *Marxism in Latin America* (Alfred A. Knopf, 1968), and author of *Cuba 1933: Prologue to Revolution* (Cornell University Press, 1972) as well as many articles for journals.

GIL CARL ALROY is Associate Professor of Political Science at Hunter College of the City University of New York. He is the author of *The Involvement of Peasants in Internal Wars* (1966), editor of *Attitudes Toward Jewish Statehood in the Arab World* (1971), and *Middle East War and Military Science* (forthcoming).

MARIO BENEDETTI is a Uruguayan author, cultural adviser to the Cuban Government, and one of the editors of the Montevideo weekly *Marcha*.

COLE BLASIER is Professor of Political Science and Director of the Center for Latin American Studies, University of Pittsburgh. He is the author of many articles and editor of *Constructive Change in Latin America* (University of Pittsburgh Press, 1968).

RICHARD FAGEN is Associate Professor of Political Science at Stanford University. He has written several books, including *The Transformation of Political Culture in Cuba* (Stanford University Press, 1969), and many articles.

MICHEL GUTELMAN, an agricultural economist, teaches at the Institut des Hautes Études de L'Amérique Latine in France. For several years he was an adviser to the Cuban Government. He is the author of the extremely useful work *L'Agriculture socialisée à Cuba* (Paris, 1967).

RICARDO LEYVA is the pseudonym of a graduate student at an American university.

C. IAN LUMSDEN teaches political economy at the University of Toronto. He has written several essays on Cuba and is the editor of *The Americanization of Canada* (University of Toronto Press, 1970).

GILBERT MERKX is a Venezuelan by birth and Associate Professor of Sociology at the University of New Mexico. He is the author of several articles.

CARMELO MESA-LAGO is Associate Professor of Economics and Associate Director of the Center for Latin American Studies, University of Pittsburgh. He has written many scholarly works on the Cuban Revolution, including *The Labor Sector and Socialist Distribution in Cuba* (Praeger, 1968), and *Cuba: A Decade of Revolution* (University of Pittsburgh Press, 1971), which he edited.

JAMES O'CONNOR is Associate Professor of Economics at San Jose State College, has served as a consultant to the Peace Corps, and is presently an editor of the journal *Socialist Revolution*. He is the author of *The Origins of Socialism in Cuba* (Cornell University Press, 1970) and has written many articles.

HEBERTO PADILLA was born in 1932 in Pinar del Río, Cuba. He has been a reporter for *Prensa Latina* in London, and is the author of many poems. Considered by many one of the outstanding poets of Cuba, he published in 1968 a book of poems, *Fuera de Juego,* which placed him in difficulty with the government. In March 1971 he was arrested for alleged counterrevolutionary activities and released a month later, after "confessing his guilt." He currently lives in Cuba.

Cuba in Revolution

ROLANDO E. BONACHEA

AND

NELSON P. VALDÉS

ANCHOR BOOKS
DOUBLEDAY & COMPANY, INC.
GARDEN CITY, NEW YORK
1972

ACKNOWLEDGMENTS

Acknowledgment to use copyrighted material has been given in the footnotes at the beginning of each selection. Our thanks are due to the distinguished scholars whose works we have been fortunate in assembling in this volume. Our grateful appreciation also goes to Dr. Janice Hopper and Dr. Luis Aguilar of Georgetown University, who stimulated our thinking and our work; and to Gilbert Merkx, Fred Padula, friends and colleagues.

The Anchor Books edition is the first publication of
CUBA IN REVOLUTION
Anchor Books edition: 1972

This book is dedicated to:
Maxine, Alisa Lynn, and Ricardo
Mary E. and Anna Maria

PREFACE

In recent Latin American history, no other event has stirred so great a controversy as the Cuban Revolution. This social experiment represents a unique model of the manner in which a group of revolutionary leaders, guided by a charismatic man, are trying to bring about a complete change in the character and substance of their own society and people. Furthermore, it is one of the most radical departures from Latin American history ever to have occurred.

The Revolution's impact, however, extended far beyond Cuban borders. It not only contributed to awakening the unfulfilled expectations of millions in Latin America (and the capitalist world) but also abruptly brought the Cold War into the Western Hemisphere and sought to spearhead continental revolution. In addition to focusing world attention on Cuba during the first decade of revolution, the process has prompted the scholarly analysis which it deserves.

Due to space limitations, we have only dealt in a limited way with the external repercussions of Cuba's social upheaval. Similarly, the relations between Cuba and the world powers, as well as the Latin American nations, are not discussed in this volume. Our concern centers mainly on the internal developments of the Revolution: social origins, politics, economics, labor, and cultural change. Unquestionably, much remains to be said with regard to the roles of women and youth, or the changes in the judicial system, the military, or religion.

Our objective in this book is to present some of the radical and thorough changes that have transpired within Cuba during the first ten years of revolution, as well as to discuss the most important aspects and issues of the Revolution.

CONTENTS

Preface   ix

Part I: SOCIAL ORIGINS OF THE REBELLION   1

    Introduction   1

    1. *Gil Carl AlRoy,* "The Peasantry in the Cuban
       Revolution"   3

    2. *Cole Blasier,* "Social Revolution: Origins in Mex-
       ico, Bolivia, and Cuba"   18

    3. *James O'Connor,* "Cuba: Its Political Economy"   52

    4. *Gilbert W. Merkx* and *Nelson P. Valdés,* "Revolu-
       tion, Consciousness, and Class: Cuba and
       Argentina"   82

Part II: POLITICS OF REVOLUTION   111

    A. GOALS AND METHODS   111
    Introduction   111

    5. "Program Manifesto of the 26th of July Move-
       ment"   113

    6. *Luis Aguilar,* "Revolution and Counterrevolu-
       tion"   141

    B. INSTITUTIONS AND STRUCTURES   153
    Introduction   153

    7. *Richard Fagen,* "Charismatic Authority and the
       Leadership of Fidel Castro"   154

    8. *Fidel Castro,* "On the Question of Revolutionary
       Charisma"   169

    9. *Cuban Communist Party,* "Bureaucracy and Rev-
       olution"   171

    10. *Richard Fagen,* "Mass Mobilization in Cuba:
       The Symbolism of Struggle"   201

xii   *Contents*

Part III: FIGHTING UNDERDEVELOPMENT   225

    A. THE ECONOMY   225
    Introduction   225
11. *Michel Gutelman,* "Cuba's Lessons on Economic
      Policies"   231
12. *Michel Gutelman,* "The Socialization of the
      Means of Production in Cuba"   238
13. *Fidel Castro,* "Report on the Sugar Harvest"   261
14. *Fidel Castro,* "The Problem of Underdevelop-
      ment"   305
15. *Fidel Castro,* "Report on the Cuban Economy"   317

    B. LABOR AND REVOLUTION   357
    Introduction   357
16. *Carmelo Mesa-Lago,* "Economic Significance of
      Unpaid Labor in Socialist Cuba"   384
17. *The Revolutionary Orientation Commission,* "The
      Problem of Absenteeism"   413
18. "Workers' Dossiers Law"   417

Part IV: SOCIAL DEVELOPMENT   421

    Introduction   421
19. *Nelson P. Valdés,* "The Radical Transformation
      of Cuban Education"   422
20. *Ricardo Leyva,* "Health and Revolution in Cuba" 456

Part V: CULTURE AND REVOLUTIONARY IDEOLOGY   497

    Introduction   497
21. *Mario Benedetti,* "Present Status of Cuban Cul-
      ture"   500
22. *Heberto Padilla,* "Out of the Game" (Poem)   527
23. *C. Ian Lumsden,* "The Ideology of the Revolu-
      tion"   529

Part I

++

SOCIAL ORIGINS OF
THE REBELLION

INTRODUCTION

Since the very moment that the revolutionaries attained power in Cuba, scholars have tried to answer the controversial question "What social class overthrew the regime of Fulgencio Batista?" Some have contended that the peasantry made the successful rebellion, while others have minimized its role. In the following essay by Gil Carl AlRoy, it is made quite clear that discussions of peasant participation depend heavily on the political ideologies of the authors one may read, and that the extent and manner of peasant participation still remain obscure.

An interpretation with numerous adherents in the United States is that the political and military struggle against the *ancien régime* was the work of the middle class. The "middle-class thesis" maintains that the desertion of the middle class caused Batista's regime to disintegrate from within and the armed forces to evaporate. The proponents of this school claim that although the rank and file of the Rebel Army was predominantly peasant in origin, its leadership originated in the bourgeoisie, and that the social composition of the revolutionary force was determined by its leadership. A variant of this thesis suggests that the revolution was led by *déclassé* middle-class revolutionaries, that is, by members of the bourgeoisie who were totally alienated from their own class. Cole Blasier, in his useful and enlightening study, surveys the literature on causes, precipitants, preconditions, and social origins of revolution in Mexico, Bolivia, and Cuba.

Several scholars, among them James O'Connor in the outstanding study presented here, have observed that the middle class tended to be a passive spectator in the island's politics, and that the rebellion against Batista had a unique classless character since it was fought by sections of *all* social classes.

The article by Merkx and Valdés comparing Cuba and Argentina, on the other hand, argues that the question of the social composition of the revolutionary groups has been posed in the wrong manner. What is important, they state, is the fact that the social roots of the Cuban revolutionaries cut across classes, and they are united by a generational consciousness. Moreover, this phenomenon can be traced to particular social structures and historical developments.

1

THE PEASANTRY IN THE CUBAN REVOLUTION*

Gil Carl AlRoy

I

The involvement of peasants in the rebellions and revolutions of the distant past has been impressive in certain respects, but never acquired quite the importance attributed to it in our own time. In terms of the sheer weight of their numbers, the vastness of the peasants' involvement in some internal wars of the past may perhaps never be duplicated. Over twenty million Chinese peasants were killed in the terrible T'ai-p'ing (1850–1864). Nor was the significance of these colossal figures limited to sheer mass, as the Mexican Revolution illustrates. But never before has so much reliance been put on the peasants for so ambitiously revolutionary plans as in our time. Particularly since the Chinese Communist Revolution, the peasantry has displaced the industrial proletariat as the crucial revolutionary class in the dogma of the most militant Marxists. We have been told repeatedly that Mao, Guevara, Giap, and their disciples have put their hopes in the peasantry and the countryside not merely for radical upheavals through revolutionary wars in underdeveloped countries, but also for global revolution. The role the peasants actually play in such revolutionary wars is among the crucial problems of our time.

* The author wishes to thank Merle Kling for his comments on an earlier draft of this article, and Lowry Nelson for his critique of a later draft and other assistance. The preparation of this article was made possible by the author's association with the Center of International Studies, Princeton University.

Reprinted with permission from *The Review of Politics*, Vol. 29, No. 1, January 1967, pp. 87–99.

The role of the peasantry in Cuba's revolutionary war has been greatly dramatized and has been discussed only less voluminously than its role in the Chinese Communist Revolution. Unfortunately, this effort has been futile insofar as it was part of a great controversy as to whether or not the Cuban Revolution was a true "peasant revolution." It has been futile not only because it failed to settle that issue, but also because the issue was pointless.[1] To achieve even general agreement on describing the Cuban revolution as a "peasant revolution," or in similar terms, would mean little more than promoting a painfully confused terminology.

This paper, here, will be devoted to a close examination of the condition of our knowledge of the actual peasant involvement in the Cuban revolution, up to Castro's assumption of power. After all, it is in their insurgency phase, when these revolutions hover in the backlands, that they appear particularly obscure. What is really known of the extent and manner of peasant participation in Cuba? How was it engendered? What are the problems encountered in exploring relationships between peasants and wagers of revolutionary war?

II

If the involvement of the peasants in the Cuban revolution has attracted almost universal attention, it has also stirred bitter controversy. In the heat of the ensuing passion, even incontrovertible fact has been slanted to match prejudice. The focus of attention in the literature is the Castro group in the Sierra Maestra, while hardly a reference exists to the involvement of peasants with other insurgent groups, such as the "Second Front of Escambray," established in the backlands of Central Cuba by adherents of the *Directorio Revolucionario* in February, 1958.

Concerning the actual extent of the active military involvement of the peasants, there is substantial agreement that, while Castro's army was neither large, nor even the sole

[1] "The Meaning of 'Peasant Revolution': The Cuban Case," *International Review of History and Political Science*, II, No. 2 (1965); and "The Meaning of 'Peasant Revolution': What Next?" in the subsequent issue of that journal.

insurgent force in the Cuban Revolution, it certainly "was recruited primarily from the peasantry,"[2] as one of the most respected military writers put it.

In accounts of other manners of peasant participation, much depends on the political views of the author you may consult. In the vein of many Marxists and other Castro-sympathizers, Leo Huberman and Paul M. Sweezy write: "At the beginning, the *campesinos* merely hid the rebels; before many months had passed the *campesinos,* as a class, were backing the rebels. They changed from passive onlookers to active participants. They became as one with the revolutionary army."[3]

On the other hand, Boris Goldenberg writes of the Cuban peasants that "even those whose lot was most miserable were not revolutionary. . . . Most of the population of the countryside remained passive throughout the struggle against Batista."[4] In the same vein, according to Ruby Hart Phillips, the peasants have, as a whole, displayed only "apathy."[5]

While much of what the two sides contest is important, it also is to a considerable degree intangible. For the peasants' real feelings toward the insurgents may be more elusive than outsiders, including urban Cubans, think. Even when insurgents move freely among peasants, "like fish in water," it may be due to reasons other than those which seem most obvious to outsiders.

Yet the controversy was not entirely in vain. It confirmed, if that was needed, that peasant revolutionism—whatever it may be—looms particularly large in the eyes of unorthodox Marxists, even outside China. More importantly, however, the contentiousness obscured the fact that not every aspect of peasant noncombatant participation is really controverted.

[2] Edwin Lieuwen, *Arms and Politics in Latin America* (New York, 1963), p. 264. Estimates of the total number of fighters in the rural areas in the whole campaign vary from 1000 to 3000. At a fairly late stage of the war, April, 1958, Castro's entire fighting force consisted of only 180 men.

[3] *Cuba, Anatomy of a Revolution* (New York, 1960), p. 57.

[4] "The Cuban Revolution: An Analysis," *Problems of Communism,* September–October 1963, p. 4.

[5] *The Cuban Dilemma* (New York, 1962), p. 95.

No one disputes the revolutionary leaders' own assertion that the peasants of the Sierra Maestra were at least initially cool toward the insurgents, who landed there in 1956. According to Guevara, this attitude persisted for "a long time." It changed gradually, mainly because of the *Batistiano* terror in the theater of operations.[6] There is little reason to doubt the guerrillas' claim to subsequent active support by the peasantry in the Sierra, but its true dimensions remain obscure.

There certainly is reason to doubt the picture of almost universal, enthusiastic peasant support painted by so many writers. On general grounds, this picture seems inconsistent with the character of the peasants of Oriente province, in which the Sierra is located. From his own explorations in the area, only ten years before the revolution, Lowry Nelson, author of the much-quoted classic, *Rural Cuba,* recalls these men as "abysmally ignorant, impoverished, and seemingly devoid of aspiration for something better," and generally "poor material for revolution."[7] Yet Nelson is right in assuming that even such men may be stirred by a charismatic leader like Castro. The question is, were they really stirred to provide active support in war to the extraordinary extent claimed?

There are more specific grounds for raising doubts, such as the picture of actual guerrilla operations emerging from the diary of the late Major Camilo Cienfuegos, parts of which have appeared in *Esprit* (Paris) in April, 1961. His account of the celebrated penetration of two Castroite guerrilla columns in the summer of 1958 into Las Villas province does not suggest that the guerrillas expected, or indeed obtained, the kind of massive peasant support so many have spoken of. Perhaps matters were much better for the guerrillas in Oriente province. The fact is, despite all sanguine assertions to the contrary, that we do not really know. The lack of a detailed account of

[6] Fidel Castro, *La revolución cubana* (Buenos Aires, 1960), p. 274 (for Castro's remarks) and pp. 428–429 (for Guevara's). Support for this contention by a Batista colonel, who for a time commanded troops fighting Castro, is cited in Boris Goldenberg, *The Cuban Revolution and Latin America* (New York, 1965), p. 145 note.

[7] Communication by Professor Nelson to the author, dated July 8, 1966.

the day-to-day struggle, which Thomas Freeman already noted some years ago,[8] unfortunately still exists.

The evaluation of the peasantry's participation in the Cuban Revolution naturally varies with the perception of its extent. Another factor with which it varies is the viewer's evaluation of the Castro group's share in the defeat of Batista, as opposed to that of other fighting groups. The almost universal effort to equate victory with the Castro group was accompanied soon after victory by a flood of writings attributing the success of the entire revolution almost exclusively to the peasantry. A typical eulogy of Castro simply asserts that the peasants "made the revolution."[9] By contrast with the urban underground, Castro's group seemed particularly "peasant"; by ignoring the former, the entire revolution could certainly be made to seem so as well.

As to the many charges that these were deliberate, planned optical illusions, we do know that the peasantry had certainly been used to promote Castro *vis-à-vis* his competitors in the *anti-Batistiano* camp at least before victory. Writing to the Council of Liberation in Florida late in 1957, Castro claimed that nobody "has suffered in his own flesh as we and, above all, the peasantry of the Sierra!" [While the peasants want to fight] "and beg desperately for rifles, there are arms hidden in Cuba which are not being used and are waiting for the police to pick them up or for the tyranny to fall, or for the rebels to be exterminated"[10]—the identity of the delinquent insurgents requiring no elaboration.

Castro's use of the victimized peasantry to elicit popular sympathy for his cause abroad is illustrated by the famous kidnaping incident. He justified (over *Radio Rebelde,* October 26, 1957) an embarrassing action of his brother, Raul, who abducted a group of United States citizens. The kidnaping, Castro argued, was necessary, for so the abducted Americans would be able to observe and verify the effects of the bomb-

[8] *The Crisis in Cuba* (Derby, Conn. 1963), p. 62.
[9] Paul A. Baran, "Reflections on the Cuban Revolution," *Monthly Review,* January 1961, p. 467.
[10] Cited in Jules Dubois, *Fidel Castro* (Indianapolis, 1959), p. 196.

ings of the peasant population with bombs and planes of
United States origin.

Writers who reduce the share of the Castro group in the
defeat of the Batista regime naturally also tend to attach less
importance to peasant participation in the revolution and
sometimes to err in minimizing peasant participation. Theodore Draper's well-known analysis of the revolution thus rejects the idea that the "minute" Castro fighting force could
alone have defeated Batista's army, holding that the regime
collapsed before the general revulsion against its terror. "The
heaviest losses were suffered by the largely middle-class urban
resistance movement, which secreted the political and psychological acids that ate into Batista's fighting force."[11] But
Draper goes beyond merely pleading for a less sanguine evaluation of the share of victory of the Castro fighting force,
which was drawn primarily from the peasantry; in the heat of
controversy he has even denied that the peasant background
of most Castro fighters mattered any more than it would in
any regular army in the world. This is a patent misconception
of guerrilla warfare, particularly where resources for warfare
cannot be pressed too conspicuously from the peasantry, as
in Cuba. Unlike ordinary armies also drawn primarily from
the peasantry, the Castro force assumed an ostentatious stance
as defender of peasants, fervidly cultivated agrarian slogans
and motifs, not to mention the postvictory display of solici-
tude for the peasants, which, Castro declared, they had amply
earned as a bounty.

Yet even acknowledging the struggle of the urban underground does not alter the fact that the small guerrilla band
in the backlands of Oriente not only dominated the whole
fight against Batista but also captured its success. While Castro's charisma and other factors have a great deal to do with
this fact, the insistence on the much greater urban martyrdom
(Draper's ratio is 19: 1) only serves to suggest even more
that the countryside has an inherent insurrectionary superiority over the cities. Comparing the urban and rural insurgencies
should help to reveal the advantages that the Castro and Es-

[11] *Castro's Revolution: Myths and Realities* (New York, 1962), p. 15.

cambray groups may have had over the former; comparing the latter two groups may reveal the special advantages that the Castro group possessed. Belief in the superiority of the rural areas for insurrectionary purposes inspired Guevara's famous blueprint for revolution in all the underdeveloped countries of the Americas.

"In the cities," Guevara wrote, "armed revolt can all too easily be smothered when customary civil liberties are suspended or ignored, thus forcing resistance movements to act clandestinely, without arms, and against enormous dangers. This does not hold true in rural areas where guerrillas and inhabitants cooperate closely, beyond the reach of oppressor forces. . . ."[12]

Furthermore, the guerrillas require

avenues of access and escape, possibilities for rapid maneuver, popular support, and hiding places. All this favors rural areas. Moreover, here the guerrilla can represent the desires of the great mass of poor farmers to possess their own land, animals, and all that makes up their life from cradle to grave. . . . Mao Tse-tung's China began as workers' uprisings that were defeated and almost wiped out. It recovered only when it took seat in rural areas and adopted the cause of agrarian reform. Ho Chi-minh's victory in Indochina was based on poor rice farmers oppressed by French colonists. In Algeria, Arab nationalism is bolstered by oppressive conditions of sharecropping imposed by French colonists. In Puerto Rico, special conditions so far have prevented a guerrilla outbreak, but nationalism is arising because the poor farmers want their land back from the Yankee invader. The same craving drove the farmers of Eastern Cuba to fight, ever since Batista first came to power thirty years ago, for the right to hold land.[13]

Where else, indeed, could one obtain essentials of revolutionary warfare as the Guevara doctrine says may be had so cheaply from the peasantry: fighters, shelter, provisions, sym-

[12] *Che Guevara on Guerrilla Warfare* (New York, 1961), p. 5.
[13] *Ibid.,* pp. 7–8.

pathy, intelligence? Moreover, the promise of land need not
even be honored, or rather honored only as the leaders alone
see fit. For when the time of reckoning arrives, Guevara
frankly avers, it is up to the leaders to "tell [the fighting
peasants] of the goals of the revolution, explain why they
fought, why their comrades died."[14] Guevara's peculiar admixture of fact and fancy certainly makes it seem too good
to be true.

III

Is it true in the case of Cuba? Guevara's statements and a
rash of similar ones have indeed diffused the impression that
land hunger was the decisive, if not exclusive, influence on
peasant attitudes toward the Castro insurgents.[15] The impression was greatly strengthened by the prominence in the Cuban
revolution of agrarian reform, with which it is inextricably
connected. Certainly, the importance of agrarian reform in
the revolution cannot easily be overstated. Certainly, no other
connection between the peasantry and the revolution has attracted so much attention almost everywhere. Certainly, the
popular conception of the reform as a clear promise of land
to the peasants was not unreasonable.

Still, the prevailing belief is debatable. A first look at the
available evidence indeed discloses numerous *allegations* to
the effect that land hunger was the alpha and omega of the
peasant support for the Castro insurgents, but, as usual, those
who speak the peasants' mind are rarely peasants. Yet, when
such allegations are made by men of authority and experience
like Guevara, they acquire a greater claim on our credibility
than is usually the case, Even so, this may mean only that
they believe it to be true (which is not entirely certain either,
as far as Guevara is concerned).[16] After all, to think that way

[14] *Ibid.*, p. 70.
[15] Cf. for instance, Joseph North, *Cuba: Hope of a Hemisphere* (New
York, 1961), p. 16; Edwin Lieuwen, *op. cit.*, p. 264; J. P. Morray, "Cuba
and Communism," *Monthly Review*, July–August 1961, p. 8; Paul Johnson, "A Caribbean Suez?" *New Statesman and Nation*, July 9, 1960, p. 43.
[16] Guevara, who has forcefully affirmed that "the *campesino* fights
because he wants land" in numerous ways (this particular phrase appeared early in *Verde Olivo* [April 9, 1961]), was alleged to have said
soon after victory, with special reference to the Sierra peasants, that "the

about peasants is not very surprising; there is an ancient, but dubious, belief abroad in many lands that the peasants have everywhere always rebelled for land, or, at any rate, almost always for land. In the Sierra Maestra, with its extraordinary concentration of "squatters," peasants with the most vulnerable land tenure in all of Cuba, such a view of peasant motivation appears particularly plausible;[17] this especially in the absence of flagrant contradictions, which the *campesinos* were not very likely to offer in any case.

But the question is not whether the promise of land displeased the *campesinos,* or even whether it had something to do with the generation of peasant support for Castro. Of course not! It is whether the promise of land was as decisive an influence on peasant attitudes as is alleged.

In addition to some functionally equivalent influences on the peasantry of the Sierra, such as their victimization by the Batista forces and other factors to be discussed below, of equal or greater import than land hunger, there are still other reasons for questioning the cogency of the prevailing belief.

Does it, for instance, explain satisfactorily why the *barbudos* (the fighting, as opposed to the more passive, *campesinos*) took up arms against Batista? Is it likely that the expectations of men such as they—usually more mobile, more uprooted, more venturesome, younger than the other peasants—are really circumscribed by land? All that we know from studies of other revolutionary wars suggests that these

---

guajiros did not really want to be landowners" (reported by Victor Franco, in *The Morning After,* New York, 1963, p. 114).

[17] The fact that land hunger was weak relative to other expressed desires of the Cuban *campesinos* generally has been noted by the more discriminating students of the revolution, following Lowry Nelson's findings to this effect and other evidence. It is believed, however, that the peasantry of the Sierra Maestra, which differs significantly from the rest of the Cuban peasantry, also differs from them in that it "shows its love for the possession of land most aggressively," as Guevara put it in one place (*Monthly Review,* July–August, 1961; but is reported to have contradicted himself in another, as indicated above). The author has sought to establish whether Nelson's data confirmed this belief. Unfortunately, Nelson no longer has the differentiated data for the several regions, which together make up Table 54 in his *Rural Cuba.* Nor could he recall any great variations for Alto Songo, the region closest to the Sierra Maestra.

men may actually be moving away from such traditional expectations as land. It is at least as reasonable to assume that many *barbudos* ran from the land, in joining the Castro revolutionaries, as to fight for it for themselves. The first substantial number certainly ran *from* the *Batistianos*, whatever else they may have been running for. The promise of land perhaps had more to do with the behavior of the more passive peasants in the Sierra. Still, if land hunger really moved the peasants as much as is alleged, one wonders why only so few actually took to arms, why so many apparently did nothing.[18]

The fact that the bourgeois revolutionary leaders were greatly attached to agrarian reform is, of course, not seriously disputed. As far as the leader of the revolution himself was concerned, the sheer consistency and persistence of his attachment fully warrant the conclusion that the "reform was central to Castro's entire conception of the revolution."[19] Castro had called for agrarian reform from the first, at least as early as the historic Moncada trial ("History Will Absolve Me") speech of October 6, 1953; he repeated the call in his famous Sierra Maestra Manifesto, a major bid for national support, issued on July 12, 1957; he not only reiterated the call for agrarian reform throughout the war, but actually promulgated it even before victory, on October 10, 1957, as one of his first two "rebel laws"; at last, he returned to the Sierra to sign the first of a series of agrarian reform laws, in a symbolic gesture of the hero crowning his chief work, as it were. Every instance was a clear promise of land to the *campesinos*.

But "agrarian reform," as a true compulsion, or *idée fixe* of the leaders, is not properly conceivable in this simple sense. Another conception, the reform as a master lever with which to transform radically both Cuban society and its relations to the United States, appears to have had a much stronger hold on them, perhaps even before victory. Afterwards, the In-

---

[18] According to Draper's later work on Cuba (*Castroism: Theory and Practice* [New York, 1965] p. 72), of the approximately 50,000 peasants in the Sierra Maestra, 500–1000 were in the Castro fighting force and "some thousands more . . . helped the guerrilla cause in one form or another."

[19] *Cuba: Tragedy in Our Hemisphere* (New York, 1963), p. 64.

stitute of Agrarian Reform (I.N.R.A.) functioned primarily in this sense.

Our argument is, of course, not inconsistent with the arousal among the peasantry of generalized expectations, or a genuine desire to uplift them on the part of the bourgeois revolutionaries. The latter assumption was borne out by the bestowal of attention and more material benefits (the gift of land was not the most conspicuous among them, however) upon the peasantry after Batista's downfall; it was so massive, unprecedented, and ostentatious as to suggest that a "revolution *for* peasants"[20] had indeed been wrought by the middle class. As for the peasants' hope for a better life generally in the event of a guerrilla victory, who can tell just how much it had affected the peasants' behavior during the fighting?

IV

It is curious that a most intriguing aspect of the connection between the peasantry and the guerrillas has scarcely been touched in the vast literature on the Cuban revolution. We refer to a certain "fit" between patterns of guerrillaism and the peasantry of the Sierra, a coincidence which should not really surprise anyone even barely familiar with the fact that guerrillaism is historically a product of the nineteenth-century Spanish peasantry.

Some students of the Cuban revolution have in fact not entirely ignored the existence of a certain relationship between the guerrillas and the peasants of the Sierra, which, while more effective than a calculated exchange of blood for soil, is not quite the same as the intense revolutionary passion exuding from the familiar propaganda either. Some writers have intimated a natural affinity between the incongruous partners, bourgeois intellectuals and backward peasants, even suggesting a certain magic in this peculiar union.

Only Jean-Paul Sartre has written about this "magic" in any appreciable manner, with language that is metaphorical, yet well worth pondering. Thus, according to him, the coun-

---

[20] Irving Peter Pflaum, *Tragic Island* (Englewood Cliffs, N.J. 1961), p. 19 (italics added).

tryside had already "imposed its form on the rebellion,"[21] even before the insurgents fully realized the need to fight the war mainly in the backlands, to involve the peasantry in it.

> In choosing to attack the scattering of rural garrisons, the rebels attacked the peasants' enemy. By their mode of life, they became peasants themselves and sought help from the peasants whom they protected. . . .
> In order for the peasants to become rebels, the rebels became peasants. They took part in the field chores. It wasn't enough to know the needs, the poverty of the rural people. It was necessary to suffer from these hardships and at the same time to combat them. The farmer would be that much better disposed to listen to them the more he recognized them as his own kind. A neat swing of the machete, cutting the stalks like a pro, will do more than a long speech.

In light of what is known of the peasants of the Sierra and similar peasants elsewhere, the affinity between these *guajiros* and Castro's bourgeois intruders which Sartre suggests may not be far-fetched at all. True, the identity of the intruders was initially strange to the peasants; but their role as outlaws and rebels was not, just as it is not in many other backward backlands in the world. The Sierra had been traditional outlaw country long before Castro—rife with smuggling, marijuana growing, fugitives from other districts, and a willful yet ineffectual governmental presence. The Robin Hood idea, which Castro so assiduously plied and cultivated there,[22] was not invented by him; he merely exploited existing conditions, among which was the invariably mentioned poverty, of course, but more importantly the prevailing orientations toward government.

Just how much these insurgents gained from filling familiar roles among the peasantry is debatable, though surely not inconsiderable. Their benefits were by no means unmixed ones, for the betrayal of rural outlaws is as traditional in the lore

---

[21] This and the subsequent quotation from *Sartre on Cuba* (New York, 1961), pp. 50–51.
[22] Dubois, *Fidel Castro*, p. 145.

of the backward as the robber heroes themselves. (Castro and his companions were the victims of treachery immediately upon their landing in Oriente.) But we can be just as certain that even strange insurgents filling such roles may be not more uncongenial to peasants in such an underdeveloped area than the government they are fighting, to put things mildly.[23] If the bourgeois insurgents indeed underwent in such a setting the process of "empeasantment" of which Sartre speaks, they certainly must have further enhanced their congeniality with the peasants. Objective conditions of the guerrillas' warfare everywhere *require* that they live close to the peasantry; why doubt that it happened in Oriente? Proximity, similarity, and familiarity may breed contempt, but also genuine sympathy.

V

Despite the voluminous literature on the Cuban revolution, we must conclude that the involvement of the peasantry in it remains in large measure in obscurity or worse. It is distressing to think that an international colloquium of the first magnitude, like that on this subject in the early 1960's, rested on so slender a base in fact. Guevara's startling call in 1964 for a "true" history of the Cuban revolution was already long overdue even then.

What have we been able to ascertain here? First of all, the need to learn more about the involvement of the peasants in the revolution apart from their relations to the Castro insurgency. As for the latter, while it is clear enough that Castro's small fighting force was recruited primarily from the peasantry, this fact only raises a number of difficult questions. True, unlike other wagers of revolutionary warfare (in South Vietnam, for instance), the Castroites could not draft their manpower, which would make them dependent on the voluntary accession of peasants to their ranks; yet how great was this dependence when so small a fighting force proved to be sufficient—and, incidentally, might also have been supplied from the cities? Perhaps no really acceptable substitute

---

[23] Nelson recalls a press report according to which the peasants came asking for gifts—according to the usual custom—from the strangers who were then waging war on their government.

was available; but are we sure that the peasants who joined the fighters were moved by reasons peculiar to the peasantry? Victimization by belligerents is a peasant problem only when warfare occurs in the countryside; in Cuba, it was an urban problem as well.

Unlike the extent of active participation, little is known of the dimensions of other peasant support for Castro. As we face a bewildering array of conflicting estimates and interpretations, we can only be sure that, while sympathetic observers probably exaggerate the noncombatant peasant support to the Castro insurgents, such support most probably existed, at least in the Sierra. The few probably candid glimpses of the countryside during the war in the literature would not, however, seem to support any sanguine estimates of the extent of that support.

Regarding the nature and sources of peasant support for the Castro insurgents, we should remember that traditional, negative orientations toward government, so typical of backward peasants, may well produce the same behavior ("support") that would also result from an appreciation of any traits peculiar to an insurgent movement. It would be easy, and often tempting, to confuse the two.

Moreover, while the assumption generally is that such support emerged from the *will* of the peasantry, as a deliberate choice (blood in return for land, for instance), there is good reason to believe that at least two more or less *in*voluntary conditions may have had much to do with it. The first may be termed the "parasitism" of the guerrillas, describing the poisoning of the peasantry's already bad relations with the government by the waging of war against it from amidst the peasantry, thus implicating peasants willy-nilly in the war. As we have seen, both Guevara and Castro attest to the miraculous effects of parasitism on their cause. The other involuntary factor may be called the "mimicry" of the guerrillas, or their more or less superficial[24] resemblance to the peasantry among

---

[24] Insofar as this may be more than skin-deep, we may have to borrow the term "mimetism" from Gaetano Mosca, as "the tendency of an individual's passions, sentiments and beliefs to develop in accord with the currents that prevail in the environment." *The Ruling Class* (New York, 1939), p. 184.

whom they move. These two conditions are better known to us from other revolutionary wars. With the latter of the two, mimicry, we are familiar only in the limited sense that an illusion of resemblance is experienced by the forces of law and order, not the peasants, and so the guerrillas thereby secure precious concealment. What the talk of the empeasantment, of the Robin Hoodism of the Castroite bourgeois insurgents has suggested in the Cuban case is that the peasants themselves may also respond to such a resemblance.

To sum up, while we do not pretend to have exhausted the role of the peasantry in the insurgency stage of the Cuban revolution, what we have seen of it here definitely impresses us as a broad pattern of advantages for the insurgents. The insurgents' manipulation of the peasantry appears even greater than is usually supposed, but so also does their representativeness of the peasantry, although this function is not necessarily performed in the conventional manner, or the manner revolutionary apologists usually want us to believe.

2

SOCIAL REVOLUTION:
ORIGINS IN MEXICO, BOLIVIA,
AND CUBA*

Cole Blasier

War and revolution are the cataclysmic events of our age
which affect man and society more profoundly than any other
human phenomenon. In Russia and China war brought revolution. Today, in an age of competitive ideologies and competitive nuclear armament, men fear that revolution will lead to
war.

The global conflicts that have wracked Eurasia in this century have not touched Latin America directly. The only international conflict of roughly comparable intensity was the
Chaco War (1932–1936) in which hostilities were confined
to two small powers, Bolivia and Paraguay. Bolivia's defeat was
part of a train of events that led directly to the Revolution
of 1952.

Despite Castro's ties with extra-continental powers, Latin
America's prospects for avoiding entanglement in wars outside the hemisphere are relatively good partly because of
geographic isolation. As the history of inter-American con-
ciliation and mediation shows, political and military pressure which can be brought to bear on potential belligerents
often serves as an effective constraint. Barring nuclear con-

* In addition to his debt to the authorities cited and to many others,
the author acknowledges with thanks helpful criticism on the text, the
bibliography, or both from: Carter Goodrich, James Malloy, José
Moreno, Stanley Ross, Harold Sims, Andrés Suárez, James Wilkie and
Howard Cline who first suggested this article. Stephen Connolly helped
prepare the bibliography, which appears at the end of the article.

Reprinted with permission from *Latin American Research Review*,
Vol. II, No. 3, Summer 1967, pp. 28–64.

flict, revolution is more likely to disturb Latin America's tranquility than war.

Social revolution as defined here is not simply a coup d'état or one of the other forms of violence which have often determined succession in political office in Latin America. Social revolution is a sudden and comprehensive change in social structure and values initiated by violence.

Many countries in Latin America, such as Brazil, Colombia, and the Dominican Republic, appear to have teetered on the brink of social revolution. Social revolution began in Guatemala, but did not run its full course. Latin America has had only three social revolutions which correspond to the great revolutions of Eurasia (the French, the Russian, and the Chinese): the Mexican (1910), the Bolivian (1952), and the Cuban (1959). In these countries revolutions have fundamentally changed property relationships and the distribution of national income; the locus and modes of exercising political power; and social structure, policies, and values.

Social revolution in Latin America, as elsewhere, may be studied in three chronological phases: 1) the socio-political breakdown of the old regime, 2) the seizure of government, including the strategies and tactics of ruling and revolutionary elites, and 3) the subsequent transformation of social structure and social values. The first two phases of the Mexican, Bolivian, and Cuban revolutions will be dealt with here. A review of the literature of the transformation of the three societies is so complex as to require separate treatment.

The purpose here is to survey and interpret the conclusions of authoritative writers on certain politically significant issues related to the first two phases of these three revolutions. New interpretations will not be advanced, but secondary sources will serve as a basis for tentative comparisons and generalizations. Works having partisan bias and serving a polemical purpose have perforce been used, but reliance has been placed whenever possible on authorities possessing a sense of scholarly detachment.

The Mexican Revolution has a vast historical literature in Spanish, English, and in other languages, but there has been little effort to re-evaluate the origins and nature of the early period with the insights of contemporary social science. Alexander's *The Bolivian National Revolution* (1958) is still the most convenient descriptive account in one volume of the Bolivian upheaval, although there are a few recent scholarly studies of specific topics. Initially some of the richest sources on the Cuban Revolution were provided by French scholars. Draper's work on Cuba deals cogently with selected issues. Good recent studies emphasizing the interaction of domestic and foreign policies include Goldenberg's *The Cuban Revolution and Latin America* (1965) and Suárez' *Cuba: Castroism and Communism, 1959–1966* scheduled for publication in mid-1967. Comprehensive evaluation of the impact of the revolution on Cuban society remains to be made.

In spite of its impact on history, we know relatively little about the revolutionary process. Historians have faithfully given chronological accounts of events and there have been pioneering studies of the natural history of revolutions, such as Crane Brinton's *The Anatomy of Revolution*. Blanksten (1958) and Lanning (1966) are among those who have applied Brinton's and other approaches to Latin America. Much attention, too, has been devoted to identifying different kinds of "revolutions" with essays on their philosophical and social implications. *Revolutions* edited by Carl J. Friedrich (1966) is among the most recent such efforts.

In the last few years two scholars, Chalmers Johnson and Harry Eckstein, have been attempting to break new ground in the study of revolution by going beyond the description of symptoms to the search for causes. In his provocative study, *Revolution and the Social System*, Johnson provides a typology of revolution with a broad historical sweep. He identifies six types of revolution, beginning with the jacquerie (such as the peasant revolts of the late Middle Ages), and ending with the militarized mass insurrection (illustrated by China, Viet Nam, and Algeria). In this study, Johnson maintains that revolutions are caused in part by disequilibrium in the social system. The condition that causes disequilibrium is "dysfunction" which, when widespread and serious, is "multiple dysfunction." If an intransigent ruling elite is unwilling or unable to relieve such dysfunction, opposing groups turn to violence.

In the resulting revolutionary situation, violence is touched off by an "accelerator," such as the rise of a charismatic leader, revolutionary parties, or defeat in a foreign war. In its most simple form Johnson's thesis held that multiple dysfunction, plus elite intransigence, plus an accelerator equals social revolution.

Harry Eckstein (1965) criticized Johnson's model on the grounds that social structure does not always determine attitudes and behavior and that revolutionary developments should not be linked mechanically to the social setting. Instead, Eckstein proposes his own paradigm for analyzing the causes of revolutions which contains four positive variables and four negative ones. Examples of positive variables are disorienting social processes and elite inefficiency and of negative variables, adjustive mechanisms and repression.

Subsequently, Johnson (1966: xi) dropped references to "multiple dysfunction" while reconfirming his contention that "revolution is inseparable from the social context in which it occurs." In *Revolutionary Change* he introduces value changing and environment changing forces as a means of analyzing the cause of disequilibrium. According to Johnson, when the value structure and the pattern of environmental adaptation are not synchronized, disequilibrium occurs. One major characteristic of disequilibrium is power deflation, a condition requiring the ruling elite to rely increasingly on force to maintain social integration. If this elite is subsequently unable to move towards resynchronization, a loss of authority ensues. Thus, power deflation plus loss of authority, plus an accelerator, produce revolutionary insurrection.

The work of Johnson, Eckstein, and others is beginning to provide more precise analytical tools for explaining revolutions. But, as Lawrence Stone (1966) makes clear, much remains to be done.

I

The distinction between preconditions and precipitants suggested by Eckstein (1965) is useful in analyzing the breakdown of the old regimes. Preconditions are fundamental, underlying causes of social unrest, while precipitants are the more superficial events which lead to the outbreak of violence. Among the preconditions which are most widely discussed in the literature are: inequitable and inefficient systems of land tenure; stagnating and unproductive economies; fiscal crises; and social discontent arising from low living standards, political repression and brutality; and foreign "domination."

Agrarian issues are central to understanding [all three] revolutions because of agriculture's importance in each country. On the eve of the revolution the rural population predominated in Mexico (c. 69%) and Bolivia (c. 73%). In Cuba, where the rural population had fallen below the halfway mark (c. 43%) by 1959, sugar, an agriculture product, dominated the economy.

In Mexico under Díaz land became concentrated in fewer and fewer hands by the process of acquisition from small holders, Indian communities, and the state. Silva Herzog (1960: 22) maintains that the large concentrations of land in haciendas were not designed to obtain the greatest return and were responsible for the failure of the nation's agriculture to produce efficiently. In his opinion (1960: 7), the fundamental cause of the Mexican Revolution was

> the existence of enormous haciendas in the hands of a few people with a mentality similar to that of the feudal masters of Europe of the 14th and 15th centuries . . . many of the evils from which the country suffered had their origin in the unjust and unequal distribution of land since the beginning of the Spanish domination.

McBride (1923: 158) called the agrarian issues a cause of the revolution, referring to General Díaz's belated statement that the land problem was the cause that lay back of the entire revolution and that he, Díaz, was ready to spend all the accumulated funds of the treasury to find a remedy. Tannenbaum (1950: 136) maintains that "the chief cause of the Revolution of 1910 was the uneven distribution of land." E. Simpson (1937: 43) holds that the social disequilibrium preceding the revolution was at bottom due to inequalities in the distribution of land and to the evil effects of the hacienda system.

Concentration of land in large haciendas, frequently at the expense of Indian communities, took place in the years preceding the 1952 Revolution in Bolivia as it had in Mexico. On the eve of the revolution many Bolivian peons were still required to render services without cash payment. One result of this system, as Alexander (1958: 58) points out, was that almost 3 million of the 3.5 million Bolivians could not properly have been considered part of the national market economy. In his opinion, the system of land holding, together with a number of other factors, held back agricultural development (1958: 10).

Unlike pre-revolutionary agriculture in Mexico and Bolivia which still followed the Spanish colonial pattern, much of Cuban agriculture was organized on a commercial basis. Large sugar plantations employed wage labor, and the sugar mills controlled surrounding lands through actual ownership, rental, or crop purchase. As Goldenberg (1965: 129) points out, Cuban latifundia were not feudal in character and had nothing in common with the big, almost self-sufficient haciendas in other Latin American countries. Yet, in its dependence on sugar, Cuban agriculture suffered from the lack of diversification, and much land was inefficiently cultivated. Dumont (1965: 32) calls attention to the insufficient utilization of land, labor and capital and stresses the great waste of productive forces resulting from layoffs and insufficiently intensive cultivation that occurred before 1959. Similar criticisms are widely voiced elsewhere in the literature.

Wide disagreement exists about the state of Cuban agriculture as a cause of the revolution. In his authoritative *Rural Cuba,* Nelson (1950: 255) emphasizes public demand for land reform and the serious consequences which may follow further delay. Similarly, Baran (1961) and Huberman and Sweezy (1960: 57) stress peasant unrest in the pre-revolutionary period.

Draper (1965: 75), on the other hand, claims that there is nothing comparable in Cuba to the "classic peasant revolutionary movement" led by Zapata in Mexico in 1910. The Soviet scholar Kalinin (Mikhailov, 1964: 23) denies that Cuban events were "a classical example of a peasant revolu-

tion" in view of the existence of a large agricultural proletariat. Goldenberg (1965: 125) rejects the thesis even more
decisively: "There was, after 1937, no longer any violent
unrest in the countryside . . . the demand for ownership of
land among rural people was low."

In all three countries before the revolution, agriculture suffered from insufficiently intensive exploitation, inefficiency,
and most of the social evils associated with underdevelopment. Many contemporary authorities blamed this situation
in part on antiquated systems of land tenure in Mexico and
Bolivia. In Cuba, the tendency is to place greater emphasis on
the failure of management to modernize and diversify.

The degree to which the system of land tenure, or agricultural conditions generally were a "cause" of the revolution is
another matter. The conditions of agriculture alone would not
seem to be decisive. Otherwise, revolutions would have broken
out in many other Latin American countries. In the case of
Cuba, it may be questioned whether the many anti-Batista
sentiments which existed in the 1950's in the countryside
were distinctively rural. In Bolivia, whatever may have been
the effects of the land tenure system and the state of agriculture generally, the peasants in the country as a whole had not
yet been politically aroused at the time the revolution broke
out.

The case for agrarian causes is strongest in the Mexican
Revolution. Yet Tannenbaum, who conceived of the Mexican
Revolution as agrarian, has always given great attention to its
other economic and political origins. In his study of the
Mexican ejidos, Simpson (1937: 43) maintains that "it would
be a mistake to assume . . . that the agrarian complex was the
only cause of the Revolution, or even a cause at all, if by this
term is meant a precipitating force." The participation of elements of the rural population in the revolutions, discussed
later, will throw additional light on this point.

In explaining the great revolutions of Europe and North
America, Brinton (1965: 28) holds that "revolutions often
come during economic depressions which follow on periods
of generally rising standards of living." According to Brinton, revolutions are not born in societies that are economically

retrograde, but in those which are economically progressive.
Under Díaz the economy had achieved rapid rates of capital
growth unprecedented in Mexican history. But this growth had
been achieved at the expense of the poorer elements of society and, as Tannenbaum (1929: 149) points out, rising
prices coupled with relatively stationary wages had lowered
the real income of Mexican wage earners. Cuba had had a
booming economy in the early part of the 20th century, but
Seers (1964: 12) maintains that the economy had been suffering from chronic stagnation since the 1920's. In Bolivia, too,
there had been a boom in tin during the early part of the 20th
century, but tin mining was threatened by declining yields of
ore. Thus, the experiences of all three countries could be
described as, in part, bearing out Brinton's thesis, loosely
interpreted. Little has been done in any serious way, however, to link these economic trends to social revolutions,
and there would appear to be so many reservations and qualifications, different in each case, as to complicate the application of Brinton's thesis to these countries.

Brinton (1965: 29) maintains that on the eve of the revolution governments are often in severe financial straits. One
could document to a greater or lesser extent such difficulties
in all three countries. In Bolivia, for example, the Keenleyside
report (UN: 1951) describes in detail the government's
fiscal plight and existing inflationary pressures. Mexico and
Cuba appear to have had fiscal problems, too, but of relatively
less magnitude. There appear to be no authoritative studies on
the relationship between fiscal issues and the revolutions in
these three Latin American countries.

Economic conditions were a source of popular discontent on
the eve of these revolutions and can be cited as a cause of
popular alienation from the ruling elites. And fiscal problems weakened the old regimes to varying degrees. The extent
of the importance of economic and fiscal problems as underlying causes of the revolutions is a somewhat different question, which can be fairly evaluated only in a larger context.

Most authorities are in agreement that broad social and
political issues were equally or more important than economic
and fiscal ones. Discontent with wages, working conditions,

and living conditions provide a bedrock of dissatisfaction with governments or regimes in all these countries, but similar economic conditions have plagued most countries in Latin America which have never experienced social revolution. In the words of Silva Herzog (1960: 169), it is an error to assume that the causes of malaise are exclusively economic, or exclusively international, or exclusively a matter of race. In his opinion, all of the various complex causes are manifested in a "political fever" and social crises focus on "the political question."

In explaining the causes of the Mexican Revolution, González (1960: 203) refers to six causes cited by Luis Cabrera: *caciquismo, peonismo, fabriquismo, hacendadismo, cientifisismo, and extranjerismo.* In describing them, the latter makes their socio-political content clear: revolt against local political bosses and their despotic methods, against feudal relations on the countryside, against conditions in the factory resembling servitude, against social and political control by a small group of financial and business magnates, and against the privileged positions of foreigners in Mexican society. The natural target of a growing opposition composed of alienated intellectuals and political activists was the commanding figure of the caudillo, General Porfirio Díaz, who had ruled Mexico since 1876.

Although few had dared to oppose General Díaz, and even on the eve of the revolution he appeared invincible, the unscrupulous methods he had used to control elections and insure his continuance in office, his use of censorship and brutality against those who sought to voice opposition, and his cynical manipulation of the levers of power from the capital were well known. Popular perception of the nature of the Díaz system was one thing, organizing opposition to it another. As Octavio Paz (1961: 137) points out, one antecedent of the revolt against Díaz was the development of a middle class due to the growth of commerce and industry: "A new generation had arisen, a restless generation that desired a change. The quarrel of the generations became a part of the general discord." According to Luís Cabrera in Ross (1966: 58), the Mexican Revolution was "nothing more than the insurrection of the Mexican people against a very repressive and wealthy regime . . . against a social, political, and economic system." Or Cosío Villegas (1964: 13): "The Mexican Revolution was in fact the revolt of the impoverished many against the wealthy few . . . the reason which made the reform irresistible came from the purest Christian source: a feeling of obvious social injustice."

The wellsprings of social discontent in Bolivia were similar to those in Mexico: peonage, exploitation of wage labor in the mines, political suppression, concentration of political and economic power in the hands of a small elite, and absentee ownership. According to Urquidi (1966: 326), the profound roots of this revolution were the "exploitation from which the people were suffering at the hands of the mining and feudal oligarchy for half a century . . . increasingly accentuated oppression of imperialism . . . and in the anti-democratic conduct of the government."

Unlike the revolution in Mexico, which followed one of the longest and stablest periods in history, the revolution in Bolivia climaxed a 20-year period of unprecedented social and political ferment which began at least as early as the 1929 depression. Alexander (1958: 22) correctly expresses the virtually unanimous opinion that the Chaco War (1932–1936) "disorganized the economy, discredited the army, spread new ideas among the urban workers and miners, and sowed discontent among the intelligentsia, [thereby accelerating] a process of social ferment which reached its high point on April 9, 1952." Interpretations of the impact of the Chaco War vary. In his study of the Bolivian economy, Zondag (1966: 25) maintains that "apart from disorganizing a national economy, [the Chaco War] was the beginning of a social upheaval, of moral disintegration and of costly political experiments which ultimately led to the revolution of 1952." Klein (1963: iii) explicitly de-emphasizes the socio-economic consequences of the war and emphasizes "political dislocations":

The war unquestionably caused the breakdown of both the traditional political party system and traditional patterns of leadership and class orientation. This breakdown was engendered by the Bolivian middle class to rebel against the pre-war upper class leadership because of their conduct of the Chaco War. As a result, the middle classes turned to new radical political solutions to resolve the dilemma of Bolivia's disastrous defeat. In so doing, the Bolivian middle classes broke a system of political organization which had endured for over half a century, and by breaking this pattern, they set the stage for the great social revolution of 1952.

Cuba differed from Mexico and Bolivia in that she had recently (1944–1952) enjoyed government by moderate, relatively progressive, and popularly elected presidents sponsored by the Auténtico party. True, Bolivia had reform-minded dictatorships in the governments of Toro, Bosch, and Villaroel, but these lacked the stability and constitutional legitimacy of the Grau San Martín and Prío governments in Cuba. The failure of the latter two presidents to come fully to grips with the nation's problems and establish a firm hold on the nation's loyalties, is fundamental to understanding the Cuban Revolution. On the one hand, Juan Bosch (1955: 141) holds that Grau's government provided for greater well being for the mass of society and had an "energetic social policy, with measures favoring many classes," a large public works program, a "dignified and strong international position," and unrestricted civil liberties. But Bosch calls attention to the Grau government's lamentable failing: "An absence of administrative honesty . . . ministers left their responsibilities carrying away millions, and an infinity of lower ranked functionaries enriched themselves in their posts." Gil (1962: 378–9) points out a number of social and political gains, but notes failure to achieve agrarian reform. He, too, tells how the Auténticos immersed themselves in "graft and corruption on a scale unsurpassed only in recent years by Batista's second regime." During this period crime, gangsterism, and other forms of violence were rife in Cuba. The symbol of the Auténtico's incapacity to retain and mobilize effective political support and strengthen government and the economy was

Batista's bloodless coup of March 10, 1952. Although opposition to Batista's return might have been mobilized, President Prío lost his "will to power and faith in himself." Bosch (1955: 144).

In a sense, the Achilles heel of the Batista government (1952–1959) was the illegal manner in which he came to power. Most authorities believe his coup in 1952 symbolized his inability to win the forthcoming election. Unable to legitimize his power, Batista relied heavily on coercion. As the revolutionary movement gathered momentum, he resorted increasingly to censorship, police brutality, reprisals and terror. According to Draper (1965: 116), "Batista, not Castro, was the indispensable revolutionary ingredient." Although few authors ignore the inequalities of wealth and living conditions, and particularly seasonal and structural unemployment, there is surprisingly wide agreement about the predominance of political factors in explaining Batista's fall.

Burks (1964: 8) maintains that "Cuba did not fall to Castro because of its excessive poverty or because of revolutionary class conscious unrest . . . economic and social conditions of the Cuba of the 1950's were in fact a mixture of achievement and persistent problems . . . corruption which characterized [Batista's] regime, the methods of terror and torture which it employed to stay in power, led to a profound and increasing revulsion among wider and wider elements of the population." Suárez (1967: Ch. 1) holds that "the overthrow of Batista was not due to any demand of the masses for the radical transformation of the socio-economic structure." Gil (1962: 385) maintains that the success of the 26th of July Movement can only be explained by "a national feeling of revulsion towards existing political habits." Zeitlin and Scheer (1963: 12) quote José Miró Cardona that "the fight against Batista was a fight against political dictatorship, not against economic conditions." Lanning (1966: 369) also stresses "popular revulsion against widespread corruption and the employment of terror, both essentially non-economic sentiments."

No discussion of the preconditions of revolution in these three countries would be complete without some reference to foreign economic and political influence. In all three countries "imperialism," especially United States "imperialism," had long been a politically sensitive subject. On the eve of these revolutions the United States was an especially important market for a variety of Mexican products, for Cuban sugar, and Bolivian tin. In addition, U.S. investments in Mexican and Cuban land, extractive industries, public utilities, and manufacturing caused friction. Discrimination in favor of North American residents and tourists in Mexico and Cuba, and against the native born, exacerbated relations. In both countries anti-Americanism was firmly rooted from the time of the Mexican War and the Platt Amendment. In Bolivia, many informed observers were extremely critical of absentee ownership of the largest tin mines and the Northamerican and other foreign managers, heavy foreign remittances, and the mine owner's manipulation of domestic politics from abroad.

Tannenbaum (1933: 137) indicates that contact with American labor and with other ideas and practices in the United States clashed with the structure of "feudal Mexico," which intensified discontent. Northamerican influence was perhaps relatively greater in Cuba than in either Mexico or Bolivia. According to Williams in Ross (1966: 193),

> American control operated to polarize Cuban politics and ideology. The system per se had to be changed before even reforms of a significant nature could be introduced . . . politics became increasingly revolutionary, not only in terms of domestic affairs but also in terms of Cuba's relationship to the United States. American policy thus functioned to create an indigenous radical movement.

Seers (1964: 18) called the contrast between relatively high living standards in the United States, especially in Florida, with those in Cuba "intolerable." Robert Smith (1960: 176) holds that anti-U.S. feelings, and the factors that caused them helped produce Castro's victory.

The Díaz and Batista governments, and the Bolivian *rosca* to a lesser degree, were closely associated with, and in part dependent on, U.S. interests and policies. And this association with foreign interests was one further source of popular dissatisfaction with these pre-revolutionary governments.

Most authors explaining the cause of these revolutions mention "imperialism," but few have attempted in any precise way to evaluate its relative importance as a precondition. How many revolutionaries would take up arms and risk their lives because of foreign ownership of specific properties or because of the leverage of the U.S. sugar quota? On the other hand, the subordination of their country to what they considered to be intolerable foreign domination was one of many reasons behind the demand for change. In Mexico and Cuba the "anti-imperialist" character of the revolutionaries' programs was less evident before the seizure of government than afterwards. The contrast is less marked in Bolivia.

Identifying the precipitants of social revolutions is perhaps less difficult than determining the preconditions conceived as fundamental causes. Difficult estimates are involved about how far back in time precipitants may occur and about their relative importance.

Singling out the most important precipitant in each case from treatment in secondary sources may seem arbitrary, but the exercise forces one to look more deeply into the revolutionary process. In Mexico, the most important precipitant was the arrest and imprisonment of Francisco I. Madero by the Díaz regime as the presidential campaign, in which the former was a leading contender, was approaching its climax. Ever since the Creelman interview of 1908, the Mexican people had been led to expect that General Díaz might step down. When his principal opponent in the election was arrested, the opposition's only remaining recourse was violence. As Silva Herzog (1960: 127) maintains, "only one route was left: armed struggle with all its consequences." Ross (1955: 06) calls Madero's arrest "a political blunder, inopportune and stupid. [Madero] became the object of sympathy and enjoyed even greater popularity."

A comparable moment in Bolivia was in mid-1951 when the incumbent government refused to permit the congress to select from the leading candidates in the presidential elections in which the candidate of the Movimiento Nacionalista Revolucionario (MNR), Paz Estenssoro, had received a plurality. Barcelli (1956: 249) said that the military junta's take-over "forced the MNR and the people to follow the route of conspiracy." Or, at any rate, the take-over tended to justify such a conspiracy since the MNR had already unsuccessfully tried insurrection in 1949. Peñaloza (1963: 256) points out that the military's nullification of the 1951 election resulted in the great increase in support for the MNR.

Although preceding by nearly seven years the victory of the revolution, the most important precipitating event in Cuba appears to be General Batista's coup d'etat of March 10, 1952. He seized power on the eve of elections in which many observers felt he had no chance of victory. Coming as it did after three terms of popularly elected administrations, Batista's unconstitutional act led to a series of subsequent assassination attempts, general strikes, and revolts allegedly designed to restore the constitutional order. The earliest and now best known of these was the foolhardy attack on the Moncada Barracks in Santiago de Cuba in 1953, which event served as the genesis of Castro's 26th of July Movement. As Draper (1965: 116) states, a catalytic agent was needed to bring accumulated social tensions into eruption and that agent was Batista's coup in March, 1952. He adds that subsequent revolutionary conspiracies were primarily against Batista rather than with Castro. A number of other events contributed to the mounting pace of revolutionary activity, such as the U.S. embargo on arms to Cuba, the Herbert Matthews interview, and the failure of moderates to arrange free elections.

In view of the historical traditions and political character of the pre-revolutionary regimes, undue emphasis on the maintenance of legality or constitutionality as popular norms seems out of place. Yet, the arrest of presidential candidate Madero on the eve of the elections, the Bolivian military's refusal to permit the congress to carry out the electoral mandate of 1951, and Batista's usurpation of power on the eve of the 1952 elections all have one attribute in common. In each case, a dictatorial figure or group openly and cynically denied the electorate the opportunity to select its own leadership. Such open defiance of the nation was more than simply a breach of constitutional norms; it showed contempt for the citizenry. In each case, the arbitrary and violent measure discredited the group involved, revealed its reliance on force rather than consent, and provided moral and political justification for revolution.

II

In the potentially explosive political climate created by the preconditions and precipitants described above, social revolution breaks out only in the presence of revolutionary leadership. Simpson (1937: 44) maintains that once the "oppressed classes are aware that some other way of life is possible and their ambitions are stirred, from then on revolt . . . becomes largely a matter of the appearance of leaders." The leader of a revolutionary group must somehow make himself visible on the national scene. Whereas Díaz had squelched other rivals, Madero was permitted to campaign against him in the 1910 elections because the mild, unprepossessing, little man seemed such an unlikely threat. Castro claimed public attention by a variety of public escapades such as his court case to force Batista's resignation, the bloody attack on Moncada Barracks, and his 1956 landing in Oriente province. Victor Paz Estenssoro had a dozen years of governmental and political experience behind him, plus a victory in the 1951 presidential elections.

The leadership of all three of these revolutions is usually described as lacking a carefully articulated doctrine as compared, for example, to the Bolshevik and Chinese revolutions. This is particularly true in the case of the Mexican and Cuban Revolutions. Tannenbaum (1950: 49) called the Mexican Revolution ". . . unadorned by any philosophy of politics, meager in its social program, and opportunistic in its immediate objectives." Simpson (1937: 46) described the Mexican Revolution as "innocent of either doctrine or theory . . . in the beginning it was largely a blind, blundering, haphazard, spontaneous outbreak." Cosío Villegas (1964: 3) maintains that the precursors of the revolution had greater "moral than ideological value" and that the Mexican Revolution "never had a definite program, nor has it attempted to formulate one now." Octavio Paz (1950: 136) points out that the "lack of ideological precursors and the scarcity of links with universal ideology are characteristic aspects of the revolution."

In Cuba the rich and varied ideological influences which played upon the revolutionary forces and subsequent efforts to interpret Cuban events in theoretical terms should not obscure the doctrinal confusion of Castro's pre-revolutionary statements, particularly when compared with orthodox Marxism-Leninism. In describing Castro's efforts to come to terms with Marxism, Burks (1964: 28) concludes that "the Castroites failed in their search for an adequate ideology of their own." Suárez (1967: Ch. I) describes Castro as having "only the most superficial smattering of ideology even in 1962." Perhaps, no one has devoted more critical attention to this subject than Theodore Draper (1965: 58) who concludes that "Castroism seemed to be a blueprint without a theory . . . Castroism has rather had only a 'retrospective' theory, in the sense that only after taking power did it begin to ask itself what it had done and how it had been done."

Unlike the Mexican and Cuban revolutionary movements, the Movimiento Nacionalista Revolucionario (MNR) of Bolivia was an organized and functioning political party for some dozen years, had participated in government, and had been developing its own political programs. The fact that the MNR had been influenced by both Fascist and Marxist thought was the source of no little political and ideological confusion. Under the circumstances, it should be no cause for surprise that its early programs foreshadowed only in part the course of the new revolutionary government. In the compilation sponsored by the U. S. Army, the *Area Handbook On Bolivia* (1963: 2), the Bolivian Revolution was characterized as "neither a coup d'état, nor a revamping of society according to the dictates of a particular doctrine . . . it is more aptly characterized as that primitive stage in which modernization receives official endorsement."

These revolutions were not generated in a day. The revolutionary leadership passed through a period of underground or openly rebellious actions that tested their strategy and courage. In Mexico there were numerous small uprisings prior to 1900 (particularly in the north) as well as in the first decade of the twentieth century, and Madero's insurrection lasted from the issuance of his Plan de San Luis Potosí of October 1910 until the fall of Díaz in May 1911. In Bolivia, the Movimiento Nacionalista Revolucionario was involved in conspiracies off and on from its formation in 1940 until the seizure of government in 1952, perhaps the most dramatic instance of which was the failure of the insurrection of 1949. The actual seizure of government in Bolivia lasted only about three days, with intense fighting confined largely to La Paz and a few other urban centers. If Castro's abortive attack on Moncada Barracks and other incidents are excluded, the Castroite insurrection lasted slightly more than two years, from the landing of the Granma in late 1956 until Batista's flight on January 1, 1959.

The revolutionary movements owe their success in no small measure to weaknesses of the armies of the old regimes, whose impressive facades concealed poor morale and leadership. Parkes (1938: 320) calls the Díaz dictatorship, despite its invincible appearance, as rotten with age and explains how the "army had been steadily weakened; nominally 30,000, it actually contained only 18,000 men, and these were unwilling conscripts badly equipped by grafting war department officials." Never having recovered from its disastrous defeat in the Chaco War, the Bolivian army continued to suffer from the wide rift between officers and enlisted men, poor morale, and weak organization. The revolt of the Minister of Government, General Antonio Seleme and the police, who turned over weapons to the rebels, was a fatal breach in the old regime's unity. With regard to Batista's army, Julien (1961: 91) attributes Batista's coup in 1952 to his subversion of unscrupulous officers. But the effectiveness of this technique also explains why these military "adventurers," concerned first about saving their own skin and enjoying the fruits of their corruption, could not be counted on in his hour of need. Draper (1965: 105) also points out that Batista's army was made up of raw peasant recruits who had little stake in the existing regime and "abandoned it at the first sign of weakening." The rank and file of the regular armies in Mexico and Bolivia had no better reason to risk their lives in the defense of tottering governments.

As the pressure of the revolutionary forces in each country increased, the professional, political, and moral bankruptcy of the armed forces of the old regimes led them to increasingly desperate and counter-productive measures. In the concluding months of his rule, Porfirio Díaz mixed brutal suppression with ill-timed concessions, only stimulating the revolutionary forces to new exertions. In Bolivia after the repudiation of the 1951 elections, the military junta, according to Ostria Gutiérrez (1952: 81), took harsh and not always strictly legitimate measures of self defense which generated sympathy for the "trouble makers" and paved the way for their victory. The military's repressive activities were perhaps most counter-productive in Cuba. Phillips (1959: 342) described in detail the brutalities, torture, and murderous reprisals for which the Batista armed forces were responsible and which had the effect of uniting the population in opposition to the Batista regime. Gil (1962: 383) describes how "the brutal revenge taken by the regime, in the form of murder and torture applied indiscriminantly to all opponents of Batista, terrorized the population" and led to widespread revolutionary activity all over the island.

The Bolivian revolutionaries used a lightning urban insurrection to achieve a classical coup d'état. The fact that the revolutionaries included important elements of the civilian population distinguished it from the typical palace or barracks revolts. In Mexico and Cuba the revolutionaries used a wide spectrum of violent techniques: demonstrations, strikes, local revolts, and armed rebellion. Castro's methods, unlike those used in the Mexican and Bolivian Revolutions (methods well known in Latin America) combined paramilitary activities with the techniques of psychological warfare. His meticulous attention to publicity, indicated in part by his "History Will Absolve Me" speech and the Matthews interview, the strict rules about proper guerrilla conduct toward the local populace, the dramatic kidnapping of racing driver Juan Manuel Fangio and of American and Canadian executives, were all part of his political strategy. In assuming the military risks of announcing his 1956 landing in Cuba in advance, Castro explicitly indicated the priority he gave "psychological warfare." (Huberman and Sweezy, 1960: 52.)

Although the techniques of revolutionary violence varied, none of the three revolutionary movements could escape direct confrontation with the military forces of the old regimes. In each case, when the revolutionaries had successfully bested regular forces in a conventional military situation, the old regimes collapsed like a house of cards.

In Mexico the confrontation took place at Ciudad Juárez on the U.S. border, after revolts and demonstrations scattered through Mexico had shaken Díaz's authority. Cut off from distant sources of supply in the south, regular forces proved no match for Madero's irregulars. According to Silva Herzog (1960: 160), "the fall of Ciudad Juárez was the *coup de grâce* of General Díaz's government. With a single battle won, by the taking of an unimportant town square, such as that of Ciudad Juárez, the revolution begun in November, 1910 had triumphed. It was not the army but public opinion which had won." While recognizing the vast repercussions of the Madero revolt, Cline (1953: 121) calls it "scarcely the mass uprising of a downtrodden people . . . not the instrument of rapacious foreign capitalism . . . the Madero revolution was essentially a colossal bluff that succeeded . . . even by Mexican standards it was a small affair."

In Bolivia the confrontation with the army took place in La Paz itself. With the support of the police, the revolutionary forces hung on in La Paz and defeated the most courageous defenders of the old regime, the cadets from the military school. According to Peñaloza (1963: 279), when the commanding general, Torres Ortíz, learned of the rebel victory in Oruro, was informed of his troops' reluctance to fight, and faced a dwindling supply of munitions, he capitulated to the MNR's demands. As Patch (1961: 127) indicates, "The revolution did not follow the rules. . . . there was little loss of life, there was little fighting outside of La Paz."

In Cuba the decisive military confrontation of the revolution took place in Santa Clara in Las Villas province. Detachments of Castro's 26th of July Movement marched west from their sanctuary in the Sierra Maestra mountains, harassing Batista's army, subduing small garrisons, but avoiding a direct confrontation in force. At Santa Clara, troops from the 26th of July Movement and other resistance organizations under the leadership of Ché Guevara met and attacked a heavily armed military detachment in force and won. Subject to a variety of other pressures such as a U.S. embargo, the unwillingness of troops to fight, and the demands of his own general staff, Batista fled the island within a matter of hours.

Until the revolutionary forces were ready to face and defeat the regular armies in direct combat, they could not dislodge the old regimes. When these armies were defeated in single encounters at Ciudad Juárez, La Paz, and Santa Clara, the old regimes collapsed from within. Agreement about the military insignificance of the coup in La Paz is virtually unanimous. Authorities also tend to play down the military significance of Madero's victory, even though the local revolts of Orozco, Zapata, Villa, and others should not be ignored. The significance of Castro's paramilitary activities, however, is one of the most controversial issues of the Cuban Revolution.

Controversy about the military significance of Castro's victory relates primarily to two questions. First, how important were Castro's resistance activities as compared to those of other Cuban revolutionary groups? According to MacGaffey and Barnett (1965: 277), "for most of the two year period that Castro spent in guerrilla warfare, the rebels were on the defensive in the mountains . . . a much larger urban resistance movement harassed the army and police in the cities." Taber (1961: 277) explains the decision to send Guevara and Cienfuegos to the west as the means of ensuring Fidelista predominance over other revolutionary groups which far outnumbered the Fidelistas. And there can be no doubt that strikes, sabotage, demonstrations, attempted assassinations, local revolts sponsored by groups independent of Castro played an enormous role in bringing Batista down. Evidence from secondary sources, however, is insufficient for quantitative measurement of the importance of Castro's efforts compared with those of others, if in fact quantification is possible. What may be more significant is the fact that Castro's strategies succeeded where others had failed, he became the best known leader of the Cuban resistance, and imposed his will on the nation after the seizure of the government.

A second controversial issue involves the military as opposed to the political or psychological significance of Castro's revolutionary activities. Phillips (1959), the *New York Times* correspondent in Havana, gives the impression of considerable paramilitary activities throughout the country. Also the accounts of the guerrilla campaigns by Taber (1961), Pardo Llada (1960) and Guevara (1963) describe seemingly complex and far reaching guerrilla operations. Yet, it appears that Castro's armed forces on the eve of his victory barely exceeded 1,500 men. According to Pardo Llada (1960: 42) who joined Castro in the Sierra in October, 1958, Castro had succeeded in arming from 1,500 to 1,700 men. Goldenberg (1965: 162) reports that he was personally informed that there were only about 803 officially recognized members in Castro's forces in December 1958. Draper (1965: 71) quotes Castro as maintaining that the "decisive battles" of the war were fought with fewer than 500 men. Evidence available from secondary sources is thus not conclusive on this point, but a reasonable working hypothesis is that Castro's armed forces represented a tiny fraction of the number of men available to Batista.

Many of the authoritative accounts de-emphasize the military aspects of Castro's victory. Julien (1961: 97) concludes "the victory of Fidel Castro was not strictly speaking a military victory. Above all, it was a moral and popular victory." MacGaffey and Barnett (1965: 295) describe Castro's forces as being unprepared for Batista's flight since "their only substantial military victories had occurred in December, culminating in the seizure of Santa Clara." Draper (1965: 25) also describes Castro's surprise at Batista's capitulation, a capitulation to a "hostile people," rather than "a defeat by a superior force." Draper maintains that Batista's regime would not have fallen without Castro's military pressure, but military pressure itself was far from enough to bring about Batista's fall.

While there may continue to be grounds for disagreement about the extent and impact of Castro's paramilitary activities, the weight of authority gives precedence to the political rather than the military significance of his victory.

In the light of what happened later, especially in Mexico and Cuba, the initial political objectives of all three insurrectionary movements were surprisingly moderate. In Mexico Madero directed his criticism at President Díaz' unwillingness to step down after so many years in power, calling for free elections, and the restriction on suffrage. According to Quirk (1963: 3), Madero "abhorred revolution" and turned reluctantly to armed revolt. He concentrated on the implementation of democratic and constitutional norms rather than far-reaching socio-economic reform. Initially, he had been prepared for all manner of compromise with Díaz; it was only the latter's intransigence which forced him to take up arms. In Bolivia, the Movimiento Nacionalista Revolucionario did have specific ideas about political and economic innovation, but the leadership assumed that mantle of constitutional legitimacy in claiming Paz Estenssoro's right to the presidency as a result of his plurality in the 1951 elections. During the insurrection in Cuba, Castro's political platform was firmly based on a return to the Constitution of 1940; the Cuban Revolution was radicalized *after* he was in power.

On the eve of and during the insurrections the revolutionary movements in all three countries directed their fire at fairly narrow political targets. Madero fought Díaz and his inner circle. The MNR sought to wrench power from the military who represented the "rosca," the combination of mining and landed interests that had traditionally ruled the country. Unlike pre-revolutionary Mexico and Bolivia, Cuba by the 1950's no longer had a society so clearly marked by the traditional pattern of 19th century class stratification. Castro's revolt was against Batista and his military clique, not against a traditional upper class.

Although it is not too difficult to identify what group these three revolutions were against, it is somewhat harder to determine who they were for. An analysis of the groups which made the revolutions provides a partial answer.

In Mexico, almost all classes were sources of revolutionary leadership. Madero came from a rich family of hacendados, Carranza and Obregón were ranchers, Calles a school teacher. Zapata was a peasant who clung to the land and Pancho Villa escaped peonage as a cattle rustler. During the insurrection and Madero's presidency the class character of the new regime had not yet been determined; these issues were to be resolved during the civil war and thereafter.

Almost all authorities agree that the Bolivian Revolution was made by members of the middle class and industrial workers, particularly miners. Canelas (1966: 160) holds that the leadership in the 1952 Revolution was "fundamentally petty bourgeois" and the rank and file were predominantly "urban workers and miners." In the official *Bolivia: Diez años de revolución,* Dirección Nacional de Informaciones (1962) the MNR government makes explicit reference to the middle class' participation in the 1952 coup. Few if any authorities indicate any significant participation by the peasants and Urquidi (1966: 327) explicitly denies peasant participation. Most of the leading members of the MNR were middle class intellectuals and professional men, although there were a few important leaders, such as Juan Lechín, who came up through mining or other sectors of organized labor.

The social origins of the participants in the Cuban revolutionary movement are far more controversial. Agreement does exist about the important contribution of the middle class to Castro's victory. In the first place, Castro's core group, those who survived the 1956 landing, were middle class, as Taber (1961: 12) points out, and included: the son of a sugar cane planter, a grocer's son, an accountant, a judge's son, a school teacher, and a minor league baseball player. Draper (1965: 68) quotes Ché Guevara that "none of us . . . of the first group who came in the *Granma* . . . had a worker's or peasant's background." According to Draper (1965: 111), the great majority of leadership and a large part of the rank and file came from the middle class until 1957 or even perhaps 1958. Even the Soviet analyst, Kalinin (in Mikhailov, 1964: 28), leaves no doubt about middle class participation. Gil (1962: 384) and MacGaffey and Barnett (1965: 289) describe Castro's financial and other support from rich Cubans who opposed Batista.

For ideological and other reasons many commentators sympathetic to the Cuban Revolution list the participation of organized labor in the resistance movement. Much evidence is available, however, to discount the significance of labor's role. Draper (1965: 76) denies that the Cuban Revolution was a "proletarian revolution," as far as the conquest of power was concerned and MacGaffey and Barnett (1965: 179) said the Castro government came to power without the support of organized labor. Castro's advisor, Dumont (1965: 40), said that the urban working class was too Americanized and remained on the sidelines during the resistance. Goldenberg (1965: 144) described the workers as taking "less part in the struggle than any other class."

The extent of peasant participation in the Cuban resistance movement is difficult to determine in part because of the contradictory testimony. Aguirre (1964: 301) and Huberman and Sweezy (1961: 78) emphasize the role of peasants in the guerrilla movement. The latter claims elsewhere (p. 57) that ¾ to ⅘ of the soldiers in the final campaigns of 1958 were peasants, and that the "most important class" which joined the rebels was the peasantry. Draper (1965: 72) takes a contrary position, maintaining that "Castro's active peasant backing was so limited in terms of the peasantry or agricultural population as a whole that it can hardly serve to support the theory of 'agrarian revolution.'" He quotes Guevara to show that the members of the rural populace in the Sierra Maestra who joined the 26th of July Movement were atypical in that they wanted land of their own and were not wage laborers on large sugar plantations. Draper (1965: 67) points out that Guevara does not derive guerrilla warfare from the agrarian revolution, but the reverse. That is Guevara stresses fighting in the countryside because this is easier and more effective than in the cities. In comparing the role of the middle class and the peasants, Lanning (1966: 367) concludes that the revolution probably could have succeeded without the peasants, but it could not have succeeded without the middle class.

Another issue which needs to be squarely faced is the extent of Communist participation during the seizure of government in these three countries. Alexander (1958: 272) expresses what is probably the most accepted view, namely: "The Mexican and Bolivian Revolution have both been fundamentally American. Neither has been led by people owing their allegiance to any foreign government or any foreign ideology." The Mexican Revolution, of course, took place well before the Bolshevik Revolution and the Mexican Communist Party was not formed until 1919. The Bolivian Communist Party was formed in 1950 and Communist sources often claim an active role in the 1952 insurrection. But at this early date the Communist Party was extremely small and it was not until 1959 that it held its first national congress.

The nature and extent of Communist participation in the resistance movement has been one of the most controversial aspects of the Cuban Revolution. Virtually all sources agree that some Communists supported Castro and participated in the guerrilla and other activities of the resistance movement several months prior to Batista's fall. Burks (1964: 30) expresses one authoritative view:

Sometime in the summer of 1959 the PSP [Partido Socialista Popular] (Communist) old guard decided they should support Castro, since it seemed certain that he was going to win, and that Batista was on the way out. The Communists were not, however, united; some Party members continued to serve in the Batista government and others failed to oppose Batista openly. In the early summer of 1958 a Communist leader, Carlos Rafael Rodríguez, had visited Castro in the Sierra Maestra. There is no known evidence one way or another of a deal, but it would seem that Castro reassured the Party leaders that if he came to power he would not be and it would not be anti-Communist.

The major issues, then, were not whether the Communists supported Castro, but how soon, to what extent, and the significance of their participation. In general, those who tend to stress the importance of the Communists in the early phases of the Cuban Revolution come from one of two extremes.

On the one hand, Cuban and other Communists who seek credit for the Party's participation in the revolution tend to emphasize Communist participation and gloss over Castro's differences with the Party. On the other, some of Castro's harshest critics stress the Communist tie in connection with their efforts to support positions on public policies hostile towards Castro in other countries.

Communist criticism of Castro's abortive attack on Moncada Barracks in 1953 and their unwillingness to support Castro's call for a general strike in April 1958 are both a matter of record. The Soviet analyst Kalinin (in Mikhailov, 1964: 23) describes how some Cuban Communists during the preparation for the revolution maintained a "mistaken position" which kept the Party for a certain time from entering into "the active struggle." Goldenberg (1965: 166), Zeitlin and Scheer (1963: 110), Arnault (1962: 89), Julien (1961: 82) all stress the deep gulf that separated Castro and the Communists until the concluding months of the revolution. Suaréz (1967: Ch. I) points out that even by January 1, 1959, when Castro had won, the Communists had not definitely defined their position with respect to Castro. The reply given to Janette Habel (Castro and Habel, 1965: 49) by Blas Roca, leader of the Cuban Communists for many years, about what he believed to be the most important phenomenon of the Cuban Revolution may be decisive: "[The Cuban Revolution] is the first socialist revolution which had not been made [hecha] by the Communist Party."

Another question which arises in connection with all three revolutions is the nature and extent of United States influence. Madero used the United States as a sanctuary and secured weapons and munitions there, mostly at his own and his family's expense. Ross (1955: 143) denies that the U.S. government was either a supporter of the Díaz government, or a cohort of the revolutionists, but that U.S. neutrality "strengthened the Madero movement morally and materially."

The fact that troops were massed along the border as the Ciudad Juárez campaign was reaching a climax has been described as pressure on President Díaz to resign. Vera Estañol (1957: 155) maintains that Díaz's cabinet believed that it was vital to avoid at all costs "any pretext or cause for the outbreak of hostilities with the neighboring country." Silva Herzog (1960: 156) also describes how "fear of our neighbors" alarmed Díaz's government and implies that Díaz felt the need to come to terms with Madero in order to avoid U.S. intervention. Parkes (1938: 320) and Cumberland (1952: 133) describe how the presence of American troops complicated the negotiating position of the Díaz government. Treatment of this issue in the secondary sources consulted does not provide sufficient evidence for conclusive judgment.

The United States ties with Bolivia were less close than those with Mexico and Cuba on the eve of the revolution. The United States was, nonetheless, a major market for tin and U.S. dealings with the Bolivian government in the months preceding the revolution were a subject of public attention and did not strengthen the hand of the authorities in the rapidly approaching revolutionary situation. Partly because U.S. financial interests in Bolivia went less extensive, the nationalization of the large tin companies and the agrarian reform in 1952 and 1953 created less strain in relations with the United States than comparable actions in the Mexican and Cuban Revolutions.

The question of United States influence on Cuba as Batista's term drew to a close is controversial and complex. During that period the U.S. maintained close relations with Batista and was providing economic assistance. At the same time, Castro received important support from Cuban exiles in the United States, and the 1958 embargo on military aid dealt Batista a severe blow. Burks (1964: 12) describes United States policy during this period as "unimaginative if well meaning confusion of the principle of non-intervention with that of neutrality . . . the lack of interest on the part of the administration in Latin America and the general belief, held until late 1958 that Castro could not win." U.S. policies towards Castro after January 1959 are sometimes interpreted as having an important influence on the course of the Cuban Revolution; most sources dealing with the pre-revolutionary period emphasize domestic trends and events in Cuba.

III

Works on the revolutionary process by Johnson, Eckstein, and others have helped identify critical aspects of social revolution about which we know little and need to know much more. For example, under what circumstances and how do disorienting social processes, such as industrialization and urbanization, contribute to the development of revolutionary situations? What is the impact on political stability of changing social values and social structures? How does one relate the development of new classes or interest groups to revolution? What can be learned about the social origins, attitudes, and objectives of members of revolutionary or potentially revolutionary groups? Much is known about certain leaders, little about their followers. What decisions of incumbent elites tend to inflame, or dampen, revolutionary situations? What were the causes and the nature of the disintegration of the regular armed forces in countries which have experienced revolutions? Answers to such questions are likely to be found not only through the study of revolution, but as a result of increased understanding of social change itself.

Although our understanding of Latin American revolutions is at best in its adolescence, useful working hypotheses can be drawn on the basis of the foregoing survey of secondary sources. In a general way these hypotheses reflect the insight of some of the recent findings in social science about revolutions, but remain in the traditional framework of the literature on which they are based. Genuinely new conceptions about revolution await the design of sharper and more powerful analytical tools and their application to primary sources.

An underlying and fundamental cause of the revolutions in Mexico, Bolivia, and Cuba was the growing gap between the vast majority of the population and a small, ruling elite. The bedrock of popular discontent was in part due to the structure and functioning of the economic system. In Mexico and Bolivia there was an inefficient and inequitable system of land tenure on the colonial pattern. In Cuba the large sugar plantations and mills which overshadow all other productive activities proved incapable of leading the economy towards the modernization and diversification required. Díaz had done more than any other Mexican leader in history to develop the country, but he did so at the expense of Mexican peasants and urban labor. In Bolivia the traditional alliance of mining and landed interests, discredited by the Chaco War and weakened by internal division, appeared incapable of bolstering the faltering economy and maintaining peace in the mines. In Cuba the moderate and democratically oriented Auténtico leadership and its successor, Batista's military dictatorship, did not introduce the broad social and economic reforms to which they gave lip service, nor could they lead the nation confidently up the slope of economic development. All three revolutionary governments were closely linked with powerful trading and investment interests abroad which dominated the countries' foreign trade and controlled some of their important domestic industries. Popular criticism of the nations' economic dependence and of privileged positions for foreigners was already strong on the eve of the revolutions.

Popular unrest, to the extent that it was due to economic problems, appears to have been insufficient to cause a revolution. At best similar conditions exist to a greater or lesser degree in almost all the underdeveloped countries of Latin America, few of which have experienced social revolutions. Opposition to existing regimes was based on broader social, even ethical grounds which touched men's hearts as well as their appetites. In all three countries the old regimes, having forfeited a claim to legitimacy, were rooted in a setting of corruption and social injustice. To oversimplify, Díaz had ruled too long and too despotically. The Bolivian "rosca" ruled too falteringly and too ineffectively. Batista ruled too arbitrarily and cruelly.

As a result, on the eve of the revolution all three regimes maintained themselves in power less and less through popular consent and more and more through coercion. And as they attempted increasingly through violent means to strengthen their faltering grip on the country, the popular reaction grew until the opposing forces exploded into revolution. On the eve of all three conflicts an old elite had been forced to take, or had chosen to take, a dramatic step which symbolized their alienation from the population at large and served, together with the rush of events, to precipitate the outbreak of violence.

The revolutionary leadership concentrated their fire on narrow political targets: Díaz and his coterie in Mexico, the "rosca" in Bolivia, and Batista and his military clique in Cuba. Madero's slogan was "no re-election; effective suffrage," and the rest of his program gave hope to many, alarming few. The MNR's program saved its main ammunition for the government and promised something to most sectors of society, including the middle classes. Castro's pre-1959 political program, in the tradition of the middle-of-the-road Orthodox Party, sought to attract support from most sectors of Cuban society. All three revolutionary groups claimed to be the legitimate heirs of a constitutional system which had been betrayed by an incumbent government. And all secured the active support, or at least passivity, of much of the nation.

The same social class dominated each of the three revolutions, but the admixture of participation by different classes varied. In Mexico representatives of many classes participated, but ultimately middle-class elements predominated. Peasant resistance was probably more important relatively than in either Bolivia or Cuba, but peasants belatedly influenced the course of the revolution and never dominated it. In Bolivia the MNR leadership was, in the main, middle class, although miners and urban labor were important participants in the three-day insurrection. Peasants played at most an insignificant role. Castro's closest followers were middle class. His peasant support was not inconsequential, but also probably not decisive. Organized labor was on the periphery of his movement. In all three countries, the middle classes provided the core of the leadership and the core of the rank and file. To anticipate, the middle classes have dominated the revolutions in both Mexico and Bolivia to this day; in Cuba, middle class interests were later sacrificed to those of urban and rural labor.

The revolutionaries won not because of their own virtues but because of the old elite's vices. Capitalizing on what became ultimately moral issues, the revolutionary leaders succeeded because they were able to mobilize, or neutralize, the great mass of the population in a struggle against despotic regimes. Political recruitment and mobilization were the foundation of their success, but these achievements were insufficient in themselves. In the end, each revolutionary group could unseat the incumbent regime only by a military defeat of the regular army. One such victory was sufficient in each case to permit them to capitalize on their political advantage.

Expressed in broadest terms, the three social revolutions represented the revolt of a wide spectrum of the population, or of groups which claimed to represent that spectrum, against a relatively small traditional or military elite which had lost its ability to govern the country effectively. Influences from abroad played only a peripheral role. The fundamental causes were essentially indigenous, arising from a new sense of national cohesion and national purpose. What distinguished these revolutions from others in Latin America was not so much how they seized the government, but what happened afterwards. This is true even in Cuba where guerrilla tactics were an innovation. The insurrections led ultimately to a far-reaching transformation of social systems, each with distinctive character of its own.

The nature of these transformations, and how they took place, are worthy of separate treatment.

BIBLIOGRAPHY

Baran, Paul A. "Reflections on the Cuban Revolution," *The Monthly Review* (January–February 1961).

Brinton, Crane. *The Anatomy of Revolution*. New York: Norton, 1938.

Cline, Howard F. *United States and Mexico*. Cambridge: Harvard University Press, 1953.

Cosio Villegas, Daniel. *American Extremes*. Austin: University of Texas Press, 1964.

Cumberland, Charles C. *The Mexican Revolution: Genesis Under Madero*. Austin: Greenwood Press, Inc., 1952.

Draper, Theodore. *Castroism: Theory and Practice*. New York: Praeger, 1965.

Eckstein, Harry. "On the Etiology of Internal War," *History and Theory,* No. 4 (1965), 133–163.

Friedrich, Carl J., Ed. "Revolution," *Nomos,* 8 (1966).

Gil, Federico. "Antecedents of the Cuban Revolution," *The Centennial Review,* Vol. 6, No. 3 (1962).

Goldenberg, Boris. *The Cuban Revolution and Latin America*. New York: Praeger, 1965.

Huberman, Leo and Sweezy, Paul M. *Cuba: The Anatomy of a Revolution*. New York: Monthly Review, 1961.

Johnson, Chalmers. *Revolutionary Change*. Boston: Little, 1966.

Klein, Herbert S. "The Impact of the Chaco War on Bolivian Society." University of Chicago Microfilm, 1963.

Lanning, Eldon Wayne. "The Bolivian Revolution of 1952 and the Cuban Revolution of 1959; Case Studies of a Theory of Revolution." University Microfilms, Ann Arbor, 1966.

MacGaffey, Wyatt and Barnett, Clifford R. *Twentieth Century Cuba*. Garden City: Doubleday, 1965.

Nelson, Lowry. *Rural Cuba*. Minneapolis: University of Minnesota Press, 1950.

Parkes, Henry B. *A History of Mexico*. Boston: Houghton, 1938.

Patch, Richard W. "Bolivia: The Restrained Revolution," *Annals of the Academy of Political and Social Science,* Vol. 334 (1961), 123–132.

Paz, Octavio. *The Labyrinth of Solitude: Life and Thought in Mexico*. New York: Grove, 1962.

Phillips, Ruby Hart. *Cuba: Island of Paradox*. New York: Mc-Dowell, 1959.

Quirk, Robert E. *The Mexican Revolution: 1914–1915*. New York: Citadel, 1963.

Ross, Stanley R. *Francisco I. Madero, Apostle of Mexican Democracy*. New York: Columbia University Press, 1955.

——, Ed. *Is the Mexican Revolution Dead?* New York: Knopf, 1966.

Seers, Dudley et al. *Cuba: The Economic and Social Revolution*. Chapel Hill: University of North Carolina Press, 1964.

Simpson, Eyler N. *The Ejido, Mexico's Way Out*. Chapel Hill: University of North Carolina Press, 1937.

Smith, Robert Freeman. *The United States and Cuba: Business and Diplomacy 1917–1960*. New York: Bookman Associates, 1961.

Suárez, Andrés. *Cuba: Castroism and Communism 1959–1966*. Cambridge: MIT Press, 1969.

Tannenbaum, Frank. *The Mexican Agrarian Revolution*. New York: Brookings Institute, 1929.

——. *Peace By Revolution: An Interpretation of Mexico*. New York: Columbia University Press, 1933.

——. *Mexico, The Struggle for Peace and Bread*. New York: Knopf, 1950.

United Nations Publications. Report of the United Nations Mission of Technical Assistance to Bolivia, New York, 1951.

U. S. Army Area Handbook for Bolivia. Prepared by Foreign Area Studies Division, Special Operations Research, The American University, Washington, D.C., 1963.

Zeitlin, Maurice and Scheer, Robert. *Cuba: Tragedy in Our Hemisphere*. New York: Grove, 1963.

Zondag, Cornelius H. *The Bolivian Economy, 1952–1965; The Revolution and Its Aftermath*. New York: Praeger, 1966.

3

CUBA: ITS POLITICAL ECONOMY*

James O'Connor

1. Class Structure, Consciousness, and Organization

In the course of the 20th century Cuba's economic class structure underwent two important modifications. It was polarized
by the penetration of foreign capital, economic depression,
war, and rising nationalism, which also modified and transformed class consciousness. Both developments advanced
Cuba's revolutionary potential but the changes in the organization and political perspective of the island's farmers and
workers were of primary significance for the emergence of a
socialist state in 1959–1961.

A cursory glance at census data, in fact, fails to reveal any
important objective changes in Cuba's class structure. By 1907
a typically "capitalist" class structure was already a feature
of the island's social economy and a rural proletariat was
already statistically well-developed; according to the census
of that year, of roughly 770,000 Cuban wage workers, about
40 per cent, or 310,000, were farm laborers. Elsewhere in
the agricultural labor force were 40,000 tenant farmers of
various kinds and 17,000 farm owners. Forty years later, the
proportion of farm owners to tenants remained slightly less
than one-half. Similarly, the rural proletariat had expanded
at about the same pace as the total working class, and in
both 1907 and 1946, about 5 per cent of Cuba's total rural
labor class were farm owners.

* Reprinted with permission from James O'Connor, "The Foundations
of Cuban Socialism," *Studies on the Left*, Vol. 4, No. 4, Fall 1964, pp.
97–117.

There were, however, sharp alterations, which the aggregative data obscure, in the composition of the owner and tenant classes. Thousands of independent tobacco farmers and sugar growers lost their farms during the crises of the 1920's and the great depression and were transformed into tenants and sharecroppers.[1] Replacing them in the "owner" column were marginal subsistence farmers and small coffee growers who inherited increasingly fragmentized plots from generation to generation. Thus the remnants of the rural petty bourgeoisie from the 19th century were to a large degree destroyed by large-scale foreign and domestic investments in sugar cultivation in the first quarter of the 20th century and later on in other sectors of the economy, and replaced by large "administrator-operated" farms or transformed into dependent tenants. By mid-century there were relatively fewer well-to-do farm owners and a large increase in the absolute and relative number of small, poor tenants.

Unlike the experiences of all advanced capitalist societies, a new petty bourgeoisie failed to replace the old; in Cuba large-scale enterprise created few new satellite industries and no widespread opportunities for small-scale investments. Investment opportunities in industries supplying raw materials, semi-finished parts, transport, packing, and distribution facilities to the sugar industry and possibilities in higher stages of manufacture were extremely limited, and, in any event, Cuban capitalists were generally conditioned by an economy of scarce opportunities and failed to seize those which did open

[1] The independent tobacco farmer, like the sugar grower before him, was the victim of large-scale capital. The mechanization of cigarette and some cigar production diverted foreign capital into the manufacturing branch of the tobacco industry. Fluctuating leaf prices introduced an element of unpredictability into the cost calculations of the manufacturers, turning their attention to tobacco cultivation itself. Were they to have effective control over supplies of leaf, they realized, costs could be stabilized. But once the manufacturers moved into tobacco cultivation they had to do so on the largest possible scale, for the product of each grower varied from year to year in quality. Only when the manufacturers owned extensive producing lands were they assured of a consistently similar product from one season to the next. What is more, by the late 1920's and early 1930's land could be purchased at rock bottom prices.

In this way, Partagas, the giant English-owned firm, came to own 18,000 acres of the finest tobacco lands in Cuba. From 1925 to 1940, the number of independent growers fell from over 11,000 to 3,000.

up. Foreign investment and control deprived Cubans of many
of the possibilities which the expansions of the sugar industry
did create and thus further conditioned the development of
the Cuban class structure by frustrating the growth of a potential new middle class. New satellite and secondary industries, which would have normally sprung up on Cuban soil
and encouraged the growth of a new petty bourgeoisie, made
their appearance in the United States. Sugar refining is perhaps the best illustration: United States duties on Cuban exports of refined sugar were always somewhat higher than
those on crude sugar, and in 1934 the Jones-Costigan Act
placed physical limits on United States imports of the Cuban
refined product.[2] Of the island's total quota in its mainland
market, a maximum of 22 per cent was allowed to enter as
refined sugar; this ratio remained more or less fixed until
1960 when Cuba was deprived of its United States sales altogether. Even during World War II, when Cuba had the opportunity to expand exports of refined sugar, lack of capacity
reduced the share of refined to crude exports from about
one-fifth in 1939 to roughly one-tenth in 1947.

United States commercial policy also contributed to the
"export" of the Cuban manufactured tobacco industry. High
tariffs on manufactured products encouraged the American
Cigar Company and other firms to shift some of their operations to the United States, although militant wage and anti-
mechanization policies by the tobacco workers' union were
also important in the transfer of capital from Cuba to the
mainland; caught in a tight bind, foreign capital attempted
just before the war to reduce the industry to its purely agricultural phase. Similarly, in mining industries foreign control
deprived Cuba of many processing and finishing industries,
limiting still further the growth of a new middle class.

[2] Robert F. Smith, *The United States and Cuba, Business and Diplomacy, 1917–1960*, New York, 1960, pp. 66, 160. Had the Hershey Company not produced about 50 per cent of Cuba's refined sugar, the island's
refined quota would no doubt have been lower. The northern refining interests were pleased with the legislation. According to Earl Babst of the
American Sugar Refining Company, the two pieces of legislation were
". . . a step in the direction of a sound Colonial policy" (quoted in *Ibid.*,
p. 161).

Outside of agriculture, the most significant modification of the island's class structure was the growth of the salariat in commerce and state employment; white collar workers probably comprised about 10 per cent of the total labor force in the first decade of the century and roughly 20 per cent forty years later. This expansion was due to the growth and increasing complexity of foreign trade and the mushrooming state bureaucracy associated with the growing interference of the government in the island's economic life, and was significant in that it conditioned Cubans to think of government jobs as legitimate sources of employment. Seventy per cent of Cuba's rural population looked to the government to resolve the unemployment problem (which 73 per cent said was the most important problem), according to a Catholic University survey. Thus by 1958 non-farm wage and salary workers in private and public employment made up about one-half of the total labor force, and agricultural wage workers comprised about 22 per cent of the total. Small farm owners and tenants accounted for roughly 10 per cent; the remaining 18 per cent was made up of thousands of petty bourgeois commercialists, a national manufacturing and agricultural bourgeoisie, and a tiny upper class of unenterprising landowners and stockholders, and the larger ranchers and manufacturers.

The second important development in the Cuban class structure during the 20th century was the heightening and transformation of class consciousness. Although the rural proletariat failed to grow quantitatively compared with other economic classes in the countryside, farm laborers' consciousness of themselves as members of a specific class broadened and became clearer. Around the turn of the century it was possible to describe the rural worker in the following terms: "The Spanish laborer expects little. Withal, he is a peaceful, temperate and hard working man, as a rule."[3] The class consciousness of Negro agricultural workers was even less developed, and they themselves more passive, mainly because they lacked nearly totally any political history. By 1933 this

---

[3] According to the British Consul-General in Havana.

had all changed as a result of an extreme deterioration of the
rural economy and nearly a decade of union organizational
work. In the course of the 1933 revolution there was a great
deal of peasant and worker agitation in the countryside, and
the fact that subsequent social legislation was to a degree
written in the interests of the rural laborers implies that
they were a political force of some importance. Certainly by
1959 they had become the most cohesive economic class on
the island, and potentially the strongest. Attracted by their
labor organizations and tradition of militant struggle, even
many of the smaller sugar growers came to identify more
with them than their own class.[4]

For these developments there were a number of reasons,
important among which was the ban on immigration from
Haiti and Jamaica which tended to stabilize the labor force and
ease the task of union organizers. For another thing, the depression attracted hundreds of urban-based revolutionaries
and political activists into the ranks of the professional labor
organizers and speeded the development of rural unionism.
What is more, with the concentration of capital in sugar, and
the growing importance of the large sugar farm, up to the
mid-1930's labor was hired in increasingly large units. The
job of union organizing and collective bargaining was facilitated. In the context of the decline of the oligarchy in the
late 1920's and the moral and political bankruptcy of the capitalist class generally during the great depression, it is not
difficult to understand the sources of the growing class consciousness of the rural proletariat.

There were parallel changes in the political awareness, orientation and organization of Cuba's tenant farmers, particularly the sugar growers (*colonos*). The crises of the 1920's and
1930's introduced the island's small farmers to their first contemporary political experiences; before this period they were
by and large economically and politically passive, or they had
prospered as farm owners. As tenants and even small owners they were compelled to sell their produce when and where
they were able, most of the time under conditions imposed

[4] Charles Page, *The Development of Organized Labor in Cuba,* Ph.D.,
University of California, 1950, p. 204.

on them by the mills, middlemen, or the large ranchers. Self-organization, government protection, the loss of political power by the oligarchy, and common need during the depression, all played their role in the development of the *colonos* associations and other farm groups which quickly acquired independent political power and won favorable tenure arrangements, contractual agreements with the mills and other buyers, and other important gains. Thus a polarized structure of land tenure and economic classes had for three decades been fundamental data of Cuban politics. The labor organizations of the rural proletariat had since the 1930's seized every opportunity to put forth basic economic demands. The small and middle farmers, the cane planters in particular, had acquired through their associations a more or less high degree of security by wringing basic concessions from Cuba's big and small landlords. It was around these twin questions, the "economism" of the rural laborer and the peasant's quest for security, that Cuban rural reform and revolutionary politics revolved.

Despite the political development and organization of the poorer rural classes, their social development lagged far behind that of the organized urban workers, not to speak of the better-to-do business, commercial, and professional classes. As the number and scope of the rural economic and political organizations suggest, the Cuban peasant and workers had acquired a certain degree of political literacy, but for the rest, they were kept in a primitive cultural state; 43 per cent of the adult rural population could not read or write; an imported cultural life flourished among the upper classes in Havana but, with the exception of American films, failed to penetrate the countryside, although, as later events proved, the rural people were starved for books, theater, and knowledge of all kinds. Materially, they fared little better; in the mid-1950's, 60 per cent of the island's rural families lived in dwellings with earth floors and roofs of palm leaves.[5] In

[5] These (rounded) data are from a study made by the Catholic University in 1956. A representative sample of 1000 families distributed in Cuba's 126 municipalities was taken to represent a universe of roughly 400,000 rural families (Agrupacíon Católica Universitaria, *Por qué Reforma Agraria,* n.p., n.d. [mimeographed]. While the categories are not

nearly two-thirds of Cuba's rural houses there were no water-closets or latrines; only one out of fourteen houses was wired for electricity. Poor housing was matched by deficient diets; only 4 per cent of all rural families consumed meat regularly; rice furnished 24 per cent of the average diet, kidney beans, 23 per cent, and root crops, 22 per cent. For the health of Cuba's country people diets and living conditions had terrible implications: 13 per cent of the population had had a history of typhoid, 14 per cent of tuberculosis, and over one-third had intestinal parasites. Of Cuba's social resources, country people consumed a tiny share. Their social development clearly lagged behind their economic and political development; for the sugar mill workers, some farm laborers, many cane, tobacco, and other planters, unions and peasant associations brought important benefits. There were, however, clear limits to what rural labor and farmer organizations could accomplish in the old Cuba.

Meanwhile the island's urban-based middle classes had grown and acquired more political influence, although it is difficult to draw a straight line from the increasingly important economic position of the bourgeoisie to seats of political power and decision-making. Everywhere there was competition for power and influence; from the rising rural organizations, from the giant Cuban Workers' Federation, from the relatively new but entrenched state bureaucracy with its own interests and needs. More significant for the outlook and character of the middle classes were the effects of United States influence in Cuba's economic and political life. Just as the statistical size and industrial location of the Cuban bourgeoisie were conditioned by the pattern of United States investments, so were the general orientation and class mentality of the middle classes shaped by their relationships with foreign capital, the all-pervasiveness of United States culture, and Cuba's neo-colonial political status.

---

exactly similar, the results of the full count of the island's 463,143 rural houses reported by the Population Census of 1953 roughly correspond to the 1956 sample. According to the Census, for example, 63.4 per cent of rural housing had palm leaf roofs and earthen floors; 90.5 per cent lacked bath or shower, inside or outside.

The historical bases of United States influence in island politics are geographical proximity, the attempts by the slave states to bring Cuba into the Union, United States intervention in the Cuban War of Independence, and the complementarity of the United States and Cuban economies. Both in the past and in recent years United States investments in Cuba were for the most part direct, rather than portfolio, and for the island this has meant foreign management, investment policies which were at odds with Cuba's own needs, and often a "community of interests" between domestic and foreign capital. During the key period of the 1950's, the important points of entry for North American interests were the new economic development banks and other institutions. United States influence also fanned out from established beachheads in sugar, cattle, commerce, banking, and utilities into new areas in manufacturing and mineral production and processing. Cuba's dependence on imports from the United States (they averaged four-fifths of the island's total) introduced other social and economic influences, and was the consequence of United States trade preferences, intensive advertising, after-sale service of machinery, the purchase of United States commodities by United States-controlled businesses and professionals and technicians trained in the United States, the lack of foreign exchange controls, and quickness of deliveries.

The penetration of North American capital thus had two broad effects: the first was objective, quantitative, and conditioned the making of the class structure. Existing tendencies were strengthened, the pace of the polarization of the class structure was quickened, and the Cuban economy's capitalist features were exaggerated. This was probably the United States' profoundest impact on Cuba. But North American imperialism as a "cause" of Cuba's stagnation was an even more complex phenomenon. United States influence also had a subjective, qualitative effect; the Cuban bourgeoisie lacked a sense of power, a sense of themselves as agents of progress. One reason was that some segments of the middle class were demoralized by their inability to compete with efficient foreign enterprise, or privileged imports from the United States. Elsewhere in the economy, foreign investment "typically took the form of the establishment of subsidiaries by United States companies with participation by local Cuban capital. . . . Cuban capital was thus invested not in competition but in collaboration with United States capital. The result was the structural integration of the Cuban bourgeoisie within the economy of the alien capitalism."[6] Thus the middle classes were to a degree limited by the participation of United States capital in Cuban industry, and also partly conditioned by their "partnership" status. But this was by no means the whole story; there was also a tendency for portions of the bourgeoisie to take the ideological standards of the old landed wealth as their own, particularly in connection with consumption and social standards. These old standards were mixed liberally with modern business attitudes imported from the United States, and probably most significant, were also combined with attitudes conditioned by the tight networks of market controls and the all-pervasive atmosphere of artificial economic scarcity. In some sectors of the economy, however, notably urban construction, this mixture was overwhelmed by accepted standards which placed key emphasis on the rapid turnover of capital and quick profit-taking. In this light, the sources of middle class ideology, business outlook, and morale, are difficult to trace and define with any precision; what can be said is that the Cuban bourgeoisie lacked a progressive, optimistic, and creative ideology of their own making.

As the splintering and in-fighting among the various exile groups and the desertion of most large exiled businessmen from the anti-Castro cause indicate, neither did the middle class have a sense of class loyalty. G. D. H. Cole once described the significance of this in the following words: ". . . (a man) will be able to act effectively in social matters only if he transfers his allegiance to some . . . group or class

---

[6] Robin Blackburn, "Prologue to the Cuban Revolution," *New Left Review,* No. 21, October, 1963. Blackburn's statement that Cuba lacked any (or nearly any) national bourgeoisie is too extreme. He gives as one "proof" the fact that many Cuban industrialists were naturalized Cubans; but this does not make them any the less independent or semi-independent of imperialist control.

within which he can find like-minded collaborators . . . a
class cannot be defined, when it is regarded as an active agent
of social change, simply in terms of its common economic
experience. It becomes fully a class, in this positive sense, only
to the extent to which it is permeated by a spirit of loyalty
. . . class loyalty need not imply class consciousness in the
individual. . . . Those whom the existing social and economic arrangements suit best are often least conscious of acting together on the basis of class. . . ."[7] In the old Cuba
there was no single class, or mutually satisfactory alliance of
classes which "the existing social and economic arrangements
suit(ed) best," given the nature of market organization, and
particularly the overwhelmingly redistributive aspect of public
economic policy; from these facts we can infer an absence
of class loyalty. The Cuban bourgeoisie was rarely the agent
of social change and was barred from full access to political
power by large and well-organized economic classes and
groups elsewhere in the society.

2. The United States and the Old State

The State in pre-revolutionary Cuba can be characterized
as an administrative, bureaucratic, redistributive state. Foreign policy and some aspects of domestic policy took direction
from the United States; this was another dimension to the
old state.[8] The United States government, North American
business firms operating in Cuba, and business interests with
important Cuban ties regularly interfered directly and indirectly in Cuban affairs, ordinarily to bring about resolutions
to various issues favorable to outside interests. A long cata-
logue of charges of United States interference and intervention in Cuba already has been drawn up, and it is unnecessary

[7] G. D. H. Cole, *The Meaning of Marxism,* London, 1950, pp. 37–38.
[8] "Whenever I asked President Batista for Cuba's vote to support the
United States in the United Nations, he would instruct his Foreign Minister to have the Cuban delegation vote in accordance with the U.S. delegate and to give full support to the American delegate at the U.N." (Earl
Smith, *The Fourth Floor,* New York, 1963, p. 55).

to reproduce it here;[9] United States foreign policy in Cuba is sufficiently well known, and, besides, what is given primary emphasis here are the *effects* of outside intervention and influence on the size and character of the island's class structure, and the general impact on the Cuban political and economic systems.

For the United States the "Cuban problem" had two major facets: the first was the problem of maintaining economic and political stability in order to protect investments amounting in 1958 to over one billion dollars. The second was the related problem of maintaining Cuba as a profitable market for United States exports and a source of crude sugar supplies which could be relied on more or less greatly depending upon mainland and off-shore production and the balance of these interests in the political arena. Thus it was necessary to deprive Cuba of any autonomy (including domestic monetary autonomy which might have resulted, as in other Latin American countries, in inflation) it might have had in a world of free international commerce and mutual respect for national sovereignty. This dependency status had very unfavorable implications for the island's economic growth, particularly in the area of international commercial relationships. Tariff preferences to United States exporters were an obstacle to industrialization and to effective trade bargaining with third countries. "The single most important decision to the Cuban economy, the size of the American sugar quota [was] determined by legislative authorities with whom Cuba [had] no official standing. The affront to national sovereignty inherent in this satellitic relationship should be . . . obvious."[10] In the hands of the United States Secretary of State were placed life and death decisions over the Cuban economy: The Sugar Act of 1948, for instance, gave the Secretary of Agriculture

[9] Smith, *op. cit.,* pp. 19, 46–48, 51, 81, 98, 102, 121, 165, 202–221. Benjamin H. Williams, *Economic Foreign Policy of the United States,* New York, 1929, pp. 56, 169, 201–202. Leland Jenks, *Our Cuban Colony,* New York, 1928, *passim. INRA,* I, No. 1, diciembre de 1960, pp. 56–57. Juan Noyola, "Principales objectivos de nuestro Plan Económico hasta 1965," *Cuba Socialista,* II, No. 13, septiembre de 1962, *passim.*

[10] Boris Swerling, "Sugar and Sympathy," *The Nation,* February 13, 1960, pp. 142–143.

power "to withhold or withdraw any increase in the share of
the domestic consumption requirement provided for (a country which the Secretary of State found to deny fair and
equitable treatment to nationals of the United States, its commerce, navigation, or industry)."[11] The effects of this power
were far-reaching; the Sugar Act of 1951, for example, reduced Cuba's quota for 1952–1956, and led to a drop in
world sugar prices and a multiple decline in Cuba's national
income.

In the course of international commercial negotiations, the
United States rarely hesitated to use its superior bargaining
power. In return for limited Cuban access to the mainland
sugar market, United States exports to Cuba enjoyed wide
tariff preferences; yet this did not stop Washington from
time and again unilaterally reducing Cuba's sugar quota. Of
the many negotiations between the two countries, the Reciprocal Trade Agreement of 1934 was perhaps the most one-
sided and prejudicial to Cuba's interests. Cuba left the bargaining table with modest cuts in United States duties on
sugar, tobacco, and a handful of other agricultural products,
and thus slightly increased its foreign exchange earnings. In
return, Cuba raised United States preferentials by wide
margins, agreed to refrain from increasing duties on large
numbers of mainland products during the life of the treaty
and to reduce or abolish internal taxes on many American
products, and accepted a ban on any quantitative restriction
on any item receiving the benefit of tariff reductions, together
with any transfer and means of payment for commodities.[12]

It is true that 1934 marked a low point in United States
foreign policy in Cuba. The Grau government had just fallen,
thanks chiefly to United States disfavor. In other periods both
before and after the revolution and counter-revolution of
1933–1934, Cuba was able and willing to follow more independent policies conceived more in the island's own interests.
The 1927 tariff, for example, which lifted the prospects of
domestic economic development at the expense of established

[11] U.S. Statutes at Large, 61 Stat., 80th Congress, 1st Session, Ch. 519
(August 8, 1948), p. 195.
[12] Smith, *op. cit.*, pp. 158–159.

United States markets in Cuba, was an authentic expression of Cuban nationalism.[13] At that time Machado's "businessmen's government" was not under any pressure from popular forces, which lacked any coherent organization until the next decade, and on behalf of the restless national bourgeoisie could safely feel its oats vis-a-vis the United States. By the early 1930s, the reaction to Machado's terror had placed Cuban capitalism itself in danger, making Cuban businessmen and commercialists more amenable to United States demands as the price of Washington's political support.

Similar situations characterized other periods of Cuban-United States relationships; now the left (and/or independent labor unionism) would be weakened by internal or external political developments, and the Cuban government could court disapproval with independent nationalistic or quasi-nationalistic economic policies—during World War II, for instance, when Cuban communists were allied; now the government would be in trouble and compelled to turn to the United States for support, usually at the price of more concessions—during the first years of the Batista coup, for example, the United States agreed to alleviate the threatening economic crisis by purchasing large stocks of surplus sugar, apparently at the price of fat concessions to new foreign investments. The short-run needs of the United States also conditioned its Cuban policy: to take an example, with the materialization of a large shortage of jute supplies during World War II, the United States helped to establish in Cuba the Cooperative Fiber Commission to expand the production of a substitute commodity, kenaf. When jute supplies were normalized after the war, the United States lost all interest in the incipient industry, but in the early 1950s when underdeveloped countries were again receiving attention from the United States, Point Four aid was granted to Cuban kenaf producers.

[13] Smith (*Ibid.*, p. 51) argues that Machado was compelled to suspend sugar production and market controls introduced in 1927 the following year after protests by American producers and banks. On the surface, Machado was bowing to United States interests pure and simple; in fact, his policies conformed to Cuban interests as well.

These ups and downs in Cuban-United States relations were superimposed on a long-run tendency: from the mid-1920s on, American businessmen began to recognize that they must identify, or at least appear to identify, with Cuban nationalistic sentiments and aspirations in order to secure political stability on the island.[14] For Washington this was the second and related facet of the "Cuban problem." In the 1950s, the logic of this position was carried to the end; United States capital began to profit from a close collaboration with Batista's quasi-nationalistic economic development program. Thus Cuba remained under the wing of United States imperialism—whose interests had shifted and more closely corresponded to Cuba's own. Until the early 1950s, Cuba's main attractions for the United States were the island's markets. With the drying up of investment opportunities in Europe and elsewhere at the end of the postwar reconstruction period, and with increasing competition and pressures on the profit rate at home, United States capital revived its interests, dormant since the 1920s, in Cuba as an outlet for investments. Thus foreign capital moved into virgin territory in manufacturing, commerce, and agriculture; this corresponded precisely with the needs of Batista's quasi-nationalism—the development of manufacturing industries and the diversification of agriculture.

That this policy was destined to be an economic failure was inevitable given the structure of market organization, together with the contradictions contained in the policy itself. Economic development required total national autonomy; political stability (the pre-condition for foreign investments) in the absence of a strong, stable class basis for bourgeois rule, required dependence on Washington. Economic development required an independent monetary system and monetary autonomy; political stability required that Cuba be secured against inflation, and that the peso be kept on a par with the dollar by retaining the island as a monetary colony of the United States. Economic development required that Cuba be able to postpone, adjust, modify its international payments;

[14] *Ibid.*, p. 113.

political stability required prompt, full payments (in 1957–1958, 70 per cent of United States credit collections were termed "prompt," and 90 per cent were paid within thirty days). Economic development required that Cuba be able to seize the advantages of common instruments of national economic policy—multiple exchange rates, import quotas, and so on; political stability required that Cuba's international commercial arrangements be arranged in the interests of United States traders. Economic development required that Cuba liberate itself from the sugar quota system; political stability required that Cuba's fate be linked to the interests and mood of the United States Congress.

Thus in the long run a durable, stable politics and a fragmented demoralized bourgeoisie were necessarily incompatible social forms in the context of Cuban capitalism. The national bourgeoisie was not able to free itself totally from United States tutelage, and the United States hesitated to allow it to walk on its own power. The alternative was to build up the middle classes, and create opportunities for new investments; this was the policy which the United States half-heartedly followed without success during the second Batista period. A kind of Point Four program was applied to Cuba, its aim to provide a technical basis for the growth of agriculture and the development of light industry. The World Bank team, most of them prominent North Americans, continuously stressed the need for widening the horizons of the Cuban middle classes, creating new opportunities for domestic capital, and other policies under which Cuban capitalism could flourish. Batista attempted to implement many of these policies with minor successes, and with the help of foreign capital which for the first time entered manufacturing industries producing import substitutes, utilizing local raw materials and labor skills, and generally engaging in activities which could be expected to redound to the benefit of national economic development.

In some other countries where foreign investment figured importantly, foreign interests joined hands with local feudal or neo-feudal rulers, strengthened the prevailing political system, and gained temporary stability; Mexico between 1880 and

1910 is a prime example of the potentialities of such an alliance. But this kind of solution was not available in Cuba because the island did not have a feudal or neo-feudal economy. No single class, or alliance of social classes with corresponding interests, not the remnants of the old landowning oligarchy, not the big class of capitalist landlords, not the urban national bourgeoisie, not the commercialists, was powerful enough to gain and retain political power, even with United States backing.

This is why the old Cuban state can be characterized as bureaucratic, opportunistic, and redistributive. Cuban governments, whether elected to power (1940–1952) or formed on the basis of a political revolt or coup (1933–1939 and 1952–1959), increasingly drew their support from all classes, and representatives of all classes could be located in key decision-making positions in all governments since 1935. This includes labor leaders "bound by personal, official, and financial ties to the members of the Batista regime."[15] It also includes representatives of the rural associations of tenants and landlords who ordinarily answered to the largest of the island's farmers. And it includes representatives of Cuba's mill owners, and manufacturing, commercial, and financial interests, and professional classes. Lacking a solid class base, the old regimes rose to power on whatever support they could obtain. The balance of class forces—taking into account size, organization, and morale—created a political nexus in which no class had political initiative. The destruction of the old-line army in 1933–1934 and its reconstruction as Batista's personal machine left the oligarchy powerless, and it went into a political decline. The depression meanwhile bankrupted economically and politically the national bourgeoisie and gave impetus to the organization of popular forces. The 1933 revolution resembled the political upheaval of 1959 in the sense that "the Machado dictatorship had been so ruthless . . . that it brought about a coalition of heterogeneous forces" opposing

[15] Maurice Zeitlin and Robert Scheer, *Cuba: Tragedy in Our Hemisphere,* New York, 1963, p. 23. The authors go on to say that labor officials "cooperated with [Batista's regime] and served its ends." This is overly simplified; Batista was also compelled to "serve the [economic] ends" of organized labor.

it. But Cuba's first revolution was an uprising which took place "spontaneously, almost accidentally."[16] The period of 1953–1958 is the history of a hard-fought political and military struggle. Thus the two revolutions depart in this one important respect: the latter period was characterized by greater economic prosperity. Far more important, by the 1950s representatives of each class had firmly entrenched themselves in the state bureaucracy. Thus the character of Castro's struggle was determined in part by the outcome of the earlier upheaval which removed a solid class basis for political rule and laid the groundwork for each class to establish some kind of stake in the national political economy. These vested interests profited both from the network of market controls and redistributive national economy policies. In this way the paradoxical situation developed that segments of each class enjoyed a large stake in the system, while others stood to gain from its annihilation. This situation was reflected in the nature of the political struggle against Batista: it was difficult to organize the civil war along class lines, yet once power was obtained, it was easy to overhaul the government from top to bottom and push rapidly ahead with a social revolution. Support for many basic reforms was forthcoming from segments of nearly all of the island's major classes. The peasants and rural workers had been made aware by their hunger and enforced idleness of the abundance of unused lands; the teacher and doctor, by illiteracy and disease, of the backwardness of the educational system and health services; the small businessman, by his sluggish profits, of state corruption, and irrational labor, foreign trade, and other legislation; many urban industrial workers were made conscious by their lack of training and underemployment of the under-utilization of both their own and the island's productive potential.

It is true that "sugar dominate[d] the economic policy of the country, and other interests [had to] stand aside in the interest of sugar."[17] But in the fortunes of the sugar industry, all classes were enmeshed. Thus Cuba was governed by men

[16] Page, *op. cit.*, p. 71.
[17] Henry C. Wallich, *Monetary Problems of an Export Economy, the Cuban Experience, 1914–1947,* Cambridge, 1950, p. 12.

who had no class interests in governing efficiently and honestly. The collection of opportunists who were willing to support the dictator were by and large neither for or against capital or labor or farmers or any other class of Cubans with political experience and organization either on principle or from the standpoint of their own concrete interests. They were instead very much out for themselves. Of course, in the ranks of the civil services, the financial institutions, and the armed forces there were many honorable men who deplored not only the excesses of the Batista regime but the very principles of the Cuban way of political life. Yet the operators, the in-group, the men who knew who to see about an investment project, a price increase, a labor problem, the men who were located on the commanding heights of the public economy, were in the game to maximize returns for themselves. If the competitive, individualistic "market mentality" was absent in the cartelized private sector, it dominated the public sector. No one in Cuba ever ran the government with the belief that what was being done was in Cuba's best interest —meaning in the best interest of the class of whom he was a representative and with whom he identified. Few were willing or able to construct honest administrations by systematically excluding from the middle and lower ranks time-servers, incompetents, and thieves. Because political power failed to be rooted in local economic power, except indirectly and imperfectly, a stable politics aimed at smoothing the path for the development of the national bourgeoisie was never realized. Instead, both domestic and foreign economic policies of successive Cuban governments contained more and more contradictions and irrationalities. In his last years of rule, Batista himself was too weak to develop a state capitalism similar, for example, to Fascist Italy; he lacked sufficient capitalist support in town and country to embark on a development course comparable to that, say of the United States in the late 19th century; and he lacked a solid base of labor and peasant support, such that he could cut the ground out from under private capital and embark on the path of socialistic economic planning. Thus he faltered and floun-

dered, at first trying to please everyone, and finally driven to
the wall, having to suppress everyone.

Cuba's system of corruption and bribery was at once one
way in which Batista maintained a consensus of support and
one source of his downfall; its inequities, irrationalities, and
hardships helped to win for Castro's 26th of July Movement
allies in all layers of society. The system was produced and
sustained by a combination of forces: the lack of opportunities associated with economic stagnation; the all-pervasive
gambling mentality which conditioned the outlook and orientation of urban Cubans, and which was rooted in the island's over-all dependence on the volatile international sugar
market; and restrictions of various kinds specifically associated with the ways in which labor, capital, and product
markets were organized. This last factor was of particular
importance: with the monopolization and cartelization of
markets, prices bore little or no relationship to supply and
demand, opening the way for a flourishing business of bribery. On the most elementary and mechanical level, this involved a pay-off by a job-seeking worker to a corrupt union
boss or an employer's personnel agent. One condition for a
state loan often was a requirement that Batista men be given
posts in the personnel offices of the new firm, and, in such
cases, it would be the height of naïveté for a worker subsequently to expect to obtain employment without a large bribe.
In the housing market, a combination of shortages and official
rent ceiling gave incentives to landlords to bribe building
inspectors in order to get tenements condemned; tenants
were then dispossessed and readmitted at higher rents. On a
more rarefied level, "entrepreneurs" transferred vast sums
to government officials for scarce public contracts and public
funds; the official family itself was expert at getting something
for nothing; parking meter revenues yielded the personal
allowance of Batista's wife, and the dictator himself amassed
a huge fortune from stolen public funds. The tax system consisted, in Castro's words, "of paying off the revenue collector
instead of paying the state."[18]

[18] "Why We Fight," *Coronet*, 43, No. 4, February, 1958, p. 85.

The corruption system was basically a symptom of the island's backwardness; the fact that it was wiped out in a few months by the Revolutionary Government confirms this. But in the old society it was also a "second order" cause of backwardness, because it diverted the attention and energies of the population from acquiring physical and human assets and productive employment. Even Cuba's official opposition political party recognized the importance of this: it is significant that the central, indeed the only important, issue in Cuba's last election (1948) was corruption. The only opposition to the Auténtico Party, which held office and sacked the public treasury from 1944–1952, was the Ortodoxo Party, founded in 1947 by Eddy Chibas specifically to oppose Auténtico corruption.

Under Batista's last government, the corruption system was extended and made more elaborate, and elevated to an everyday system of business. A confidential business report service described the system: "The 'collector' is an important man on the island. Everybody doing business, from the cabbie to a hole-in-the-wall shop must pay to the regime's and the machine's ambulatory cash register. Veritable scales have been set for anything from street vendors to big businessmen . . . [graft] probably has never risen to such heights (or dropped to such depths), nor has it even been so efficient as under Batista. In such areas as Santiago, many a small businessman has been ruined . . . because he could no longer 'deliver' the share demanded from him by his 'protector.' "[19]

In higher circles in the public economy, about one-quarter of total state expenditures was paid out in graft, according to one experienced banker who financed a number of Batista's projects.[20] This more or less corresponds to the estimate of another Cuban in a position to grasp the extent of official corruption: ". . . in the years preceding the revolution, the average amount of graft in public works (alone) cost as much

[19] S. J. Rundt and Associates, *Rundt's Market Reports,* No. 199, February 14, 1959, p. 22.
[20] Irving Pflaum, "Fidelista Finance," *Reports Service, Mexico and the Caribbean Service* (American Universities Field Staff), V, No. 8, August, 1960, p. 9.

as the works themselves."[21] About three-fifths of the budget
of the Public Health Ministry was stolen, and about one-
third of the Education Ministry budget.[22] Teachers were government officials with life tenure and full salaries; it was common for teachers and school inspectors to sell their positions
for one-half or less of their salaries; one striking indication
of the degeneration of the Education Ministry was the long-
term drop in the proportion of Cuba's children enrolled in
school from the mid-1920s to the 1950s. New schools which
were built were showcase units constructed along the Central
Highway, badly located in terms of need.

Nor was the National Lottery immune from the grasp of
government officials, both highly and lowly placed. Over $200
million worth of tickets were sold during Batista's last reign;
winning tickets collect $114 million and expenses came to
about $9 million; the rest was stolen.[23] A close student of
Cuban affairs depicted the results of the lottery as "the further
economic degradation of the poor . . . [and] the most potent
enemy of any program designed to promote thrift among the
population."[24]

Had the Cuban state been a weak and poor state, state
corruption would have been devoid of much real significance. Next to the sugar industry, however, the Cuban government was the island's largest employer, and state institutions partially or wholly owned many enterprises in the
transportation, commercial, and manufacturing sectors of the
economy. Thus public corruption had a large quantitative impact on Cuba's all-around economic performance. It is true
that the government was not entirely inflexible; when the
public budget was in trouble salaries of public employees were
sometimes temporarily cut. But successive regimes failed to
clean up the education racket, graft in the ministries and the
lottery and the quasi-public financial and other institutions

[21] Felipe Pazos, "The Economy," *Cambridge Opinion 32,* February,
1963, p. 13.
[22] Speech by Fidel Castro to Second Congress of National Association
of Small Farmers, reported in *Hoy* (Havana), 10 de agosto de 1963, p. 4.
[23] Cuba, Institute Nacional de Ahorro y Vicienda, *Revista,* 1 de no-
viembre de 1959.
[24] Lowry Nelson, *Rural Cuba,* Minneapolis, 1950, p. 218.

whose roles were important in the national economy, and the systematic corruption in the armed forces. These interests, particularly the latter, had to be respected in order to maintain the consensus. Thus the corruption system was but the most dramatic example of the ever-recurring and all-pervasive anomaly of the old political economy. Segments of all classes profited by the system, yet at the same time the system thwarted the aspirations and plans of all classes. On the market level, widespread monopolistic elements and cartel controls yielded benefits to some workers, some farmers, some manufacturers, some commercialists. On the political level, the politics of redistribution channeled income and other material gains into every corner of the island, and the corruption system embraced a diverse group of social elements. Thus it was not merely one's relationship to the means of production which determined and conditioned support for the dictator; far more significant, it was one's relationship to market controls, and the systems of state subsidies and protection and corruption.

3. The Civil War and the Economics and Ideology of the 26th of July Movement

The preceding analysis explains why there was no single revolutionary class in Cuba giving momentum to the *political* revolution against Batista, why there was no Cuban counterpart to the peasants in the Mexican Revolution or the urban workers in the Russian Revolution. Compared with the Chinese, Mexican, Soviet, and Vietnam struggles, to choose a handful of examples, the old political system in Cuba crumbled under relatively little military and political pressure. The military and political war against Batista had a distinctly classless character, and was fought by sections of all classes—peasant soldiers, middle-class intellectuals, student terrorists and strikers, workers engaged in active and passive resistance, arms financiers of wealth and modest incomes, and entire established professional and business groups in open political opposition to the dictatorship.

So far as the class content of the political revolution was concerned, there was no clear national tendency. In the Havana area, the middle classes were dominant in the struggle; the class composition of the city, weighted heavily in favor of the comprador, the employee in tourism, the domestic servant, the lumpen element, and the labor "aristocrat," limited working class participation. The Havana-based union bureaucracy, together with the fact that political strikes lacked the backing of the Rebel Army operating hundreds of miles away, also placed limits on mass, working class action. These were the basic reasons why the general strike of April, 1958 was a failure. Lack of planning, coordination, and communications—the Revolutionary Directorate and the Communist party refused to participate in the strike—were secondary factors. Yet Castro himself has maintained that the general strike in January, 1959 actually consolidated the revolution, for even in conservative Havana mass action was possible when there was no fear of reprisals.[25] And we have testimony by Batista's labor chief himself that there were rumblings of discontent in the Havana working classes as early as March, 1958.[26]

At the other end of the island, Santiago was shut down by the first general strike; earlier, in August, 1957, strikes spread out from Santiago as an aftermath to the assassination and funerals of two 26th of July leaders, Frank Pais and Raul Pujol. Anti-Batista working class sentiment ran high there; there were fewer labor "aristocrats," unemployment was higher, and the working class was more cohesive. In Cienfuegos, an uprising of naval officers in collaboration with civilian revolutionaries which took place in September, 1957 demonstrated discontent in some sectors of the armed forces. And in the mountains of Oriente province, where the Rebel Army had the initiative, Castro's guerrilla forces consisted of peasant soldiers, and were maintained by peasant families, who in turn were aided economically and socially by the rebels. In town and country revolutionary-minded intellectuals took the lead, for one reason because more than any other

[25] Monitored radio speech, June 13, 1960.
[26] *The Fourth Floor, op. cit.,* p. 27.

group they perceived clearly the substantial structural changes which would be required to get the economy and the whole society off dead center, together with the role of the United States in the Cuban economy and its implications for social and economic development.

Castro has interpreted the role of various economic classes in the revolution somewhat differently: ". . . the revolution was never a bourgeois one, as imperialist propaganda has tried to represent it. It has never been a revolution of the upper classes. Not a single representative of the upper class took part in the revolution, not a single rich man. All the participants . . . were young men with a modest, working class background; workers and peasants, the sons of working people, employees. . . ."[27] Yet sections of the middle and professional classes did have a hand in the revolution, although it is true that the "rich" man played a tiny role, because they, like those in nearly every group in Cuba, found the totality of the society's institutional structure inadequate. But each had a stake in these institutions, and thus their part in the drama was truly ambiguous; this explains the fact that anti-Batista sentiment was not widespread until the dictator's terror grew in response to guerrilla action initiated by Fidel and the ease with which the Rebel Army leader consolidated the revolution on his own terms. Political power was transformed from one relatively small group to another; no single class had the political initiative under the old system, nor in the political revolution which overthrew the Batista government, because no single class was systematically excluded from the old politics of consensus. Even Northern Oriente's coffee farmers, located near the bottom of the social structure, who formed Raul Castro's social base in 1957–1958, profited from government purchasing programs aimed at maintaining coffee prices and farm income.

Of course, the burden of the irrationalities of the old Cuban society did not fall equally on all classes. Nor, even though nearly everyone was dissatisfied in part with the Batista regime, did all Cubans share the same vision of the

---

[27] Radio interview of Fidel Castro with the Editors of *Pravda* and *Izvestia*, January 29, 1962.

future. Yet there was widespread recognition that "something had to be done" and that mild reforms here and there were insufficient. Gustavo Gutierrez, the head of Batista's own National Economic Council, wrote on Cuba's "structural deformations" and "colonial structure."[28] In May, 1958, Batista's labor boss, Eusebio Mujal, published a "National Plan for Strengthening and Developing the Economy of Cuba." The plan called for agrarian reform, price ceilings, "aggressive" trade policies to stimulate export diversifications and the development of import substitutes, higher income taxes and the elimination of indirect taxes, a new protectionist tariff aimed at United States exports of foods and light manufactured goods, and a vast housing program for workers and peasants. It is ironic that all of these measures were pushed through by the reform-minded government in 1959. The idea of putting seasonally-idle farm workers on agricultural diversification projects dates back at least to the rule of Charles Magoon, who himself proposed it to the then-powerful landed oligarchy. Even the "conservative" National Association of Cuban Industrialists, the major organization of the island's national bourgeoisie, drew up a rather far-reaching Plan for the Economic Development of Cuba, and presented it to Castro early in 1959. These schemes were symptomatic of widespread dissatisfaction with the performance and structure of the economy, and were also significant in that they (together with the plans which Batista actually implemented during the 1950s) undermined popular apathy for economic and social movement and also raised popular expectations for the future.

Historically the most significant program was that of the 26th of July, Castro's own organization.[29] The program reveals that the 26th of July Movement lacked a unifying

---

[28] *The Economic Program of Cuba,* Havana, March 1, 1955, *passim.*

[29] Fidel Castro, "What Cuba's Rebels Want," *The Nation,* November 30, 1957, pp. 399–401, a translation of an article appearing in *Cuba Libre,* a Costa Rican publication of the 26th of July Movement. "Why We Fight," *op. cit.,* pp. 80–86. Felipe Pazos and Regino Boti, "Thesis of the Revolutionary Movement of July 26th," *Political, Economic, and Social Thought of Fidel Castro,* Havana, 1959, pp. 119–166. It should be pointed out that by all accounts the program was more radical than Pazos himself wished for.

ideology and political theory; this reflects the class content of the political struggle against Batista, and is in turn reflected in the economic content of the program.[30] Two themes were stressed by the authors of the 26th of July program. An attack on the "distributive" mentality of Cuban government past and present, and related to this point, a condemnation of existing state policy aimed at restricting sugar production, was one of them. This theme had great relevance to the Cuban scene. The political implications and the implications for the organization of markets, however, failed to be worked out. The program's specific policies, in fact, contradicted its overall assessment of Cuba's problems; elsewhere in the plan, the aim was to strengthen the sugar quota system by raising the minimum quota to firm up the position of the marginal *colonos*. For industry, a profit-sharing plan was put forward, in which workers would receive 30 per cent of the profits of non-agricultural enterprises—another form of "redistributive," as opposed to "productive," state policy.

In the case of public utilities, the movement was similarly ambivalent. At first, Castro supported a plan to nationalize the electric and telephone trusts, but just before the movement seized power, he reversed himself. In another sense the program was vague: land holdings would be fixed, excess acreage would be expropriated and distributed to small farmers, who, in turn, would be encouraged to organize into cooperatives of the Western European type. The future role of the rural proletariat was uncertain; nowhere was it written that they would have a place in the projected cooperative; who would employ them, and under what conditions, was left in doubt. The movement was also vague with respect to the disposal of confiscated assets of grafters and embezzlers; there was no indication whether they would be sold at auction or operated and managed by the state.

[30] Blackburn is only half correct when he writes: "The unprecedented hallmark of the revolution—its lack of party or an ideology—were the logical products of a pre-revolutionary society which itself lacked any decisive institutional or ideological structure." In fact, Cuba's economic institutions continuously confined the Revolution to certain paths. What made the social revolution a "revolution" was the opposition of certain classes to certain reforms and social changes.

Batista came under further attack for his policy of building highly mechanized plants and creating technological unemployment; elsewhere it was suggested that agriculture be mechanized to raise labor productivity and incomes in the countryside, again raising a contradiction. These inconsistencies and ambivalencies arose because reform measures and planning were placed in the context of capitalist institutions. The gist of all of the movement's materials was "the participation of all sectors and groups" in economic planning. While this was undoubtedly partly a tactic aimed at consolidating a united front against the dictatorship, it is significant that the movement felt that it could profitably appeal to varied interests in the old Cuba because the existing political economy thwarted in one way or another the realization of these interests. Had the dictatorship had a solid social base, and had the movement had its own social base—one fundamentally antagonistic to the other—the latter's appeal would have been unambiguously directed to its base.

The second theme running through the program was the stress on mobilizing domestic savings for productive investments, and related to this, protecting manufacturing interests. This evidently appealed to many industrialists big and small, and helped to offset the specter of the profit-sharing scheme, itself the program's chief appeal to Cuba's workers. What gave the mobilization of domestic savings its fundamental importance was the movement's unwillingness to "compromise our economic and political future with the importing of capital." The fear of foreign influence and control was also reflected in the emphasis given to market diversification and the production of substitutes for imported commodities. The latter weighs heavily in the movement's program, and the former figures prominently in early speeches by revolutionary leaders. In a talk by Commandante Guevara before the Sociedad Nuestro Tiempo on January 27, 1959, for example, it was stressed that current dependence on United States trade was dangerous for Cuba's autonomy.[31] The anti-foreign stress

[31] *The Havana Post,* January 28, 1959.
Boti and Pazos attempted a concrete analysis of the amount of domestic savings required to finance a level of investment which would in

and, beginning in 1960, the anti-imperialist theme was the one element binding together the diverse groups and classes engaged in the struggle against the dictatorship. There was always a strong nationalist sentiment in Cuban labor agitation, which took the form less of a direct economic struggle against foreign firms (although it is significant that unions of workers employed in the foreign monopolies, particularly in banking, were the most radical in Cuba) than of agitation directed at foreign political control.[32] Pushed to the point of the expropriation of United States properties, however, this theme alienated many in the middle classes; and Cubans who were close to United States business interests were always wary of Castro's anti-Americanism.

The liberals and moderates in the middle classes who involved themselves in nationalistic, anti-yankee sentiment clearly were unaware that they were playing with a loaded gun. They *wanted* there to be a sizeable national bourgeoisie capable of at once building up Cuban capitalism on a reformed basis and withstanding pressure from the United States, but they failed to recognize the implications of the absence of one. This political confusion was mixed, as we have seen, with confusion over the causes of Cuba's stagnation and backwardness, which in turn led to contradictory policies and proposals. Felipe Pazos, an economist who was one of the best-known of the group of liberal reformers, wrote after going into exile: ". . . the economic and social tensions . . . that gave rise to the original non-Communist revolution

---

ten years wipe out unemployment. Taking into account estimated existing capital: labor ratios in agriculture and industry, existing idle capacity, and the low productivity of social capital, they concluded that $200 million annually was required, exactly equal to then-current total savings with the current distribution of income. This equivalency suggests that there was some wishful thinking in their analysis, which, in fact, contains two serious errors: First, given that existing market organization placed limits on capital efficiency, marginal capital/labor ratios and capital/output ratios would surely be less than average ratios. Second, given that a reallocation of capital to more productive employments would affect the distribution of income, it was unrealistic to assume a constant level of savings. In short, their estimates had a mechanical character.

[32] Page, *op. cit.*, p. 67; Dana Gardner Munro, *The Latin American Republics, A History*, Second Edition, New York, 1950, p. 501.

. . . were not those of poverty and extreme inequity."[33] This judgment clearly has some validity, as far as it goes. But he continues, "economic stagnation, chronic unemployment, corruption, and frustration—these seem to me to have played the largest part in bringing about the revolution." But this explains nothing; there is no theory of stagnation, and no explicit realization that corruption, frustration, and unemployment were secondary causes which obscured the real problems of the island. Like all reformers whether democratic-minded such as himself, or crude opportunists such as Mujal, or, for that matter, such as Batista himself, Pazos shied away from analyses of market and political structures and the explosive implications of such analyses. Thus liberal thought and reform remedies concocted from the theories of reformed capitalism in advanced industrial countries were totally bankrupt as applied to Cuba; liberal theory in Cuba was little more than pure rhetoric. Years ago, another Latin American, the Peruvian Marxist, José Carlos Mariátegui, opposed the liberal rhetoric: he said that the agrarian problem (and we can add, the trade, labor, and other problems) was a "socio-economic (and therefore political) problem . . . and it is useless to attempt to convert it . . . into a technical-agricultural problem under the control of agricultural experts."

4. The Origins of Cuban Socialism: A Summary

"High level stagnation" is an appropriate description of the old Cuban social economy; its fundamental causes were market and political organization. Cuba's markets were organized along specifically capitalist lines; official cartels and outright monopolies were the dominant forms. Neo-mercantile or neo-feudal types of organizations were not prominent features of the island's economy. The root cause of the malorganization of markets were technical conditions in the export sector, particularly the sugar sector, which encouraged domestic and foreign capital to exploit economies of large-

[33] Pazos, *op. cit.,* p. 13.

scale production. Placed in this frame of reference, the development of a *socialist* social revolution in 1960–1962 is a more comprehensible phenomenon. Socialism was both possible and suitable in Cuba, for related reasons.

Socialism (in the sense of public ownership of the means of production and a political alliance between the rural proletariat, "advanced" segments of the working classes in the cities, and the poorer peasants, able to break or reduce the independent political power of the large ranchers, growers, manufacturers, bankers, commercialists, and labor aristocracy) was possible because of the relative size and character of the island's economic classes. While Cuba's middle-class, compared with those in many other Latin American countries, was relatively large, placed next to the proletariat and marginal peasantry, it was tiny. Fragmented and demoralized, it failed to systematically employ state power for its own ends; Cuban governments were made up of opportunists, pure and simple. For these reasons, there was no significant organized resistance to the rapid socialization of the Cuban economy.

Related to this point is the fact that nearly all were dissatisfied to one degree or another with the old Cuba, and that there was widespread support for steps taken to get the economy off dead center. In the heat of a social revolution it is difficult for participants and observers alike to distinguish between reform measures and measures which inherently threaten property relationships themselves. For this reason the Revolutionary Government could count on a near-unanimous national consensus even when it began to implement policies with a specifically socialist character.

Socialism was suitable and desirable for Cuba because of the monopolization and cartelization of the island's markets, and because of the failure of capitalism to fulfill its economic and social potential. Cuba's socio-economic institutions were political by-products of the composition, outlook, and balance of class forces. It is thus in this sense that what was possible merges into what was desirable, and it was this synthesis which gives Cuban socialism the air of inevitability.

4

REVOLUTION, CONSCIOUSNESS, AND CLASS: CUBA AND ARGENTINA*

Gilbert W. Merkx and *Nelson P. Valdés*

One of the classic topics of sociology since Karl Marx has been the relationship between social structures and forms of consciousness. Like many things which are classical, the topic is primarily honored by neglect. In part this is because discussion has tended to degenerate into polemics, and in part because the nature of the topic discourages those who are accustomed to the safety of survey research.

Nonetheless, it is the intention of this paper to examine class structures and political consciousness. On the basis of two cases we can only generate hypotheses, to be sure, but these may be useful for understanding events in other nations. The countries we shall discuss are Cuba and Argentina, which produced remarkable nationalist leaders in the persons of Fidel Castro and Juan Perón. We shall attempt to relate the consciousness which resulted in such leaders to historical processes that produced distinctive class structures. We shall further suggest that class consciousness may have a negative impact upon the radicalization of a revolution,† whereas the absence of class consciousness may promote radicalization.

* This is a revised version of a paper presented at the 1970 Annual Meetings of the Rural Sociological Society, Washington, D.C.

† By the "radicalization" of a Revolution, we mean the rapid and abrupt restructuring of the economic and social order as a result of efforts by the revolutionary government.

Similarities

Before discussing differences between the two cases, it may be useful to point out some of the similarities. Foremost is that both countries are heavily dependent on the export of one or two agricultural commodities, Cuba on sugar and tobacco and Argentina on beef and wheat. Both nations suffered heavily from the Depression, experienced a long-term decline of markets, and have been hurt by short-term price swings.

Nevertheless, Cuba and Argentina stand near the top of most indices of Latin American development, thanks in large part to advances made before the Depression. In 1958 Cuba and Argentina had the lowest rates of mortality in Latin America, and were second and third lowest in terms of both birth rate and infant mortality, while being third and first in terms of physicians per capita.[1] Argentina was first in percentage of literates, Cuba was third.[2] They held the same position in terms of newspapers sold per capita.[3] They were in the top six Latin American nations in terms of national income per capita.[4]

The sequence of political events preceding the emergence of Castro and Perón is also similar. In both countries military dictatorships had been followed by corrupt and discredited civilian governments which were in turn replaced by new military regimes. In each case the second round of dictatorship was followed by the rise of the nationalist leader. Both Perón and Castro are distinguished for their anti-U.S. policies, which generated not only U.S. Government opposition but an extremely bad press in the United States (though they were hung with different labels).

The list of similarities could easily be extended. Nonethe-

[1] Cuban Economic Research Project, *A Study on Cuba* (Coral Gables: University of Miami Press, 1965), pp. 440–441, Tables 309 and 311.
[2] *Ibid.*, p. 441, Table 312.
[3] *Ibid.*, p. 443, Table 316.
[4] *Ibid.*, p. 444, Table 319.

less, it is misleading, since underlying such resemblances are key differences of social structure and consciousness. To these we shall now turn.

Agricultural Development and Independence

The starting points for analyzing differences between Cuba and Argentina are the patterns of agricultural development which preceded their independence. In Argentina, vast expanses of prairie encouraged ranching and the export of hides and tallow to Europe.[5] Ranching was further stimulated in the 1780's by the establishment of meat-salting plants on the River Plate.[6] Despite prohibition by the Spanish Crown, the flourishing trade with Europe created a class of merchants in Buenos Aires and gave the Argentines a sense of autonomy from Spain.[7]

This finally led to the famous Cabildo Abierto of 1810 which set up both local government and free trade.[8] Argentine ranchers and merchants alike were enthusiastic about independence, and as a result the monarchy could find no powerful adherents to help stop the revolution, which triumphed easily. Argentina's War of Independence did not so much alter Argentine social structure as free it to develop further.

In Cuba, agriculture developed rapidly along plantation lines after the British occupation of 1762. During the nine months of British military rule nearly 10,000 African slaves were imported into Cuba.[9] The Haitian revolution of 1790

[5] Juan Hipólito Vieytes, *Antecedentes económicos de la Revolución de Mayo* (Buenos Aires: Editorial Raigal, 1956).

[6] James R. Scobie, *Argentina* (New York: Oxford University Press, 1964), p. 78.

[7] See Vieytes, *op. cit.,* and Jorge A. Ramos, *Revolución y contrarrevolución en la Argentina* (Buenos Aires: La Reja, 1961), pp. 25, 63.

[8] It is worth noting that while Argentina was the seat of the independence movement in southern Spanish America, this role was played by Venezuela in the north. Venezuela was also a cattle country, but the cattle population there was almost exterminated by the wars which followed, whereas the vast herds in Argentina were left untouched.

[9] C. H. Haring, *The Spanish Empire in Latin America* (New York, 1947), p. 340, and Ramiro Guerra y Sánchez, *Azúcar y población en las Antillas* (La Habana, 1944, 3d edition), p. 54. Cited by Robin Blackburn

eliminated the world's major producer of sugar and coffee, leading to a further expansion of plantation agriculture in Cuba. By 1817, as revolution was sweeping the mainland of Spanish America, which was only 2% African in population, the black population of Cuba outnumbered the whites 340,-000 to 291,000.[10] Independence for Cuba carried with it the specter of slave revolt, and was rejected by plantation owners and merchants, as well as the large population of French exiles from Haiti and Spanish exiles from the mainland.

The following decades were highly profitable for Cuban sugar and coffee growers. Sugar plantations were large in area and used slave labor, whereas coffee cultivation was amenable to smaller-scale production in the rugged country of eastern Cuba. After 1840, however, coffee planters were hard hit by the tariff war between the United States and Spain, although sugar was not affected. In 1868 the beleaguered coffee growers of Oriente province joined in a call for independence from Spain. Most of those who signed this manifesto held no slaves at all, those who did were not large-scale holders. In the war which followed the sugar planters, who did have large slave holdings, supported the Crown.

Spain responded to the call for independence with a ruthless program of "pacificación." During the ten years which followed before a temporary peace could be established, Spain lost 81,000 soldiers in Cuba. More significant, however, was the devastation wrought upon the Cubans. The landowners in the coffee sector who had supported the revolution were wiped out as a class by the struggle, which passed into the hands of lower-income groups. The sugar sector emerged dominant and more Spanish than ever.

Three years after the end of the First War of Cuban Independence in 1878, Spain began to emancipate the slaves at last, settling the formal issue of slavery. Then in 1895 the United States extended tariffs to sugar. For the first time sugar planters began to join the independence movement. War

in his brilliant article, to which we are deeply indebted for much of our interpretation, "Prologue to the Cuban Revolution," *New Left Review*, No. 2 (October 1963).

[10] Ulpiano Vega Cobiellas, *Nuestra América y la evolución de Cuba* (La Habana, 1944), pp. 74–75, cited by Blackburn.

erupted again. The Spanish threw twice as many soldiers into Cuba as they had used in all the mainland of Spanish America during the earlier wars of independence. One fifth of the Cuban population died in concentration camps or during the fighting.[11]

The war came to a sudden end in 1898 with U.S. intervention, which was soon to complete what Spanish repression had begun: the shattering of the Cuban social order. American capital moved swiftly into Cuba under the aegis of U.S. governors and then the Platt Amendment. The Spanish were joined and partly replaced in key areas such as sugar and commerce. By 1929 one fourth of the cane land was owned by four American companies.[12]

The struggle for Cuban independence had several marked social effects. 1) It eliminated the coffee growers, who were closest to being a genuinely Cuban agricultural elite. 2) It decimated the rural population of independent farmers, playing havoc with land tenure. 3) It freed land for the expansion of sugar plantations. 4) It terminated with American intervention and increasing American influence over Cuba. The peculiar character of Cuban society must be understood as a product of these structural changes.

Argentina: Social Change After Independence

The course of Argentine social change in the 19th century was entirely different. After independence the expansion of foreign trade proved devastating to the handicraft manufacturing of the Argentine interior, and a series of revolts broke out.[13] Unrest continued until crushed in the 1830's by the dictator Rosas, who allowed the expansion of exports to proceed unhampered. After Rosas agriculture grew even more rapidly with development of wheat as an export crop. Then

[11] Blackburn, *op. cit.*
[12] Guerra y Sánchez, *op. cit.*, pp. 94–95.
[13] The causes of these are thoroughly explored by Myron Burgin, *The Economic Aspects of Argentine Federalism, 1820–1852* (Cambridge: Harvard University Press, 1946).

beef exports began to grow also, thanks to breakthroughs in refrigerated transport. Argentina became one of the most prosperous nations in the world.

Argentina's economy required increasing amounts of labor, as had been the case for Cuba. In Argentina, however, laborers came as voluntary migrants rather than slaves, attracted by the available opportunities. A large foreign population was established and a massive inflow of foreign investment began. This investment took place mostly in the economic infrastructure, such as utilities, communications, and railroads.

The native Argentine elite retained control over their key source of wealth, the land. As vast amounts of new land were brought into use between 1870 and 1914 they succeeded in obtaining ownership of this also. Between 1895 and 1914 the amount of land in use increased from 5 million to 25 million hectares,[14] but the percentage of hacendados and estancieros who were Argentine dropped only slightly, from 83% in 1895 to 80% in 1914.[15] Their haciendas and estancias were not the feudal estates of some Latin American countries, but market-oriented commercial enterprises. In addition, many commercial farms were established by foreigners, particularly in the coastal regions. Except in the far north, subsistence agriculture was not a part of the Argentine pattern.[16]

In Buenos Aires a new middle class blossomed. The prosperity and very existence of this middle class depended upon the export sector, since Argentina had no industry. Argentina was probably the first nation to have a large middle class *before* having an industrial bourgeoisie. The white-collar urban middle class grew so rapidly that between 1869 and 1914 it jumped from 6% to 21% of the total economically active population, an increase in real numbers of about thirteen times.[17]

Underneath the largely Argentine upper and middle classes

[14] Gilbert W. Merkx, *Political and Economic Change in Argentina from 1870–1966* (Yale University: Ph.D. dissertation, 1968), p. 56.

[15] *Ibid.*, p. 91, data taken from censuses.

[16] Horacio G. E. Giberti, *El desarrollo agrario argentino* (Buenos Aires: Eudeba, 1964).

[17] Merkx, *op. cit.*, pp. 85–86.

88   *Gilbert W. Merkx and Nelson P. Valdés*

developed a massive foreign working class. The dimensions
of the immigration were such that the 1.7 million Argentines
of 1869 were joined over the next forty-four years by 4.7
million foreigners, of whom 3 million became permanent
residents.[18]

These changes led to concurrent changes in political life.
After Rosas, the agricultural elite ran the country with a parliamentary system conducted in the tradition of liberal pa-
ternalism. There were no true political parties, and as late as
1910 only 3% of the population voted in presidential elections.[19] The foreign working class presented no political
threat, despite Socialist attempts to organize them. But a
middle-class political party, called the Radical Civic Union,
was founded in 1890 and proceeded to fight vigorously for
power, couching its appeals in highly nationalist and idealistic
terms.

After an extended debate, the Argentine elite decided to
expand the franchise and allow the Radicals to take power,
as a means of avoiding revolution and social unrest. The
change of power came with the elections of 1916, which the
Radical Hipólito Irigoyen won by a landslide. This peaceful
transition was a classic example of reform and cooptation
along the British model. Like the Liberal governments in
Britain, the Radical governments of Argentina proved not to
be very radical.

Nevertheless, the commitment of the Argentine upper class
to democracy was fragile. When the Radicals proved unable
to respond effectively to the threat posed for Argentina's
foreign trade by the world depression, they were ousted in a
bloodless coup by upper-class officers.[20] The resulting Conservative government undertook policies intended to safeguard
export markets and increase agricultural production, which
had the side effect of massively stimulating industry.[21] By
1935 industrial investment had increased 68% from the 1932

[18] *Ibid.*, p. 73.
[19] The political system at this time is described by Cantón in his excellent work. Darío Cantón, *El parlamento argentino en épocas de cambio:
1890, 1916, y 1946* (Buenos Aires: Editorial del Instituto, 1966).
[20] Merkx, *op. cit.*, pp. 148–165.
[21] *Ibid.*, pp. 165–177.

low. Between 1935 and the fall of the last Conservative government in 1943, the number of manufacturing establishments increased by 60%, the number of industrial workers and employees by 83%, and the value added by industry by 110%.[22] The Conservatives succeeded, where the Radicals had failed, with the industrialization of Argentina. By the middle forties there were more than one million persons employed by industry, largely in the Buenos Aires area.

Despite the economic successes of the Conservative governments, the Radical party maintained its popular strength, although it did not return to its earlier tactic of revolution. The Conservatives found themselves obliged to govern by electoral fraud throughout the thirties. Argentina entered the 1940's with a political system that still contained the forms but no longer the substance of parliamentary democracy.

Cuba: Social Change After Independence

The U.S. takeover of Cuba, which terminated the Cuban War of Independence, accelerated the social changes begun by the fighting. Under the protection of U.S. military governors at first, and then supported by continued U.S. interventions, North American capital flowed into the sugar sector. The amount of land under sugar cane increased rapidly, as did mechanization and the value of sugar exports. By 1926, foreign-owned sugar mills ground over 90% of the island's sugar cane.[23] During this period the national product rose rapidly in over-all terms, although the benefit to the bulk of the rural population was marginal.

The impact of the Great Depression upon Cuba was devastating. Sugar prices, wages, and incomes plunged, and thousands of independent small farmers lost their land. The remnants of the rural petite bourgeoisie that had survived

[22] CEPAL, *El desarrollo económico de la Argentina* (Mexico: Naciones Unidas, 1959), Anexo estadístico, pp. 4 and 81. Also República Argentina, *Censo Industrial de 1946*, p. 16.

[23] James O'Connor, *The Origins of Socialism in Cuba* (Ithaca: Cornell University Press, 1970), p. 13.

the War of Independence were thus further decimated. Cuba's period of economic growth based upon sugar production had come to a stop, and the decades which followed witnessed a halting, uneven recovery of production. By the time that Batista fell, per capita income was still at the same level as fifty years earlier.[24]

During this period of stagnation, there was some withdrawal of U.S. capital in the sugar sector, but the close import-export relationship with the United States continued. The lack of economic development was paralleled by a lack of social change. The Cuban agricultural censuses of 1907 and 1946 showed almost the same proportions of farm owners to tenants, rural wage workers to urban laborers, and farm owners to the total population.[25]

TABLE 1
Cuban Farms by Size Groups, 1945

Size Groups (Hectares)	Farms		Area	
	Number	Per Cent	Thous. Hect.	Per Cent
0.4–24.9	111278	69.6%	1021.9	11.2%
25.0–99.9	35911	22.5	1608.0	17.7
100–499.9	10433	6.5	2193.6	24.1
500–999.9	1442	0.9	992.5	10.9
1000 and over	894	0.5	3261.1	36.1

Sources: Cuban Agricultural Census, 1946. Cited by Andrés Bianchi in Dudley Seers, ed., *Cuba: The Economic and Social Revolution* (Chapel Hill: The University of North Carolina Press, 1964), p. 75.

The Cuban agricultural system combined the worst features of minifundismo with immense sugar holdings, as shown in Table 1. The largest part of the rural labor force were employed on the sugar plantations, as shown in Table 2. But this employment was seasonal and unstable.

The Agricultural Census of 1946 gave, however, some indication of the magnitude of the problem which affected

[24] *Ibid.*, p. 17.
[25] *Ibid.*, p. 22.

TABLE 2

The Agricultural Labor Force in Cuba, 1952

	Thousands of persons	Per Cent
Farm laborers	596.8	72.9%
Paid workers	520.9	63.6
Unpaid family workers	66.7	8.1
Administrators and foremen	9.2	1.1
Ranchers and farmers	221.9	27.1
Agricultural labor force	818.7	100.0%

Sources: Censos de Población, Viviendas y Electoral, 1952. Cited by Andrés Bianchi in Dudley Seers, ed., *Cuba: The Economic and Social Revolution* (Chapel Hill: The University of North Carolina Press, 1964), p. 80.

the more than 400,000 paid temporary workers who constituted about one-half of the gainfully occupied agricultural population: 52% of them had worked no more than four months of the year, and only 6% had been employed for nine months or longer.[26]

The minifundist farmers were hardly better off. Their situation was so bad that they were not a conservative force, as small farmers are often considered to be. Kulaks simply were not a part of the Cuban scene. To begin with, only one third of farms were owner-run. Most of them were rented, sharecropped, or squatter-held. This is shown in Table 3. In addition, the size of farms made them marginal or submarginal. Lowry Nelson's comments in 1949 are very much to the point:

Small farmers, although numerous, have a pitifully small share of the land. Those with farms under 25 hectares in size (about 63 acres) constitute 70 per cent of all operators and have only 11 per cent of the land—about 9 hectares (22 acres) each, on the average, but most of them much less. This is a matter of grave concern in Cuba, where

[26] Andrés Bianchi, "Agriculture: The Pre-Revolutionary Background," in Dudley Seers, *Cuba: The Economic and Social Revolution* (Chapel Hill: The University of North Carolina Press, 1964), pp. 81–82.

TABLE 3

Tenure Class of Cuban Farms in 1946

Tenure Class	Number	Per Cent
Manager	9,342	5.8%
Owner	48,792	30.5
Renter	46,048	28.8
Subrenters	6,987	4.4
Sharecroppers	33,064	20.6
Squatter	13,718	8.6
Others	2,007	1.3
Total	159,958	100.0%

Source: National Agricultural Census, 1946, preliminary release. Cited in Lowry Nelson, *Rural Cuba* (Minneapolis: The University of Minnesota Press, 1950), p. 164.

thousands of small operators are clamoring for possession of land. The political implications are such that no government can long ignore them.[27]

In addition to a partial recovery of agricultural production, the years following the Depression saw a slow growth of the modest industrial sector, oriented toward the replacement of certain import items on the Cuban market. The urban population was largely occupied, however, in the service sector, which was in turn dependent upon the fluctuations of the import-export trade.

The general instability of the Cuban economy was reflected in the unstable character of the Cuban political scene, despite repeated U.S. efforts to impose the formulas of parliamentary democracy. A series of unstable governments led in 1925 to the imposition of order by the dictator Gerardo Machado. His bloody regime was met by the formation of terrorist groups. Murders on both sides became common, and remained a part of the Cuban scene until the triumph of Castro.

Machado was finally overthrown in 1933 by an alliance of students, intellectuals, labor, and army sergeants, who deposed

[27] Lowry Nelson, *Rural Cuba* (Minneapolis: The University of Minnesota Press, 1950), p. 139.

the officer corps under the leadership of Fulgencio Batista. The government of Grau San Martín which followed was soon overthrown by Batista, who ruled between 1934 and 1944, at which time he voluntarily left the country. The subsequent eight years of Grau's Auténtico party served primarily to discredit parliamentary democracy in Cuba, as graft and venality reached new highs. When Batista resumed power in 1952 there was little opposition from the organized parties. The stage was set for the struggle to come.

Contrasts in Social Structure

The differential patterns of development in Cuba and Argentina further accentuated the dissimilarities of pre-independence social structure. Argentina had undergone an impressive growth of manufacturing and national income in the decade before Perón's rise to power. Cuba before Castro, on the other hand, was characterized by the lack of social change and economic expansion which O'Connor has aptly termed the "permanent crisis."[28]

In the urban sector, the two countries were distinguished from each other by the differential development of the industrial labor force, large and unsatisfied in Argentina, small and privileged in Cuba. Argentina had virtually full employment, whereas Cuba had chronic unemployment. In the rural sector, the dissimilarity of structure can be seen by the 1946 figures on farm size: 74.8% of Argentine farms were over a thousand hectares, whereas only 36.1% of Cuban farms were that large. Most Argentine agricultural units were large and prosperous, whereas most Cuban farms were small and poor.[29]

The differences between Cuban and Argentine social structure are illustrated in Table 4. Agriculture accounted for 25% of the Argentine work force in 1947, as compared with

[28] O'Connor, *op. cit.*, p. 12.
[29] Cuban Economic Research Project, *Cuba: Agriculture and Planning* (Coral Gables: University of Miami Press, 1965), p. 182. The Argentine figures are presumably from the agricultural census of 1947.

TABLE 4

Argentina and Cuba: Percentage of Economically Active Population According to Sector of Occupation*

Country	Agriculture[a]	Mining	Construction	Manufacturing	Commerce	Transport[b]	Other
Argentina	25.2%	0.5%	5.2%	22.1%	13.3%	6.0%	21.8%
Cuba	41.5	0.5	3.3	16.6	11.8	5.3	20.5

Sources and Comments: a) Includes hunting and fishing. b) Includes warehousing and communications.

* The years referred to are Argentina in 1947 and Cuba in 1953, and the original sources of the data are the censuses of each country in the respective years. Cited in Cuban Economic Research Project, *A Study on Cuba* (Coral Gables: University of Miami Press, 1965), Table No. 321, p. 445.

TABLE 5

Estimates of Argentine and Cuban Class Structures

Argentina (Merkx) Social Class	% of Family Units*	Cuba (Blackburn) Social Class	% of Work Force
I. Upper Class	2%	I. and II.: Exploiting Classes	20%
II. Professional and Business Class	33%		
III. Skilled and White Collar Working Class	52%	III. Urban Proletariat and Petite Bourgeoisie	25%
IV. Unskilled Working Class (inc. agric. labor)	10%	IV. Rural Workers	21%
V. Marginal Underclass (inc. unemployed, tenant farmers, retired, etc.)	5%	V. Unemployed and Minifundist Peasantry	34%

Sources and Comments: The Merkx estimates on Argentina are from Gilbert W. Merkx, "Sectoral Clashes and Political Change: The Argentine Experience," *Latin American Research Review*, Vol. IV, No. 3 (Fall 1969), p. 104. The Blackburn estimates for Cuba are from Robin Blackburn, "Prologue to the Cuban Revolution," *New Left Review*, No. 21 (October 1963), and are calculated as percentages using Blackburn's figures for each group and his estimate of the total work force. See also his footnote 69. The Argentine estimates are for 1961, and the Cuban estimates apparently for 1959.

* The Argentine figures add up to 102% due to authors' rounding off the numbers.

42% of the Cuban work force in 1953. Construction and manufacturing occupied 27% of Argentines and only 19% of Cubans. These figures do not account for the unemployment in each sector, which was high in Cuba and non-existent in Argentina.

If we make even a rough attempt to compare economic classes, the differences become even more evident. Although no hard data exist on class membership, it is possible to compare Blackburn's estimates of Cuban occupational group size with Argentine income group statistics.[30] These data are shown in Table 5. Unskilled and marginal working classes made up 13% of Argentine family units, but equivalent groups constituted 55% of the Cuban work force. Groups in the skilled working class and above made up 87% of the Argentine population and only 47% of the Cuban population. If we recall that the per capita product of the two countries is not greatly different, the far higher inequality of Cuban society is apparent.

Consciousness and Class

As a result of these different histories of development, Cuba and Argentina did not resemble each other either in class structure or forms of social consciousness.

By the 1940's Argentina had developed into a rather European society. In addition to an aristocratic but liberal rural elite, she possessed a new industrial bourgeoisie. There was a sizable rural middle class of landowning farmers and a very large urban middle class. Both the industrial bourgeoisie and the urban middle class were strongly nationalistic. Local ad-

[30] Blackburn, *op. cit.*, bases his estimates on a variety of Cuban sources, primarily the censuses of 1953 and 1946.

This material is presented and discussed in greater detail in Gilbert W. Merkx, "Sectoral Clashes and Political Change, the Argentine Experience," *Latin American Research Review*, Vol. IV, No. 3 (Fall 1969), pp. 102–104.

vertising campaigns were based on the theme, "Buy Argentine."[31]

At the time of the 1943 colonels' coup, the new industrial working class was only partly organized into labor unions. Perón realized the potential this represented.[32] As minister of labor he promoted the unionization of virtually the entire urban working class between 1943 and 1945, and then organized his political party, which resembled the labor parties of Europe in base and program.[33] Once formed it joined the Radicals as a permanent force in Argentine political life, even after Perón's fall. Voting analyses show that the Radicals continue to draw middle-class support and the Peronists to draw working-class support.[34]

One product of Peronist influence was the conspicuous degree of working-class pride in Argentina. Even non-Peronist workers have said of Perón that "he made us feel we were somebody," a statement echoed in the upper-class complaint that "since Perón the workers have no respect for anyone."[35] A wide range of workers' clubs and associations existed in addition to labor unions. Conversely there was little association across class lines, and student-worker coalitions were never a prominent part of the Argentine scene. The old landed elite also kept its distance from the nouveaux riches and middle class, through its own network of social clubs. One of the rather English features of Argentine social stratification was

[31] This is described at some length by Thomas C. Cochran and Ruben E. Reina, *Entrepreneurship in Argentine Culture. Torcuato Di Tella and S.I.A.M.* (Philadelphia: University of Pennsylvania Press, 1962).

[32] The influence of labor upon Perón's program is recently coming to light. See Juan Carlos Portantiero and Miguel Murmis, *El Movimiento Obrero en los origines del Peronismo* (Buenos Aires: Instituto Di Tella, Documentos de Trabajo, April 1969).

[33] James W. Rowe, *The Argentine Elections of 1963* (Washington, D.C.: Institute for the Comparative Study of Political Systems, no date). Also, Timothy Mellon, "The Peronist Movement in Argentine Politics," Yale University Library, Scholar of the House Paper (m.s.), 1964.

[34] Merkx, *op. cit.*, pp. 209–224. The inaccurate labeling of Perón as a fascist has obscured the labor party-populist character of his thought and program.

[35] Personal communications from Juan Gatti, automobile mechanic, Buenos Aires, and from a female member of one of Argentina's aristocratic families, August 1969.

(and is) the multiplicity of such clubs and voluntary organizations at each social level.

In addition to stable party institutions and a sense of class identification, Argentina had a remarkable absence of political violence until very recently. Most Argentine military coups involved only symbolic shows of force—civilian deaths were unheard of until 1955. There are no documented cases of executions attributed to Perón or most military presidents, with the notable exception of Aramburu, and political assassinations were virtually unheard of in Argentina until two years ago. Neither the Peronist nor the Radical parties have espoused revolution as a tactic since shortly after their inceptions.

Another prominent feature of Argentine political and intellectual life was its truly national quality. The flourishing character of Argentine cultural life produced some of Latin America's outstanding composers, writers, and artists, both in the popular and refined arts. This has long had a political side; Argentines have a strong nationalistic bent, and the celebrated anti-Americanism of Argentine foreign policy dates back to before World War I. The dynamic character of the Argentine industrial bourgeoisie and middle classes, expressed in cultural as well as economic productivity, nicely fits the Marxist picture of what a modernizing bourgeoisie ought to be.

The nationalistic character of Argentine popular thought is probably one of the main reasons for the notorious failure of the Communist party to make an impact upon Argentina either before or after Perón. Despite the fact that a majority of Argentine intellectuals call themselves Marxists, and most political analysis is along class lines, the Communists are primarily conspicuous by their failure.

A final feature of Argentine society that must be cited is the prestige and high professional caliber of the Argentine Armed Forces. In 1899 the army embarked upon a program of modernization and professionalization which most other Latin American armies only received at U.S. urging after

World War II.[36] As a result the Argentine Army maintains a high level of unity and morale, despite its frequent involvement in politics since 1930.[37] The armed forces view themselves as the final arbiters of Argentine politics, and as they have a monopoly on the instruments of force, they do in effect play that role.

In summary, Argentine political culture features 1) a strong landed elite, 2) a dynamic, nationalist bourgeoisie, 3) a large, nationalist middle class, 4) strong, class-based political parties, 5) a general tendency to think and behave along class lines, 6) a strong military with a propensity for defending its interests, and 7) a surprisingly civil politics of little personal violence.

Cuban political culture in the Batista years could accurately be described as the polar opposite on every variable. Its key features were 1) the absence of a traditional Latin American aristocracy, 2) a denationalized bourgeoisie, 3) fragmented middle-income groups, 4) weak political parties of uncertain life and belief, 5) a tendency to think politically in terms of personalities or generations rather than class, 6) a demoralized and unprofessional army, and 7) a political atmosphere charged by a high degree of personal violence.

We have already discussed the procedures whereby the Cuban landed elite in the coffee sector were destroyed, as sugar remained in the hands of Spanish interests and then American corporations as well. A corollary effect of the U.S. presence was that urban upper-income groups in Cuba did not develop into a national bourgeoisie.[38] Instead they were something of a tail on the dog of the American business class, maintaining apartments in New York or Miami, sending their children to Ivy League schools, and generally identifying with

[36] Darío Cantón, "Notas sobre las Fuerzas Armadas argentinas," *Revista Latinoamericana de Sociología*, Vol. 1, No. 3, pp. 290–313.

[37] Robert Potash, *The Army and Politics in Argentina* (Stanford: Stanford University Press, 1969).

[38] Among those who have laid stress on this are Blackburn, *op. cit.*, and Dennis B. Wood, "The Long Revolution: Class Relations and Political Conflict in Cuba, 1868–1968," *Science and Society*, Vol. 34, No. 1 (Spring 1970), pp. 1–41. See also Jorge Ibarra, Manuel Moreno Fraginais, and Oscar Pino Santos, "Historiografía and revolución," *Casa de las Américas* (Havana), November 1968, pp. 101–119.

the United States rather than Cuba.[39] A good many observers
have commented on the denationalized quality of the Cuban
upper class, but perhaps the best label for them was given by
Fidel Castro himself, who called them the "lumpen bourgeoisie."

Cuba not only lacked a nationally oriented elite, it also
did not possess a middle class worthy of the name. The famous remarks of the sociologist Lowry Nelson in 1949 are
very much to the point: "This observer is not at all certain
that a middle class exists in Cuba. . . . One has the general
feeling that Cuban society has not set or jelled."[40] Some
twenty years later, the University of Massachusetts historian
Ramón Ruiz added the following emphatic comments:

> Theodore Draper errs when he ascribes a "middle-class
> way of life" to "middle-class" Cuban families. Further-
> more, contrary to his claim, Cuba had not already under-
> gone its "bourgeois revolution." That nebulous stratum
> between the upper and lower echelons of Cuban society
> was made up of not one but several sectors, none of which,
> either separately or as a whole, had a consciousness of
> class. . . . No consensus or unanimity of opinion united
> the various sectors . . . the middle sectors were united
> only in their desire to join hands with the more
> affluent.[41]

The amorphous quality of the Cuban middle class was
reflected in the nature of Cuban political parties. They were
short-lived, ill-defined, and inconsistent. Blackburn's description is typical: "The Cuban political scene was an inextricable
confusion of volatile and venal factions, devoid of any program or ideology, competing avidly for office and wealth."[42]
When Batista ran for office in 1940 after six years as dictator,
he was supported by a coalition including the National party,

[39] Jorge Fraga, Manuel Moreno Fraginals, and Carlos Romeo, "The
Ideology of the Cuban Revolution," *Problemi del Socialismo* (Rome),
February 1968, pp. 206–220.
[40] Nelson, *op. cit.*, p. 41.
[41] Ramón Eduardo Ruiz, *Cuba: The Making of a Revolution* (Am-
herst: The University of Massachusetts Press, 1968), p. 13.
[42] Blackburn, *op. cit.*

the Democratic party, the National Democratic party, the Communist party, the Conservative party, and the Liberal party.[43] Virtually all observers have pointed to the weakness of Cuban parties as a principal feature of pre-Castro politics.[44]

One of the curious features of the Cuban scene was the absence of the class relations and class-oriented thought found in most of Latin America.[45] This was evidenced by Batista's rise to power despite his Afro-Chinese background, and is expressed by the Cuban term "choteo," which refers to brash or flip behavior, which was more likely to characterize inter-class relations than humility or respect. A typical Cuban political party would be likely to contain a cross section of intellectuals, workers, gangsters, students, farmers, and soldiers of fortune.[46] Membership in Cuban political groups was likely to follow family ties, marriage, and friendship, as well as simple avarice.

Instead of class-oriented thought, most Cuban political analysis focused on two themes: U.S. imperialism and the role of political generations in Cuban history. To this day, some materials published by the self-proclaimedly Marxist government are not organized around the historic role of classes, but around the historic role of the generations of 1868, 1895, 1933, and 1953.[47] Interestingly enough, most Cuban authors comment on the generational theme in Cuban analysis, whereas few U.S. writers on Cuba have done so.[48]

The major exception to the non-Marxist scene of the Batista period was the Communist party, which had a strong

[43] *Ibid.*

[44] See, for example, Andrés Suárez, *Cuba: Castroism and Communism, 1959–1966* (Cambridge: M.I.T. Press, 1967), Chapter 1. See also Blackburn, Wood, and Ruiz, *op. cit.*

[45] Ruiz, *op. cit.*, p. 15.

[46] Julio de Riverend, "Cuba: las dos historias," *Marcha* (Montevideo), July 12, 1969, pp. 7–9; Diego de Pereda, *El nuevo pensamiento político de Cuba,* Havana: Editorial Lex, 1943; and José A. Duarte, *Historiologia Cubana,* Vol. 4, Hollywood, California, 1969 (mimeographed).

[47] See the special issue "Cien años de lucha," *Cuba* (Havana), October 1968.

[48] The authors are preparing a bibliography of materials discussing the generational theme on Cuba.

base in a portion of Cuban labor.[49] But the Communists made their impact on Cuba through bread-and-butter issues rather than as an intellectual force.[50] Their deals with Machado, Batista, and the Auténticos gave them a record for opportunism as marked as any Cuban party's, and intellectually they seemed curiously isolated from the main currents of Cuban thought.[51] The Communists managed to misjudge most political developments in Cuba, from the strikes against Machado to Castro's guerrilla campaign, which they denounced as adventurism.[52]

Another important feature of Cuban political culture was its high level of endemic violence, characterized by "action groups" or "bonches" which existed parallel to and independent of political parties.[53] Originally founded to combat Machado, such groups took on a life of their own as semi-gangster terrorist organizations, despite their high-sounding names. These organizations fought each other, the police, and the army. Bombings, assassinations, and kidnappings were common in Havana, and the roster of Cuban politics is studded with dozens of violent deaths—Guiteras, Mella, and Menendez, to name three.[54]

In this chaotic situation, the Cuban Armed Forces played the stabilizing role, at least in theory. But the Cuban military was demoralized, faction-ridden, and venal—and singularly isolated within Cuba. Ruiz sums up the situation as follows:

> By deposing the officer clique whose background identified it with the ruling groups, Batista divorced the military from the traditional power structure; by race and social position, Batista and his men belonged to the lower classes. Yet Batista's betrayal of the revolutionaries in 1934 . . . destroyed what mass popularity the army had won in its earlier coup. Born of mutiny and betrayal, the post-

[49] See Wood, Blackburn, and Ruiz, *op. cit.*
[50] Boris Goldenberg, *The Cuban Revolution and Latin America* (London: George Allen and Unwin, 1965), pp. 113–119.
[51] Suárez, *op. cit.*, pp. 7–8.
[52] Goldenberg, *op. cit.*, p. 115.
[53] *Ibid.*, pp. 143–171, and Suárez, *op. cit.*, pp. 11–18.
[54] William Stokes, "National and Local Violence in Cuban Politics," *Southwestern Social Science Quarterly,* September 1953, pp. 57–63.

Machado army became the puppet of Batista, a military establishment shorn of professional ties with the elite, an opportunist, predatory army of professional soldiers of the lower class but devoid of any class loyalties, distrusted alike by the populace and the affluent.[55]

Analysis and Interpretation

With these features of Cuban and Argentine politics in mind, the subsequent development of their politics becomes explainable. In the Cuban case, the weakness of Batista stands out. Batista represented no group in Cuban society except his clique, and he offered other groups only one thing: his ability to maintain order. As such he had commanded the support of the two most privileged groups in Cuban society: organized labor and the Americanized economic elite. But when Batista proved unable to suppress the growing urban terrorism or Fidel's rural guerrillas, he was completely dispensable. No group identified with him, and no group thought they would fall with him. He simply represented no social class.

The success of the guerrilla movement in the countryside is also understandable in terms of the absence of a rural middle class. Virtually everyone in the Cuban countryside was a semi-employed plantation worker or a land-hungry marginal farmer. The key factor was not, as some Marxists have claimed, that the cane workers were a rural proletariat, but simply that few people in the countryside had anything to lose from a revolution. Those who did not support the guerrillas did not oppose them. This would not of course be the outcome in rural societies with a viable peasantry or commercial farming, such as Bolivia and Argentina, in which cases one might predict that rural guerrillas would get a short shrift.

Also explainable is the lack of social definition of Castro's revolutionary movement. It was neither middle class, as some have claimed,[56] nor peasant, as others claim.[57] It was a typi-

[55] Ruiz, *op. cit.*, p. 158.
[56] Theodore Draper, *Castroism, Theory and Practice* (New York: Praeger, 1965); Hugh Thomas, "Middle Class Politics and the Cuban

cally Cuban mixture of individuals from all sorts of back-
grounds united by personal ties and opposition to the status
quo.[58] The real shakedown did not occur until the revolutionary regime began to make hard decisions. Once this process
began, the regime moved to the left more swiftly than anyone had anticipated. This ideological flexibility was also due
to the lack of any firm class base.

The failure of Cuban bourgeois and middle-class groups to
mount an effective counterrevolution, despite frantic U.S.
assistance, illustrates their own social and ideological frac-
tionation. It also reflects their isolation from the rest of Cuban
society. Such groups had more in common with their U.S.
counterparts than with semi-literate cane workers and small
farmers, and were unable to generate much of a following.
Expectations of a U.S. intervention may also have played a
role in dampening their actions.

The one social group which might have effectively opposed
the revolution was organized labor. But the long history of
Communist labor leadership enabled the Communists to provide both know-how and influence in dealing with urban labor, once they had decided to jump on Castro's bandwagon.
Even though Castro would later purge most old Communists,
the C.P. was invaluable to his government during its early
years.

One striking feature of the Cuban revolution has seldom
been commented on: its relatively bloodless character. In a

Revolution," in Claudio Véliz, ed., *The Politics of Conformity in Latin
America* (London: Oxford University Press, 1967).

[57] Gil Carl AlRoy, "The Peasantry in the Cuban Revolution," this
volume; and "The Meaning of 'Peasant Revolution': The Cuban Case,"
International Review of History and Political Science, Vol. 2, No. 2, 1965.

[58] See Rolando E. Bonachea and Nelson P. Valdés, ed., *The Selected
Works of Fidel Castro* (Cambridge: M.I.T. Press, forthcoming), especially the Introduction. Between 1946 and 1960, according to Eckstein,
Cuba experienced fifty events of large- or small-scale terrorism. No
other Latin American nation experienced more than seventeen such
events. In Eckstein's tabulation of incidents of internal war, Cuba's total
score was twice that of the next Latin American nation. H. Eckstein,
"Internal War: The Problem of Anticipation (Appendix i). " A report
submitted to the Research Group in Psychology and the Social Sciences
(Smithsonian Institution, January 15, 1962). Cited by I. L. Horowitz in
"United States Policy and the Military Establishment," *The Correspondent*, No. 32, Autumn, 1964, p. 49.

nation which had had the highest rate of political murder in Latin America, the triumphant revolution was followed by a reduction of political violence. Major revolutions such as the Mexican and Russian had death tolls in the millions; in Cuba the official figures are in the hundreds (or low thousands if counterrevolutionary raids and guerrilla activities are considered—i.e. the Bay of Pigs). When the entire structure of land tenure was overhauled, neither a viable counterrevolution nor a pogrom resulted. The wealthy left early in the revolution, and many educated professional Cubans have left since.[59] But the Castro government appears to enjoy a continued working-class support that is remarkable, given the regime's economic difficulties.

The considerable unity of the Cuban public under Castro has been made possible, we suggest, by the absence of class consciousness in Cuban society. The generational theme and the anti-U.S. stance of Cuban thought made it possible for Castro to become the representative of all dispossessed groups in Cuba. As leader of the generation of 1953 he is leader of Cuba, from a generational perspective, having taken up the mantle of Martí and Guiteras.[60] A corollary to the absence of class consciousness in Cuba is the absence of race consciousness as an important political variable. Classes and races exist in Cuba as elsewhere, but the impact of Spanish and U.S. domination prevented forms of consciousness based upon them from developing, and thus made it possible for a revolutionary government to unify the country.

The establishment of strong class consciousness in Argentina gave political events there a rather different tone. Perón and his wife Evita appealed to the class identity of the industrial working class to generate popular support, and in fact, they helped to shape that identity. At the same time Perón appealed to the nationalist sentiments of the Argentine middle class and industrial bourgeoisie. He offered the Argentine military and industrialists a program of economic develop-

[59] José I. Rasco, "Sociología del Exilio," paper presented at the Primera Reunión de Estudios Cubanos held in Washington, D.C., on April 2–6, 1969.

[60] Bonachea and Valdés, *op. cit.*

ment based on industrial expansion and national autonomy. The only class group which Perón did not court was the landed aristocracy.

Perón's strategy was to raise wages as a means of stimulating demand on the local market, which would in turn be met by expanding industrial production, thereby freeing Argentina from dependence on the world market. National income would expand as a result of this "growth inward," and Argentina could enjoy full employment, prosperity, and economic independence.

This approach worked brilliantly during the first three years of Perón's government. But stagnating agricultural investment and exports eventually led to a foreign-exchange bottleneck. Economic growth stopped. A series of short-run recessions began, and the income groups that had enjoyed a sharp growth of real income now began to suffer reductions.

Probably the first group to defect (not counting the landowners, who never joined) was the middle class, which suffered most directly from austerity measures and in any case had been repelled by the working-class style of many Peronist officials, including the President's wife. This supposed vulgarity was of course enormously popular in the working class, for whom even today Evita is a sort of folk saint. But as the recessions continued and the industrialists began to suffer, they too withdrew support from Perón. At this juncture enthusiasm in the armed forces began to waver. Perón became increasingly dependent upon labor, which alienated other groups even further.

Perón faced the typical dilemma of coalition politics in a system of declining payoffs: how to keep one group satisfied without alienating other groups. It became apparent that the regime was nearing a revolutionary watershed in spite of Perón's attempts to heal the breaches with his former supporters. He swung to the right in economic matters and to the left by attacking the Church, but without avail. In the end Perón could depend only upon labor, and the instruments of violence were in the hands of the armed forces. Rejecting the one chance left to him, of a Spanish-style civil war pitting the working class against the armed forces, Perón withdrew from the scene.[61]

Perón left a country organized and divided along income and sectoral dimensions, or in a word, class.[62] The economic issues which were so prominent in his rise to power became the focus for the next fifteen years of indecisive struggle between Argentine classes. The representation of such interests through political parties has continued, and the Radical and Peronist movements show no signs of withering away, although they work through the army as often as through electoral mechanisms. The real Argentine parliament at present is the army, which maintained and strengthened its position both during and after Perón. But partly because of its own divisions the army has been unable to resolve the power standoff between Argentine classes to the permanent advantage of any group.

Conclusions

In summary, the weak character of the Cuban class structure helped shape both a political system without strong institutions and a political tradition without class consciousness. A popular leader could arise without having declared himself ideologically, and once having taken power, could radicalize and reshape the country without serious internal opposition. The absence of class consciousness resulted in the absence of an effective defense of class interests by those groups threatened by the radicalization of the Cuban revolution.

The rapid and vigorous development of the Argentine class structure created a political system with strong parties, a highly

[61] In an interview with one of the authors, Perón discussed the analogy with Spain and indicated that it had weighed heavily on his thinking at the time of his decision. Perón had been military observer with the Franco forces during the later stages of the Spanish Civil War.

[62] This material is presented and discussed in greater detail in Gilbert W. Merkx, "Sectoral Clashes and Political Change, the Argentine Experience," *Latin American Research Review,* Vol. IV, No. 3 (Fall 1969), pp. 102–104.

politicized military, and a political tradition in which class-linked issues became of paramount importance. As a result a popular leader could arise by fomenting both bourgeois nationalism and working-class pride at the same time. Once in power, however, such a leader was a prisoner of the coalition which he established and was unable to alter the social order without destroying the coalition. The high development of class consciousness in Argentina meant that all groups knew what was at stake and guarded their interests carefully. The Peronist revolution had no room for maneuver.

The Argentine and Cuban patterns are perhaps more common than they appear at first glance. Peronist-type military leaders who took power by combining the support of an emergent industrial bourgeoisie with an urban working-class base include Ataturk in Turkey, Nasser in Egypt, and Sukarno in Indonesia. This type of political evolution is likely to emerge in countries where a modernizing elite develops export agriculture or mining that in turn makes possible the development of import-substitution manufacturing and the growth of an urban working class. But once such a leader exhausts the room for economic maneuvering which he has at the start, he is likely to be ousted. The class conflict remains.

The ingredients of the Cuban sequence are to be found where imperialist domination has prevented the development of a strong native bourgeoisie, where national culture and class consciousness have not emerged, and where the popular lines of social and political thought are likely to unite the bulk of the population against the dominant foreign power. Such a consciousness was generational in Cuba, but in other countries it might be ethnic, linguistic, or racial.

If this consciousness is found in conjunction with plantation agriculture and minifundist plots, giving the rural population little to lose, the scenario for a successful guerrilla war is about complete. This pattern has characterized Kenya, Algeria, and Vietnam, where it produced guerrillas and charismatic leaders in Kenyatta, Ben Bella, and Ho Chi Minh. It also characterizes the Philippine Islands, where we predict the rise of the next such leader.

As these cases suggest, and as the Cuban and Argentine examples illustrate, the absence of class consciousness of a Marxist type is no barrier to the radicalization of a revolution, and the presence of traditional forms of class consciousness is likely to impede the radicalization of a revolution.

Part II

POLITICS OF REVOLUTION

A. GOALS AND METHODS

INTRODUCTION

In 1956 the 26th of July Movement issued a manifesto (re-printed in this volume) explicitly stating its goals. The motivating ideas were economic independence as a fundamental basis for political independence; the need for economic development; agrarian reform to create small landowners; agricultural diversification; industrialization; the nationalization of public services; and the expansion of foreign trade. The ideology was defined as nationalist, anti-imperialist, and democratic, a fulfillment of the frustrated ideals of past generations.

It was easy to agree on what was needed for Cuba, but not upon how to go about achieving it. Thus the measures of the revolutionary government were destined to meet disapproval from the supporters of the Revolution itself. It is demanding and difficult to live in a revolutionary society. If at the same time the country is rapidly trying to throw off the shackles of underdevelopment and imperialism, life can become agonizing, although the dramatic changes provide a certain hope. People sacrifice to build a better society, a good community with freedom, justice, and fulfillment for all. There are those, however, who question premises, who have doubts about the efforts they make, who disagree with the revolutionary leadership. This is a phenomenon which has received little attention until now; it is the painful, sometimes tragic process of those Cubans whose initial support of the Revolution changed to a position of doubt and criticism, and then to a final break with the revolutionary government.

Beyond our agreement or disagreement, their reasons and arguments, voiced in Cuba at the time, help us to understand the attitude of a segment of the Cuban people who had to define their own roles as individuals in a revolutionary process.

We offer here summaries of some articles by Luis E. Aguilar published in Cuba during 1959–60, when the Revolution swiftly moved from a radical democratic movement toward a socialist system. They express dramatically the mounting tension of a Cuban intellectual forced to face the unavoidable dilemma posed by the revolutionary government at that time: total support or total rejection of its decisions.

5

PROGRAM MANIFESTO OF THE 26TH OF JULY MOVEMENT*

1. The Present

The 26th of July Movement is resolved to take up the un-fulfilled ideals of the Cuban nation and to realize them. To accomplish these aims, the movement counts on its credential and its distinctive feature: the contribution and presence of the reserves of youth who are anxious for new horizons in the chronic frustration of the Republic.

By declaring itself a continuation of the revolutionary generations of the past, it defines the reason for the present struggle and the direction guiding it toward the future. This is a path of national affirmation, human dignity, and democratic order. Those of us who make up the 26th of July Movement, as free men, are guided solely by a compromise of honor with our consciences. We are not moved by stubbornness or insanity but by a well-thought-out conviction in justice, in the necessity of revolution, and a faith—well proven by blood—in the worthy destiny of Cuba.

That destiny has been crushed by an immoral and anti-Cuban power which has concentrated in itself all the vices and negative elements opposing the liberty and dignity of our land throughout the years. *The colonial mentality, the foreign economic domination, political corruption, and unlimited military control*[1] have united into one, like apocalyptic riders, to impose a regime of oppression and exploitation, gro-

---

* Manifesto issued in November 1956. Source: *Manifesto programa del Movimiento 26 de Julio*. Editors' copy. All emphasis and headings appear in the original. Footnotes have been provided by the editors.
[1] The phrase used is "desorbitación castrense."

tesquely disguised as a republican government, upon the country.

In fact, a republic does not exist. Those calamities, tied by the unpersonal knot of the crudest provincialism, hinder the functioning of a democratic system while submitting the people to a deliberate and effective process of debasement. The failure of the most conspicuous means of public opinion is patent. The political parties and the press in particular, with few exceptions, have publicly backed down in the face of governmental coercion or bribery. Consumed by incompetence, conformism, and cowardice, they have been totally ineffective to serve the nation at its most difficult hour. Thus, Cuba has become a defenseless colony,[2] entirely at the mercy of armed bandits who lavishly enrich themselves and deal with the national patrimony as if it were private property.

The March 10 coup radically suppressed the law of the land. Arbitrary brute force (which is not even capable of inventing an ideological pretext) prevails over enemy law, judge, or tribunal. All human rights are disregarded, and the most elemental guarantees (home, property, moral integrity, and life) assured by any civilized society are crushed by the brutal weight of the repressive hordes. The outrages and tortures of SIM[3] or the Bureau[4] or of any of the innumerable official agencies, barracks, and police stations that hire murderers throughout the island have no need to envy the torture chambers of totalitarian regimes.

But to those attempts against civilization, against legal order, and against human dignity (with the consent and complicity of the submissive courts) must be added the assaults of the country's economic resources. That aspect of government banditry has not only reached incredible extremes of robbing the public treasury and exploiting in an organized manner vice and smuggling, but even steals from the vital agencies such as the National Bank the funds for retirement and the gold reserves of the nation. The tremendous amount of credit owed to the "armed forces," the rapid increase in the public

[2] The term used was "factoría indefensa."
[3] Servicio Militar de Inteligencia—military intelligence.
[4] Bureau of Investigations.

debt, the nickel concession, the telephone concession, the secret oil concessions of the Isle of Pines and many others, such as the fantastic concession of the Cuba canal, characterize the irresponsibility of the clique of crooks who, led by Batista, have usurped power since March 10, 1952. They have caused irreparable harm to the present and future national economy.

Only the reserves of the country's youth have resisted this storm of horror and shame without bowing. This is highly significant and demonstrates the urgent necessity for renovation which the nation demands. With the failure of natural civic defenses—the parties and their leaders, the organs of publicity, and the courts of justice—the youth literally have had to come forward to take combat position. With that authority, sealed with blood and the lives of comrades fallen in the struggle or killed by the dictatorship's executioners, we declare that nothing and nobody will make us surrender the responsibility that rests upon us and that we will be faithful to the ethics and program of the Revolution.

A TRUE REVOLUTION

Let it be clear, then, that we are thinking about a true Revolution. We are not fighting simply to oust a gang of thieves from power nor are we going to substitute some bosses for others. We are not struggling to propitiate a return to the vicious stage that gave rise to the March 10 coup. We are not resigned, whatever the form used to conceal it, to having a colony for a fatherland and a clique of exploiters for democracy. We aspire to something else. We want a true and worthy nation within the American community of nations. We want a just and functional democracy. We want an independent and productive economy.

That is why we cannot be satisfied with puerile words. We are working on a program of serious political, economic, agrarian, and educational transformations. We move resolutely toward the roots of Cuba's problems. We are going to set up in an effective manner its democratic mechanism. We will apply technical norms and honesty in public administration and will study and intelligently administer our natural wealth. We will establish a just and scientific system of land distribution, and we will effectively nationalize public services. We will also create an intensive plan to foment agricultural and industrial development, a new foreign trade policy, and the structural planning of the educational system.

THE "NECESSARY WAR"

That is fundamentally the essence of our struggle. We are now occupied with removing the obstacles from our task. The spurious power that today blocks and frustrates Cuba's destiny presents features similar to or worse than those of the colonial past. That is why the insurrection is as justified today, perhaps more so, as it was in 1868 or 1895.

We are resuming the unfinished Cuban Revolution. That is why we preach the same "necessary war" of José Martí for exactly the same reasons he proclaimed it: against the regressive ills of the colony, against the sword that shelters tyrants, against corrupt and rapacious politicians, against the merchants of our national economy. We fight against the ills produced by that sorrowful amalgam.

We are aware that the struggle is difficult. The enemy recklessly squanders the public treasury to surround itself with powerful weapons and pretends to strengthen itself in two other ways: first, by attracting North American aid by simulating "order" and "anti-communism" (the old and worn-out arguments used by Latin American dictators); and secondly, by encouraging and entertaining a false political opposition with those whose complicity presents the necessary institutional and electoral façade.

It is interesting to note that at this moment encouraging signs are absent from the public of the United States, and the government officials of that country are beginning to see the deceit behind "strong men." They see how the false Cuban opposition—incapable and shortsighted—is ready to play the game of a decadent Batista who is condemned to disappear.

All these indicate that we alone are facing the usurpers. The positions are perfectly defined. On one side are the *nega-*

tive forces representing colonial backwardness; on the other, the *positive* forces of the Revolution.

Such distinction is historically fruitful. It will enable the nation to know, without any risk of confusion, who serves and who betrays. The ruling crooks rely on their power and their natural allies—the selfish and professional politicians. We rely on our dignity as free men and on the justice of our revolutionary cause.

That is our essence.

2. The Cuban Nation

Cuba has all the geographic, historic, political, economic, and sociological reasons to justify its right to constitute itself as an independent and sovereign nation. Without that right the historic process of the Cuban people in the last hundred years has no meaning.

If the struggle has not yet ended, it simply means that the conditions of *territorial sovereignty, an independent political structure, a national economy, and a differentiated culture* —bases upon which the nation must be founded—have not been achieved. Those conditions exist in an imperfect and incomplete manner due to negative factors that have always intervened in Cuba's national destiny.

The Cuban historic process can be clearly understood by noting the presence of three great political forces in its development. Those forces are *Spanish, Cuban,* and *North American* and have manifested themselves in the colonial period, the Republic, and the intervention. Their reciprocal action has been experienced from the outset when the embryonic Cuban consciousness was formed in the early days of the nineteenth century, and has existed until the present.

THE COLONIAL PERIOD

Félix Varela,[5] "the first who taught us to think," was also the first to express the idea of an independent Cuba. His

---

[5] Nineteenth-century Cuban priest and philosopher.

thought represents the third force competing in shaping the island's political destiny in his time. Already, at the beginning of the nineteenth century, Jefferson had stated in a famous letter to President Monroe (1823), "I confess that I have always looked upon Cuba as the most important acquisition we could make." On the other hand, Varela, in one of his articles for the *Habanero,* replied straight to the point (1825): "I am against the union of the island with any other government. I would like to see it as independent politically as it is geographically."

Those were the positions during the Spanish colonial regime of the three political forces of Cuba's future. The words of Jefferson and Varela posed an important dilemma to the colony. Although the subsequent history of Cuba developed around this question, rigorous geographic logic and the tangible fact of national desires undoubtedly proved that the independent position was correct and the only one convenient for the country.

THE REVOLUTION

In 1898 we witness another historic event of extraordinary importance. The three forces met at the same time. After more than thirty years of struggle (fifty years if we begin with Narciso López[6]), Spain was forced to relinquish its last possession in America. During the struggle, Cuba paid for its freedom with a high price in martyrs, heroism, ideals, and program. Nonetheless, at the symbolic moment when the war terminated, Cuba was not allowed to participate in the discussions setting its political status.

That was a sad precedent. The final outcome was determined more by the United States' intervention than by the bloody effort of the Cubans. The island seemed liberated from Spain's political yoke thanks to the aid of the "powerful neighbor." The antecedents and consequences of the episode perhaps could be explained within the context of the natural development of events, but the old colony became a

[6] Secessionist leader in the 1840's until his death in 1851, financed by United States Southern interests.

protectorate; and an ironic and costly "debt of gratitude" was acquired which served as an excuse for innumerable arbitrary injustices.

THE REPUBLIC

The history of republican Cuba continued to be written to a large extent by the unequal activity of the three forces. It is true that Spain disappeared as a political entity, but its influence remained as an active presence in the colonialist formation of the most important and powerful sectors of the society—all of which, feeling nostalgia for the colonial period, successively moved toward the United States.

Then, under the pretext of the Platt Amendment, interventions occurred. When no interventions took place, American ambassadors ruled Cuba. Messrs. González, Crowder, Guggenheim, Welles, and Caffery exerted more power than Cuba's presidents. Sometimes they had the consent and blessings of the presidents! Washington is the center of power to which all the servile rulers, caudillos, and Cuban politicians turned.

We have no right to complain. If the political and economic expansion of the great power can be considered as a natural phenomenon, characteristic of that epoch, it must be recognized that on our side (with the exception of some courageous but isolated voices) no resistance was presented. On the contrary, the great power was invited and even welcomed.

Thus, the Republic, due to the faults of Cubans, was a sad caricature. The political parties were mere personalist groupings lacking ideology and even a clear idea of the nation's goals. Politics was understood as an exhibitionist tournament of ambitions, or as a tropical rehearsal of Machiavellianism. Meanwhile, national wealth passed without difficulty into the hands of foreigners. Land, mines, the sugar industry, and public services were acquired by men who saw in our country only a rich and promising land to exploit. The Cuban became an outcast, living as a beggar in his own land. Independence disappeared ever more under the crushing weight of betrayal and apostasy.

THE 1930 GENERATION

Then another outbreak of the primitive and unfinished Revolution took place. The 1930's signaled a new contribution of the reserves of youth of the fatherland against the intact chains of the past. Workers and students marched this time in the vanguard of the movement, thus showing the rebelliousness of the second republican generation violently divorcing itself from the remains of colonialism embodied by the regime of Gerardo Machado.

Despite the romantic immaturity of that "1930 generation," it is necessary to note a favorable credit balance in the account of the Republic. In the "hundred days" that the revolutionary forces held power, they did more in defense of the interests of the nation and the people than all the governments of the preceding thirty years. Not only was the Platt Amendment abolished, but measures were established which, although common and natural in the more developed countries, were very progressive "conquests" in Cuba. The eight-hour workday, the right to strike, the nationalization of work, university autonomy, and reduction of electric rates gave the Cuban people the sense of finding themselves for the first time. It also proved that it was possible, without a catastrophe taking place, that we could rule ourselves.

Nonetheless, the colonialist elements predominant in the armed forces and in the cliques formed by exploiters of politics captured power once again and strangled the recently initiated attempt at national affirmation. Without experience or organization the leaders of the 1930 generation drowned in their own naïveté. Its leaders were unable to defend the Revolution from its traditional enemies—the armed forces and the corrupt and deceptive politicians—and allowed Batista, Mendieta, Menocal, and all the other reactionaries to take power.

However, the revolutionary movement—though precarious in its organization and rather imprecise about its goals—managed to leave marks in the juridical epilogue that ended it.[7]

[7] Refers to the 1940 Constitution, which adopted many of the revolutionary ideals of 1933.

The incipient feeling of sovereignty awakened in the people was sufficient to bring about a constitutional order that adopted the movement's social ideals and established an acceptable democratic mechanism. For the first time in the Republic, the will of the populace was considered, and a system based on popular suffrage and the open competition of the political parties functioned effectively.

It was this that permitted the group which appeared to be most identified with the movement to come to power: the Partido Revolucionario Cubano, "auténtico." But the event also served to prove once again what has always been a weak point in the Cuban struggle: the lack of organization, discipline, and revolutionary mentality.

The two "auténtico" governments of Grau San Martín and Prío Socarrás were tremendous frauds. Magnificent opportunities were incredibly wasted. Not only did they leave unresolved the basic problems of the country—the economic, industrial, agrarian, educational, judicial, military, etc.—but also they opened an immense floodgate of frivolity and scandal through which the anti-revolutionary forces sneaked back into power, significantly led once again by Fulgencio Batista.

If one member of the revolutionary force of the thirties remained alive, the reactionary March 10 coup extinguished him completely. The Republic was defenseless, lacking efficient instruments for civic resistance—political parties, courts of justice, and the press—and due to the counterrevolutionary forces which had united in a sinister alliance of military ambitions, political garbage, and large financial interests lacking any type of scruples, the weak democratic frame fell. The conspiracy had no difficulty in using the costly and corrupt apparatus of the armed forces, which happily joined this new treason.

Everything else was a logical consequence. Gangs of degenerate politicians, some improvised, others taken from the dustbin of the past in which they lay, all happily responded in order to join the civil bandwagon of the military dictatorship. Cuba suddenly moved backward to the point where it had begun its historic development. The country became in fact (not in theory because of the total absence of political thought in the seditious coup) a Caribbean version of the "police state." The armed forces assumed its true role as a mercenary army of occupation. Democracy ceased to exist.

FAILURE OF THE POLITICAL PARTIES

The case of the political parties requires a special section. One of Cuba's ills consists in never having had a true political party. The Partido Revolucionario Cubano founded by Martí was only a simple structure exclusively created for the immediate necessities of the Revolution. Therefore it did not exist when the unhappy Republic was born, nor did it participate in its miserable childhood.

It is ironically sad that the closest thing to a real political party was, precisely at the very outset of the Republic, the Partido Autonomista, an organization which negated independence, formed by arrogant intellectuals who had no use for or faith in the fatherland.

During the first thirty years of the Republic, the political parties were simple groupings of ignorant and innocent masses formed around some caudillo-like figure. Those groupings, whatever their names, were manipulated by cliques of political opportunists who fought over their turn to take the power conceded from Washington.

After 1930 the definitive profile of a true political party appeared: the PRC "auténtico."[8] Soon, however, the party achieved power and destroyed by recent and very well-known deeds the false hopes of those who saw it as a revolutionary instrument.

The discredit of "autenticismo"[9] forced Chibás,[10] one of its most prestigious and respected leaders, to create the Partido del Pueblo Cubano, "ortodoxo." As its name implied, the goal of the party was to fill the place that the "autenticismo" had lamentably deserted. In fact, however, the new party was only a curious phenomenon of political psychology, lacking in practice an ideology and a program of its own. Only the vigorous personality of Chibás, his image of honesty

---

[8] Refers to Partido Revolucionario Cubano.
[9] "Autenticismo" was the political movement formed by the PRC.
[10] Eduardo Chibás.

and rebelliousness, and his clean history of struggle against the Machado dictatorship managed to give coherence to what was a heterogenous amalgam of incompatible elements.

The persistent harangue of public honesty at a very opportune moment permitted the "ortodoxo" movement to amass the most formidable volume of popular support that the country remembers.

Against the happy spree of reckless waste by the "auténticos," Chibás' symbolic broom was impressive. But the premature death of the popular leader, and the March 10 military coup, showed the great internal weakness of the "ortodoxo" movement. Not only was it unable to oppose the calamity provoked by Batista and the military, but it was not even able to keep intact its own structure or use in any manner the popular and gigantic volume of support at its command.

THE LABOR ORGANIZATIONS

The passivity of the labor organizations, in addition to the ineptitude of the political parties, the surrender of the judiciary, and the submission of the press in the face of the March 10 coup, was also to blame for the fact that the nation was not defended. The behavior is the consequence of a class philosophy (which is indifferent to national problems unless it can exploit them) that has prevailed in the formation of the concept of work in Cuba. Although the worker, as a citizen and as a man, is capable of feeling and comprehending the country's problems, collectively he cannot operate, overwhelmed by *deceptive* arguments and by "leaders" who have submitted to official banditry.

Hypocritically posing as mere defenders of "class interests," the false leaders of the proletariat—exemplified by Eusebio Mujal—maintain the workers under a terror regime. They use against the workers the repressive state apparatus, and intervene in the labor unions or federations that refuse to follow their "discipline." In the Labor Ministry they also negotiate the supposedly legal coercive measures with which their labor union dictatorship is maintained.

Elections in the labor unions are indefinitely postponed, or they are held with hand-picked candidates. The same occurs at labor congresses and other meetings which are held with puppet delegates under police protection, in the style of the prefabricated assemblies held in totalitarian regimes. Since 1952 the Cuban workers have not held their traditional May Day parade because the government impedes it and the collaborationist leadership of the confederation of labor agrees.

It is amazing that in spite of that steel ring, civic and patriotic disquiet finds a sounding board in many Cuban workers. This has been proven by the sugar and bank strikes carried out under the most ferocious government repression, and the patent rebelliousness, *among the rank and file*, in the electric and telephone sectors, despite the abuses executed by the dictatorship through Mujal.

Those positive signs encourage the hope that the Cuban worker will incorporate himself, in an organized fashion, into the national struggle, whose stability and well-being directly concern him. The worker should not be alien to the fatherland's sorrows, and should abandon his class isolation and negative passivity which have been sponsored by the dishonest and treacherous leadership of the labor movement.

THE COLONY

The gang of anti-national elements that took power during the March 10 coup canceled ipso facto all hope of Cuba for its economic independence. The colonialists' interests have imposed on the country a type of subordinated economy that presents as its main aspects the following: 1) a system of concessions and of large monopoly over public services, 2) new and gigantic concessions such as the canal across Cuba, 3) unconditional surrender to foreign interests of our most important mineral resources (nickel, manganese, iron, and oil), 4) a policy of privileges and *laissez faire* with regard to foreign capital,[11] and 5) a plan to suppress and annul the laws helping the worker.

It is easy to comprehend that a reactionary plot transfers abroad the decisions that shape our economy; it establishes an exploitative regime without limits and suppresses the people's right to work and their social conquests. It trades inde-

---

[11] In the original the phrase is "gran capital inversionista."

pendence, with all its political, cultural, and spiritual implications, for the colonial status.

The hypothetical basis for this stand is a frightening, brutal, and coarse materialism. It consists of declaring that the employment opportunities and the circulation of money that will be produced as a consequence, despite the ostensible remittance of profits and sacrifice of the future for the sake of the present, will immediately compensate for any subjective loss of national integrity.

But the fallacy of the statement is as great as the cynicism of those who sustain it, because it is not true that the values of national integrity are exclusively *subjective,* nor is it true that the best method of creating more jobs and the material well-being of the people is the surrender of the economy to foreign domination.

Basically, this is not a dispute between economic theories. The root of the matter lies in the government's banditry, anxious to obtain foreign backing at any price. The government does not hesitate to gain that support in a criminal and irresponsible manner by surrendering the economic sovereignty and natural wealth of the country.

SIERRA MAESTRA

The Cuban nation can only be saved from all these ills and dangers by the decisive and active eruption of its youth, formed and indoctrinated in a firm national and patriotic conviction. They have the urgent task of completing the unfinished revolution, and of repairing the harm done to the country by the March 10 coup and by the conformity, cowardice, and submission of those who had the unavoidable duty of repelling it.

The paths of democratic recuperation are closed; only the dignified road of insurrection remains, justified today as it was justified during the independence struggle. The reasons are similar.

That is why, together with its epic realism, the action of the Sierra Maestra is highly symbolic. It represents the battle of the new and pure sap of the nation against the poisonous fumes that are undermining and destroying it. Whatever may be the outcome of insurrection at the moment, it has been proven that the insurrection is not a chimera and that the highest mountains of the rebellious region[12] have simply witnessed another episode of the *"necessary war."*

It must be emphasized that the Revolution is not a simple restoration or punitive movement, aimed solely at the bandits controlling power. Its scope is much broader. If today it is necessary to use a knife to cut the cancer at its root in order to stop its consequences, later it will be even more necessary to apply the adequate treatment of reconstruction.

The Sierra Maestra is the first and indispensable step toward a worthier and brighter future; it is the logical antecedent of the revolutionary program.

The struggle, then, has two complementary phases: one is destructive, the other constructive. In one phase the damned apparatus of the tyranny has to be reduced to rubble; in the other the free and true Republic must be built over ruins. We are on the first stage today. For how long we do not know, although we should all prepare for an eventually long and cruel fight. There is one thing we are sure about: we will triumph, and then the constructive phase of the Revolution will begin so as to build a great fatherland.

3. Doctrine of the Revolution

The Revolution is the struggle of the Cuban nation to reach its historic goals and accomplish its complete integration. That "integration" consists in the harmonious development of three elements: *political sovereignty, economic independence, and a differentiated culture.* The first defines the condition of the state, the second affirms the necessity for its own maintenance, and the third relates to the character and appropriate mental attitude of the people.

The Revolution is not precisely a war or an isolated episode, but the continuous historic process which presents different moments and stages. The landings of Narcizo Lopez

[12] Refers to Oriente province.

in the middle of the nineteenth century, the 1868 and 1895 wars, the movement of the 1930's, and today the struggle against Batista's banditry are all parts of the same and only national Revolution.

Armed struggle is not a necessary and substantial element of the Revolution. In theory, even in situations of institutional normalcy, the ideal can be carried out through democratic procedures. But once that channel is spoiled and obstructed by the presence in power of negative anti-national elements, represented by military dictatorship and its political accomplices, then revolutionaries have only one remaining path, that of insurrection.

The Revolution simply seeks *the establishment of a state of affairs in which man will have justice and dignity, in which he will find well-being, and in which all legal and necessary aspects of life will be agreeable.* In this case, of course, we will realize this ideal in the island of Cuba and for the benefit of the Cuban people.

The revolutionary ideal is composed of political, economic, social, and cultural aspects. Therefore, it covers all areas where the *human person* lives. Man has as much right to a free land as he has to his bread. He has the right to live in a society directed by norms recognizing his rights, and to enjoy cultural opportunities compatible with his particular character.

Taking this concept as a basis, the essential aims of the Cuban Revolution are the following: 1) a free and sovereign fatherland, 2) a democratic republic, 3) an independent economy, and 4) a culture of its own.

None of these goals can exist in isolation from each other. There is no fatherland without economy, no republic without culture, nor the opposite. Each is a part of the others, and the integral presence of all is necessary if the national goal is to become a tangible reality.

IDEOLOGY

"A Constitution is a lively and practical law that can not be constructed with ideological precepts."

Martí.

With regard to ideological definitions, the 26th of July Movement prefers to avoid abstract formulations or pre-established clichés. The ideology of the Cuban Revolution must arise from its own roots and the particular circumstances of the people and the country. Therefore, its ideology will not be something imported from other places, nor will it be discovered by a mental process that will later be applied to reality. On the contrary, its ideology will come forth from the land and the Cuban people.

Nonetheless, beginning from the stated principle and taking into consideration the essential goals already expressed, the 26th of July Movement can be defined as guided by the *ideals of democracy, nationalism, and social justice.*

These concepts need to be clearly defined because political categories are frequently distorted and twisted. In recent history many crimes have been committed in the name of those ideals.

With regard to *democracy,* the 26th of July Movement still considers valid the Jeffersonian philosophy and fully identifies with Lincoln's statement, "government of the people, by the people and for the people." Democracy cannot be the government of a race, class, or religion, it must be the government of *all* the people. The Cuban Revolution is also democratic due to the tradition established by our forefathers. "All men are equal," stated the proclamation of October 10, 1868. And the same idea was later maintained in the Montecristi Manifesto [of 1895], and in all the documents and Constitutions of the Republic.

Nationalism is the natural outcome of geographic and historic circumstances which from the outset determined Cuba's independent status. It refers to "wanting to be a nation" of a people that has been capable of conquering its own freedom. Cuba achieved nominal independence in 1902, but it has not yet accomplished its economic independence. The land, mines, public services, credit institutions, the transportation sector—in other words, the most important sectors of the national economy—send the greatest percentage of their profits abroad. The nationalist position, in this case, consists of rectifying that unjust situation so that the country will benefit from its own wealth and economic resources. As an adequate complement to that task, the nation will also have expression in education and culture.

With regard to *social justice,* the 26th of July Movement foresees the establishment of an order in which all the inalienable rights of a *human being*—political, social, economic, and cultural—will be fully met and guaranteed.

That premise established, some considerations relative to material well-being are necessary because they constitute the *sine qua non* of any other human right. The experience of the economic development of other nations in the nineteenth and twentieth centuries has demonstrated that the capitalist system of free enterprise inevitably leads to the accumulation of wealth in a few hands, while the majority is exploited. This experience has forced the most advanced nations, including the country most representative of the capitalist system— the United States—to resort to economic planning techniques that will guarantee the production and consumption of goods in accordance with the needs of the social order.

The 26th of July Movement favors a system of economic planning that will be capable of freeing the country from the ills of monoculture, concessions, monopolist privileges, latifundia, and other expressions of a colonial economy. In short, a system that will offer each Cuban the opportunity for material progress and dignity enjoyed today by the citizens of the great developed countries.[13]

In summary, the 26th of July Movement declares that the above-stated principles emanate from the political thought of José Martí, who once stated that the essential principle was that of the *full dignity of man.* All human relations— fatherland, politics, economy, education—converge at that point. In that position, in the following of Martí's ideas,[14] the philosophical base of our struggle must be found.

This ideological position can be divided into the following points.

---

[13] The phrase used is "países civilizados."
[14] "Culto martiano."

1) National Sovereignty

"If the family of American republics have a specific function it is not to be servants of any other."

Martí.

Sovereignty is the right of a nation to orient and shape its
own destiny. Without it, everything else—state, government,
culture—lacks national meaning; it is false. The first objective
of the Revolution, therefore, is to assert the full sovereignty
of Cuba.

This condition is officially recognized in terms of international politics, especially since the abrogation of the Platt
Amendment in 1934. But Cuba still suffers from a situation
which, although not direct political intervention, constitutes
essential violations of its sovereignty. The presence of foreign
bases and missions in the national territory, the different economic pressures, and the interference of diplomats who publicly take sides and issue declarations about our internal affairs
are clear and eloquent examples [of intervention]. These
things demoralize and impoverish our national spirit and make
more difficult the true understanding that should exist between neighboring countries.

The nation must be fully sovereign with regard to its territory, form of government, national and international
political decisions, economic orientation, education, culture,
and any other activities related to its historic process.

Sovereignty is perfectly compatible with the ideal of continental and universal fraternity. In fact, it is an indispensable
condition and guarantee of the cordial relations and peaceful
coexistence of nations and governments.

2) Economic Independence

"The only fruitful and lasting peace and freedom are those
accomplished by one's own effort."

Martí.

Economic independence is understood as the capacity of a
country to take care of itself within the natural system of
international relations. This independence is the indispensable

foundation for political sovereignty. Cuba possesses sufficient resources to aspire to its economic independence like any other sovereign nation in this world. This aspiration does not hinder in any way; rather it aids the development of a rich, productive, and satisfactory trade for all.

The principle of economic independence essentially consists in the *investment in the country of the greatest possible percentage of nationally produced profits*. When, for some reason or other, the majority of the profits goes abroad, this is superseded by a mathematical disequilibrium of the monetary reserves and the subsequent tendency to subordination and impoverishment. In such cases the means of production are not developed according to the national interest, but according to the convenience of the exploiting private capital. That is the moment when the country loses its economic sovereignty and falls into the practical condition of a colony.

With the aim of avoiding such disastrous consequences and assuring a stable economic development which will not be vulnerable to abrupt changes or foreign contingencies, the state will exert a policy of controls over natural resources, public services, banks, insurance, capital investments, and all other forms of production and credit. It will also reserve for itself the right to orient and plan, within international common understanding, the conditions of foreign trade.

3) Work

"The general happiness of a people depends on the individual independence of its inhabitants."

Martí.

Although the 26th of July Movement does not defend the doctrines of economic determinism, it proclaims that there cannot be democracy or social justice if man does not have the means to satisfy in an honorable way his material needs. Consequently, we maintain that the state is obliged to provide those means, principally in the form of adequate production instruments and well-paid opportunities to work.

Hence, work is considered a right and a way to achieve individual progress. More than a pretext to fragmentize the social unity of alien groups, it will be a factor indispensable for production and national unity. Work should be guaranteed at all times by a just and progressive compensation, and by a body of legal measures that will regulate its conditions, having as its point of departure the full dignity of every human being.

The law will also guarantee, of course, the right to organize and strike. But once labor is defined as an integral part of the production process, class conflicts with regard to capital will cease or decline to an extraordinary degree. In this manner, elevating the functional importance of "labor," and limiting the privileges of "capital," we will reach a state of solidarity and harmony between the two which considerably will increase productivity and will benefit everyone.

4) Social Order

"We must impede the distortion or exploitation of Cuba's interests by the interests of one group, the excessive authority of a military or civil organization, a given region, or of one race over another."

Martí.

The 26th of July Movement takes its ideas with respect to social problems from Martí. Its ideal about this is the *organic unity of the nation.* According to this concept, no group, class, race, or religion should sacrifice the common good to benefit its particular interest, nor can it remain aloof from the problems of the entire social order or one of its parts. Ancient civilization recognized this principle in the expression *salus populi suprema lex,* which meant that the commonweal was the norm guiding the practice and spirit of the law.

The concept of organic social order[15] will incorporate all, without privilege or exception, to the advantages and responsibilities of progress. The incorporation will be done through a more just and dynamic conception of property (especially land), capital, and production, and through the elevation of labor to the category of cooperating agent in the direction and

[15] The phrase used is "organicidad social."

profit sharing of the enterprise. In this way the causes that provoke class antagonisms are eliminated or reduced, and the cohesion of all on the basis of the common good is made easier.

Social unity rests on what can be considered the supreme goal of the Revolution: *the moral and material welfare of man.* This implies all human rights, including the natural right to a dignified standard of life. In that manner, when promoting the happiness of the individual and his harmony in relation to the community, the necessary conditions are established for the ideal of *national integration* and the subjective values of the fatherland are affirmed.

5) Education

"The measure of responsibility is related to the extent of one's education."

Martí.

Education is the radical solution to be implemented by the Revolution (the immediate or urgent one is political insurrection). Since we cannot have a fatherland without a national consciousness, nor democracy without citizens, it is necessary to have a thorough and systematic instrument dedicated to provide the people with those indispensable instruments.

From this it can be concluded that the state must concern itself with education. For the 26th of July Movement this will be *the intelligent and systematic process of educational and environmental factors which, together with the function of instructing culture and skills, will be directed at forming in the individual the fundamental traits for citizenship and patriotism.*

That definition comprises the four aspects that should be covered by Cuban education: 1) cultural, 2) vocational, 3) civic, and 4) national.

Understood as such it is easy to see that education cannot be simply reduced to a pedagogic technique. In a country like Cuba, still struggling to achieve its *national* fulfillment, education must be aimed toward the achievement of important goals, some of which are *subjective,* while others are *objective.* The subjective goals are the values of freedom and fatherland, both of which are complemented by the basic principle of the *dignity of man.* Among the objective goals can be found, at the forefront, the cultural, vocational, and technical preparation of the citizen which will make him a capable and aggressive instrument in the face of the country's social and economic problems.

All this explains the great revolutionary importance of the educational process. It also shows why the state must pay special attention and interest to the philosophy that will guide this process.

If education pretends to have national and civic ends, it cannot limit itself to a technical function, but requires a certain moral and philosophic content; this content cannot be of a sectarian or confessional type, because it will gravely endanger the democratic freedoms. The morality that will animate our education will be universal in character, common to all men in spite of belief differences. It will be a natural ally of the principle of freedom. Also, the essential characteristic of the democratic state demands that public education be *absolutely secular,* so that there will be no room, due to reasons of conscience, for undesirable discriminations or distinctions among the future citizens.

The 26th of July Movement, in expounding these ideas, emphasizes the exceptional value it grants to public education, and announces its intent to dedicate to it the most serious attention in terms of studies and programs.

6) Politics

"To govern is to direct the national forces in such a manner as to allow each man to fulfill himself in a dignified way, and to make good use of public prosperity."

Martí.

The 26th of July Movement is determined to achieve the ideal of a democratic republic, inspired in the credo of freedom and founded in the character and capacity of its citizens. It aspires to establish in Cuba a form of government and a system of public and individual rights that will be fully practiced in real life and not forgotten in written Constitutions and laws.

To reach that end, however, it is first necessary to carry out a thorough eradication of arbitrary procedures and evils that debase Cuban politics. The principal causes for this particular situation are: *political parties without doctrine, immoral politicians, personalism, the low level of civic consciousness among the masses, abstentionist neutralism; and all their consequences, such as: electoral mercantilism, the mocking of elections, police power, military hegemony, providentialism, and dictatorship.*

The eradication of all these ills supposes a twofold task: on the one hand, revolutionary action in the form of a series of decrees directly aimed at severely punishing crimes committed against political freedom or against human rights; and on the other hand, a systematic campaign of civic education capable of giving the masses the indispensable minimum of political education acquired in a democratic system.

The next step will be the adoption of a politico-electoral structure (or code) that will establish adequate guidelines, as well as measures that will assure its functioning and practice. The 26th of July Movement will propose a juridical project to guarantee as a fundamental issue the validity of the citizen's vote, providing at the same time the necessary educational means that will secure the certainty that that vote is at all times the spontaneous manifestation of a conscious and constructive public opinion.

This stand by the 26th of July Movement arises from its ideological aim of inaugurating in Cuba the practice of true political democracy, i.e., the competition of ideas between political parties and a representative government based on the genuine expression of the general will.

7) Civil Authority

"Governmental power should be only in the hands of civilian men. . . . A nation is not established as one runs a military camp."

Martí.

All the guarantees of the democratic system contained in essence in all the great historic documents of the West, from the Declaration of Independence (1776) to the Déclaration des Droits de l'Homme et du Citoyen (1789) to the present Declaration of Human Rights of the United Nations, are based on the establishment of a firm civil authority that will assure their fulfillment.

With the increment of the military-police power as a determining factor in public life (a salient cause and consequence of the March 10 coup), Cuba has returned to a very primitive political level. So much so that, except for the absolute ideological vacuum that characterizes it, the bandits ruling the country, led by Batista, reproduce one by one all the horrors of totalitarian regimes.

This state of affairs is in direct contradiction to the purest national tradition. The founders of the fatherland always were, by conviction and temperament, profoundly civilian-oriented. Céspedes, Aguilera, Agramonte, Gómez, Maceo, García, Sanguily, Varona, Martí . . . even those like Gómez and Maceo, who won innumerable laurels on the battlefront, were men who subordinated their authority to civilian leaders. But there is more. The civilian position is not only delimited by biographical sketches; we also have the Constitutions and other juridical documents of the Revolution expressing its political thought. The October 10, 1868, Proclamation, the Montecristi Manifesto, the bases of the Partido Revolucionario Cubano, and the Constitutions of Guáimaro, Jimaguayú, and La Yaya are filled with the civilian outlook which shaped the formation of Cuba at every moment.

These ideas and this historical summary are sufficient to establish the civil orientation of the 26th of July Movement, and to foresee the type of pragmatic action that will be carried out once the Revolution achieves power.

8) Freedom of Conscience

"Freedom is the right every man has to be honest and to think and speak without hypocrisy."

Martí.

The Revolution considers as one of the essential elements of democracy the principle of freedom of conscience. Each citizen will be free to sustain whatever creed or religion he might want, or none at all, as long as his attitude does not diminish human dignity or endanger the rights and freedoms of others.

When the state makes any religion official or gives it privileges, or permits it to intervene in areas that are of public concern alone, then the principle of freedom of conscience disappears and democratic equilibrium becomes unstable.

This position has its roots in Western democratic thought. In Cuban history it appears jointly with the thesis of civilian control, and is also found in the thought and behavior of the founding fathers as well as in the juridical literature of the Revolution. In the same manner, the names of all of our great patriots could be cited; but it would suffice to remember the abundant references made by Martí, whose belief, in summary, is that "there can be no happiness without the separation of Church and State."

Nonetheless, state secularism suffers constant violations in Cuba, especially in the form of privileges—many of them economic and granted to religious groups. Under the banner of charity the unequivocal separation of the state from religious creeds—so essential to any democratic system—is being undermined and weakened.

On this matter, the 26th of July Movement adopts and proclaims the ideas of Martí, declaring that it will fight at all times for those conditions which would make the principle of freedom of conscience effective. In political terms this means a secular state.

9) Public Morality

The Republic was born carrying the colonial germs of political corruption. At the same time it lacked the moral or philosophical strength to counteract corruption, and time has done nothing but aggravate the evil. It is not surprising, therefore, that public matters in Cuba constantly fall prey to profiteers and thieves for whom the institutions of democracy are only a profitable market.

That is why the Cuban Revolution must complement its ideology with serious ethical concerns. The corruption of public affairs could not in itself constitute an essential evil if it could easily be eradicated (in theory at least) by legal and educational means; but it certainly is of great danger as it frustrates constructive work and opens the gate to worse evils. Crimes against public morality remain unpunished. They destroy the civic faith of the masses and undermine our institutions.

The 26th of July Movement maintains that the problem demands the action of a double program. First, we need a thorough investigation and sanctions that would purify the responsibilities contracted by those in power with the threat of confiscation, among other things, to those who are guilty of enriching themselves illegally. Secondly, there must be a joint plan of electoral and administrative reforms that would eliminate, or at least minimize, the possibilities for crime. The law would point out in due time the details of the procedure. What is important is to have in mind that the revolutionary task cannot reach its objectives if it is not accompanied by intense, firm, and systematic action.

10) International Position

The Cuban Revolution is historically situated within the purest American tradition. The common ideals and interests which necessarily unite the republics of the hemisphere—both north and south—are a reality that should be developed and maintained cooperatively by all the nations of the continent.

The independence of Cuba, therefore, as well as that of all the other countries of America, cannot be taken as an isolated event. It is part of a process whose supreme objective must logically be the integration of all in a higher unity of freedom and mutual understanding.

That is, then, in a few words, the international position (mainly inter-American) that the 26th of July Movement adopts. Therefore, in its relations with the other American republics, including, of course, the United States, Cuba's attitude is not one of separation but rather friendship. This attitude, as long as the common historical ideals demand it, will have priority over the rest of our international relations, that is, extracontinental.

Having laid down certain basic points, we must now make some other clarifications. Just as it is true that independence can be considered a step toward plural integration (not yet realized), this does not mean that it can or should be omitted or reduced at any time. On the contrary, this desirable state of harmonious unity for all could never be attained without the full maturity of all its parts—a maturity that in this case is *national integration.* In other words, independence is not an obstacle but a path. It is conceived as good and beautiful, a possible fraternity among homogeneous republics, not as colonies or satellites.

With regard to the specific matter of the relations between Cuba and the United States, the 26th of July Movement formulates a doctrine of *constructive friendship.* By this we mean mutual respect, particularly in the economic and cultural areas.

In good political terminology, it is improper in America to utilize the word "imperialism"; but forms of economic penetration still persist, accompanied generally by political influence. These cause irreparable damage to the moral, as well as material, well-being of the country that suffers them.

Fortunately, such a situation can be overcome without damage to any legitimate interest. Through *constructive friendship,* Cuba can truly become, as is indicated by a multitude of geographical, economic, and even political factors, a loyal ally of the great country to the north, yet at the same time preserve its ability to control its own destiny. Through new and just agreements, without unnecessary sacrifices or humiliating sellouts, it can multiply the advantages that are derived from our neighborhood.

Constructive friendship can be expressed fully in one simple formula: combine the process of national integration with an increase in relations on a scale of equity and justice. That is, in reality, a "healthy Americanism." On the one hand, it gives reality to the postulates of the national Revolution, and on the other, it opens the door to a reasonable, profitable, and lasting understanding.

4. The Future

Today (five years after March 10, 1952) Cuba is undergoing the most critical juncture of its history. Either the Revolution triumphs—thanks to the effort, almost the only one, of the youth reserves—and inaugurates a new order of dignity, freedom, and national reconstruction, or the banditry of Batista prevails (even though it dissimulates its appearance by a false change of façade in complicity with elements of the pseudo-opposition) and adds new frustration to the destiny of the fatherland, obliging itself to continue the struggle indefinitely.

As a revolutionary force, born and baptized with blood in the midst of the tragedy, the 26th of July Movement aspires not only to the overthrow of government banditry and the renovation of the rotten political atmosphere that nourishes and supports it, but also to the development of the indispensable program of transformations that constitute the positive part of the Revolution.

The history of republican Cuba shows an unfavorable balance for the political organizations and parties. The slogans and promises were never anything other than electoral promises or demagoguery.

One of the reasons that the 26th of July Movement exists is due to the necessity of overcoming this reality. The Cuban people will not find their true destiny until they have a political instrument which represents the national will with a sincere ideology and sensible program. Leaving aside the theatrical language of the merchants of cheap politics, the 26th of July Movement proposes to reach the very root of each problem, and to offer in accord with its position and doctrine the corresponding solution.

6

REVOLUTION AND COUNTERREVOLUTION

Luis Aguilar

1. The Revolution, the Economy and the Counterrevolution

*The economic measures adopted by the Revolution have provoked a certain alarm in several sectors of the nation. We could say, to be more exact, that the alarm has been produced more by the tone with which the laws have been proclaimed than by the laws themselves. It was natural that the deep and radical course taken by the revolutionary government would produce profound tremors in our economic structure, hypersensitive to every political change.

Those who believed that this regime was going to limit itself to the restoration of the Constitution of 1940, those who forget the old and bitter social problems which Cuba had and is still suffering from are quite alarmed by the unexpected urgency with which the Revolution wants to cure and heal ancient and national injuries. They speak of "irresponsibility," and of rash measures. Before jumping to conclusions and abandoning all faith, they should consider that every revolution is essentially a matter of acceleration and impetuosity, for those are the essential ingredients of which successful revolutionaries are made. They fail to remember also that perhaps the ablest hands of this government—Felipe Pazos, Rufo López Fresquet, Justo Carrillo, Cepero Bonilla, and

* From "La Revolución: La Economía y la Contrarrevolución," *Prensa Libre* (Habana), March 21, 1959, p. 2.

Regino Boti[1]—are in control of the economic helm. They
should thus recognize that urgency does not always mean lack
of judgment, and that rush does not necessarily imply lack of
deliberation. The Revolution has solemn historical pledges,
and wants to honor them at its normal pace, a revolutionary
pace, charged with urgency and avid for reforms.

It is possible to accept, nevertheless, that certain tendencies
of the Revolution have contributed decisively to the confusion
and dismay of those national sectors. We could mention one
which, because of its negative results, should and could be
easily rectified. That is the excessive facility with which the
term "counterrevolutionary" is flung in every direction, as if
it were not quite possible to make a distinction between a
poisonous censure and a criticism or dissent which is honest
and sincere. This tactic not only stifles advice which could be
positive, but plays right into the hands of the enemies of the
Revolution. The cry of the dethroned oligarch or the broken
"latifundista" is basically an isolated and echoless cry. But
if the Revolution classifies in that same counterrevolutionary
category the lawyer who demonstrates the arbitrariness of a
disposition, the architect who only asks for the revision of a
regulation, the small property owner hurt by some law, the
employee who protests his dismissal, the worker who demands
too much, or the journalist who merely insinuates a warning,
then it is the Revolution herself who adds allies to those who
criticize in bad faith and out of resentment. It is the Revolution herself who makes appear as her declared enemies many
who consider themselves as her sincere allies. It is the Revolution who pushes them into a group they despise, allowing
that group then to disguise its reactionary and unpopular
voice by joining a chorus which, though supporting the
Revolution, is still capable of dissent. . . . This Revolution
which has rallied all the Cuban people, enthralled individuals
from all classes and positions, and which can, with only one
gesture, assemble raving multitudes has few, but very few
enemies and the people know them well. This Revolution

---

[1] Pazos, Carrillo and López Fresquet are now in exile. Cepero Bonilla
died in a plane crash in 1962, while still working for the Cuban Government. Regino Boti is in Cuba in an unimportant administrative position.

can therefore confidently accept the sometimes productive and positive jar of some criticism and censure, and has no reason or need to suspect dark, malignant intentions in anyone who asks, protests, or advises. To listen to some warnings or counsels is not to cease being a revolutionary.

*Even those of us who are not versed in economy, that mysterious science fraught with statistics and figures, know that one of its most dreaded characteristics is its total absence of emotion. An economist judges the efficiency of a law not through the good or bad intentions of its authors, but through the cold data which his graphs show. That is why many of us, Cubans who are not "latifundistas" and who do not own a single inch of land, Cubans who have hailed the Revolution as the fulfillment of an old national dream, and who know the mountain of abuse suffered for so long by our peasant population, are somehow disturbed by some of the arguments offered against the Agrarian Reform Law in its present form. Some of them sound as if they deserve better attention.

Against the argument that we don't have enough technicians to carry on the Agrarian Reform in one single thrust, or that our peasant population lacks the knowledge and the resources to substitute immediately for the present managers, or the warning that every agrarian reform produces an initial decline in productivity with the inevitable result of unemployment and misery, we would like to hear better counterarguments than the usual adjective of "reactionary" or "counterrevolutionary." Just as a criminal on trial can give the police useful and valid information, so even a "latifundista" could be pointing out an economic truth or offering some reasonable economic argument. And if it is treason against the Revolution not to act for fear of the reactionaries, it is also treasonable to jeopardize the Revolution by pushing it toward a dangerous economic setback simply because one refuses to listen to some adverse argument.[2]

* From "Proa a la Tormenta," *Prensa Libre* (Habana), June 12, 1959, p. 18.
[2] It should be remembered that years later the leaders of the Revolution themselves, including Fidel Castro, have recognized the initial economic "mistakes" of the Revolution, which they consider now the result

But beyond and above all of us, as a goddess only looking at the future, the Agrarian Reform Law has been proclaimed. With it the Revolution has crossed the Rubicon to lead the nation to the deepest and most dangerous adventure of its entire history. With the firm hands of those fully convinced of the justice of their cause, the revolutionary government has turned the helm of state to steer its course toward a problematic horizon. The government has not hesitated in assuming the tremendous responsibility of radically transforming a country without any other guide than its own criteria and its own program. . . . If it succeeds in the enterprise all the glory and the blessing of future generations will belong to it; if it fails the government itself will have been the architect of the disaster. For all the rest of us who with our duties and with our hopes travel in the same ship, to be saved or doomed with it, it remains only to repeat the old invocation of Phoenician sailors: "Let the wind be favorable and let us be equal to our task."

2. A Mounting Dilemma: Devotion to the Leader or to the Nation?

*Every honest Cuban who at the present hour bears his quota of patriotic concern, who vibrates with the hopes and risks of these moments, who wants to keep his enthusiasm alive but free of fanaticism, feels himself gripped in the pincers of an expected dilemma. On one side, like a torrent of energy, the Revolution displays its accomplishments and its programs, its dream of justice and its will to heal, and this invigorating force makes the soul thrill with love for Cuba and gives rise to a loyal devotion to duty.

On the other side there appear the inevitable negative aspects of every movement, the excesses, the tactical mistakes which could jeopardize the entire formidable task . . . and one feels the temptation to raise his voice humbly and se-

---

of a first "romantic" or "anarchical" period of the Revolution. (Note of the author.)

* From "El Dilema," *Prensa Libre* (Habana), June 27, 1959.

renely to warn, advise, or dissent. Ah! but one is immediately reminded that to point out a mistake of the Revolution means to cooperate with the somber legion of enemies who inside and outside of Cuba are planning a sinister revenge. To dissent, they say, is to join the ranks of the parasites who oppose the Revolution to defend lost and sordid interests. . . . To disagree, they say, is to weaken the Revolution and to strengthen our northern neighbor whose imperialist beak has more than once cut deep into Latin American flesh. . . .

And who does not balk, facing that terrible dilemma, at giving any sort of aid to those who once usurped power, escaped loaded with crimes, and blinded by resentment are plotting against the country? Who wants to see his loyal and honest criticism mixed and confused with the criticism of those trying to defend the permanence of unjust situations? Who wants to weaken our sovereignty and will not add his effort to keep in full force our awakened national dignity? . . . If those are the terms of the dilemma, then there is not even the possibility of a doubt: the duty is to silence all opinion and quietly continue our own personal task.

But a closer look at the problem shows that there is no such dilemma, or that, at least, its edges are not so sharp. We begin to surmount the limits of the situation if we move beyond the narrow and tense present toward a wider historical perspective. We realize then that governments and political movements are but periods in the history of every nation. They pass, but the nation remains. And it is the nation, that supra-individual entity, permanently reinvigorated by the injections of successive generations, which finally measures the actions of governments and men. And the final balance is based only on the benefits or damages that they have brought to or inflicted on the collective body.

Sometimes, in dramatic historical circumstances, a man or a party seems to incarnate the highest aspirations of the fatherland, and they rally around them the last fiber of national enthusiasm and energy. But even in those moments of supreme elation it is good to remember that the basic spur of popular fervor is the faith in the capacity of those men to bring a radical improvement of the national standard. This is the tremendous responsibility of those who enjoy power in those moments, and their duty to be alert not to fall into tempting mirages. For the intoxicating popularity and the massive response of millions of citizens are not irrevocable concessions of the people; they are temporary loans given to those leaders who have managed to gain the supreme confidence of the people. And those loans demand, in order not to disappear quickly like the foam, concrete and visible results. And if the positive or negative signs of those results for the collectivity are going to be the ultimate criteria, then the initial dilemma is reduced to acceptable terms.

Keeping in mind the high set of national values which is at stake, it is the clear duty of every citizen not only to applaud, support, and encourage every action which seems aimed at the betterment of the social conditions of the people, but also to express his concern over every governmental action which could jeopardize or harm the common effort.

In moments charged with high political emotions, there is nothing more tempting and easier than to renounce our own criteria, yield to our own dosage of collective passion, and applaud everything or criticize everything. I think, nevertheless, that even in those moments it is much more useful to make an effort to keep a just balance, and thus to be able to express our unrestricted applause or our restrained criticism each time we face a beneficial or a dangerous program. At the end, as usual, the extremes are equally harmful. To applaud a wrong position because we benefit from applauding is as counterrevolutionary and anti-patriotic as to oppose a just law because it harms us.

In the entire dangerous process, the decisive factor is to be honest with oneself. Only by basing the judgment on our good faith can we discern where to join the collective effort of the nation. United, yes, totally united against the attack of the "Batistianos," or against foreign intervention from wherever it might come . . . but united without an imposed uniformity, united by convictions and not by force, united in our roots, but allowing every branch to preserve its capacity to decide, its right to criticize without excesses, its respect for the person who dissents. . . . At the end, above leaders and parties, history will only classify in two groups the men who have lived these dramatic times: those who were beneficial, and those who were harmful for the nation. All the rest is transitory.

3. Paredón, Paredón . . . ! The Somber Voice of the Revolution

Editors' Note   In October 1959, Major Hubert Matos, one of the top officers of the Rebel Army and a veteran of the struggle in the mountains, was arrested after protesting Communist infiltration of the Rebel Army. His arrest was followed by a huge popular meeting in Havana where drastic measures were announced against "all the enemies of the Revolution." After a succession of similar, if less important crises, this event was for many Cubans the turning point in their attitude toward the Revolution.

*Many Cubans opposed Batista's regime, few took arms to fight and topple it. And because they were few, and heroic, and gallant, the day that the indomitable warriors came down from the mountains holding in their victorious hands the future of Cuba, a vast and deep feeling of gratitude and admiration swept the island. We all knew how numerous were our national problems; we knew that Batista's dictatorship had been the result and not the cause of basic social inequalities; that the time had come to apply radical solutions to the very heart of the nation. Because we all knew that, we applauded the initial decisions of the Revolution and its more regenerative and drastic laws.

But we had also a burning hope: the hope that after seven years of abuse and oppression by an insolent military cast, choked by an atmosphere polluted by base insults and daily invectives, a new era was going to begin, an era of generous and collective effort, which could heal the injuries of hate and resentment. We believed, and we still do, that a Revolution

* From "Los que construyen y los que destruyen," *Prensa Libre* (Habana), November 24, 1959.

so fervorously and unanimously received could have applied the most drastic measures without displaying a concentrated hate against any national sector, without using the system of inflaming popular rancor against those who were simply exerting the right that the Revolution itself had brought back: the right of dissent. We hoped that the Revolution against a dictatorship would know how to restrain itself so as not to become a revolutionary dictatorship. . . . Each day that passes seems to snip parts of that hope.

**This last week was darkened by somber events which fill the heart with an oppressive sensation. I am not referring to the repulse that provokes the news of the discovery of certain plans made by the representatives of the past regime, and which we have already denounced publicly and energetically. I am thinking of more profound and essential emotions. . . . First it was the spectacle, the terrible spectacle of a multitude shouting rhythmically one single, ominous word: "Paredón! Paredón!" The word resounded with the air of a popular tune, but it referred to a wall pierced by bullets and to silent men waking at dawn to their deaths. . . . The chorus was cheerful, but it meant a decision over the life and death of a number of imprisoned fellow citizens. And as I deeply believed that existence is the supreme value of every human being, as I believed that under exceptional circumstances society has the right to suppress that value, but never in such a way, during a public rally in a public place, under the fragile irresponsibility of a frenetic mob, I felt a deep sorrow.

And hearing the rhythmic and unanimous cry, with the persistence of a nightmare and the tenacity of a beating anguish, my inner agony broke into several bitter questions: where were all these people when the man against whom they were shouting was risking his life for Cuba? What were they doing then when he was fighting, all these "fanatics" who now, under the easy impunity of their massive number, applaud and demand the execution of a man against whom not a single proof has been offered, and who has not yet even received the opportunity to defend himself? . . . Is this going to be the

** From "Hora de Pesadumbre," *Prensa Libre* (Habana), November 1, 1959, p. 7.

method? . . . The life and prestige of six million citizens are going to depend on the shouts in a public square of a frenzied fraction of the population? . . .

Then came the uncertainty of the whereabouts of Camilo Cienfuegos.[3] Camilo, the one of the friendly smile and the cordial attitude. Camilo, the hero of so many combats lost now in what seems to be a trivial and tragic mechanical accident unworthy of his legend and his history. . . . The week closes with a somber balance. The revolutionary tribunals have been reinstated, a hero disappears, the ominous precedent of a man condemned by the howling of a multitude still shakes our mind. And behind all these events, as in a Greek tragedy, a dark and implacable chorus keeps hammering on every conscience one single, terrible word: "Paredón! . . . Paredón! . . ."

4. Social Justice, Yes, Totalitarianism, No!

*A massive and impressive meeting of Cuban Catholics has raised its voice against the atmosphere of hate which is mounting in Cuba. It was about time. . . . It was about time that the other voice of the people should be heard. It proclaims that the true road toward progress is one based on a firm respect for the individual, for the human person as such, as an end in itself, and not as another figure in a statistic of production. . . .

Social justice, yes, totalitarianism, no! . . . That was the slogan which provoked a mad enthusiasm. Social justice without social or class hatred. Resolute effort to improve the lot of the worker without beheading the employer. Collective participation in the profits, without transforming the state into the only employer, the owner of everything, for against that state there is no possible protest or demand. Full social jus-

---

[3] Camilo Cienfuegos, one of the great heroes of the Revolution, disappeared in a plane which was never found, when en route to Havana. His "accident" was and is a source of speculation in and out of Cuba.

* From "Por la victoria sobre el odio," *Prensa Libre* (Habana), December 1, 1959, p. 8.

tice, without capitalist exploitation or state totalitarianism. That is the clean doctrine of Christianity. . . . The reactionary Right should forget its old dream of spreading religiosity as a means to check the just aspirations of the proletariat. And the totalitarian Left should learn that it won't be easy to conduct a people with religious convictions toward the mirage of a dictatorship only theoretically proletarian. . . . And let us also hope that the rulers of the nation hear this voice and avoid pushing us toward that road. . . . This could be, perhaps, the only way to win a victory over hate.

5. The Curtain Falls*

Editors' Note   In May 1960, among public denunciations of an imminent landing of the American Marines in Cuba, the Diario de la Marina, *the oldest and most conservative of the Cuban newspapers, was "occupied" by its workers. Two days after the publication of the following article by Luis Aguilar,* Prensa Libre, *the newspaper in which it was published, suffered the same fate.*

> "I thoroughly disagree with what you say, but I shall defend to the death your right to say it."—Voltaire

> "I want a hundred ideas to germinate in my country, and a hundred buds to sprout."—Mao Tse-tung

Freedom of speech, if it is to be real, must be extended to all and not be the prerogative or special gift of anyone. That is the crux of the problem. It is not a question of defending the ideas maintained by the newspaper *Diario de la Marina*. It is a question of defending the *Diario de la Marina*'s right to express its ideas, and the right of thousands of Cuban citizens to read what they think is worth reading. Hard battles have been fought in Cuba on behalf of that freedom of expression and freedom of choice. And it has been said that if

* From *Prensa Libre* (Habana), May 13, 1960, p. 1.

one began by persecuting a newspaper for maintaining an idea, he would end up persecuting all ideas. And it has been said that there was a desire for a regime in which there would be room for the newspaper *Hoy,* of the Communists, and the *Diario de la Marina,* of conservative leanings. Despite that, the *Diario de la Marina* has disappeared as a vehicle of thought. And the newspaper *Hoy* remains freer and more firmly established than ever. Evidently the regime has lost its determination to maintain balance.

For those of us who long for full freedom of expression to be crystallized in Cuba once and for all, for those of us who are convinced that in this country of ours union and tolerance among all Cubans are essential for carrying forward the purest and most fertile ideals, the ideological death of another newspaper produces a sad and somber echo. For, however it may be presented, the silencing of a public organ of thought or its unconditional enlistment in the government line implies nothing less than the subjugation, by one means or another, of a tenacious critical posture. All the massive propaganda of the government was not enough. There was the voice and there was the argument. And since they did not want or were not able to debate the argument, it was indispensable to choke off the voice. The method is an old one, the results are well known.

Now the time of unanimity is arriving in Cuba, a solid and impenetrable totalitarian unanimity. The same slogan will be repeated by all the organs of news. There will be no disagreeing voices, no possibility of criticism, no public refutations. Control of all the media of expression will facilitate the work of persuasion, collective fear will take charge of the rest. And underneath the sound of the vociferous propaganda, there will remain . . . the silence. The silence of those who cannot speak. The implicated silence of those who, being able to speak, did not venture to do so.

But, it is shouted, the fatherland is in danger. Well then, if it is, let us defend it by making it unattackable both in theory and in practice. Let us wield arms, but also our rights. Let us start by showing the world that here there is a free people, a truly free people, and that here all ideas and attitudes

can coexist. Or is it that in order to save our national liberty
we must begin by suffocating civil liberties? Or is it that in order to defend our sovereignty we must limit the sovereign
rights of the individual? Or is it that in order to demonstrate
the justice of our cause we must make common cause with the
injustice of totalitarian methods? Would it not be much more
beautiful and much more worthy to offer all America the example of a people that makes ready to defend its freedom
without impairing the freedom of anyone, without offering
even the shade of a pretext to those who suggest that we here
are falling into a government of force?

Unfortunately, that does not seem to be the path that has
been chosen. Instead of the sane multiplicity of opinions, the
formula of a single guide, a single watchword, and common
obedience is preferred. This way leads to compulsory unanimity. And then not even those who have remained silent will
find shelter in their silence. For unanimity is worse than censorship. Censorship obliges us to hold our own truth silent;
unanimity forces us to repeat the truth of others, even though
we do not believe it. That is to say, it dissolves our own personalities into a general, monotonous chorus. And there is
nothing worse than that for those who do not have the herd
instinct.

B. INSTITUTIONS AND STRUCTURES

INTRODUCTION

The revolutionary system of Cuba, although consisting of specific structures, institutions, and organizations, is essentially shaped by the charismatic leadership of Fidel Castro, who in most cases has correctly interpreted the moods and desires of his followers while providing them with new views and goals. In the following selections Richard Fagen analyzes Castro's utilization of his magnetism, the mass media, and the mass rallies, and the way he has bound to his side a large part of the island's population. The selection by Fidel Castro (an excerpt from a speech) is an interesting one since it replies to arguments based on Max Weber's concept of charisma. According to Fidel, the revolutionary leaders have the support of the people not because of their personal appeal but as a consequence of the Revolution's achievements.

An inevitable corollary of a social system based on charismatic authority is its anti-bureaucratic attitude. Bureaucracy is considered a social evil, an obstacle to what is truly radical in any revolution: its permanent dynamism. The selection on "Bureaucracy and Revolution," published in the official newspaper of the Cuban Communist Party, reveals in all its facets the Government's position on the matter, and outlines what the new society will be like.

A socialist society can be achieved, Cuban revolutionaries maintain, only through a constant struggle where every man lives in permanent asceticism while developing society's wealth and its own consciousness. In this struggle Cubans fight in the trenches of production or against backwardness, ignorance, or imperialism, and from all of these will surface the man of the twenty-first century. Richard Fagen, in his penetrating essay on Cuba's "mobilization system," describes the history, evolution, and instrumentalities created to implement this vision.

7

CHARISMATIC AUTHORITY AND THE LEADERSHIP OF FIDEL CASTRO*

Richard Fagen

No part of Max Weber's sociology has been as thoroughly overworked in discourse about politics as has his concept of charisma. The appellation "charismatic" has been applied to leaders as different as Stalin, Nkrumah, Hitler, and Gandhi, and there has been a general tendency to equate the charismatic in politics with the demagogic, the irrational, the emotional, and the "popular."

This luxuriance of meanings and attention is not, as one commentator has already pointed out, simply a result of intellectual faddism.[1] Rather, it represents in part a very genuine groping about for a conceptual framework which might be of service in the analysis of twentieth-century politics. However, if the concept of charisma is to serve in scientific political inquiry, it cannot refer in blanket fashion to leadership styles as disparate as those mentioned above. There is a need for explication and parsimony. This paper attempts to provide a first step toward that explication and to indicate, by example, how the concept might be used in empirical inquiry.

* From the *Western Political Quarterly*, Vol. XVIII, No. 2, June 1965, pp. 275–284. Reprinted by permission of the University of Utah, copyright owners.
[1] Carl J. Friedrich, "Political Leadership and the Problem of the Charismatic Power," *Journal of Politics,* 23 (1961), 3–24.

WEBER'S FORMULATION OF CHARISMATIC AUTHORITY

As conceptualized by Weber, charisma (the gift of grace) referred to "a certain quality of an individual personality by virtue of which he is set apart from ordinary men and treated as endowed with supernatural, superhuman, or at least specifically exceptional powers or qualities."[2] The concept was, of course, taken from the idiom of early Christianity, and in Weber's sociology charismatic authority was one of the three pure types of legitimate authority—the other two being rational-legal and traditional.[3]

There are at least five elements of Weber's formulation of charismatic authority which must be taken into account in any political research using the concept. These elements, stated in propositional form, follow:

1. The charismatic leader is always the creation of his followers. That is, charismatic authority (in common with all other types of legitimate authority) is rooted in the belief system of the followers rather than in some transcendental characteristics of the leader.[4] When no one is disposed or

[2] Max Weber, *The Theory of Social and Economic Organization*, trans. A. M. Henderson and Talcott Parsons (Glencoe: Free Press, 1947), p. 358.

[3] Weber's three-part typology of legitimate authority has been discussed so frequently that there seems to be no need to summarize it here. For a particularly compact and cogent explication of the typology see Peter M. Blau and W. Richard Scott, *Formal Organizations, A Comparative Approach* (San Francisco: Chandler, 1962), pp. 30–36. The most recent critique of Weber's typology is Peter M. Blau, "Critical Remarks on Weber's Theory of Authority," *APSR*, 57 (1963), 305–16. Blau's essay contains a useful listing of earlier critical appraisals of the typology.

[4] "It is recognition on the part of those subject to authority which is decisive for the validity of charisma." Weber, *op. cit.*, p. 359; see also p. 382. This aspect of the charismatic relationship was stressed in an important article by James C. Davies, "Charisma in the 1952 Campaign," *APSR*, 48 (1954), 1083–1102. Using data from the Survey Research Center of the University of Michigan, Davies identified and analyzed 32 respondents (out of 1,799), who perceived Eisenhower as a charismatic leader. Davies' insights and approach do not seem to have been followed

able to believe in the omnipotence, omniscience, and moral perfection of the leader, he cannot be said to exercise charismatic authority no matter how strong, wise, or moral he perceives himself to be.

2. An "individual personality" or leader capable of generating a charismatic authority relationship in one context may fail completely to generate that relationship in some other context. There are no universal charismatics. This is clearly a corollary of the first proposition and suggests that the set of followers is always bounded by at least two factors. There are some who are never reached (physically) by the messages of the leader and thus remain at best what we shall call *potential followers*. And there are others who, although reached, do not for a variety of reasons respond in the prescribed manner. These individuals we shall call the *non-followers*.

3. The leader does not regard himself either as chosen by or as solely dependent on his followers, but rather as "elected" from above to fulfill a mission.[5] He perceives his followers as having obligations and duties toward him and he perceives himself as deriving his morality and legitimation from his special relationship with some more abstract force such as God or history. Furthermore, those who resist or ignore him—the non-followers—are regarded as "delinquent in duty."[6]

4. The behavior of the charismatic leader in power is anti-bureaucratic—"specifically outside the realm of everyday routine and the profane sphere."[7] Daily affairs, whether economic, political or administrative, are treated with disdain by the leader. He surrounds himself with disciples chosen for their devotion rather than a staff selected by more formal means.

5. Charismatic authority is unstable, tending to be transformed (routinized) through time.[8] This "natural entropy of

---

up by scholars interested in the rapidly changing political environments where the concept would be of more research value.

[5] Weber, *op. cit.*, pp. 359–61.

[6] *Ibid.*, p. 360.

[7] *Ibid.*, p. 361.

[8] See H. H. Gerth and C. Wright Mills (eds. and trans.), *From Max Weber: Essays in Sociology* (New York: Galaxy, 1958), pp. 248–50.

the hero's charisma"[9] occurs in part because his image of infallibility cannot be maintained in the face of inevitable failures, and in part because the demands of ruling cannot be met through time without more rationalized involvement in the mundane affairs of state.[10]

These five propositions serve to direct us toward a set of empirical questions which should prove useful when confronted with a suspected instance of charismatic authority in the real world. The first proposition focuses our attention on the attitudes and perceptions of the followers as crucial determinants of the existence or non-existence of the charismatic relationship. The second proposition suggests that deeper understanding of the relationship will result if we can map these perceptions and attitudes against the distribution of social and personality characteristics in the society. The third directs us to an examination of the leader's perceived relationship both to his mission and to his followers. The fourth and fifth propositions are predictive; the former states that the leader in power will behave in certain ways, and the latter states that the charismatic relationship will inevitably be transformed.

This is clearly a mixed bag of propositions, and any thorough investigation of one or more cases would of necessity have to concentrate on some elements to the partial or complete exclusion of others.[11] Nevertheless in the following examination of the Cuban case whatever data were at hand—no matter how unsatisfactory—are presented in order to offer

[9] The phrase is from Immanuel Wallerstein, "Evolving Patterns of African Society," in Immanuel Wallerstein et al., The Political Economy of Contemporary Africa (Washington, D.C.: George Washington U., 1959), p. 6.

[10] Notice that our five propositions say nothing about the social and political conditions conducive to the establishment of charismatic authority. This reflects a gap in Weber's thought structure which has been succinctly pointed out by Blau: "In short, Weber's theory encompasses only the historical processes that lead from charismatic movements to increasing rationalization and does not include an analysis of the historical conditions and social processes that give rise to charismatic eruptions in the social structure. He has no theory of revolution." Blau, op. cit., p. 309. Davies, op. cit., discusses the genesis of the "charismatic phenomenon," but only in the context of politics in the large modern state.

[11] Except for the first proposition which cannot be ignored because it is at the core of the definition under which we are operating.

at least a brief exploration and discussion of each proposition. This exploratory posture is assumed because it best serves the twin purposes of suggesting investigatory strategies appropriate to the propositions and of organizing what little we actually know about the leadership of Fidel Castro.

THE CUBAN CASE

1. The Charismatic Leader Is the Creation of His Followers

There is no lack of reports which mention that in the early stages of the Cuban Revolution Castro was regarded by large segments of the population as the heaven-sent savior of the nation.[12] The religious overtones of this relationship have

[12] Among the book-length studies in English which stress the charismatic elements of Castro's relationship with his followers I would mention the following ten: Teresa Casuso, *Cuba and Castro* (New York: Random House, 1961); Jules Dubois, *Fidel Castro* (Indianapolis: Bobbs Merrill, 1959); Leo Huberman and Paul M. Sweezy, *Cuba, Anatomy of a Revolution* (New York: Monthly Review Press, 1960); Herbert L. Matthews, *The Cuban Story* (New York: Brasiller, 1961); Warren Miller, *90 Miles from Home* (New York: Crest, 1961); C. Wright Mills, *Listen Yankee* (New York: Ballentine, 1960); R. Hart Phillips, *Cuba, Island of Paradox* (New York: McDowell, Obolensky, 1959); Nicolas Rivero, *Castro's Cuba, An American Dilemma* (Washington, D.C.: Luce, 1962); Jean-Paul Sartre, *Sartre on Cuba* (New York: Ballentine, 1961); William Appleman Williams, *The United States, Cuba, and Castro* (New York: Monthly Review Press, 1962). These books, which otherwise represent a wide range of interpretations of the Revolution, are in consensus on the charismatic basis of the leader-follower relationship—at least in the first year or two of Castro's rule. For two brief scholarly analyses which make the same point see Russell H. Fitzgibbon, "The Revolution Next Door: Cuba," *Annals*, 334 (1961), 113–22, and George I. Blanksten, "Fidel Castro and Latin America," in Morton A. Kaplan (ed.), *The Revolution in World Politics* (New York: Wiley, 1962). The two most scholarly sources on the Revolution and its antecedents are Wyatt MacGaffey and Clifford R. Barnett, *Cuba, Its People, Its Society, Its Culture* (New Haven: HRAF Press, 1962), and Dudley Seers (ed.), *Cuba, The Economic and Social Revolution* (Chapel Hill: U. of N. Carolina Press, 1964). A critical and well-documented treatment of many aspects of the Revolution can be found in International Commission of Jurists, *Cuba and the Rule of Law* (Geneva: The Commission, 1962).

been emphasized by many commentators, and one prominent Presbyterian minister in Cuba published an article in which he wrote: "It is my conviction which I state now with full responsibility for what I am saying, that Fidel Castro is an instrument in the hands of God for the establishment of His reign among men."[13]

Only one study, however, is actually based on the type of systematic data needed for a more thorough analysis of the charismatic elements in the relationship of Cubans to Castro during the first few years of the Revolution. This is a sample survey conducted by Lloyd Free in Cuba in April and May of 1960.[14] Under the direction of Free, a Cuban research organization interviewed a cross section of 500 residents of Havana and another cross section of 500 residents of other urban and semi-urban centers. The 40 per cent of the Cuban population living in rural areas was not represented in Free's survey.

Free classified 86 per cent of his respondents as supporters of the regime. Of all supporters, one-half (or 43 per cent of all respondents) were sub-classified as *fervent* supporters. In "more-or-less typical quotations from the interviews" Free suggests the articulated content of fervent support: "'Fidel has the same ideas as Jesus Christ, our protector and guide.' 'I would kiss the beard of Fidel Castro.' '[My greatest fear is:] That some mean person might kill Fidel. If this happens, I think I would die.'"[15]

Now these are clearly responses with charismatic over-

[13] Rafael Cepeda, "Fidel Castro y el Reino de Dios," *Bohemia* (July 17, 1960), p. 110 (my translation). An American observer noted: "In many Cuban homes a picture of Fidel has an honored place; in some of them it is a photograph of a bearded youth who seems to be wearing a kind of halo; the resemblance to portraits of Christ is notable." Irving P. Pflaum, "By Voice and Violence," Part I, *American Universities Field Staff Reports,* Series V, No. 3 (August 1960), p. 16. See also MacGaffey and Barnett, *op. cit.,* pp. 284–85.

[14] Lloyd A. Free, *Attitudes of the Cuban People Toward the Castro Regime* (Princeton: Institute for International Social Research, 1960).

[15] *Ibid.,* p. 6. Free makes the point that such expressions of devotion were not dictated by the political exigencies of the open-ended interview situation. If a respondent simply wanted to give a "safe" answer, it would have been quite sufficient simply to express admiration for Castro and the regime.

tones. But it would be an unwarranted inference simply to assume that *all* of the fervent supporters are also charismatic followers. Rather, in the absence of an analysis specifically designed to identify the sub-set of charismatics we can only speculate on how closely it might coincide with the set of all fervent supporters. In any event, two points stand out: First, in the early stages of the revolution Castro was perceived as a charismatic leader by some "sizable" fraction of the Cuban population. Second, in the absence of survey research designed especially for the purpose, it is impossible to determine with exactitude just how sizable this fraction was, or how it might have changed in size and composition through time.[16]

2. The Distribution of Charismatic Followers Illuminates Important Characteristics of the Relationship

One striking aspect of the Cuban Revolution is the thoroughness and frequency with which the voice and visage of Fidel Castro have blanketed the island. Through the extensive television system and the mass rallies—which have on occasion drawn as many as one million of Cuba's seven million inhabitants into the plaza of Havana—the messages of the maximum leader have been brought to almost 100 per cent of the population.[17] In our terminology this suggests that there

[16] Of course the problems of conducting survey research in areas undergoing rapid political and social change are immense. Free mentions that the Cuban organization which originally promised to undertake the field work backed out at the last moment when informed by a government leader that it would be "suicidal." The organization which finally undertook the research did so only because it felt its days in Cuba were already numbered. *Ibid.*, p. i.

[17] I have developed and documented this theme of the modernity and pervasiveness of the Cuban communication system in two other papers. See Richard R. Fagen, "Calculation and Emotion in Foreign Policy: The Cuban Case," *Journal of Conflict Resolution*, 6 (1962), 214–21, and "Television and the Cuban Revolution" (Stanford: Dept. of Political Science, 1960), mimeo. For a useful evaluation of Castro's television talents see Tad Szulc, "Cuban Television's One-Man Show," in CBS (ed.), *The Eighth Art* (New York: Holt, Rinehart and Winston, 1962), 197–206.

is only an insignificant number of *potential followers* (persons not reached by the leader's messages) in Cuba. We can therefore direct our entire attention to the *non-followers,* those who have been reached but do not respond in a charismatic manner.

Once again we must return to Free's data as the best available for an analysis of the distribution of charismatic followers in Cuba. As before, we cannot identify the sub-set of charismatics from the set of all fervent supporters, but the patterning of fervent support by education, social class, and place of residence is revealing. The tendency for fervent support to be associated with low education, low social class, and semi-urban residence is clear.[18] If rural respondents had been

TABLE 1

Support for Castro in 1959 by Education, Social Class, and Place of Residence*

(*in percentages*)

(*N=1,000*)	*Fervent Supporters* (43 per cent)	*Moderate Supporters and Non-supporters* (57 per cent)
Education:		
Elementary or no schooling	49	51
Secondary schooling	35	65
University training	1L	6Z
Social class:		
Lowest socioeconomic class	48	52
Lower-middle class	39	61
Upper-middle and upper class	34	66
Place of Residence:		
Outside of Havana	49	51
In Havana	34	66

* Adapted from Lloyd A. Free, *Attitudes of the Cuban People Toward the Castro Regime* (Princeton: Institute for International Social Research, 1960), p. 7.

[18] Our inability to isolate the charismatics from the fervent supporters is not too crucial here for it seems safe to assume that, if anything, the charismatics would exhibit these tendencies to a greater degree than the fervent supporters do.

included in the sample, we would expect the associations to emerge even more strongly. Finally, Free found that the distribution of fervent supporters was sharply skewed toward the lower end of the age continuum—43 per cent of all fervent supporters were between 20 and 29 years of age.[19]

Confirmation of this pattern of support for Castro also emerges from data on a systematic sample of Cuban refugees in Miami—a group which is presently unanimous in its expressed hatred of Fidel.[20] When asked how they *originally* had felt about Castro when he came to power in 1959, 42 out of 191 refugees replied that they thought "he was the savior of Cuba." Since the refugee community represents a highly skewed sample of Cubans, a sample comprised substantially of members of the middle and upper classes, Table

TABLE 2

Refugee Support for Castro in 1959 by Education,
Place of Residence, and Age*

(*in percentages*)

(N = 191)	"Castro was Savior of Cuba" (N = 42)	All other responses (N = 149)
Education:		
High school or less	25	75
At least some college	12	88
Place of Residence:		
Outside of Havana	27	73
Havana	19	81
Age:		
40 or younger	26	74
41 or older	18	82

* All respondents currently in exile in Miami.

[19] Free, *op. cit.,* p. 8.
[20] This derives from an unpublished study by the author and Professor Richard Brody of Stanford University. As part of the study, a self-administered questionnaire was given to a pre-selected sample of male Cuban heads of household living in Miami (in March 1963). The data in Table 2 are taken from the completed questionnaires. Complete demographic data on the refugees are reported in Richard R. Fagen and Richard C. Brody, "Cubans in Exile: A Demographic Analysis," *Social Problems,* 11 (1964), 389–401.

2 is of special interest. Thus, even in this refugee sample the association of strong support with lower education, semi-urban and rural residence, and lower age is found.

But should we expect these particular socio-demographic patterns of fervent support (and the less frequently encountered—though similar—patterns of charismatic support) to be found in all cases of charismatic leadership? That is, whenever a charismatic political relationship is identified will the followers tend to come from among the rural, the younger, the less educated, and the lower classes? There is no simple answer to this question, but at least three points should be noted:

First, as emphasized previously, the communication system of Cuba has brought all members of the society into contact with Fidel, giving them at least the *opportunity* to become charismatic followers. In less developed and less homogeneous societies, it would be precisely the lower classes, the rural, and the poorly educated who would tend to be cut off from the national channels and therefore from the messages through which the leader might establish his claim to legitimacy. Second, both the ideological focus and the actual accomplishments of the Cuban Revolution have come to center on the rural and less privileged sectors of the society.[21] It is natural to assume that those who perceive themselves as the prime beneficiaries of Castro's leadership should also tend to relate most frequently to him in a charismatic manner. However, just as all nations do not have Cuba's well-developed communication system, so all charismatic political movements do not necessarily benefit the rural, the poorly educated, and the lower classes. Finally, the social groupings most likely to relate charismaticly to Castro may well contain a disproportionate number of persons who *as individuals* are predisposed to make a charismatic response. Davies, for instance, hypothesizes four characteristics of the "charismatic aspect of

[21] By actual accomplishments of the Cuban Revolution we refer to such social gains as the educational, health and welfare, and housing facilities which have been built since 1959. For examples of the manner in which the Revolutionary Government uses the themes of egalitarianism and social welfare, see Richard R. Fagen, *Cuba: The Political Content of Adult Education* (Stanford: Hoover Institution, 1964).

personality structure,"[22] and Doob has suggested that the less educated and less westernized members of a society perceive and behave toward authority figures quite differently than do their more educated and westernized countrymen.[23] It is perhaps at this level of "personality in social structure" that the Cuban experience will prove to be most similar to other instances of political charisma.

3. The Leader Regards Himself as Elected from above to Fulfill a Mission

Only a close analysis of Castro's published and unpublished thought could supply the richness of detail which a full investigation of his self-image would require. In the absence of such an analysis, we can only note a few recurring and interrelated themes.

First, Castro perceives the Revolution as part of a greater historical movement against tyranny and oppression. Castro developed this theme long before he became a professed Marxist-Leninist. More recently, of course, capitalism and imperialism have replaced (domestic) tyranny and oppression as the prime obstacles to a revolutionary cleansing of the world's political landscape. Second, the Cuban leadership and Castro in particular are seen as blessed and protected by the larger historical movement of which the Revolution is a part. Castro's famous speech ending, "condemn me, it doesn't matter. History will absolve me," is a classic, early articulation of this idea.[24] Finally, because the leader is seen as acting in

[22] Davies, *op. cit.*

[23] Leonard W. Doob, *Becoming More Civilized: A Psychological Exploration* (New Haven: Yale U. Press, 1960).

[24] This speech was delivered by Castro at his trial for leading an attack on the Moncada Army Barracks in 1953. It is available in English under the title, *History Will Absolve Me* (New York: Lyle Stuart, 1961). The attack and the trial are well treated in Dubois, *op. cit.* The theme of historical blessedness and protection received popular reinforcement from the circumstances surrounding Castro's return to Cuba from Mexico in 1956 with 82 men and the avowed purpose of overthrowing Batista. Only Castro and 11 others escaped to the Sierra Maestra where they launched the guerrilla action which culminated in the downfall of Batista

concert with larger historical forces not always visible to more ordinary men, he alone retains the right to determine "correct" behavior in the service of the Revolution.

It is important to realize that these overtones of intellectual Marxism and political authoritarianism preceded by many months the introduction of Marxist economic determinism and Soviet bloc alliances into the vocabulary and practice of Cuban politics. Castro's growing impatience during 1959 with his political opposition was only one early manifestation of this particular self-perception. More recently, as is suggested by his attack on Aníbal Escalante and the "old-line" Havana Communists, he has exhibited much the same determination to maintain his position as chief interpreter of the correct meaning and interrelatedness of events.[25] However, now it is (some) Communists in addition to (all) anti-Communists who are being rudely schooled in what it means to be a follower in Castro's Cuba.[26]

4. The Behavior of the Leader in Power Is Anti-bureaucratic

Once again we find striking agreement among the various interpreters of the Revolution that Castro is (or at least was) highly disdainful of and uninterested in the routine processes

---

two years later. All the elements of high drama and miraculous escape were attached to the story of the guerrilla band during these two years. At one time, Castro was reported dead, and subsequently a price of $100,000 was set on his head.

[25] The crucial document here is Castro's television speech of March 26, 1962. This is available in English under the title *Fidel Castro Denounces Bureaucracy and Sectarianism* (New York: Pioneer, 1962). See also the discussion in Theodore Draper, *Castro's Revolution* (New York: Praeger, 1962), Appendix Three.

[26] I am simplifying a very complex and poorly understood relationship (between Castro and the old-line Communists) for purposes of emphasis. However, I think that the essential point remains valid; i.e., Castro has fought very hard to maintain his position as the prime interpreter of the larger historical importance and meaning of events in Cuba, and thus he sees himself as a leader who is not obligated to accept the interpretations of others with regard to what his or their political roles should be.

of public administration. Friends and foes of the Revolution differ on whether this disinterest is "good" or "bad," "creative" or "uncreative," but few deny its existence.

This characteristic of Castro is thrown into ironic relief by the immensity and pervasiveness of the bureaucratic structures which have been created to direct the reorganization of Cuban society. For instance, the National Institute of Agrarian Reform (INRA), once headed by Castro and often called the heart of the Revolution, directly or indirectly controls 80 per cent of the farm land on the island.[27] But Castro's behavior, both while chairman of INRA and after, hardly fits Weber's model of rational-legal leadership. On the contrary, his leadership was highly personalized and un-hierarchical, and his choice of second-level administrators was based primarily on ascription (is he a trusted follower from the Sierra?) rather than achievement criteria.

Nowhere is the personalized and un-hierarchical nature of Castro's leadership better drawn than in an episode reported by Jean-Paul Sartre. In a chapter called "A Day in the Country with Fidel," Sartre tells how on a stopover at a rural tourist center Castro became upset because his soft drink was warm.[28] According to Sartre, Castro's ire was not aroused by his personal inconvenience but rather by his generalized irritation with a bureaucratic structure which was created to serve "the people" but which frequently succeeded only in frustrating them. After "rummaging passionately around in a refrigerator that was out of order . . ." and being unable to fix it himself, "He closed with this growled sentence: 'Tell your people in charge that if they don't take care of their problems, they will have problems with me.'" And this, Sartre maintains, was typical of the manner in which the "maximum leader" invested his energies in the administration of Cuba.

[27] International Commission of Jurists, *op. cit.*, p. 61.
[28] Sartre, *op. cit.*, see pp. 122–3.

5. Charismatic Authority Is Unstable, Tending to Be Routinized through Time

Now we come to a set of questions which we have in part glossed over by pretending that the legitimacy of Castro's rule has been relatively stable since 1959. This is not the case, for there have been changes along at least two dimensions. First, there has been some shrinkage of the set of followers, both the charismatic and the non-charismatic. Most simply, Castro's rule is not now as legitimate for as many Cubans as it once was. However, we lack the data needed to document and quantify the extent and distribution of this partial disintegration of legitimacy.

Second—and this bears most directly on Weber's concerns—there has been at least a partial shift as predicted from authority relationships based on charisma to relationships based on rules, law, and a nascent "revolutionary tradition." This shift cannot be adequately described in brief compass, but central to the partial routinization of charisma in Cuba has been a movement *away from* Castro as the prime popular symbol of the Revolution and a concomitant movement *toward* a heterogeneity of symbols which includes other leaders, a whole spectrum of martyrs, revolutionary organizations, and achievements. This movement away from Castro as the organizing symbol of the Revolution incarnate is illustrated in Table 3, which compares the frequency with which Castro's picture appeared in two successive sets of *INRA,* the official monthly magazine of the National Institute of Agrarian Reform.[29] Although these data do not constitute a test of Weber's hypothesis, they do suggest that his statement that "in its pure form charismatic authority may be said to exist only in the process

[29] *INRA* is a large-format popular magazine of 108 pages. It contains both pictures and text much in the manner of *LIFE.* Although *INRA* concentrates rather heavily in the areas of current events and recent history, it does publish essays, reviews, fiction, and poetry. The original intent was to compare Volume I (1960) with Volume II (1961), but two issues of Volume I could not be located so the 22 remaining issues were split into two equal sets of 11 each.

TABLE 3

Pictures of Castro in 22 Available Issues of *INRA*

First 11 Issues	No. of Pictures	Second 11 Issues	No. of Pictures
Vol. I (1960)		Vol. II (1961)	
#1	11	#2	5
2	6	3	1
3	4	4	2
5	8	5	4
6	5	6	8
7	6	7	1
8	7	8	5
9	18	9	4
10	9	10	0
11	6	11	1
		12	0
Vol. II (1961)			
#1	12		
Total = 92		Total = 31	
Mean* = 8.36		Mean* = 2.82	

* For difference between the means, t = 3.85, d.f. = 20, p = .001.

of originating. It cannot remain stable, but becomes either traditionalized or rationalized, or a combination of both"[30] may be susceptible to more rigorous investigation than it has hitherto received.

Certainly our understanding of politics and political change in the emerging nations of the world would be much enhanced by systematic research designed to explore the validity of this and other segments of Weber's model of charismatic authority. This paper has attempted to explicate that model in a way which might prove useful for research. A brief look at the leadership of Fidel Castro leads to cautious optimism regarding the usefulness of Weber's ideas for the investigation of charismatic politics. But much work is still needed before we can claim with any confidence to understand the processes by which politicians like Castro bind to themselves and their causes the men and women who as charismatic followers constitute the primary resource of such regimes.

[30] Weber, *op. cit.*, p. 364.

8

ON THE QUESTION OF
REVOLUTIONARY CHARISMA*

Fidel Castro

Someone, I believe a foreign reporter, spoke with a comrade of ours and told him that he was interested in analyzing the problem, or better yet, the reasons that "made Castro such an attractive individual," "what it was that the masses felt toward Castro." You all know very well that we are not capable of imagining that this phenomenon is the mere consequence of personal magnetism.

The reply, the only answer to the attraction, does not lie with Mr. Castro but with the Revolution. The reason why the masses support the Revolution must be sought in the history of our revolutionary laws. The answer cannot be found in the personality or character of an individual. The answer can be found in the accomplishments of the Revolution, because this is not a country of fanatics, but of men and women who think and feel; a people that have made thinking and feeling one and the same thing.

This is not a people with the habit of worshiping anyone. The opposite was the case, this was a country where men and women believed in no one. What was difficult was to return faith to the people. And on July 26, 1953, when our history entered a dramatic stage, we were completely unknown to the people.

Only events have awakened the faith of the people; their faith is the product of a struggle in which we participated. Faith was not recovered with words or personalities. Only

* July 26, 1964, speech (excerpt). Translated by the editors.

events and accomplishments did that. It is in the events that an explanation must be sought. . . .

A revolution is not the work of a man, a revolution is not made by a man or a group of men. Revolutions are the work of an entire people. And what we are doing today in our fatherland, for good or evil, better or worse, is the work of the people, of all of us.

9

BUREAUCRACY AND REVOLUTION*

Cuban Communist Party

It is necessary to ponder deeply the problems posed by the existence of a bureaucratic stratum to the process of constructing socialism and communism. This is a phenomenon of universal validity. It is a danger we must abolish from our country since the complete success of the Revolution depends to a great extent on its elimination.

Bureaucracy, without any doubt, constitutes a special sector with a specified relationship to the means of production. We can affirm that, with the triumph of the Socialist Revolution, bureaucracy acquires a new character.

On what basis do we affirm this? Under capitalism bureaucracy holds the same positions and apparently has the same relationship to the means of production. Nevertheless, in such a regime, it plays a subordinate role to the administrative and political power and authority of the dominant class, the bourgeoisie.

Capitalist bureaucracy is made up of public employees and the functionaries and employees of private enterprises. Neither group is directly concerned with political or governmental policy. In fact public functionaries and employees as well as those in private enterprise are trained to think of their activity as a specialized professional function, removed from politics, and even to view political activity with a certain disdain. Thus capitalist bureaucracy serves as an intermediary, totally submissive to the domination of the bourgeoisie.

But what happens following the triumph of the Revolution?

---

* From "The Struggle Against Bureaucracy: A Decisive Task," editorial in *Granma Weekly Review* (Havana), March 5, 1967, Year 2, No. 10, pp. 2–3, and March 12, 1967, Year 2, No. 11, pp. 2–3.

In the first place, all of the formerly dispersed bureaucratic apparatus is vertically re-deployed into the State apparatus and, to a certain extent, organized and strengthened. If we add to this the problems of lack of experience and knowledge on the part of revolutionaries, the tendency toward centralization or the application of bureaucratized foreign patterns, it is clear that bureaucracy will grow, develop and gain strength during the early years of revolutionary power.

However, there is much more to the question than this. In addition to greater organization and growth in size, bureaucracy takes on a new character in its relationship to the means of production and, therefore, to political activity as well. When the Revolution triumphs and the direction of the economy passes into the hands of the State, bureaucracy intervenes in the administration of production, in the control and governing of the material and human resources of the nation.

Minor functionaries, who previously were not entrusted with making decisions on political and administrative questions, move into posts which require political decisions and decisions affecting the means of production. That is, a change occurs in their relation to the entire life of the nation.

The fact that many workers begin to hold administrative posts does not give a class content to State administration. On the contrary, when a worker or farmer takes over an administrative post, he is in danger of being influenced politically and ideologically by this administrative job, of becoming one more bureaucratic functionary. A worker transformed into a position of authority in the direction of production is not necessarily thereby transformed into a leader of the working class.

As long as the State exists as an institution and as long as organization, administration and policy are not all fully of a communist nature, the danger will continue to exist that a special stratum of citizens will form in the heart of the bureaucratic apparatus which directs and administers the State. This apparatus has given relationship to the means of production, different from that of the rest of the population, which can convert bureaucratic posts into comfortable, stagnant or privileged positions.

And this is the most profound and serious problem to be considered in the campaign against bureaucracy!

Socialism and communism are not spontaneous phenomena. Arrival at these higher stages of social development is achieved by following a correct policy and orientation. The fact that a Revolution triumphs and proclaims its intention to construct a new society is no guarantee that this society will become a reality.

To achieve socialism and communism, two factors must be combined: the development of the new man with new awareness and attitudes toward life, and the advance of technology to a level which will multiply productivity and bring about abundance of material goods. In order to reach this high goal in human society, a policy consequent with the principles of Marxism-Leninism, with the concepts developed by Marx, Engels and Lenin and other great leaders of the working class, is essential. A policy which will lead to the disappearance of the concepts and ideology of the exploiting classes and of petty-bourgeois mentality is essential. This demands the existence of a Party which is always youthful, always alert, never stagnant. The Party must be ever creative and united with the masses, never a Party which is simply resigned to repeating what has been done by others without first evaluating this critically in the light of the concrete situations under which it must exercise its function of leader and guide.

Starting on the road to communism is no guarantee of arrival. At the least, it could happen that the Revolution's ascendant movement be frustrated and that stagnation and decomposition appear in the earliest stages of the process.

A number of factors are involved in this problem which, taken as whole, depend upon the general conception that is held of how socialism and communism are to be constructed.

If we allow certain categories characteristic of the capitalist system to survive within the organization and development of our economy, if we take the easiest way out, using material interest as the driving force in the construction of socialism, if merchandise is held up as the central core of the economy, if the presence of money remains omnipotent within the new society, then selfishness and individualism will continue to be the predominant characteristics in the conscience of men and we shall never arrive at the formation of the new man.

And if such concepts prevail within the society, if an individualist and petty bourgeois ideology survives, a bureaucratic mentality will likewise survive, together with a bureaucratic concept of administration and politics, but with the aggravating factor that now this concept will prevail among a special stratum of men whose relation to the means of production and political decisions places them in a position of leadership. Thus there is nothing strange about the fact that the desire to belong to this bureaucratic stratum of society is kept alive or that this becomes a material objective for those seeking comfort and privilege.

If the Party does not win this battle over bureaucracy, if this danger is not eliminated through the formation of the new man and the application of an unyielding policy, consequent with Marxist-Leninist principles, the Party will end by bureaucratizing itself. And a Party which stagnates is a party in decomposition.

What does this mean? What occurs if the Party organization sinks into this bureaucratic morass? When that occurs, a special stratum consolidates itself in the administration and direction of the State and in political leadership, a special stratum with aspirations toward self-perpetuation that draws constantly farther away from the masses, divorced from fruitful productive labor and from those who perform it, to become a privileged body, incapable of impelling the people forward, incapable of leading the conscience of the people toward higher levels.

And when this occurs the construction of socialism and communism has already been abandoned. As long as certain functions of an administrative nature, necessary in the transitional period, continue to exist, certain measures can be taken to aid in the avoidance of this danger. One of these is to maintain mobility in the posts of administrative officials and public employees, to prevent their becoming fossilized and to avoid the formation of a special stratum of society.

The apparatus for the direction of the State must be kept simple and at the same time dynamic, informed in the technical processes involved in production, capable of coordinating efforts of stimulating activity, and of inspiring the spirit of work in those who function under their leadership.

Danger also exists that, within political organizations and the Party itself, a special category of citizen be created among professional cadres, differentiated from the rest of the population. This is a danger that must be assessed and taken into consideration, because the historical and social process is a result of certain laws and principles which we must understand extremely well or run the risk of falling into grave errors.

The way to avoid functionaries and administrative cadres within the Party becoming a special sector of society is by confronting them directly with problems of production. This danger will be avoided to the extent to which the cadres face up to the concrete tasks of agriculture and industry in the closest possible contact with production itself. And this rule is valid for functionaries and administrative employees, as well.

In our own present reality, since the Party is a product of the Revolution and grew out of the Revolution, the need has arisen for the Party cadres to dedicate themselves to tasks of production and management in the most direct and immediate form. They must be in contact with technical problems as they come up in the fields, on State Farms, in industrial plants. We are aided in this task by the fact that our party is young, without professional experience in most cases.

Thus, measures are being taken within the Party to avoid the development of a special stratum of professionals, which in any case should always be as limited and reduced in size as possible, and as close as is possible to production. We will be helped in this task by the constantly increasing trend toward the formation of new cadres which will provide greater movement among them from production to the Party, and from the Party to production.

The struggle against bureaucracy is of decisive importance in the progress of the Revolution. Fidel Castro has given this definition: "The struggle against the bureaucratic mentality is almost as difficult as the struggle against imperialism itself. More difficult than the struggle against the landowners, of course, since these were the minority, and there are many more people with bureaucratic mentalities than there were landowners in this country."

This is a long and complex struggle that cannot be won in one day. The mere establishment of revolutionary measures and laws is not enough. Action is necessary on the part of the masses and the Party, as well as the constant application of a policy based on the principle of maximum reduction in numbers and maximum increase in efficiency. As Fidel has said, ". . . the only way to lend dignity to administrative work is to liberate it from bureaucratic concepts and methods . . ." Bureaucracy is a legacy from the capitalist system. Its complete and radical elimination is fundamental in achieving the complete triumph of the Revolution.

Only if we are clearly aware of the danger posed by the existence of the petty-bourgeois mentality within the state apparatus can we properly understand, in all its magnitude, the importance of this key struggle in a country such as ours that proposes to achieve the maximum aims of revolution: the construction of the communist society. This is why we cannot detain ourselves in a mere struggle against the most obvious, quantitative aspects of this evil. We could make the mistake of reducing all of the personnel in a given place without taking their methods of work into consideration, thereby, even with a minimum of employees and functionaries, permitting bureaucratic work to continue, allowing obstacles to action, divorce from the masses and from the real problems at hand, to prevail. This is well-known by all who have thought over this matter. What does this ideological origin reveal? It reveals that the problem of bureaucracy has ideological origins, that it originates in a concept and a mentality, not only of excess administrative personnel. Fidel Castro expresses this clearly when he says, ". . . the principal cause is the petty-bourgeois mentality, the lack of awareness of the importance of a country's human resources, of a country's material resources."

Since this is the case, we must complement the struggle

against bureaucracy's external manifestations—such as the proliferation of administrative personnel, inertia, red tape, the "run-around," etc.—with ideological struggle against the concepts that engender these evils, against the petty-bourgeois mentality within the revolutionary State.

This editorial, as well as those that will be appearing during the next few days, proposes to collaborate on this struggle.

Where and when did bureaucracy arise? In what social system did it originate? This is the first question we must analyze, because bureaucracy is not a product of our society, but rather one of the most unsavory holdovers from the past we have had to deal with. The rise of bureaucracy is closely related to the capitalist system. Its development has taken place parallel with that of the bourgeoisie in its rise to the position of the ruling class in contemporaneous capitalist states. Although in former societies there did exist some incipient forms of bureaucratic work, such as that of functionaries, scribes and priests, it cannot be said that a highly-developed bureaucracy existed under slavery or feudalism. Why not? Because in those societies, such activity did not favor the growth and consolidation of a social stratum that would exercise power in the name of the ruling class. But such parasitic stratum does exist in bourgeois society. The basis for its existence is the greater complexity in administration and government demanded by the centralized bourgeois state—which involves multiple forms of mercantile and financial relations determined by an active domestic and world trade requiring numerous controls, a government with a complex fiscal system, and finally a state apparatus with forms of organization that must necessarily be complex in view of the veiled character of exploitation in bourgeois society.

Bureaucracy also constitutes the most negative product of the division between manual and intellectual labor.

This division, between the productive work of society and that of the members of the ruling class—dedicated to political or cultural activities—arose at the onset of class society. The slave system's ruling class, owners of great extensions of land and slaves, was exempt from all physical productive work. This they relegated to the great masses of the people, considering it "unworthy of true men." This also was a characteristic of the feudal regime, in which the landowning aristocracy considered the work of the agricultural serfs as unfit for them.

Under capitalism, this division is sharpened to even greater extremes by the bourgeoisie. Bureaucracy, a bourgeois creation, is profoundly steeped in this attitude toward manual labor. Educated in the petty-bourgeois ideology, bureaucrats disdain productive activity and consider themselves an intellectual stratum on a level with the bourgeoisie, situated above the working people.

Indeed, it must be stressed that even if we go so far as to classify bureaucratic work as "intellectual," if it is "intellectual" at all, it is one of the most simple and mediocre forms of intellectual work. Of this there is no doubt. There is nothing creative about bureaucratic work: deviation from the beaten path of routine can cost any functionary or employee his job.

There are other products of the division between physical and intellectual work that can be considered as historically necessary, since they have played a very important role during class society in the development of science, art and literature. But bureaucracy, on the contrary, is a sterile entity that can claim no important accomplishment in the history of human culture.

Where could the bourgeoisie discover a social base to use in the establishment of this bureaucratic stratum? The bourgeoisie had no interest, nor were they in the position, to take over intermediate posts in government and business, since they were busy with the running of their own private affairs. They reserved high offices in the State and business for themselves. Therefore, they needed a specified sector of society to be used as instruments in the running of government matters and the management of the companies they owned, with the purpose of organizing, controlling and administering their exploitation of wage earners. Moreover, the bourgeoisie, although they were masters of the nation's economy, were a rather small group numerically. A wider social stratum was required to give them support, one allied to their own interests, which could be used in the exercising of their dictatorial class power, as a direct instrument against the working classes.

The creation of a bureaucratic stratum was one of the solutions seized upon to fill this need. Together with the bureaucracy, we also had the "labor aristocracy," set up with the same end in mind, the strengthening of the basis of power and extension of social influence.

Both the bureaucracy and the labor aristocracy in a bourgeois regime became mere extensions of the capitalist class into the petty bourgeois sectors and the proletariat. Both groups served as supports to the dominant power, carrying on political maneuvering, causing division in the ranks of the proletariat and hampering any kind of popular movement.

In the early days of capitalism this stratum was drawn from middle class urban groups whose position was neither that of the feudal aristocrats nor of the workers and poorer artisans. In this environment the bourgeoisie created and nurtured the appropriate ideology and outlook on life. It developed a petty-bourgeois mentality in this social sector.

This was achieved through a hierarchy of officials and employees. Each of these was subject to the authority of an immediate superior, and all were trained to stick to routine work, obey more or less inflexible rules and regulations and to abhor the introduction of innovations. They sought security and rank in society which would give them certain "respectability," placing them above the working class.

This gave rise to the criteria of the bureaucratic post as a profession, and the concept became ingrained that the duty of one holding such a post was to blindly abide by the orders of superiors in the hierarchy. The bureaucrat was given the guarantee of a secure livelihood in exchange for his absolute submission to the bourgeoisie's planning. This explains why bureaucracy was born and grew identified with the capitalist class ideology, possibly to a greater degree than any other sector of the petty bourgeoisie.

Bureaucrats were formed by the division between manual and intellectual work. They were trained to completely ignore and despise production and those who made it possible.

What is bureaucracy?

As Lenin points out, it is "that particular stratum holding power . . ." It is the intermediary entrusted by the dominant class with the handling of affairs of State and administrative work in capitalist enterprises; an intermediary which reflects faithfully the thinking and the conceptions of the capitalist class. That is, in a bourgeois regime bureaucracy constitutes a social stratum playing a role subordinate to the political and administrative authority of the dominant class. It is an intermediary stratum that executes the decisions of the bourgeois dictatorship. It is the administration of power by employees and officials placed between the capitalist and the working masses. This stratum is invested with power and government by the exploiting classes whom it serves.

Therefore, we should define bureaucracy on the basis of its relations with the capitalist class and its participation in the government of that class, rather than on the basis of its concrete administrative functions.

We have analyzed the origin of the bureaucratic stratum, have determined at what moment in history it arose and have shown what classes it merged with: This proves Lenin's idea that, ". . . owing to its historical origin as well as to its contemporary sources and its mission, bureaucracy is always a purely and exclusively bourgeois institution."

Engendered by and serving the interests of the bourgeoisie, bureaucracy reaches the zenith of its reactionary, anti-popular nature under imperialism.

Impersonal bureaucratic functions reach their highest degree of dehumanization. There is a veritable army of clerks and offices, acting as a machine of international oppression.

The phenomenon that had appeared with the rise of capitalism grows more pronounced: in industry, in commerce, in the trade unions, in social institutions; on every hand, bureaucracy manifests itself and becomes entrenched. Its end is always the same: alienation of the worker—turning him into an object, a cipher, one more item of merchandise—expediting the exploitation of man by man.

In underdeveloped countries, the problem of bureaucracy takes on very particular characteristics. It is tied to and facilitates exploitation by foreign monopolies; it is steeped in the imperialist ideology and often comes into conflict with the interests of the nation itself.

Servitor of neocolonial governments, bureaucracy is allied with administrative corruption and the sinecures typical of countries under the national domination of militarists and land barons.

It no longer serves only as a social bulwark of the bourgeoisie, but has become an international mainstay of imperialist policy and exploitation.

While this may not be so in each and every case, it is a widespread reality affecting bureaucracy in underdeveloped countries.

The bourgeois states formed their armies in keeping with their particular organizational concepts. The armies of the capitalist states took on a bureaucratic structure. The growing use of artillery, complex troop movements, the formation of enormous armies, required the presence of an extensive apparatus of officers, liaison men and many other command cadres, directed from the top down through a hierarchy.

In the era of bourgeois revolutions, these armies represented a force superior on organization to the feudal forces. Obviously, the methods brought into play were not the only determining factor; many others determined the superiority of the bourgeois armies over their feudal counterparts. But the establishment of bureaucratic methods in modern armies is sufficiently important for us to pursue the matter further.

Side by side with expansion of its sphere of action and development in its highest stage—imperialism—capitalism needed to augment its entire military apparatus, to create a large war industry and to operate transports that could move its armies anywhere. As this took place, the bureaucratic structure of the armies expanded.

The military forces of any imperialist nation have thousands of command cadres; there are modern armies that need seven men in the rear to back up three men in the front lines.

Besides the administrative or command function realized by this entrenched bureaucracy in the armed forces, it also fulfills the function of a stratum closely tied to the military caste and to the monopolists of the regime; that is, from the army, this stratum serves the political interests of the most reactionary class.

Bourgeois ideologists claim that there is no organization technically superior to that of an imperialist army, and they point to the structure of modern armies as an example of the efficiency and superiority of bureaucratic methods.

But history teaches us something else. The peoples who fight for liberation organize their armed forces without resorting to bureaucratic techniques.

We are not going to enter upon an analysis of all the factors moving the struggle forward nor all the elements present in a victory in a war of liberation. We only wish to stress that there exist organizations which are not constituted bureaucratically and which are capable of standing up to armies set up with the highest techniques of bourgeois organization.

To take only a few examples, we have the War of Liberation of the Algerian and Vietnamese peoples against the French army, and the present battle of the Vietnamese guerrillas against the hierarchically super-organized forces of the imperialists.

The armies of the underdeveloped countries are characterized by their swollen staffs.

In an article entitled "Latin American Viet Cong" in the Canadian newspaper "Toronto Star," appearing on November 5, 1966, it is stated:

"U. S. officials in Guatemala City are astonished at the rapid tendency of Guatemalan officers, returning after months of tough training in the United States, to develop large stomachs and settle down in easy, secure office jobs which they do not seem to want to relinquish."

The article later describes the Guatemalan army as: "An overgrown corps of top-ranking officers, with 400 out of the thousand officers assigned the high rank of colonel." This army has tried and failed on numerous occasions to destroy the popular forces organized into guerrilla detachments.

Of course, this bureaucratic tendency typical in all spheres in underdeveloped countries is not the essence of the phenomenon, but it is one of its most injurious manifestations. It is an element that comes to have a determining character in the decomposition of these regimes.

We Cubans know this situation very well. The pro-imperialist army of the tyranny was completely rigid in structure. Among the consequences of the decomposition of the capitalist system under the exploitation of Yankee capital was the bureaucratizing of the army, a sort of fossilization, an inability to face a new form of struggle. Our Rebel Army—the popular forces—dispensed with everything superfluous, conducting the war in a direct, very concrete way, bringing into play a non-bureaucratic organization that showed organizational superiority over the bureaucratic military apparatus.

We can draw a conclusion from the confrontation of the Liberation Forces, based on the incorporation of the masses, with the traditional armies: it is possible to excel bureaucratic ways of organization. There are organizational forms which are far more efficient than bureaucratic ones.

In socialism, the incorporation of workers via the militias— the revolutionary origin of the armed forces—and the system of an army of technically-trained cadres, with large numbers of young men coming in through conscription, makes possible an army free of the evil of bureaucracy.

In January, 1959, the Revolution found itself confronted with a society characterized by vestiges of feudalism in agriculture, incipient capitalist development, extensive domination of our economy and commerce by imperialism, and an extraordinary concentration of the population and administrative apparatus in Havana, contrasting with neglect, depopulation and misery in the countryside.

Alongside the large U. S. companies had developed a great variety of small enterprises such as insurance companies, banking agencies, businesses, private health institutions, private schools, etc., staffed with administrative personnel to assure their operation: traveling salesmen, bill collectors, publicity agents, office workers, etc.

The pro-imperialist, bourgeois-latifundist Cuban State was corrupt to its very core. Daily, new posts were created and public offices multiplied to favor elements allied to the regime in power. Those who held government office prospered on public funds. "Botellas" (fictitious posts with salaries attached), embezzlement and graft were common from the office boy right up to the chief of State.

That pseudo-administrative apparatus was consolidated into an enormous bureaucratic army. It was for many—and quite markedly so in a country like ours, without job possibilities for hundreds of thousands of men and women—a hope, a goal. Institutions designed to train people in unproductive tasks sprang up all across the nation; business schools, typing and secretarial academies. This mentality was deep-rooted among the petty bourgeoisie.

The Revolution did away with graft and "botellas"; it wiped out administrative corruption and conducted a general clean-up campaign in public administration. This was one of the important achievements at the beginning of the Revolution. But obviously the young revolutionary power could not at that time eliminate the bureaucratic concept, the petty bourgeois spirit in the administration of a State designed to serve the interests of the workers and farmers.

Later we had to confront the phenomenon of bureaucracy within the process of constructing socialism and communism. The experiences gained in this struggle and the pitfalls that have come to light are of extraordinary importance and should be food for thought for all revolutionaries in our country, especially for Party members.

With the nationalization of the major foreign and national enterprises, this immense bureaucratic army, until then scattered, became State employees and functionaries. Many of them, those closest to the bourgeoisie and to Yankee imperialism, chose to leave the country. In contrast, the Revolution offered men and women of the people opportunities to hold these positions, in many cases as a way—a poor way—to alleviate the serious problem of unemployment and the lack of job sources.

At the same time the need to control the different enterprises and organizations—many of which were new, products of the revolutionary process—led to the development of a policy of centralization which resulted in the excessive growth of central administrative organisms, such as consolidated enterprises and ministries. In this, an important part was played by the inexperience of many revolutionary leaders placed in positions of responsibility, who did not know how to organize or administer efficiently. In trying to solve the problem of poor functioning, constant backlog, lack of controls and bureaucratic shackles, they could think of nothing better than to create new departments, increase office personnel, appoint more and more functionaries and constantly invent new forms to fill out.

All they accomplished was to add more fuel to the fire. And who got burned? The people.

Another element aiding the development of bureaucracy in the first few years of the Revolution was the introduction of some administrative systems and organizational procedures, copied from countries of the socialist camp, that were weighted down with bureaucracy. At the same time, we lacked sufficient experience and a sense of criticism, which led us to accept as good structures from economically advanced countries that did not correspond to our needs, to the situation of a country just undertaking its development.

Fidel has pointed out that perhaps the greatest merit of this generation of revolutionaries has been to accomplish all these successes in production, education, and defense, despite our own ignorance. Lenin also stressed that if revolutionaries, on assuming the responsibilities of power, do not have the background and concepts to oppose bureaucracy, it will continue to dominate because of its greater background and superior knowledge of "how to do things"—naturally, according to the capitalist pattern. Something like that happened in our country. Bureaucracy, to a certain extent, imposed its background of experience on us, its concepts of how to organize the new State, and what institutions are necessary. As Fidel pointed out in his address at the closing of the conference on the Long-Range Sugar Production Plan in Santa Clara, "at first we imitated everything done by the bourgeoisie, the capitalists, the old State. That's true. Unconsciously we were influenced by the idea that a ministry was a ministry and a minister a minister, that an office was an office and an organizational diagram an organizational diagram, and so the world advanced. And the world advanced, and everybody retained this concept, followed these ideas."

As can be seen from what our Prime Minister said, bureaucracy in a socialist State has much to do with our conception of that State. It has much to do with the economic categories prevailing in that society. It has a lot to do with the structures that are created within that State. Bureaucracy was born with capitalism. Its origin closely links it with the existence of a mercantile economy, with the commercial operations and tax system of the bourgeois financial system.

For the gradual elimination of bureaucracy we must transform the State apparatus inherited from capitalism into an instrument appropriate to socialism. This requires gradual elimination of the activities of those categories that our society has inherited.

We are therefore trying to simplify operations between State organizations as much as possible. We are trying to eliminate mercantile operations between organs of the socialist economy. We will be inflicting decisive blows on bureaucracy to the extent that our economic concepts shake themselves free of the norms and methods regulating the capitalist economy and we adopt truly revolutionary measures on our path toward communism. What would happen in our country if we permitted each enterprise to buy from and sell to other State organizations, conduct private accounts, divide profits and pay taxes to the socialist treasury, or if we gave encouragement to a mercantile type of economy? We would never rid ourselves of bureaucracy! On the contrary, it would grow right along with the growth of our economy.

Valuable orientation on many essential problems in organization of the new revolutionary State can be obtained through the profound study of Marx' conclusions on the Paris Commune and Lenin's original statements on the soviets of workers, peasants and soldiers.

These statements essentially indicate the need not only for a new type of State, but an agile, simple, executive State, without a huge central apparatus, without bureaucracy, and with permanent and direct participation by the workers. All the great founders of Marxism-Leninism coincide in this view. This is what Lenin had in mind when he said: "The essence of the question lies in whether the old State apparatus (tied by thousands of threads to the bourgeoisie and filled to the core with routine and inertia), is to be maintained or destroyed, replaced by a completely new one. The Revolution must consist not in having the new class command and govern with the help of the old State apparatus, but in destroying that apparatus and governing with the help of a completely new one."

"We must teach the people, down to the humblest sections, the art of governing and administering the State, not only through books, but through immediate practical application everywhere of the experience of the masses."

Lenin himself expressed important views such as rejection of all veneration for ministries, and their replacement by work commissions, by teams of specialists and technicians.

Bureaucracy Creates More Bureaucracy

Bureaucracy engenders bureaucracy. An overgrown central apparatus continually demanding reports and data, much of which is meaningless for practical purposes and determining concrete measures, engenders the need to staff the lower level of the hierarchic structure with a shocking number of employees and functionaries. Therefore, a decisive aspect of the direct, immediate struggle against bureaucracy is an analysis of organization. For in many cases the problem does not consist simply in analyzing exactly what work is done by each individual employee or official. What we must also concern ourselves with is whether that office, that department, that branch or enterprise itself should exist at all.

We must check each paper, each form, and ask ourselves what purpose it serves. We must check the function of each employee and official, what he does, the whys and wherefores of his work. And together with this, we must analyze the entire structure of our State, from the organization and operation of each department to entire branches and ministries.

A Brake on Revolutionary Action

Bureaucracy leads to a brake on revolutionary action. Perhaps this is one of its most serious immediate consequences.

Hemmed in by a rigid and inoperative hierarchy, no one dares to decide, to act, to solve problems.

"I have to take this up above," is an eloquent and all too familiar answer. The bureaucratic conception suffers from a generalized malady: lack of confidence in the masses, lack of confidence in the grass roots, the level at which real production takes place, where the Revolution's great goals are decided. Thus, practical executive decisions are reserved in many cases, for intermediate or central echelons where at times they are put off indefinitely.

Our policy must be directed toward bringing those in direction as close as possible to production units. This is extremely important for agricultural production in particular, where rapid decisions are essential due to unpredictable factors such as rain. As our commander-in-chief pointed out: ". . . agriculture cannot be directed with abstract ideas, agriculture cannot be directed in an abstract manner. Agriculture can only be directed right there in the province, at the farm aggregation, on the individual farm, on the lot. For there is where all the headaches are, all the problems . . ." The bureaucrat, on the other hand, is an alienated being. He shuffles around among forms, memorandums, orientations and plans; he substitutes "discussion" for "action." Solutions are put off while problems are chewed over on all levels, going from one department to another. Thus, many times the real, practical problem, the problem affecting the people, is relegated to a secondary plane, forgotten, and attention is concentrated on papers, plans, discussions and "levels" that supposedly exist to solve it.

The bureaucrat turns means of solving problems into ends, objectives of his work. This causes him to work in an impersonalized manner, and he becomes detached from the real needs of the country. He completely loses the political sense of his work and draws away from the masses.

Bureaucratic work lacks sensitivity to human beings; it is characterized by inability to analyze a situation from a political standpoint. Its very conception makes it dogmatic and mechanical to the core.

Bureaucracy denatures revolutionary work methods: it turns collective leadership into a convenient means of disclaiming individual responsibility; criticism and self-criticism shift from methods of overcoming deficiencies, to superficial confession and self-absolution of errors. New and revolutionary work principles cannot be carried out where this petty bourgeois conception exists.

One of the greatest damages produced by bureaucracy is in its repercussion on the workers—not only production workers, but also many administrative employees, victims themselves of the bureaucratic system. As for workers and farmers, bureaucracy hits them by affecting production and frequently affecting distribution of consumer articles or the provision of services needed by the worker and his family.

What could be worse than for a worker or farmer to see problems that he understands and knows how to solve—in many cases simple matters—remain unsolved or badly handled because of bureaucratic functionaries and procedures?

What is more likely to dishearten those who must make the greatest effort to produce the nation's wealth? What is so capable of affecting the workers' faith and confidence in their Revolution?

Many times an organism gives instructions that "must be fulfilled," and although in practice, in real life, at the grass roots, they shy far from the needs, the mental make-up of the bureaucrats comes into play and forces its will. The result: failure, discontent, non-fulfillment, astonishment . . . and "meetings for analyses" with an abundance of "self-criticism." Bureaucracy causes us more damage than imperialism. Imperialism is an open and external enemy. Bureaucracy corrodes us from within and attacks the healthiest, firmest elements of the masses, those who must suffer the most from it. It is clear that our people have an extraordinary sensitivity in detecting these problems and full confidence in the leadership of the Revolution. Our people do not believe in the omnipotence of any bureaucratic functionary.

They react immediately when something goes wrong, when it is necessary to discover and fight these errors of administrative overgrowth. For that reason the masses and our Party, their vanguard, must lead the constant, stubborn battle against bureaucracy.

Bureaucracy also permeates numerous social sectors whose work is not in itself bureaucratic. In other words, bureaucracy is not limited to administration only, but transcends this, corrupting other spheres of work.

The work of a teacher, for example, is not in itself bureaucratic. It may even be considered an indirect form of productive work, since it trains the future productive members of society to handle technology. Education provides people with a new social awareness and prepares them for life. In other words, the work of a teacher is of exceptional value for society: it is at once creative and formative. Now, what happens when we swamp a teacher with a torrent of circulars, forms and other bureaucratic manifestations? We often succeed in turning him into a bureaucrat. He begins to feel that the most important part of his job is to fill out all of the forms correctly, and loses sight of his real role in the training, study program and progress of students. He falls prey to formalistic detail—to bureaucracy.

Those who direct education in our country are waging an all-out offensive against bureaucracy. This struggle is decisive for achieving good quality in teaching, which runs the risk of being thwarted, held back and sidetracked by the petty-bourgeois and bureaucratic mentality of certain functionaries in education.

This same bureaucratizing process may affect a restaurant worker, a train conductor, an agricultural expert—in short, any worker. The bureaucratic concepts and mentality of the hierarchy above him can thwart the worker's ability to think, create and reason, as well as dampen his eagerness to solve problems, rendering him a simple robot that executes orders, circulars and instructions: annihilating him as a man, recreating him as a bureaucrat.

In other words, the bureaucratic mentality, in practice, is a corrosive acid that penetrates and denatures the most important activities in the life of a country: the economy, education, culture and public services.

Because they are well aware of this reality, those at the helm of education, production and other principal fronts of the Revolution, led by Fidel Castro, are waging a steady combat against this. As Fidel has said, "When we say bureaucracy—and let's clearly understand this—we do not mean administration; but rather the overextension of administrative work, the massive, useless, parasitic and unproductive concentration involved."

We must not underestimate the importance of administrative work. An agile, dynamic administration, based upon direct participation in technology and the concrete problems of production, is of extraordinary political value.

It is true that our administration needs accountants and office workers of the highest caliber, but what is essential is that revolutionary administration be in the hands of technicians and economists who really understand the productive process. The value of administrative work can be truly appreciated only when it is based upon the technical processes of production at the grass roots. This is what we are striving toward.

The struggle against the petty bourgeois and bureaucratic mentality must not categorically reject the necessity and importance of organization and control in productive activities and social services.

Our immediate struggle is to reduce the personnel working on these fronts to a bare minimum, instilling in that personnel a new outlook stressing technology, stressing the real problems of the masses, concentrating on revolutionary action and flexible ready means of solving problems. In short, a new dynamic and aggressive style of work must be developed. Along with this, the struggle includes maximum simplification of the structures of the State apparatus as well as achievement of maximum efficiency from minimum personnel.

One of the major tasks included in the struggle against

bureaucracy is to find enthusiastic, tireless individuals capable of carrying out the plans of the Revolution. We do not propose a sporadic, chance discovery of such people, but rather a very concrete policy designed to produce such people with an aggressive, direct style of work. We are going to depend less on schemata, on theoretical organization, and instead place our trust in the practical and executive ability of people who carry out and control plans efficiently without resorting to a bureaucratic apparatus.

Experience has taught us that there is no better control than that guaranteed by a job headed by someone capable, steeped in the revolutionary spirit and eager to further the construction of the new life. More can be accomplished by one revolutionary cadre, linked with the masses he directs, and fully dedicated to the problems of production and technology, than all the organizational diagrams, forms and bureaucratic "braintrusts" put together.

One man with executive ability, directing a plan with a spirit of unwillingness to put up with obstacles, is worth more than any traditional form of control.

Ample experience has taught us that it is necessary to place our most competent cadres, with the exception of those engaged in some centralized jobs, as near as possible to the actual process of production or of public services.

The example of our leading revolutionary figures, principally Fidel Castro, stands before us. All of us must become steeped in this new approach. This consists in working with concrete realities, going to state farm after state farm analyzing each problem in all possible detail, orienting, discussing, conversing with the workers themselves, living their problems and difficulties.

Of course, in order to do this properly, we must have a very thorough knowledge of the technical problems of agriculture and industry. It is the most difficult road, but, without a doubt, the most effective, economically and politically.

No one should deceive himself about the Revolution's campaign against bureaucracy. It is not a battle that can be won in a few months' time. It is a complex and difficult task with certain practical operative aspects which can be dealt with directly and immediately. However, there are ideological aspects involved as well, and this is where it is much more difficult to triumph rapidly. It will be necessary to mobilize all the Revolution's resources, our labor movement, women and young people, all, under the leadership of the Party, for an effort to strike out against bureaucracy on all fronts, in all its manifestations.

The fact that this is an ideological struggle does not mean that the problem can be solved with propaganda campaigns, through the proclamation of slogans or political phrases. In addition to the always necessary information campaigns, serious work must be undertaken among our masses to help them develop a full understanding of just what this top-heavy phenomenon and this petty-bourgeois mentality truly represent within our revolutionary state.

We must confront this bureaucracy directly with militant working class spirit. Past experience in struggle against this evil indicates that bureaucracy tends to operate as a new class. Certain bonds are formed among bureaucrats themselves, close ties and relationships characteristic of every social class.

They work hand-in-glove protecting each other against revolutionary rules and regulations. If the Party and revolutionaries in general let down, if they lower their guard for a single moment, bureaucracy tends to spring up again, regulations are violated, and once more the same group installs itself in places of influence. And this occurs because bureaucratic functionaries have nothing to defend except their own positions and these they defend as would any class.

We must launch a program of revolutionary action against all this and prepare ourselves for a day-by-day, month-by-month struggle. And this combat must be continued as long as necessary, until this impediment to the Revolution's progress is completely eliminated. Specifically, first consideration and highest rank must be given to those who are doing productive work, to technicians, to workers and farmers alike. For they are the ones who are doing the most useful work, and the hardest work as well. Their efforts will go farthest in solving the problems fundamental to the construction of socialism.

The advocates of such an ideology, an alien ideology, inadmissible under socialism, must be sought out and ousted from their posts. And care must be taken to assure that bureaucratic "solidarity" does not substitute the old practice of "kicking people upstairs" for one of transferring them to similar jobs.

The increase in new administrative posts must cease. Infractions of revolutionary norms must be detected and sanctions applied.

We must track down every printed "form" to see what it really is like, what it solves and what end it serves. We must simplify supervision to the maximum. And whenever possible, participation of the masses in the selection of administrative personnel should be encouraged.

Commitments to the masses must be strengthened in place of commitments to a bureaucratic hierarchy alone.

We must continue to develop our policy of promoting new cadres based on political considerations. While this policy advances, administrative posts must be rotated. A principle of mobility must be put into effect in order to prevent job rigidity, a tendency to settle in and consider oneself "indispensable."

The Havana Provincial Committee of the Party, together with students from the Revolutionary Instruction Schools, has been carrying out an investigation of cases of failure to enforce the government's labor policies.

These investigations have revealed a number of irregularities which the Ministry of Labor is now studying with the idea of applying the necessary sanctions. Those who have committed infractions of regulations laid down or general orientations must be subject to sanctions. This is one of the measures which must be adopted in our campaign against bureaucracy.

Thus, under Party supervision, the Havana Provincial Committee and the Ministry of Labor are studying the stabilization of the entire system of employment practice and considering what measures are required for strict supervision of the naming of new personnel in administration, services and production in general.

It is absolutely vital that the Ministry of Labor lay down exact labor rules and regulations and that these be adhered to most precisely. For, as we have stated, excess of administrative personnel is one of the more obvious manifestations of bureaucracy.

It is absolutely essential that all of the nation's work centers and each and every administrative office have only the minimum indispensable personnel needed to carry out their functions.

Accordingly, it has been decided that a very reduced number of persons, an absolute minimum, may have the authority to employ additional personnel or put new workers under temporary contract. Moreover, this minimum must be determined by the actual operational problems at service and production centers.

And this reduced group of functionaries authorized to contract new employees must have an absolutely clear conception of what bureaucracy means.

All those who have the authority to hire new employees must be comrades fully aware of what the anti-bureaucratic campaign means. Party branches on all levels must develop this awareness. Administrative leaders must delve deeply into the subject. It will never be enough merely to deal out sanctions. What we must do is develop the social consciousness and sense of responsibility of those authorized to appoint personnel. Moreover, at work centers throughout the nation, workers should seriously discuss what the campaign against bureaucracy signifies, where its roots lie, and a campaign without quarter must be launched against any who break those administrative norms. That is why worker participation, under the guidance of union locals and members of the Party, is a cardinal factor.

The Party nuclei have, among other duties, the responsibility of making a profound study of the ideological roots of bureaucracy in order to increase anti-bureaucratic consciousness in the masses and to make certain that every center of work is fulfilling Party policies in this important campaign.

Vigilance on the part of communists and workers in the application of employment practices is very important in the fight to do away with excess personnel and eradicate violations of employment policy in general.

The greatest concentration of bureaucrats and consequently the greatest stronghold of the petty-bourgeois spirit is in metropolitan Havana. The investigation results show that there is a total of nearly 74,000 employees and administrative officials with a yearly salary fund of $140,000,000. That is why our main battle against this evil within our State apparatus must be carried out here, following a revolutionary policy and in such a way that no one need feel worried or insecure about his future.

Thus, the struggle against bureaucracy has become the most important task for our Party in the capital.

Because of its importance and the vigor it has gathered, the struggle against bureaucracy has come to be a veritable revolution within the revolution. It is, possibly, the kind of revolution that has never before taken place anywhere. This is the revolution that lies ahead of us and we can carry it out successfully insofar as we can combine the struggle against bureaucracy and the struggle for self-improvement, technological training, and massive participation in the tasks of production, especially agriculture. The development of agricultural and cattle raising programs in the various provinces and the consequent demand for technicians result in a permanent deficit of technicians and workers on every farm or farm aggregation in our country. On the other hand, an increase in educational plans and the extension of important public services offer a wide field for self-improvement and for incorporation into more useful work which will result in greater satisfaction and moral stimulation for those who participate in it.

The greatest thing that Havana and other large cities can do for the countryside is to offer the services of technicians, economists, and manpower in general.

Administrative and directive officials must be incorporated, actively, and in a spirit of militancy, into this battle. Nothing will reflect so clearly their capacity to occupy positions of responsibility as a clear awareness of and a determined attitude toward these problems.

In many instances, these comrades have become the victims of a situation which has condemned them to routine and inertia. Their only way to give their work a new meaning and a new style is to join the front ranks of the battle against bureaucracy.

And at the head of this battle, setting the example, will be militants of the Party.

Party organisms in the province of Havana have started a movement to incorporate hundreds of communists, now doing administrative work in the capital, to the tasks of agriculture. Six hundred communists in the capital have registered for agricultural work. Many of them have a certain amount of technical skill and political development. This is a very important step in the struggle against bureaucracy and a significant contribution to the work of agriculture.

Communists and workers in work centers who have registered for agricultural work must consider, when they are called, whether it is necessary for these industrial or administrative centers to hire new personnel to substitute them.

Communists already doing agricultural work as well as the workers who stay behind must demand that no new personnel be hired unless it becomes absolutely imperative.

Party workers should be assigned to work at the base, that is, on farm lots and cattle rotation pastures, as these are places where the battle of production is either won or lost.

The movement of city militants of a higher cultural and ideological level to the country can be a factor of extraordinary importance for the strengthening of the Party in each lot, department, or farm. This is the honorable and revolutionary task confronting Havana Party militants, since the Party must be strengthened on the farms, where it is still weak.

The correct thing would be to have a Party nucleus in each farm lot. Until this becomes a reality we cannot speak of an organized Party in agriculture. The incorporation of hundreds of Party militants proceeding from unproductive sectors in the capital will be a great contribution to this task of organization.

Thus we will strengthen our Party membership and we will be prepared to send thousands upon thousands of workers to a more dignified, useful work, urging them toward a higher education and technology, and investing their new activity with a new context that will be a source of satisfaction and happiness for those who have been the victims of a system that chained their energies to sterile, enervating work.

Certain expressions of bureaucracy take on frankly negative aspects. One of them, for instance, is the employment of young people in bureaucratic, unproductive work. This constitutes a crime against the future of these youths as well as against the interests of the Revolution.

Young people should either be studying, doing productive work, particularly in agriculture, or serving in the Revolutionary Armed Forces (FAR). It is hard to conceive that a young person today should fail to participate in one or more of these activities.

Our duty and our policy should be not to hire any young person for unproductive work. As a matter of principle, we should struggle hard to implement this concrete policy. It should be the task of every Party and Young Communist organization in each province, region or municipality to check the activities of every young person; what he does, where he works and where he studies. And to struggle, permanently and systematically, to have these people study, serve in the FAR or do productive work, if possible in agriculture. The Young Communist League plays a leading role in this battle, directing and leading the young people toward agricultural work. In the Camagüey and the Isle of Pines agricultural programs, in places such as Juraguá, all through our countryside, this accurate policy constitutes a significant factor in the eradication of the bureaucratic concept and in the formation of the new man. It means the materialization of the principles set forth by our Commander in Chief in the sense of more "ruralization" and less "urbanization."

A study must be made at each production unit to decide if it is absolutely necessary that the young people going into agricultural work be replaced. This is a task for the appropriate administrative organism. However, the working masses, inspired by the example of the communists and the youngsters, must demand that no personnel be hired unless their

BUREAUCRACY AND REVOLUTION

services are indispensable to production or the service in question.

Our attack on bureaucracy within the State includes taking the necessary measures for the education of future generations under quite different principles, principles that will make them impervious to the petty-bourgeois spirit. The "school goes to the country" program is a very good example. Every year, thousands of youngsters combine education with participation in productive agricultural work. As Fidel has pointed out, in the formation of our children, this principle must be applied beginning in early childhood. Only thus will we be able to eliminate the "dead weight" of bureaucracy as an ideological factor within the new society.

On the other hand, the immediate, direct attack on this evil has entered a new stage. The Commissions for Struggle Against Bureaucracy are now on the offensive, with a new spirit and a new force. Serious and careful work lies ahead: that of simplifying to the nth degree all structures, paper work and regulations within the Revolutionary State. This will require the examination of every instrument of administrative power since many of them correspond, in essence, to a society that no longer exists in our country. This analysis will be the determining factor in deciding whether or not the departments, branches, and even ministries and State organisms of our central apparatus are really needed.

The work of the officials must be made more concrete and direct, closely bound up with production and given content directed toward technology and control.

A great step forward would be on the spot technical and control teams which could help organize work centers without the need of hierarchies and bureaucratic echelons.

The wars of liberation have given us great lessons. We have already cited some of these.

There are superior forms of organization, based on different principles, which have given rise to methods far more efficient than those stemming from the bureaucratic structures typical of bourgeois military institutions, beloved example of ideologists of capitalism.

The revolution is now on the offensive in its war against

bureaucracy. We are making advances in our struggle, supported by the masses and our Party.

It will be a long fight. We cannot let down our guard for one single minute. But we will do away with the danger of a special stratum within our revolutionary society. We will confront this danger with the formation of a new man and victory will be ours.

In order to succeed, we must increase the awareness of our entire nation. It is only when the young cadres and workers in general have acquired an ample, profound understanding that we will win this decisive battle, that is, that we will be victorious in the revolution that is yet to be made: the anti-bureaucratic revolution!

10

MASS MOBILIZATION IN CUBA: THE SYMBOLISM OF STRUGGLE*

Richard Fagen

> Imperialism wants to do battle, mobilize its nest of worms, promote subversion, it doesn't matter. There is also virtue in this; it invigorates the revolutionary, it excites him, it quickens his fighting spirit. We have seen this a thousand and one times: A unit is doing nothing, the enemy has scarcely arrived and then it acts differently, it reacts differently. The Revolution needs the enemy, the proletariat does not flee from the enemy, it needs the enemy. To develop himself, the revolutionary needs his antithesis, which is the counterrevolutionary.[1]
>
> FIDEL CASTRO

It is impossible to spend more than one-half hour reading or listening to any of Fidel Castro's speeches without being struck by the degree to which the language of combat and struggle permeates his discourse. The list of persons, institutions, and behaviors against which the battle must be joined seems end-

* Copyright by the Board of Editors of the *Journal of International Affairs*, reprinted from Vol. XX, No. 2, pp. 254–271, 1966. Permission to reprint in this volume is gratefully acknowledged to the editors of the *Journal*.

This article is based on the introductory and concluding sections of a much longer study entitled "The Cuban Revolution: Enemies and Friends" to be published in David J. Finlay, Ole Holsti, and Richard R. Fagen, *Enemies in Politics* (Chicago: Rand McNally, forthcoming). The author wishes to acknowledge the financial support of the Social Science Research Council.

[1] *Revolución*, February 23, 1963, p. 5. All Spanish language newspapers and periodicals cited are published in Havana. *Gusano* (worm) is the generic term applied by the revolutionaries to other Cubans, whether in exile or still on the island, who are "enemies of the Revolution."

less: counterrevolutionaries, slackers, profiteers, imperialism
and the remnants of pre-revolutionary consciousness, to name
only a few. The following song provides an example of the
tone and content of this rhetoric:

> In the certain danger of this hour
> —with claw and fang on the horizon—
> it is necessary to dress with a knife
> and to dress with a machinegun.
>
> Because if at Playa Girón and at Playa Larga
> the invading trash
> was liquidated by the charge, by the terrible charge
> of our redeeming force,
> those who attempt now
> to come to tread upon our unsoiled roads
> will receive the same,
> whether they be vile mercenaries
> or imperialism's marines.
>
> Although planes fly over Playa Girón
> —Yankee planes in cowardly formation!—
> No one here has weak knees!
> No one here is afraid!
> Yankee boats and planes! Fascism disregards
> law, and, trampling it, navigates our coasts!
> It threatens us! But, here no one surrenders!
> Here no one surrenders or yields!
>
> Hitler and Mussolini live again, and cast themselves
> with Kennedy and the swastika! It is nazi-fascism!
> except that there are other powerful forces that advance
> to destroy it: the new forces of socialism!
>
> The days of the empire of the North are numbered,
> like those of all rotten empires!
> Socialism advances! And they will be beaten,
> exterminated
> and swept away
> by unleashed hurricanes!

Cuba will be a crossroad of wounds! That we know!
But nailed in our trench,
without taking a step backward, we will resist;
without taking a step backward, we will defend
the flag to the last drop of blood.[2]

Similar expressions of conflict can be found in the speeches
of Fidel and other leaders, in textbooks, in the graphic arts,
in revolutionary literature, and in parades and other symbolic
displays. Almost all public communication in Cuba bears the
stamp of this language and political style. It is part and parcel
of the political system established by the Revolution. More
formally, the symbolism of struggle is functionally related to
the conduct of the Revolution through the instrumentalities
of mass mobilization. It is the purpose of this paper to analyze
this functional relationship.

First it is necessary to get some clearer picture of what
type of political system exists in Cuba. In short, to what
analytical class of systems does the Cuban belong? An easy
answer is that it is a communist system. Unfortunately, this
confuses more than it clarifies, for despite Castro's belated
public embrace of Marxism-Leninism, the society is still far
from communized; and even when it becomes communized, it
promises to be a Latin variant differing in significant ways
from the Soviet and Chinese models. Rather, the most useful concept would seem to be that of the "mobilization system"
as developed by Apter. His description is worth quoting at
length:

The mobilization system contains an implicit assumption:
that which divides men from one another is due to unnatural
causes—colonialism, neocolonialism, classes which derive
their differences from hostile relationships centering around
property. Men must be freed from these unnatural differences by both acts of leadership and exceptional public will.
Harmony in the political sphere derives from the messianic

[2] From "The Flame," a revolutionary song, published in *Trabajo*, second fortnight of March, 1962, p. 66. Playa Girón and Playa Larga were
two beaches which figured prominently in the Bay of Pigs invasion of
April, 1961.

leader who points out the dangers and noxious poisons
of faction. Many such leaders are charismatic who represent
the "one." They personify the monistic quality of the
system.

To achieve such oneness, mobilization systems begin by
politicizing all political life. As a result, politics as such
disappears. This is in keeping with monistic political belief.
Conflict is not only bad but also counterrevolutionary. It
runs counter to the natural evolution of human society,
and ideas of opposition downgrade and confuse the power
of positive thinking. . . .

Mobilization systems are characterized by what Durkheim
called repressive law. Punitive and symbolic, it is political
crimes which are punished with great severity. Such
regimes are humorless. Their model of society is an organic
one. Although it does not always fit exactly, Marxism or
some variant thereof is appealing because it satisfies these
conditions theoretically and Leninism supports them
organizationally. Such systems represent the new puritanism.
Progress is its faith. Industrialization is its vision. Harmony
is its goal.[3]

This definition allows us to view the brief history of Cuba
under Castro in perspective. The conditions for a mobilization system—the presence of a charismatic leader and the semi-
colonial relationship with the United States—existed in 1959
when Castro came to power. But the real development of the
present regime did not begin until sometime later in the year.
The suppression of opposition, reform of education, control
and exploitation of the communication media, creation of the
mass organizations, the felt need for a functioning Leninist
party and the open antagonism with the United States all
followed in the early 1960's. Furthermore, these changes,
although massive, were only the structural outcroppings of the
leadership's more fundamental drive for unanimity, control
and the total utilization of human resources. *It is this elite
commitment to total exploitation of human resources in the*

---

[3] David E. Apter, "Political Religion in the New Nations," in Clifford
Geertz (ed.), *Old Societies and New States* (New York: The Free Press,
1963), p. 78.

*service of revolutionary goals which both indexed and moti-
vated the transformation of Cuba in less than five years from
a standard repressive dictatorship under Batista to a mobilization regime under Castro.*

Thus, the dominant ideal of political development in Cuba
today is what Pye has called the model of mass mobilization
and participation.[4] Every Cuban a revolutionary and every
revolutionary a militant is the goal. To accomplish this, an
impressive new institutional order has been fashioned, and
it is through these institutions that the symbolism of struggle
is carried to the masses in the hope that they too will be
mobilized in the service of the Revolution. On the following
pages we shall look first at the institutions that have been
developed since 1959 to aid in the creation of "the new Cuban
man," and then we shall examine the manner in which the
symbolism of struggle is used in the mobilization of the
masses within the context of revolutionary goals and Cuban
history.

New Images of the Political Environment: the Scope of the Cuban Effort

Even casual observers of the Cuban scene have been struck
by the extent to which social and political life have been re-
organized under Castro in order to provide the Cuban citizen
with a carefully controlled view of the world. The carriers
of the officially approved images fall rather naturally into the
following five categories: (1) mass media, (2) armed forces,
(3) mass organizations, (4) special schools and structures,
and (5) the Party. These are the institutions being used to
forge the new Cuban man and to tell the masses the story of
the Revolution.

Mass media. When Castro came to power, Cuba was already well endowed with mass media facilities. There has been
some expansion under the Revolutionary Government,

[4] Lucian W. Pye, *Aspects of Political Development* (Boston: Little,
Brown and Co., 1966), pp. 39–40.

particularly in the electronic media, but basically the physical plant in use is the one inherited from the Batista regime. With the exception of Japan, no Asian or African nation enjoys such a well-developed mass media system. And in Latin America itself, only three other countries—Argentina, Uruguay and Venezuela—approach or surpass Cuba in media facilities.

As might be expected, the regime now exercises complete control over the mass media. Of the three most important newspapers in the early 1960's, *Revolución* and *Noticias de Hoy* were respectively the organs of Castro's 26th of July Movement and the pre-Castro Communist Party. In 1965 they were merged into a new daily, *Granma,* published as the official organ of the party. *El Mundo,* the third important paper, was a flourishing daily under Batista. The Revolutionary Government took over the property early in 1960 and has continued to publish the paper since that time. Control of radio and television facilities was also completed by the middle of 1960.

Castro's most striking innovation in the use of the media came in his marathon television dialogues. As is well known, he would often speak for three or four hours, explaining, cajoling, exciting, inciting and lecturing the populace. The effectiveness of this method of communication between the leader and the masses is difficult to evaluate in detail, but the overall impact must have been enormous, particularly in the early years. Certainly there is no question that the Cuban leadership perceives the mass media as being of prime importance for political mobilization and character formation. Writing in the theoretical journal *Cuba Socialista* in 1964, José Antonio Portuondo expressed the revolutionary media philosophy concisely:

. . . the desire of all the revolutionary leaders, beginning with Fidel Castro, is to transform radio and television into educational instruments through which the masses may be both *informed* and *formed*. Each appearance of the leaders of the Revolution is always a lesson in economics, politics, history, and even in specialized techniques, with a profound

Marxist-Leninist revolutionary meaning. . . . What is sought. . . . is the formation of a new type of intellectual, of socialist man, a conscious actor in the formidable tasks of his time.[5]

The revolutionary elite has made every effort to bring media practice into line with this ideal.

Armed forces. It was on the shoulders of the Rebel Army that Fidel Castro rode to power. Although few in number, the _barbudos_ (bearded ones—popular name for those who fought in the Rebel Army against Batista) were both politically and symbolically of utmost importance during the first years of the Revolutionary Government. Many of the _barbudos_ and much of the symbolism remain important today, but the enduring significance of the armed forces as agencies of mass mobilization derives from more recent developments.

Particularly significant was the creation of the national militia late in 1959. By 1960, the militia numbered more than 200,000 men and women, and it continued to grow through 1961 and 1962. In one analysis its functions and composition have been characterized as follows:

. . . through it, popular support for the regime was organized and popular education furthered. Peasants in rural districts, wearing as part of their uniform the _guajiro's_ straw hat, and workers from industrial plants were formed into militia companies. . . . Professional and trade associations formed support units, such as the medical corps, which were gradually integrated with the regular militia. In this way every important occupational group was reconstituted as a branch of an armed Fidelista movement. By joining the militia, men and women who had not fought in the revolution itself ("in the mountains") could actively associate themselves with the revolution's symbolic figure, an armed peasant or factory worker defending his right to build a better future. People who were unable to fill prestigious roles in the old order, including a noticeably

---

[5] José Antonio Portuondo, "Los intelectuales y la Revolución," _Cuba Socialista,_ June, 1964, pp. 62–63. Emphasis in original.

high proportion of both Negroes and middle-aged women, could see themselves as members of a new elite.[6]

Thus, it was in the militia that vast numbers of otherwise non-participant men, women, and youth were first actively made to feel part of the Revolution. And there, in addition to the informal lessons learned in the course of preparing to defend their homeland against "counterrevolutionaries and imperialists," more formal training was offered in revolutionary history, politics and economics.

In November, 1963, the Revolutionary Government promulgated a compulsory military service law. In the preamble to the law it was stated that "rendering military service in the Revolutionary Armed Forces, in addition to encouraging military learning, foments the sense of revolutionary discipline and morals, and contributes effectively to the cultural and technical formation of the enlistees."[7] This was merely a formalization of an already well-institutionalized policy of regarding the armed forces as, in part, centers for the political training of young adults. The added scope and thoroughness given to the existing efforts by the compulsory military training program thus do not indicate a basic shift in policy but rather only an intensification of programs begun several years earlier.

Mass organizations. Like other mobilization systems, Cuba has developed a large number of mass organizations. Youth, women, workers, farmers, teachers, students and other groupings are organized into federations or associations "for the accomplishment of revolutionary tasks."[8] These tasks include communication, coordination, control, education and—perhaps most importantly—what we call "education through participation." In the Cuban view, it is largely through participation in the mass organizations that the average citizen and

[6] Wyatt MacGaffey and Clifford R. Barnett, *Cuba, Its People, Its Society, Its Culture* (New Haven: HRAF Press, 1962), pp. 281–82.

[7] *Noticias de Hoy,* November 29, 1963, p. 7.

[8] Among the most important revolutionary mass organizations are the *Confederación de Trabajadores de Cuba Revolucionaria* (workers), *Federación de Mujeres Cubanas* (women), *Federación Estudiantil Universitaria* (university students), and *Unión de Juventud Comunista* (youth).

particularly the younger people come to understand the Revolution and their own particular place in "the historic transformation." Through participation comes political consciousness, a prime requisite for correct revolutionary behavior.

On the organizational side, the Cubans have developed one set of institutions that deserves special mention. These are the Committees for the Defense of the Revolution (*Comités de Defensa de la Revolución*). The creation of the CDR dates from September, 1960, when Castro, faced with mounting counterrevolutionary activity both from within and from without, called for the formation of vigilance committees to act as a grass roots defense against *gusanos* and their collaborators. The CDR are organized on a geographical basis, and in densely populated areas there would typically be one committee for each residential block. Although originally charged with defense functions, they soon became in addition multipurpose citizen groups which were used by the leadership for recruiting, administering and proselytizing.

Perhaps the most significant aspect of the entire CDR structure is its sheer size. Organized as a capillary system, the goal is island-wide coverage. Even after allowance is made for the probable inflationary effect of revolutionary enthusiasm, the official statistics published during 1963 are impressive.

TABLE 1

The Size and Composition of the CDR in 1963[9]

Number of Committees	102,500
Total Number of Members	1,500,000
Number of Women Members	660,000
Number of Youth (15–25 years of age)	500,000

Since the total population of Cuba is approximately seven million, the regime thus claims that better than one out of every five Cubans is a member of the CDR. In terms of the adult population, the claim is that 34 percent of the urban

[9] *Sources: Revolución,* January 21, 1963, p. 7; *Revolución,* September 27, 1963, p. 2.

residents and 30 percent of the rural residents belong to the
CDR. When these membership figures are added to the
figures from the other mass organizations and the militia, the
total exceeds four million. Of course there is overlap in membership: a true militant would probably be a member of the
militia, a member of a trade union or farm group, and a
member of the CDR as well. Nevertheless, a conservative
estimate would suggest that at least one out of every two adult
Cubans now participates directly in mass activity under the
revolutionary banner. The net impact on political values, attitudes and behavior must be very considerable.

Special schools and structures. Early in the Revolution,
Castro said that "the most important education is the political
education of the people."[10] It is doubtful that he has since
changed his mind. The institutional innovations resulting from
this philosophy have been massive and continuous. For our
purposes, the most important changes began in 1961 with the
"Year of Education" and the campaign to eradicate illiteracy.
Political education was an integral part of this effort, and a
large scale adult education program with a strong political
component has continued since then.[11]

Since the beginning of 1961, there have also been special
schools for the teaching of Marxist-Leninist theory and practice. Known as Schools for Revolutionary Instruction (*Escuelas de Instrucción Revolucionaria* or EIR), they have as
their fundamental task, "the ideological training of the
revolutionaries and, in turn, of the people."[12] There are now
three types of EIR: National, offering an eighteen-month

[10] Quoted in Universidad Popular, Sexto Ciclo, *Educación y Revolución*
(La Habana: Imprenta Nacional de Cuba, April, 1961), p. 2.

[11] In a monograph, *Cuba: The Political Content of Adult Education*
(Stanford: Hoover Institution, 1964), I have introduced, translated and
annotated some Cuban adult education materials used in 1961 and 1962.
The best single English language source covering the organization, ad-
ministration, and accomplishments of education of all types in Cuba
under Castro is Richard Jolly, Part II of Dudley Seers (ed.), *Cuba, The
Economic and Social Revolution* (Chapel Hill: University of North
Carolina Press, 1964).

[12] Castro, as quoted by Lionel Soto in "Las Escuelas de Instrucción
Revolucionaria en una nueva fase," *Cuba Socialista*, February, 1964, pp.
62–77. Quotation on p. 63. This article has been used as the primary
source for the discussion which follows.

course; Provincial, offering a nine-month course; and Basic, offering a five-month course. By the end of 1963 it was claimed that more than 86,000 persons had been graduated from these schools. Of those graduates, approximately 85 percent had been trained in the Basic Schools, and 6 percent and 9 percent in the Provincial and National Schools respectively.

The quality of the academic training is probably not very high—for instance, in 1963 in the Provincial party schools, only 21 percent of the students had more than a sixth grade education. But the making of experts is only one task of the schools. They are also used for experimentation. In the EIR's are brought together in concentrated form most of the techniques—competition, criticism and self-criticism, productive work and intensive study—that are also used in other agencies of mass mobilization. Thus, the potential importance of the EIR's derives not only from the heightened political consciousness of the graduates, but also from the spread of organizational and pedagogical innovations developed in the course of training.

The Party. As of the first part of 1966, Cuba did not yet have a fully functioning Marxist-Leninist party. However, the philosophical and organizational outlines of the Party had already been laid down, the central committee had been named, and recruiting at the local level was in progress. In common with other governing communist parties, the newly created _Partido Communista de Cuba_ (earlier called _Partido Unido de la Revolución Socialista de Cuba_ or United Party of the Cuban Socialist Revolution) will coordinate, educate, communicate and control:

> The Party is the vanguard that guides the masses in the construction of Socialism. In order to perform its leading role, it is of no importance whether it has so many more or less members, but only that it will be capable of carrying out the directives from the National Directorate of the Revolution, of applying these creatively to specific conditions, of maintaining a close relationship with the working masses, and of leading them onward.

In order to organize and mobilize the masses, in addition to its cadres, the party depends upon the mass organizations, which are like its arms and legs.[13]

When recruitment is complete and the Party fully operative, it should give new unity and coherence to the other institutions of political education and mass mobilization. In addition to being the primary agency through which its own members become imbued with the revolutionary world view, the Party will also oversee the programs of political training carried on through the mass media, armed forces, mass organizations and schools. Organizationally, the Party represents the final (or at least the most recent) step in the drive for unanimity, control and the total utilization of human resources. How successful it will be in these tasks remains to be seen.

History, Mass Mobilization, and the Conduct of Cuban Politics

In order to understand the appeal and the uses of the current Cuban symbolism, it is necessary to appreciate its historical antecedents and its development. Primary among these antecedents is seven decades of anti-Americanism. Since at least the time of José Martí and the Spanish-American War, antagonism toward the United States has been a recurring theme in Cuban politics, although its earlier volume and pervasiveness never approached the level attained under Castro after 1960. The most fully institutionalized pre-Castro expression of anti-Americanism came in the first years of the Party of the Cuban Revolution or *Auténticos,* founded in the 1930's. The 1935 program of the *Auténticos* was organized around the three themes of "nationalism, socialism, and anti-imperialism."[14] By nationalism was meant national independence and

[13] "El PURS en las Montañas de Oriente," *Cuba Socialista,* August, 1963, p. 118.

[14] Theodore Draper, *Castroism: Theory and Practice* (New York: Praeger, 1965), p. 7. In the first chapter of this book, entitled "What is Castroism?", Draper argues convincingly that Castro's original program was deeply rooted in what might now be called the nationalistic demo-

development, and by anti-imperialism was meant disengagement from North American political and economic control. But long before the *Auténticos* began to broadcast their own particular brand of anti-Americanism, publicly expressed dislike for the "Colossus of the North" was heard on the island. For instance, in 1922, after developments in the sugar trade and the sugar industry which were considered by many Cubans to be inimical to their interests, one Havana newspaper printed the following two-page headline: "Hatred of North Americans will be the Religion of Cubans." "The day will have to arrive," the paper continued, "when we will consider it the most sacred duty of our life to walk along the street and eliminate the first American we encounter."[15] Fidel Castro has seldom used more virulent language.

The character of Cuban anti-Americanism from Martí through the *Auténticos* to Castro has not, however, always been the same. Much of the rhetoric and symbolism—the bloated Uncle Sam, his pockets stuffed with dollars and guns, the Wall Street millionaires, hand-in-hand with corrupt Latin American politicians and landowners—are common to most varieties of Cuban nationalism. Similarly, the themes of North American economic exploitation, political domination and the necessity for Latin solidarity in the face of Yankee aggression have not changed much during the twentieth century. But the specific sins attributed to the Yankees have changed through time, as changing political and economic relations in the hemisphere have offered first one and then another "target of opportunity" to the nationalists. Furthermore, the involvement of Cuba with the Soviet Union and Eastern Europe has added an entirely new dimension to the situation. Cuban anti-Americanism before 1960 was not thrown into relief by positive references to any other country or any other form of social organization. Except for a pantheon of idealized Cuban and Latin American heroes, the rhetoric introduced no abstract good guys, only bad. At that time, Cuban nationalism

cratic left of pre-Castro Cuban politics, namely the *Auténticos* and, more particularly, their offshoot the *Ortodoxos*.

[15] Quoted in Robert F. Smith, *The United States and Cuba: Business and Diplomacy, 1917–1960* (New York: Bookman Associates, 1960), p. 103.

looked to indigenous sources for a definition of what was right, proper and civilized, whereas it looked north of the Rio Grande for a characterization of what was evil, immoral and barbaric. After Castro, however, and particularly after the Bay of Pigs, positive models for the construction of the new Cuba were sought not only in the Cuban past, real and imagined, but also in Soviet theory and practice. While anti-Americanism continued unabated, Cuban nationalism became admixed with internationalism, albeit internationalism of a very special type.

With the advent of Castro to national prominence in 1953—the date of his abortive attack on the Moncada Army barracks—a new generation of post-Martí revolutionary heroes appears, doing battle against dictatorship at home and imperialism both on the island and abroad. Castro and his lieutenants stand at the head of the new gallery of heroes, but the ranks are filled with hundreds of lesser-known Cubans, mostly young and mostly dead. Typical are José Antonio Echeverría and Conrado Benítez. Echeverría was president of the Student Federation of the University of Havana and was shot and killed by the police in 1957 while participating in a student attack on the presidential palace and on Batista. Benítez was a young Negro literacy worker who allegedly was murdered by anti-Castro forces in 1961 while teaching in the mountains of Las Villas. There is hardly a factory or school in Cuba that does not now carry the name of some modern revolutionary martyr like Echeverría or Benítez, and the Cubans are constantly called upon to emulate the dedication of such heroes.

Thus, the Castro regime has drawn selectively on Cuban history for both gods and devils to inform its current mobilization efforts. To these historical symbols, as we have seen, have been added others, overwhelmingly positive, which evoke no such echoes from the past. There are new actors on the stage, the Soviet Union, East European states, "national liberation movements" in all parts of the world, and a host of Cuban heroes created by the Revolution itself. But the dominant theme of mobilization symbolism continues to be the inevitable antagonism between Cuba and the United

States. Why should this be so? Is the hemispheric political environment in which the Revolution moves really as hostile as the Cuban leadership claims?

It is extremely difficult to separate the real from the imagined Cuban grievances against the United States. Speaking of the pre-Castro period, apologists for the Cuban side argue that for sixty years the United States controlled the politics, plundered the resources, humiliated the population and crippled the economy of the island. Defenders of United States policy, on the other hand, list manifold social and economic benefits that accrued to the Cubans because of the American presence. Yet for our purposes we need attempt no detailed reconciliation of these two extreme interpretations of the historical record, for consistent with both are three key assertions. First, the degree of American political involvement in Cuba was considerable. For instance, the Platt Amendment, in which "Cuba consents that the United States may exercise the right to intervene for the preservation of Cuban independence, the maintenance of a government adequate for the protection of life, property, and individual liberty," was in effect from 1901 to 1934. Second, the degree of American economic involvement in Cuba was even greater. A U.S. Department of Commerce survey published in 1956 stated that in Cuba "The only foreign investments of importance are those of the United States. American participation exceeds 90 percent of telephone and electric services, about 50 percent in public service railways, and roughly 40 percent in raw sugar production. The Cuban branches of United States banks are entrusted with almost one-fourth of all bank deposits."[16] Third, without considering the morality or immorality of this political and economic involvement, without taking sides with either those who claim that the American presence stunted Cuban development or those who claim that it accelerated the economy, we can note that it must have been extremely galling to Cuban nationalists to live for sixty years in the political and economic shadow of the United States.

In 1959, the Castro regime's first year in power, there was

[16] Quoted in Leland L. Johnson, "U.S. Business Interests in Cuba and the Rise of Castro," *World Politics,* Vol. XVII, No. 3, April, 1965, p. 443.

a rapid disintegration of Cuban-American relations and a concomitant rise of anti-Americanism. By January of 1961, when the U.S. broke diplomatic relations with Cuba, the revolutionary image of the United States was already being presented in negative and strident language. Once again, to explain the course of events leading to this antagonism, apologists for both sides point accusing fingers at the other. Referring to 1959 and 1960, the Cubans cite American aid to Batista, opposition to the first agrarian reform and later nationalization laws, attacks by Miami-based exiles, termination of military and technical aid, refusal to refine Soviet crude oil, reduction of the U.S. quota for Cuban sugar, economic embargo on U.S. goods shipped to Cuba, and espionage and subversion by U.S. agents. The American spokesmen can muster an equally long list of Cuban provocations and misdeeds: illegal executions, communist infiltration in government, expropriation without compensation, destruction of press autonomy, recognition of Communist China, increasing economic dependence on the Soviet bloc, export of revolution to the hemisphere and unjustified attacks on U.S. officials, citizens, policies and property. Again, however, for our purposes we need not attempt a reconciliation of these two points of view. Whichever side was "right" and whichever "wrong," it is clear that an interactive and self-supporting system of threat and counter-threat, misunderstanding and counter-misunderstanding, and retaliation and counter-retaliation was established between Cuba and the United States in 1959 and 1960. By 1961, the antagonism had hardened, and further moves by both sides—the Bay of Pigs invasion, Castro's embrace of Marxism-Leninism, the missile crisis, U.S. overflights and Cuban hemispheric insurrectionism—only served to reinforce existing hostility.

Still, however, we have not come to grips with the important functional questions. Why, as Castro says, does the Revolution need enemies? Or conversely, in addition to the necessity of military protection and economic aid, why does it need friends? Put more generally, in what manner is the revolutionary map of the political environment related to the dynamics of the Cuban system? *History, nationalism and the surge of radicalism have provided the symbols and the opportunities exploited in programs of mass mobilization, but these factors do not by themselves fully explain the thorough-going commitment to mobilization as a political strategy.*

The revolutionary map of the political environment is intended to serve the regime's mobilization efforts in the following four ways: (1) by establishing the identity and the meaning of the Revolution; (2) by legitimizing the revolutionary leaders and their programs; (3) by providing a spur to action and a rationale for participation; and (4) by defining new models of development and new modes of behavior. Success in all of these tasks is considered crucial to the continuation of the revolutionary system.

Establishing the identity and meaning of the Revolution. Consistency is not one of the virtues of Fidel Castro and his lieutenants. The recent history of Cuba is characterized by rapid shifts in revolutionary policies, personnel, tactics and expressed goals. Some admirers of the Cuban style profess to see in this turbulence the organic growth and maturation of the Revolution, the victory of the "true" revolution over the forces originally impeding and qualifying it. But such explanations ignore the pragmatism, the experimentation and, at times, the lack of any sense of direction on the part of the leadership. The continuity of the Revolution is not to be found in its policies and practices, but rather in the core of symbols around which it has been organized. Struggle (*lucha*) has been at the heart of the revolutionary rhetoric since Castro first took up arms against Batista. Over the last decade, the Cuban people have been called upon to struggle against dictatorship, illiteracy, low productivity, *gusanos,* imperialists, counterrevolutionary habits, discrimination, bureaucratism, sectarianism, absenteeism, colonialism, neocolonialism and much more. Always the struggle implies enemies, something or someone to do battle against, some "foreign" (*i.e.,* non-revolutionary) institution, group, or behavior which must be eradicated if the Revolution is to triumph. Although the tactics employed and the targets against which the struggle must be waged change, the *lucha* itself is continuous. In a mobilization system such as the Cuban, the revolutionary leadership makes certain that the ranks of the enemy never grow thin.

It is not only the common and continuous struggle, however, that gives identity and meaning to the Revolution. As Bittner has commented, "The usefulness of an adversary's image is not exhausted by making him the recipient of all blame and hostility. He also makes it possible to moralize by counter-example. Assaulting him means to deal him the fate that he deserves, which is precisely the opposite of what is in store for the believer."[17] To the dedicated, the Revolution means not only a struggle, but also the creation of a new and far superior social order. What are the dominant characteristics of this new social order? The new Cuba is to be a land without social and racial discrimination, where all are free to work, study and advance, where the masses are literate, healthy and dignified, and where the political, economic and cultural domination of the United States has been shattered forever. The new Cuba, child of the Revolution, is largely defined as the antithesis of the old Cuba, bastard child of the United States. The Revolution, of course, cannot destroy the United States, but it can repudiate by word and deed almost everything that the colossus stands for. In the act of repudiation, guidelines for the reconstruction of society are established and the goodness of the Revolution is made manifest.

Legitimizing the revolutionary leaders and their programs. In 1959 and probably throughout most of 1960, Fidel Castro and his followers could do no wrong so far as the vast majority of Cubans was concerned. In a sample survey conducted during the spring of 1960, Lloyd Free found that 86 percent of the combined urban and semi-urban populations supported the regime. Of these, Free classified approximately one-half as *fervent* supporters.[18] The personal popularity of

[17] Egon Bittner, "Radicalism and the Organization of Radical Movements," *American Sociological Review*, Vol. 28, No. 6, December, 1963, p. 938.
[18] Lloyd A. Free, *Attitudes of the Cuban People Toward the Castro Regime* (Princeton, N.J.: Institute for International Social Research, 1960). Under the direction of Free, a Cuban research organization interviewed a cross section of 500 residents of Havana and another cross section of 500 residents of other urban and semi-urban centers. Although the 40 percent of the Cuban population living in rural areas was not rep-

Castro was overwhelming. He was viewed by the masses as the Revolution incarnate, the charismatic leader who miraculously had led his people out of the *Batistiano* wilderness and into the promised land.[19] But the honeymoon did not last, as the flow of exiles and Castro's own speeches attest. The charismatic bond is inevitably eroded by time and circumstance. The frenzy of adulation and the image of the hero's infallibility cannot remain undamaged by the failures, disappointments and hardships which always accompany attempts to rule. Cuba proved no exception, and when new miracles were not forthcoming—with the exception of the Bay of Pigs victory—part of the legitimating charismatic myth was destroyed. Such decisive actions as the embrace of Marxism-Leninism, political repression, indoctrination in the schools, nationalization, expropriation and pressure on the Church also contributed to a falling away of support for both the leader and his regime. Furthermore, pervasive shortages of food, clothing and services compounded popular discontent. Thus, the charisma of Castro began to diminish from "natural causes" at the same time that the revolutionary elite was both tearing the social fabric apart and demanding new levels of sacrifice from the citizenry.

The maintenance of legitimacy during this period of declining charisma, massive social change and widespread personal hardship has not been easy. It is impossible to estimate with precision how successful the leadership has been since 1961 in engendering support for itself and its policies. Much of the early euphoria is gone, but certainly large segments of the population continue to follow the revolutionary elite and

---

resented in Free's survey, the countryside has always been if anything more pro-Castro than the cities. Thus, the 86 percent level of support may well be conservative if extended to the total population of Cuba in the spring of 1960.

[19] For bibliography and an analysis of the bases of Castro's charisma, see Richard R. Fagen, "Charismatic Authority and the Leadership of Fidel Castro," *Western Political Quarterly*, Vol. XVIII, No. 2, June, 1965, pp. 275–84. For a good discussion of the sources of charisma and the purposes it serves in evolving political systems, see Ann Ruth Willner and Dorothy Willner, "The Rise and Role of Charismatic Leaders," *Annals of the American Academy of Political and Social Science*, Vol. 358, March, 1965, pp. 77–88.

give at least tacit approval to its programs. The new legitimacy is in part based on negative rather than positive appeals. Why are there shortages? Why are there hardships? Why must we do voluntary labor? Why is political control so strict? Because, the regime argues, we are surrounded and infiltrated by powerful enemies who, if we relax for one moment, will surely seize the opportunity to weaken or destroy us. This rationale, as presented to the Cuban people, is more than an attempt to divert attention from pressing domestic problems and the quality of leadership by blaming others for the failures and broken promises of the Revolution. It also represents one version of the classic "emergency" argument. When the nation is in trouble, when powerful enemies are all around, then extraordinary measures are justified, and the common defense must take precedence over individual liberty and well-being. In the Cuban case, this argument is related to the definition of the Revolution presented above. During a struggle, a *lucha,* in which the survival of the Revolution is at stake, is it not immoral or even treasonous to question the wisdom of the leaders? Moreover, is it not inevitable that in a struggle of such magnitude many must sacrifice and some must die before the ultimate victory is won?

   Providing a spur to action and a rationale for participation. Ordinary men are not often moved to action by a direct appeal to abstract ideas. Not "building socialism," but rather comradeship, ambition, social pressure, or fear probably motivate the Cuban office worker who volunteers to cut sugar cane on the weekend. Similarly, visions of a brave new world may be instrumental in keeping a few agricultural reformers working after hours, but the average Cuban peasant is probably kept in harness by some combination of necessity, habit, ignorance and hope of material gain. The Cuban leaders are well aware that wide-spread popular participation cannot be achieved by appeals to nineteenth or even twentieth century abstractions. On the other hand, for both political and ideological reasons, they are committed to a mobilization strategy that includes the use of ideas as well as the use of the carrot and the stick. Thus, in common with all politicians who seek to move the masses with some mixture of ideology, threats, bribes, promises and rewards, the Cuban leaders must translate the great issues into language easily understood by the common man. The elite definition of the Revolution as a continuing struggle against a never-ending series of adversaries represents a first attempt at translation. The motivational side of this effort involves giving the struggle a personal and highly individualistic focus. Thus, the bureaucrats are urged to fight against wastage and absenteeism, the workers against low production, the teachers against illiteracy, and the party cadres against wrong thinking. By so doing, each individual can become a soldier in the revolutionary army and contribute his share to the inevitable victory over backwardness, injustice and imperialism. As Bittner has remarked, "Because of its concreteness, the fight against the adversary may represent the only version of the doctrine accessible to believers who lack the intellectual capacity to appreciate its loftier aspects."[20]

The mobilization rhetoric thus links concrete individual efforts to the accomplishment of the most abstract revolutionary goals. Cubans are constantly reminded that the titanic struggle between good and evil now being played out on the world stage can be found in microcosm in the factories, fields and offices where they work. Through full participation, every Cuban, no matter how humble his origin, can become a revolutionary; and through sustained excellence, every revolutionary, no matter how menial his task, can become a hero. The joy of belonging to the movement, the joy of being righteous in action, and ultimately the joy of victory are within reach of all who are willing to do battle against the local manifestations of the common enemy.

Defining new models of development and new modes of behavior. Because Cuban history, culture, and political practice do not suggest a clear picture of what the new Cuba will look like, the Revolution needs models. As we have seen, these models are of two basic types. The first type derives directly from the negative evaluation of the United States and its imperialist friends and allies. This is what we called "moraliz-

[20] Bittner, *op. cit.*, p. 938.

ing by counter-example." The Revolution is in part defined as the antithesis of its enemies. A second type of model is more positive. The Soviet Union and its allies have come to be presented as good, powerful and worthy of imitation. The Revolution is now also defined by its friends.

This shift in identification is rooted in and responds to international developments, but it signifies more than new political alignments. The embrace of the Soviet Union opens up new possibilities for the guidance and the education of the masses. To understand these possibilities, it is necessary to appreciate the new demands placed on the Cuban people. The transformation of the Cuban polity, society and economy cannot be accomplished by enthusiastic but untutored citizens. It is no longer sufficient to gather in the plaza and shout *Patria o Muerte, Venceremos* (Fatherland or Death, We Will Win). This does not put bread on the table or tractors in the field. What is needed, the regime argues, is a technological revolution which will support and continue, but *not* supersede, the political revolution. The technological revolution must produce the cadres of specialists who will lead in constructing the new socio-economic order. These cadres will combine both material and political expertise, and through them the masses will eventually grow in political and technological sophistication. The models for this new man and the society he is to create have been, in large part, taken over from East European theory and practice. The Soviet industrial hero and the Soviet technological order are examples held up to the Cubans. The more inclusive image of the international environment explains and justifies these importations while, at the same time, it provides concrete examples of what the new patterns of behavior should look like.

Throughout this paper we have concentrated on the institutional matrix and the functional importance of mass mobilization efforts in Cuba. The focus has been on *strategies* of political mobilization, their historical roots and their relation to the conduct of revolutionary politics. Noticeably lacking has been a systematic attempt at evaluating the outcomes of these strategies. It is one thing to claim that the revolutionary elite uses the United States and the Soviet Union to define and give meaning to the Cuban experiment; it is quite another thing to claim that the Cuban masses accept what they are told and act accordingly. Lacking studies of the attitudes and political behavior of the Cuban population, we cannot evaluate in detail the successes and failures of the extensive mobilization campaigns. In any event, such evaluation is in part premature, for no generation of Cubans has yet grown to political maturity exclusively under the tutelage of the present regime. The leaders have reaped certain short-term benefits from increased public participation in revolutionary activities, but the long-term consequences of the drive for total participation and commitment are not yet known.

Part III

+++

FIGHTING UNDERDEVELOPMENT

A. THE ECONOMY

INTRODUCTION

The problems of a revolutionary government, of course, are far more complex than the simple acquisition of power through armed struggle. After the rebellion was over in Cuba, the entire population had to be radicalized, attitudes changed, traditions destroyed, the popular support maintained and deepened, the society restructured, viable organizations and institutions created, and social justice distributed. Meanwhile, the enemy, seeking to reverse the process of history, carried out its campaign from abroad or from inside the island. A watchful eye had to be kept over everyone—even the revolutionary ranks.

At the same time the battle against underdevelopment began. In May 1959, the first economic step was taken with the Agrarian Reform, which was believed to be an essential condition for the diversification of the economy, and an instrument with which to form the large internal market needed for accelerated industrialization. By late 1960 capitalism disappeared from most economic sectors as large industrial and business enterprises, sugar mills, oil companies, banks, public services, and 37% of the land were socialized.

Soon thereafter Cuba drew up extremely optimistic industrialization plans aimed at doing away with the sugar monoculture (prior to 1959 sugar accounted for 82% of the value of foreign trade) and its concomitant dependence on the United States. Declaring war on sugar, the revolutionists deliberately reduced the amount of land devoted to the crop, substituting for it a myriad of other crops.

It was a disastrous policy. As Michel Gutelman attests in his essay on "Cuba's Lessons on Economic Policies," the mistake was recognized in 1963 by the revolutionary government. Sugar production had fallen from close to 6 million tons in 1959 to less than 4 million tons in 1963. This brought about a foreign-exchange crisis. Further, the diversification programs in agriculture were just partial successes, and little progress was made in the industrialization drive (a romantic and impracticable venture), launched without the necessary skilled personnel or raw materials, and with the necessity of importing very costly factories.

Sugar Production
(in metric tons)

1959	5,964,100
1960	5,861,800
1961	6,767,000
1962	4,815,300
1963	3,821,100
1964	4,397,800

Thus, a change in economic policy came in 1963. The major area of Cuba's economic effort and concentration once again was to be in the exploitation of the island's sugar potential. Agriculture, which was becoming the most important sector of the economy, was further socialized, as Michel Gutelman shows in his second essay, for economic and political reasons. Through this measure medium-sized farms were confiscated, leaving only about 150,000 small farmers with control over less than 25% of the arable land. At that point Cuba became the country with the largest degree of land collectivization in the world (70% state-owned).

The emphasis on agriculture was a unique Cuban interpretation of Marxism. Although Marx's classical notion envisioned socialism as a system founded on heavy industry, the revolutionary leaders of the island argued that due to Cuba's special historical and natural conditions (lacking iron ore, oil, or any major source of power), socialism could be constructed by introducing highly advanced technology into agricultural production. Industrialization would not be abandoned, but postponed, and would grow from a healthy agricultural base and the expansion of traditional exports. Further, the requirements of agricultural production would determine which industries would have priority.

In 1964 intense and costly efforts started to increase the volume of sugar output. New methods of cultivation, intensive fertilization, extensive weeding, irrigation, and some degree of mechanization were introduced. Millions of dollars were spent as a solid agricultural infrastructure was created, and special calls were issued to the population to participate in volunteer labor and other unpaid work, as Carmelo Mesa-Lago describes in his illuminating study.

On June 7, 1965, Fidel Castro disclosed the "Sugar Plan" for 1965–1970, which was to produce a total of 46 million tons of sugar. In the succeeding years, however, despite the high cost of material and human input, Castro had to concede one time after the other that the economy failed to meet the production targets.

Agricultural goals were obstructed by management disorganization and ignorance, the weather, lack of spare parts, considerable decline in crop yields, transportation problems, inefficient use of machines, labor absenteeism, and low productivity among the rural workers. The output of consumer goods also declined due to the Government's premeditated policy of investing larger portions of the gross national product in economic development. Interestingly, while the GNP declined (1964–1968), gross investments increased.

This impressive investment brought about austerity and the inadequate supply of consumer goods, creating more rationing, long lines in front of stores, and the gradual increase of a black market. On March 13, 1968, Fidel Castro recognized the growing mood of confusion, dissatisfaction, and protest among the people. And, as he had done previously in times of difficulties, Castro stepped up his revolutionary campaign. The disappointing economic problems and the popular discontent seemed reasons enough for taking further revolutionary steps against all manifestations of private enterprise—regarded by the Revolution as the refuge of corruption, parasitism, and counterrevolution. Hence all groceries, cafes, bars (alcoholic beverages were prohibited), meat and poultry shops; clothing, furniture, hardware, glassware, and book stores; cleaning and hairdressing establishments, and other shops and small businesses were nationalized. In mid-1968 Cuba became the socialist country with the highest percentage of state-owned property, controlling almost all production, distribution, and services.

The Cuban Sugar Plan

	Production Target (in metric tons)	Real Production	Deficit
1965	6,000,000	6,050,000	——
1966	6,500,000	4,455,000	1,045,000
1967	7,500,000	6,128,000	1,372,000
1968	8,000,000	5,164,000	2,836,000
1969	9,000,000	4,459,000	4,541,000
1970	10,000,000	8,500,000	1,500,000

Having failed to fulfill most of the five-year Sugar Plan, throughout 1969 and 1970 the revolutionary government mobilized all the country's human and material resources to meet a single goal: the production of 10 million tons of sugar by July 1970. This was not a mere economic matter, but a political and psychological objective too. It was a question of national honor, a yardstick by which the capacity of the Revolution to carry out its plans could be judged. The "Zafra de los Diez Millones" also reflected the revolutionary leadership's desire to restore confidence to a people that was growing more disgruntled and disillusioned after so many unfulfilled promises and so many failures.

The 10 million tons was envisioned as a plan for the total eradication of the trade deficit plaguing Cuba since 1962. Additional foreign exchange was to be used to make payments on loans, to import machinery, and to increase consumer goods. It was a colossal effort to put an end to horrible sacrifices, to attain rapid economic development, and to improve the standard of living of the people.

To assure victory, drastic steps were taken. The labor force was placed under virtual military control, and the Ministry of the Interior was put in charge of most sugar mills. Nonetheless, the 10 million tons were not produced, and as Fidel Castro bitterly notes in his "Report on the Sugar Harvest," this failure represented an unquestionable moral and economic defeat which had to be attributed to errors of the Government and the irresponsibility of many in the sugar production process.

On August 8, 1970, the Cuban Labor Minister disclosed that the productivity of the labor force of 2 million during the sugar harvest that year was extremely low. The 8.5 million tons of sugar, he asserted, represented only seventeen tons of sugar produced by each worker engaged in the harvest, or $400 less than the annual average wage of the Cuban people. In fact, the cost of the 1970 sugar harvest was close to three times higher than its true sale value on the world market. Thus, the huge harvest was a great financial loss to the nation.[1]

The politics of austerity, constant sacrifice, and regimentation seem to be the high political price a revolutionary and underdeveloped country has to pay to oust backwardness. The island has just found that the struggle against underdevelopment is the most important, and at the same time, the most difficult thing to accomplish. The paper by Fidel Castro on "The Problem of Underdevelopment" gives the reader an incisive understanding of this terrible problem. In the meantime, the economic future of Cuba, to say the least, remains gloomy.

The effort to produce the 10 million tons has had disastrous political and economic consequences. Production has declined and absenteeism continues to grow. Moreover, Cuba

[1] Cuba's gross national product in 1969 was estimated at about $2.8 billion by U.S. analysts, that is, equal to 1958 when the island had 6.6 million inhabitants instead of 8.5 million. See: George Valsky, "Cuba Mobilizes for Sugar," the New York *Times,* January 26, 1970.

is becoming a victim of population growth. In a very courageous and honest speech ("Report on the Cuban Economy") Fidel has pointed this out. The unbalanced age structure of the population impedes economic development, and this situation is going to worsen even if birth control (which the Revolution opposes) is introduced. Unfortunately, many years of sacrifice and regimented labor still await the people of Cuba.[2]

[2] This would not be the case if the Soviet Union and the Eastern European countries furnished Cuba with the capital it needs. This alternative, however, is unlikely to materialize.

11

CUBA'S LESSONS ON ECONOMIC POLICIES*

Michel Gutelman

Immediately after taking power the revolutionary government did away with the economic conditions that institutionalized underdevelopment. From the outset it directly and exclusively controlled economic and agricultural policy-making, and plans were made to achieve industrialization and diversification of agricultural production. At first glance those goals seemed quite logical; industrialization is a common and justified aspiration—in general terms—of the Third World, and agricultural diversification sought an end to Cuba's dependence on only one product.

The agricultural policy was based on this fundamental principle: the importation of agricultural products had to be replaced by national production and exports had to be increased and diversified. Moreover, there were objective conditions that forced the revolutionary leadership to carry forward diversification beyond what was considered desirable. Three things contributed to "forcing" diversification.

First, after attaining power, the economy of the country suffered considerable monetary pressure. The rapid elimination of unemployment and the nominal salary increase expanded the wage-earning mass. Also, some social reforms permitted the movement of money to other sectors. For example, when house rents were reduced by 50%, or some public services and transportation rates were reduced by 80%, a large amount of money became available to be used in

* From Michel Gutelman, "Las lecciones de la política agrícola cubana," *Foro Internacional* (Mexico), April–June 1968, pp. 394–404. Reprinted by permission.

other sectors of the economy. In an underdeveloped country like Cuba, where the level of consumption is low, the elasticity of demand for agricultural products is very great, especially for meat and milk. Thus, the supplementary demand was principally directed toward the agricultural sector of production, which suffered an important monetary pressure. It was then necessary to freeze prices and establish rationing. But it should be noted that, for some products, the global and rationed supply was superior—as a consequence of partial increases in production—to the period prior to the Revolution. In other words, before 1958, rationing was done through prices and the low incomes of most of the population, while afterward it was organized administratively. Naturally, the distribution was now much more egalitarian. It could be argued, nonetheless, that the monetary pressure had a great psychological effect which demanded an increase in production and diversification.

The second factor contributing to the diversification drive was the economic blockade. It forced the introduction of new crops at a rate and extent larger than feasible. For example, prior to the Revolution, 10% of Cuba's consumption of oils was fulfilled by national production. The other 90% came almost entirely from the United States. In a week 90% of all oil supplies disappeared from Cuba. Such a shortage could be produced in the island because no one ever thought of building up reserves since exporters could be easily reached by telephone and demands were rapidly met. To solve the problem the revolutionary government had no other recourse than to put forth large plans for internal production. The same thing had to be done in an extensive manner with regard to agricultural products, since 30% of Cuban imports prior to the Revolution were constituted by agricultural products mainly purchased from the United States.

The last factor that contributed to the diversification drive was the creation of a light industry. This industry, born from the industrialization policy, rapidly created an important demand for agricultural products, primarily fibers. This demand could not be easily satisfied by imports due to the blockade and the scarcity of foreign exchange. Thus, new plans for diversification had to be made. Cotton could be cited as a particular item that developed between 1961 and 1963.

All these factors, whether based on principles or on objective needs, set the stage for the rapid and massive introduction of new crops, some of which were little known in Cuba. Also it forced the increment of some old crops which in the past had been cultivated at a small scale.

It should not be forgotten that side by side with this diversification an intensive industrialization policy was being carried out. Without having the same priority it had in the Soviet Union, this industrialization policy represented a colossal effort between 1960 and 1963. During that period Cuba invested $850 million in that sector, which was approximately the same amount Americans had invested in the country for fifty years.[1]

The results of these simultaneous policies of immediate industrialization and thorough agricultural diversification, without being completely negative, were not what had been expected. In 1963 the Cuban revolutionary leaders recognized that the economic situation was not too good. With reference to the industrial sector a series of unforeseen factors diminished the interest in continuing the policy. Due to the absence of a basic industrial superstructure the rate of import substitution was very low. The apparently increased value of each Cuban industry was deceptive; for example, wire was imported to make barbed wire. In reality, the policy of industrialization, which by necessity was implicitly conceived as a policy of autocracy, suffered from dispersion.

The reasons for the relative failure of the policy of agricultural diversification must be sought in the weight of the past.

The difficulties of diversification were created by the many years the structure of the Cuban economy was deformed and oriented toward monoproduction, and the low level of development of the productive forces. Concretely, the weight of the past could be found in the absence of skilled

---

[1] This assertion could be proved or disproved according to the years chosen. In 1897 the United States had $44 million invested in the island; but by 1929 it amounted to $919 million. (Eds.)

personnel (of the 300 agronomists working in Cuba in 1959, approximately 270 left the country with the American enterprises in which they worked), the focus of knowledge in sugar production, and the lack of a technical mentality among the peasants which would have permitted moving from a monoculture into diverse agriculture.

Finally, we must consider the distorted economic and technical infrastructure of agriculture, which was almost exclusively North American in origin. All these factors explain the difficulties encountered by the Cuban revolutionary government in reorienting its foreign trade after taking power and transforming all the technology of its agriculture with the aid of the socialist countries.

In the <u>industrial</u> sector the weight of the past manifested itself, above all, in the <u>total absence of engineers and middle-level technicians, and in the attempt to change abruptly an entire technology.</u> These structural factors which put a brake on the industrialization drive must be considered in conjunction with reasons that are not necessarily economic or technical, although the tendency is to forget them.

Cuba was and is a country on war-footing. From 1959 to 1963 there was at least one general mobilization yearly. In 1958 it was the struggle to take power, in 1959 it was the struggle against the opposition movements, more or less armed, and to fight the invasion of a group of Dominicans; in 1960 it was a mobilization to defeat the internal counter-revolution; in 1961 it was the mobilization of the people to stop the Bay of Pigs invasion; in 1962 the missile crisis mobilization; and in 1963 the landing of Menoyo,[2] who led a counterrevolutionary guerrilla group, thereby forcing a mobilization of the people for three weeks while the sugar harvest was going on.

These factors cannot be dismissed when internal production is examined. Some unfavorable climatic factors should also be considered. In 1961 Cuba had the driest year in the last half of the century; in 1963 Hurricane Flora, which killed

[2] Major Eloy Gutiérrez Menoyo, who fought against Batista and later fought against the Revolution for turning Communist. (Eds.)

twelve hundred persons, crossed Oriente province, the agricultural region par excellence.

In addition, we must consider the technical errors of the revolutionary leadership and the serious deficiencies in the planning system.

During the years 1962–1963, with the benefit of experience, the Cuban leaders reached the conclusion that it was not realistic to attempt to transcend industrial underdevelopment in one jump, or to diversify beyond certain limits. The past has to be taken into account when making economic policy. It was demonstrated that socialism only eliminated the institutional and political conditions impeding development, but in no way guaranteed or automatically allowed development. All sorts of obstacles had to be overcome and the principal sectors for development had to be cautiously chosen, following the points of less resistance to development. Evaluation and criticism terminated in 1963 with the launching of a new economic policy and especially a new agricultural policy.

Alarm was first expressed by the Ministry of Foreign Trade, which foresaw the beginning of a serious foreign exchange crisis. Contrary to what was expected, the export of agricultural products had not augmented. Thus, the import capacity remained stationary or declined since it was still fundamentally tied to sugar exports. From that moment on a series of technical studies was conducted aimed at finding the earning capacity of foreign trade. Comparative calculations were made to determine whether it was opportune to continue producing specific items which could be imported. The objective of the calculations was to show to what extent the autocratic tendency should be maintained in the diversification process.

At first glance, the data provided surprising results. They presented an order of priorities in agricultural production which, generally speaking, was very similar to the agricultural system prior to the Revolution. The products with greater earning capacity were sugar, tobacco, coffee, cattle, and fruits. It was a vicious cycle to be expected since it reflected, once again, the weight of the past. In the realm of principle, however, it was a discouraging situation. Should one give in to the laws of the world market dominated by imperialist powers? The options were presented in those general terms in 1963. One factor, in fact, complicated the problem.

While the production priorities were studied, important discussions were held between Cuba and the socialist countries, especially the Soviet Union. In January 1964, these discussions culminated in the signing of a commercial agreement, unique up to now, between the Soviet Union and Cuba. The agreement established that the Soviet Union would purchase Cuban sugar under conditions completely different from those prevailing in the preferential and world markets before the Revolution. First, the purchasing price was firmly set at 6 cents per pound. Purchases were planned for the next six years. The agreement covered important quantities, since Cuba would sell 5 million tons of sugar to the USSR in 1970. (The total amount of commercial sugar in the world is about 20 million tons.) This type of commercial arrangement is essentially what all underdeveloped countries producing only one product would like to have—although they have not achieved it yet.

Similar agreements signed with other socialist countries succeeded in assuring Cuba of the sale of 7 million tons of sugar for 1970, that is, more than the historic averages, not only in exports, but in production too.

The practical consequences for the stability and economic development of Cuba were considerable. A new economic and agricultural policy could be elaborated on the basis of a planned capacity for imports for a six-year period, with the aid of the priority studies made. The general lines of the new policy were that industrialization and the diversification of agriculture would remain as general objectives, but the drive would no longer be to accomplish these goals immediately or simultaneously. For those sectors of production not related to agriculture, industrialization was postponed until after 1970, except, of course, for the projects already begun which could not be abandoned without hurting the economy. In this manner the plans to develop iron and steel industries were postponed for a second period. The present and immediate goal is the development of agricultural production to meet internal needs and for exports. This agricultural production, especially that destined for exports, would be the major source of capital accumulation for the future development of industrialization. A special effort would be made to produce the items with greater earning capacity abroad, keeping in mind priority studies and the agreements with the socialist countries, and without considering the laws of the international market.

The fundamental pillar of this new economic policy is sugar production. This is the number one sector of the Cuban economy in terms of foreign trade. Schematically, Cuba will produce industrial goods in the socialist countries and those countries will produce their sugar and other tropical products in Cuba. . . .

This general strategy of development based on the need to accept historic facts has been translated into concrete priority plans. Thus, the first plan centers on sugar production, the second deals with foodstuffs production, then to be followed by the production of tobacco, coffee, and tropical fruits. Finally, a particular plan for industrial development, closely related to agriculture, is under way.

What are the results up till now and what can be foreseen for this new economic strategy? What can be said about its logic? The considerable investment in agriculture leads us to think that in five to ten years Cuba will have the most modern agriculture in Latin America. The first fruits of this policy are encouraging: in 1965, 1966, and 1967 Cuban agricultural production returned to its historic levels. The leap in sugar production has been of some importance since 6 million tons were produced in 1965. . . .

Cattle production increases regularly and in some sectors has made spectacular progress. Finally, fruits and tobacco production also move forward. The production of agricultural foodstuffs advances slowly or even remains at past levels. Naturally, to judge these results we must not forget the extraordinary effort at capital accumulation taking place today in Cuba's agriculture. Perhaps one could even consider such an effort excessive; nonetheless, that is the price to be paid to overcome underdevelopment. . . .

12

THE SOCIALIZATION OF THE MEANS OF PRODUCTION IN CUBA

Michel Gutelman

I. THE LAND REFORM

The law of May 17, 1959, which established land reform, was preceded by the law of October 1958, given in the mountains of Oriente at a time when the revolution had not yet achieved power. In the eyes of the leaders, the two laws were identical, but the first one was different from the second in that it included some important tactical objectives: it intended, on the one hand, to mobilize more intensively the small farmers in order to incorporate them massively in the ranks of the revolution and, on the other, to neutralize the reactionary forces who were to be kept expectant.

This first law conceded "land ownership to the tiller"; it was very careful about not mentioning the problem of foreign-owned properties. Likewise, it was ambiguous about the fate reserved for the latifundia, saying simply that they would be forbidden, but without specifying any formal limits to the extension of privately owned land.

The tactical results obtained corresponded entirely to expectations: from October 1958 to January 1959, the mass of peasants and the agricultural proletariat, persecuted by

Taken from Chapter 2 of *L'Agriculture socialisée à Cuba* by Michel Gutelman (Paris: François Maspéro, 1967), with permission of the author and the publisher. Also published in *Agrarian Problems and Peasant Movements in Latin America,* edited by Rodolfo Stavenhagen (Garden City: Doubleday Anchor Books, 1970).

Michel Gutelman is an agricultural economist who teaches at the Ecole Pratique des Hautes Etudes in Paris and who spent several years as an adviser to the Cuban government.

Batista's troops, rallied to the revolutionary cause and thus contributed to the rapid disintegration of the regime. Simultaneously, the lack of specifications in the law about the future of the latifundia led many national and foreign landowners to believe that, according to a solidly established political tradition in Cuba, the law would never be implemented. Consequently, several large landowners aided the *guerrilleros* of the "26th of July Movement" in the hope that their properties would not be affected after the fall of the Batista regime, which they now saw coming closer. Three months later, in January 1959, their hopes began to fade, and seven months later, on May 17, 1959, they fell apart completely.

1. *The Land Reform Law* (*May 17, 1959*)

The principal characteristics of the law of May 17, 1959, at least formally, are those of a reformist political document. Thus it could be placed together with the basic land reform texts of Mexico in 1911 and of Bolivia in 1952. Only some of its provisions are clearly more radical.

The land reform law is opposed to the existence of latifundia, but also to that of minifundia. The first aspect has become classical in many Latin American land reform projects. The second aspect is much less so. Probably drawing upon the Mexican and Bolivian experiences, the Cuban revolutionary legislator wanted to prevent the excessive fragmentation of the land which, when technological levels are low, lead inevitably to an inefficient agriculture. In order to forestall this roadblock, the law adopts the notion of "vital minimum" (2 *caballerías* = 27 hectares) and forbids the partial or total subdivision or alienation of the redistributed land.

Latifundia are prohibited. The maximum area that a physical or moral person may own is fixed at 30 *caballerías* (402.6 hectares). Land in excess of this limit, which belongs to one owner, must be expropriated and distributed among landless peasants or those who own less than the vital minimum. Properties up to 30 *caballerías* in size are not expropriable, except for those parts that may have been rented out to tenant farmers or sharecroppers or that are occupied by *precaristas* (squatters).

The land reform law is concerned with the economic efficiency of agriculture. In order to avoid a decrease in production and productivity, which was, however, expected at the beginning, and in order to maintain and accelerate, on the contrary, the development of agriculture, the law permits various exceptions to the expropriation of latifundia and large properties. These exceptions are due to concern over the need to maintain "model" agricultural enterprises. The text is, indeed, quite liberal, in that it considers as model farms those on which yields are 50 per cent higher than the national average, when only crops are concerned, and those cattle ranches where the number of head of cattle per *caballería* is simply higher than the national average. In no case, however, may these enterprises possess more than 100 *caballerías* (1,342 hectares).

The same concern over technical and economic efficiency was the reason, at least partly, for the relatively novel decision in the history of agrarian reforms not to subdivide or redistribute all of the lands belonging to the expropriated latifundia. We shall see that this decision led to the formation of an important state sector which was not formally outlined in the text of the law. Finally, according to the law, the National Institute of Agrarian Reform (INRA) was not to limit itself merely to the distribution of land to the small peasants, but was also designed to offer them powerful technical and economic aid. This naturally implied a certain state control over the small farmers, which was justified by the futility of granting the poor peasants lands which they would be unable to farm adequately because of lack of resources and of technical assistance.

We have shown that the Cuban Revolution, due to the economic structures that existed at the time, was oriented toward "national recuperation." In the agrarian reform law, the nationalist aspect is evident; but we need not exaggerate its influence. In order to really suppress the latifundia, it was necessary to affect foreign-owned landholdings. But the law treats of these in the same fashion as it does with Cuban properties. Thus, Article 15 stipulates that only Cuban citizens may acquire rural property; but it does not state anywhere that the foreign landowners of holdings which are within the maximum size limit permitted by the law, are not allowed to keep their property. Furthermore, exceptions similar to those referring to farm units with higher-than-national-average productivity are also set down for foreign-owned enterprises which, under certain conditions, may possess up to 100 *caballerías*. Thus it is not the agrarian reform law itself which eliminates foreign property from Cuba, but a series of legal measures taken between 1960 and 1961, to which we will return later.

Land reform was to be cheap. The law did not say that social justice was to be established by drawing upon the public budget; neither were the reform beneficiaries made to pay for land distribution. On the financial question, the law essentially determined that the estimated value of the land for purposes of indemnification, was based on the owners' own assessment for tax purposes. As can be imagined, declared values were very low, and the amount of indemnification calculated on this basis was not a danger to the public budget. On the other hand, it was decided that indemnification would be paid through the issue of "Land Reform Bonds" payable in twenty years with an interest of 4 per cent.

Finally, the land reform was to be efficient and quick. The experience in other Latin American countries proved that a law which was consciously or unconsciously ill conceived permitted the sabotage of the land reform process itself.[1] The law of May 17 therefore included a series of precautions designed to prevent shipwreck on the reefs of legal procedures or judicial maneuvers.

Fundamentally, the law prevented the fraudulent reconstitution of latifundia by prohibiting all sales (except to the state), exchange and transfers of privately owned land. All divisions, sales or legal acts of various kinds, carried out after the revolution came to power (January 1959) were declared null. The

---

[1] See particularly R. Dumont, *Terres Vivantes* (Paris: Plon, 1961), pp. 86–101. English edition, *Lands Alive* (New York: Monthly Review Press).

renting of land that had been distributed by the land reform
and the creation of agricultural companies the shares of
which were not nominal, were forbidden. In the calculation of
the maximum area in the hands of a single owner, all of
his properties were taken as a whole and not each unit by itself.
Finally, in order to prevent delays in the process of expropriation and redistribution of land itself, the judgment and
powers attributed to the National Land Reform Institute
(INRA) were such that the large landholders were hardly able
to slow down or distort the land reform process by getting it
bogged down in legal formalities.

2. The Political Process of the Agrarian Reform

In June 1959, INRA applied the provisions of the law
which had just been published, and divided the island into
twenty-eight Agrarian Development Zones (ZDA). These
became an intermediate administrative unit between the
municipality and the province, in which the concrete process
of confiscation and redistribution of land to the small peasants was to take place. The implementation of the agrarian
reform was entrusted to the Rebel Army as well as to civilian
revolutionaries.

The expropriations and land distribution began rather
slowly. Ten months after the promulgation of the law, not
more than 850,000 hectares had been confiscated, and
only 40,200 hectares had been distributed to 6,000 beneficiaries. At this rate, it would have taken twenty years to
satisfy the needs of some 150,000 potential beneficiaries.

However, in January 1960 the rhythm of confiscation and
distribution was suddenly accelerated. During the first half
of January, the latifundia in the center and the east of the
island were attacked. In one week, more than 600,000 hectares
were confiscated. By June 1961, 3,800,000 hectares had been
expropriated and 101,000 peasants had obtained property
titles to 2,725,000 hectares.[2]

The acceleration of the rate of land confiscation and dis-

[2] Juan Marinello and Nikolai Petertsev, *Los rasgos principales del
período de transición del capitalismo al socialismo* (Havana, 1963), p. 63.

tribution was due to both internal and external causes. It was related to the level of development of the productive forces and to the relations of production of Cuban agriculture, as well as to certain aspects of the class struggle on the international level. These factors of radicalization of the agrarian reform changed its essential character to such a point that the legal text itself was quickly left behind, as far as the original objectives of the revolutionary forces were concerned.

The purpose of the law of May 17, 1959, was, above all, to create and strengthen a small peasant bourgeoisie. It did not attempt to suppress private property of the land, nor to create state farm enterprises. But the prohibition of latifundia, given the limited number of potential beneficiaries of land distribution, and the limited amount of land which was granted to them, implied that an important part of the confiscated area would not be distributed individually. This specific situation came about because of the high degree of land concentration and the relative scarcity of farm units considered according to the criteria of the "vital minimum."

The law of May 17 had foreseen this situation: it stipulated that the expropriated land which was not granted individually would be handed as indivisible property to cooperative groups. The National Agrarian Reform Institute was to create, develop and supervise these cooperatives. The Institute also had the obligation to provide them with important technical and financial assistance. However, it would be an error to suggest that the creation of cooperatives was a consciously taken political first step toward ulterior state control of agriculture. A careful reading of the texts shows well that the revolutionary leaders who wrote the law did not conceive of the cooperatives as a form of state-run enterprise. True, INRA reserved the right to appoint a "coordinator," who was administratively dependent upon the Institute, to work together with the elected administrator. But this was considered as a provisional measure, the reasons for which were political (to prevent the sabotage of the reform by potential agents of the expropriated latifundists) as well as technical (frequent lack of capability among the elected managers).

In practice, and contrary to the explicit intentions of the law, the cooperative sector became very quickly closely dependent upon the state. The coordinators appointed by INRA, who were frequently members of the Rebel Army, became more important than the elected administrators, mainly due to their greater prestige. Very often, indeed, the elected administrator and the appointed coordinator were one and the same person. Finally, the centralization of power in these cooperatives was strongly accentuated because of the economic blockade which made the administrative distribution of scarce resources a necessity. We shall return to this point later.

But to this "intrinsic" factor, if it can be called that, of socialization (a surplus of confiscated land in relation to the number of beneficiaries), were added other factors linked to the conditions of the class struggle on the national and international levels.

The sudden acceleration of land confiscations in January 1960 can be explained by the systematic opposition of the large cattlemen to the new social policy. After the first confiscations, they refused to buy cattle from the small breeders, who were forced to sell because they lacked sufficient pastures for fattening. Faced with this menace of a boycott, which was about to create a political crisis due to the economic strangulation of a social class which had been favorable to the revolution, the state was forced to buy cattle. As it did not itself own sufficient land for feeding these animals, it was forced to rapidly expropriate the necessary pastures. For the first time, it was necessary to disregard the formal stipulations of the law, as in the case of the province of Camagüey, where cattle ranches were expropriated which had benefited from the exceptions established in the law.

If the revolutionary government had not acted as it did, if it had hesitated to pursue firmly its policy of economic and social reforms, it is probable that, even among the small peasantry, a movement of political withdrawal would have taken place, the result of which would have been, under the menace of sabotage by the large landowners, to slow down considerably the process of expropriation.

In the sugar sector, the process of acceleration of the agrarian reform, leaving behind the text of the law, was identical. Here, however, the socioeconomic links between the Cuban sugar sector and the American economy contributed in giving the class struggle a new aspect. In July 1960, the Congress of the United States authorized President Eisenhower to decide a halt of Cuban sugar imports. It was no longer a particular class of the population (the small cattle-breeders) but the whole Cuban nation which was threatened by economic strangulation.

This external menace was so much stronger in that internally it was based on the economic and political power of the American sugar-mill owners. Of 165 sugar mills on the island, 61 belonged to North Americans; they were the most important because they handled approximately 50 per cent of the annual sugar production. Their natural reticence in supporting the Cuban government only pushed the revolution into adopting a firmer attitude: nationalization; or else forcing it, through compromise, to betray the sociopolitical objectives it had set itself. Thus it was that the Law of Nationalization of foreign-owned enterprises (Law No. 851) established on July 6, 1960, the confiscation of all American enterprises. Under this law, all sugar mills and their attendant land, as well as all foreign-owned agricultural enterprises, were seized. A part of this land would have been expropriated anyway under the agrarian reform law, but less completely and less brutally. It should be noted that the payment of indemnification was foreseen; but it was tied to the suspension of the sanctions taken by the U.S. against Cuba.[3]

The "sugar bourgeoisie" of Cuba, supported morally and militarily by the United States, also passed over into open counterrevolution: fire by arson of sugar fields and public

[3] Article b, paragraph 5, of the law stipulates, in fact: "For the payment of indemnification the Cuban state will create an Indemnification Fund which will annually be provided with 25% of the foreign currency obtained through the sale to the United States of sugar in excess of 3,000,000 tons and at a price not inferior to 5.75 cents per English pound; the special account opened in the National Bank of Cuba will be called 'Fund for the payment of goods and enterprises of the United States.'"

buildings, assassination attempts and various kinds of sabotage took place during 1960 and 1961. In reprisal to this hostile attitude which endangered the national economy, the government decided upon the nationalization of all the large private enterprises in the country. The Law of October 13, 1960 (No. 890), thus resulted, in the agro-industrial sector, in the confiscation of about a hundred sugar mills and their attendant land—in other words, approximately one million hectares. Finally, an amendment to Article 24 of the Constitution allowed the confiscation of the property of moral or physical persons who left the country or who carried out activities judged to be counterrevolutionary.

If we add to these various confiscations those which were effected according to the law on the "recuperation of ill-gained wealth," as well as "voluntary sales" and "donations" to INRA,[4] we see that the land affected in 1961 amounted

TABLE 1

Land Expropriations
Situation in May 1961[5]

	Surface in Hectares	%
1. Agrarian Reform Law	1,199,184	27.0
2. Recuperation of Ill-gained Wealth Law	163,214	3.7
3. Donations to INRA	322,590	7.3
4. Voluntary sales and article 24	581,757	13.1
5. Nationalization law (No. 851)	1,261,587	28.4
6. Nationalization law (No. 890)	910,547	20.5
	4,438,879	100.0

[4] The Law of "Recuperation of Ill-gained Wealth" (December 22, 1959) allowed for the confiscation of the wealth of Batista and his family, as well as that of people who enriched themselves notoriously under cover of the dictatorship.

"Donations" came principally from municipalities and a number of revolutionary peasants who gave their land to INRA.

"Voluntary sales" were carried out by proprietors who renounced their rights to land which they were authorized to keep under the agrarian reform law. These sales still continue at present, but of course at a slower rhythm.

[5] *Source:* Departamento Legal de Tierras, INRA.

to 4,400,000 hectares, of which only 1,199,000 hectares were expropriated according to the agrarian reform law.

3. The Balance of Interventions in the Agrarian Sector

Of the total amount of land confiscated between 1959 and 1961, the area administered in some way or other by the state represented about 3,816,600 hectares. By the end of 1962, it represented 3,903,000 hectares, if we disregard certain unregistered woodlands.

The different laws which permitted the confiscation of privately owned lands all respected those farm units which were smaller than thirty *caballerías* in size (except of course those which belonged to foreigners and to sentenced counter-revolutionaries, and which were nationalized in their entirety). At that time, the land tenure situation appeared as follows:

State sector:	3,903,300 hectares – 44%	
Private sector:	5,173,800 hectares – 56%	

The private sector itself was composed of properties of less than five *caballerías,* representing 36 per cent of the agricultural surface, that is, 3,331,000 hectares, and of properties holding between five and thirty *caballerías,* representing 20 per cent of the agricultural surface, that is, 1,863,000 hectares.

On October 13, 1963, a second agrarian reform law was promulgated. It affected farm units of over five *caballerías* in size and thus transferred to the state 1,800,000 hectares of land. The proportion of land between the state sector and the private sector was thus turned around:

State sector:	5,513,700 hectares – 60.1%	
Private sector:	3,563,100 hectares – 39.3%	

From that point on, more than 60 per cent of the sugar fields and 60 per cent of the cattle were in the hands of the state sector.

The fundamental and official reasons for this second intervention of revolutionary power were political. They were linked to the elimination of the economic base of the internal counterrevolution, which was at that time involved in guerrilla warfare in the center of the island. But, as we shall see later, this second agrarian reform certainly was also the result of purely technical causes, in the sense that it permitted a consolidation of state farm units which up to then had been much dispersed and fragmented.

Between 1963 and 1967, land tenure underwent various transformations. A number of arbitrarily confiscated holdings, particularly in the province of Matanzas, were returned to their owners after 1962, whereas others, which had been more or less abandoned, were confiscated. Anyway, these were minor changes and did not affect the relative figures quoted above.

It is now useful, before studying the organization and management of the agrarian property that was restructured through the intervention of the revolutionary government, to examine briefly the historical evolution of the different kinds of land tenure forms that were set up.

II. THE TYPES OF STATE FARMS AND THE CONTROL OF THE PRIVATE SECTOR (1959–1967)

In the first place, we shall examine the different types of state farms which were established successively on the land that was confiscated but not redistributed; then, the organization and forms of control of the private sector; then the very particular, but brief, status of "Administered Farm Units"; finally, the cooperative sector.

1. State Farms

The status and name of the enterprises organized on confiscated land varied from year to year, from 1959 to 1963.

SOCIALIZATION OF THE MEANS OF PRODUCTION

From then on, the state sector became stabilized, found its equilibrium and definitive form.

During a first phase, from 1959 to 1961, three types of agricultural enterprises were organized by INRA: the "Cooperatives," the "Farm Units under Direct Administration," and the "Sugar Cooperatives."[6]

The term "Cooperatives" was a misnomer for the units of the first type, because they were neither well organized nor did they have a well-defined status. In fact, they were agricultural production units placed under the authority of administrators, generally soldiers of the Rebel Army, appointed by INRA. The complete transformation of the public administration shortly after the revolution came to power, helped to give them, if not formally, at least in fact, great technical and organizational autonomy. The majority of these "Cooperatives" were former large specialized or semi-specialized landholdings. They generally derived their name from their principal activity, thus: "Tomato-producing Cooperative," "Cooperative of Sisal Fiber Producers," "Cattle-raising Cooperative," etc. The constitution of these "Cooperatives" came about through the double need of quickly giving work to the unemployed and of raising production of foodstuffs through the opening up to cultivation of hitherto uncultivated land.

The "Farm Units under Direct Administration," the second type of state farm, were created almost exclusively on former large cattle ranches. Their creation was decided upon when the state was forced to buy the cattle of the small breeders who were in danger of being economically strangled by the latifundists. These production units were managed by administrators appointed by INRA, and their operation depended quite closely upon the directives given by the Institute. Given the way the land was acquired, as well as the type of organization and the kind of payment received by the workers, who were salaried laborers, these units could well be considered as true state farms.

The massive nationalizations of July and October 1960

[6] We have translated as "Sugar Cooperative" the Cuban expression: "Cane Cooperative."

were to lead to the creation of a type of production unit, the life of which was longer than that of the ones mentioned previously: the Sugar Cooperatives. These enterprises were given a specific statute which at least formally likened them to real production cooperatives.

The directive organ of the "Sugar Cooperative" was the "board of directors," elected by the general assembly of the cooperators. The board was directed by a "coordinator." Every member of the cooperative, if he had been a permanent worker of the former latifundium, could vote and be elected to office. In return for his labor, he received a monthly wage, called "advance," which was supplemented at the end of each cycle by an amount corresponding to the distribution of profits.

In fact, the general assembly, the board of directors and the coordinator did not have full powers to decide about the cooperative's policy. The state, in fact, had decided, in view of the fact that the members lacked administrative experience, and in order to prevent "enterprise egotism," to appoint an administrator next to the elected coordinator, who received and implemented instructions from INRA. All important decisions had to be taken both by the coordinator and the administrator. Such a two-headed management could not but lead to management difficulties and proved to be particularly unstable. In reality, the system evolved rapidly toward a transfer of power from the elected coordinator to the appointed administrator. This tendency of the concentration of power in the hands of the administrative hierarchy of INRA was reinforced further by the policy of diversification of agricultural production and by the economic blockade. Both implied an effort at coordination of the technical and quantitative guidelines, as well as of the distribution of scarce products and resources. In fact, the sugar cooperatives rapidly changed from almost authentic cooperatives, which they were at the beginning, into real state enterprises subordinated to administrative management.

This tendency toward a centralized and administrative management was accelerated after June 1961, due to the decision to create the "People's Farms." These farms resulted from

the simple fusion of the cooperatives and the Farm Units
under Direct Administration, in terms of their legal statutes,
as well as geographically and as to their organization.

The People's Farm was a unit of production comparable
to the Soviet sovkhoz. The land belonged to the state, labor
was paid for independently of the results obtained by the
farm, on a wage basis, without any participation in eventual
profits. Investments, working capital and social funds were
financed by the general budget of INRA, which in turn simply received a part of the national budget.

Every People's Farm was headed by an administrator appointed by INRA and by an administrative council. The administrator and the council were responsible for the management of the People's Farm and received their instructions
from a "General Administration of People's Farms," located
in Havana, through a local administrative agency, the "Provincial Delegation of People's Farms."

The reason for the transformation of the cooperatives and
Farm Units under Direct Administration into state farms,
and the progressive abandoning of the cooperative formula,
was principally technical, as we have said. On the one hand,
it became more and more necessary to assure a centralized
distribution of rationed means of production, and on the
other, to coordinate technical assistance and the plans for
agricultural diversification. When in April 1961 the socialist
character of the revolution was officially declared, the ideological factors became increasingly important. It is difficult to
state that they constituted an important factor in the evolution toward state control, inasmuch as they reflected an inevitable evolution, given the political and social situation in
which Cuba found itself at that time.

In August 1962, the sugar cooperatives were transformed
into "Sugar Farms." This legal transformation into state
farms only legalized a *de facto* situation. The two-headed
power structure, which had become merely formal, was
eliminated, and only the administrator was maintained. A
wage policy identical to that of the People's Farms was established, and the centralized nature of management was ac-

centuated by giving the former administrative structure a pyramidal form similar to that which existed in the "General Administration of People's Farms."

These two administrative organs were nevertheless quite independent of each other, because one of them existed in the area of sugar production and the other in the area where agricultural diversification prevailed. Each one had its own specific problems. However, at the moment when this decision was taken, the difference between Sugar Farms and People's Farms tended to decrease, because the former participated increasingly in the effort of diversification, whereas the latter had been frequently called upon, for technical reasons (for example, if they owned land near sugar mills) to plant sugar cane.

Whatever the reasons, we can say that after 1961 in deed —and, since 1962, institutionally—almost all of the confiscated land which had not been redistributed, was managed within the framework of the state farms. Their management was highly centralized and was carried out through two quite distinct administrative structures.

In 1962, the 280 People's Farms covered 2,844,000 hectares, and the 600 Sugar Farms covered 900,000 hectares. The size of the production units varied considerably: some People's Farms were no larger than 200 hectares, whereas others had up to 60,000 and even 90,000 hectares. The same can be said about the Sugar Farms.

This situation was due to the historical context of the agrarian reform, which had seized the latifundia as they existed at the time of confiscation, and had transformed them by and by into state farms, cooperatives, etc., not being able always to carry out rational consolidation of farm units, given the speed of the process. In 1962 there were about 120,000 permanent workers on the Sugar Farms and 200,000 on the People's Farms. These figures, however, are simply indicative and not exact, because statistics were deficient at that time.

In 1963 it was decided to reorganize the state sector once again. The administrative differences between People's Farms and Sugar Farms were eliminated. The two former types of

TABLE 2[7]

	Total	Less than 3,000 Has.	From 3,000 to 7,000 Has.	From 7,000 to 12,000 Has.	From 12,000 to 18,000 Has.	From 18,000 to 25,000 Has.	More than 25,000 Has.
Pinar del Río[8]	31	4	10	6	4	2	5
Havana	16	6	5	1	2	1	1
Matanzas	25	5	10	3	3	4	3
Las Villas	48	5	19	12	6	3	3
Camagüey	69	8	12	15	19	4	11
Oriente	90	8	33	13	16	8	12
	279	36	89	50	50	22	32

[7] *Estadísticas Agropecuarias*, Junta Central de Planificación, 1963, p. 4.

[8] It should be mentioned at this point that in Pinar del Río Province a group of ten People's Farms were administratively regrouped into one "*Agrupación*," called PR 2, and is considered as a single statistical entity. Likewise, in Havana Province, the "Agrupación Camilo Cienfuegos" really comprises eight People's Farms. Finally, in the Province of Las Villas, a particular administrative unit, known by the name of "Plan Escambray," contains 29 People's Farms, which are also considered as a single statistical entity.

farms got a single statute and were now simply called "State Farms."[9] Furthermore, they were regrouped into large regional administrative units called *Agrupaciones*. This form of regional organization, which was the exception before 1963, has since become the rule.

The *agrupaciones* represented a sort of federation of state farms, with highly centralized powers. In 1966, there were 575 state farms, regrouped into 58 *agrupaciones*,[10] whose area varied from 13,000 to 100,000 hectares.

This new organization, which is still valid at present, seems to be, on the one hand, the definitive form of organization of the state sector, and is, on the other, the point of departure of an effort at administrative decentralization which is quite original and continues to the present time.

[9] "Granjas Estatales."
[10] The original number was 80, but it was reduced in 1965.

2. *The Process of Control of the Private Sector*

Up to the second agrarian reform of 1963, there were in Cuba three types of private properties: the small peasants who owned less than 5 *caballerías* (67 hectares), the medium-sized agriculturists owning less than 10 *caballerías* (134 hectares), and the rich landowners who possessed up to 30 *caballerías* (402 hectares). Properties larger than this were considered to be latifundia and except for a few rare cases, had been eliminated.

TABLE 3[11]

Categories	Number of Properties
From 0 to 5 cab	150,140
From 5 to 10 cab	3,855
From 10 to 30 cab	5,970
	159,965

[11] Departamento Legal de Tierras, INRA, May 1961.

The poor peasantry, made up of old and new landowners (as a result of the land redistribution carried out by the revolutionary government), represented 94 per cent of the postrevolutionary private peasantry. The owners of farm units of less than 5 *caballerías* were the great beneficiaries of the agrarian reform. It must be pointed out in this respect that the revolution created at least two-thirds of the members of this part of the private sector.

The creation of small private properties was the result of the law of agrarian reform which, on the subject of the poor peasantry, stipulated that: (1) no one who owned less than 5 *caballerías* could be affected by the agrarian reform law and all of these owners remained in possession of their prop-

TABLE 4
Small Private Peasantry in 1961[12]

	Number of Owners	Surface of Old Properties of Less Than 5 Cab. (in Hectares)	Surface Granted to Land Reform Beneficiaries (in Hectares)	Total Surface (in Hectares)
Old owners of up to 5 cab	48,315	805,493	—	805,493
Land reform beneficiaries of up to 5 cab	101,805	—	2,725,910	2,725,910
Total number of properties of up to 5 cab	150,120	805,493	2,725,910	3,531,403

[12]During the year 1962, about 30,000 supplementary hectares were further distributed to the small peasantry, which increased the surface in the hands of owners of less than 5 *caballerías* to 3,563,000 hectares.

erties; (2) every agriculturist who did not own land received 2 *caballerías* of land free of charge and if he so wished he could buy additional land up to a total of 5 *caballerías*, if regional conditions permitted. (It should be pointed out that the distribution of land through sale was not very frequent, and that such land was never seriously paid for. This was due principally to a certain lack of financial discipline and to the difficulties encountered in assessing the value of land.)

The medium-sized farmers and the rich peasants who subsisted up to 1963 were not very numerous, inasmuch as the first group included 3,855 peasants, and the second, 5,970. It will be understood how politically easy it was for the revolutionary government, which had the support of the small peasantry, to eliminate these several thousands of landowners during the two agrarian reforms.

In contrast, the small peasantry, who were the first beneficiaries of the agrarian reform and represented a firm support of the revolution, were efficiently organized in new syndicalist structures.

From 1930 up to the time of the revolution, numerous farmers' syndicates had appeared. Quickly dominated by the large landowners, they became obligatory and thus veritable instruments of domination over the small peasantry. Thus a dozen trade-unions or syndicates were created, such as the Association of Rice Producers, the Association of Tobacco Producers, the Association of Cane Producers, etc.

Under the impact of social struggles, they broke up internally and disappeared spontaneously during 1960. On May 17, 1961, the revolutionary government, in order to replace these syndicates, created a single agricultural syndicate: the Association of Small Agriculturists, known in Cuba under the name ANAP.[13]

Organized along class lines, and no longer according to differences in the crops produced, ANAP was at first conceived as an instrument for the class struggle. Its first role was to fight against the counterrevolutionary activities of the former latifundists and the rich landowners. Only the peasants who owned less than 5 *caballerías* belonged to the Association, or exceptionally those medium-sized farmers who, during the struggle against Batista, had proven beyond a doubt their allegiance to the revolution. It must be pointed out that membership in ANAP was not obligatory and that even today not all the private farmers belong to it. However, we may consider that about 90 per cent of all small private farmers are members of the union.

The Association was organized according to the same pyramidal model of all socialist mass organizations: at the base there was the "nucleus" of about one hundred small peasants. These nuclei were federated on a regional basis, and then on the provincial level. A national directorate, located at INRA till 1964, but which became autonomous thereafter, supervised the whole organization.

Very quickly, ANAP began to play an economic role. Basically this consisted of orienting private production according

[13] Asociación Nacional de Pequeños Agricultores.

to the national agricultural plans. Later, these economic activities became more diversified and widened their scope. The Association became the normal channel through which credit, scarce materials or spare parts, and so forth, were distributed. Though ANAP cannot be considered strictly as an organization for the control of private agriculture, given the fact that it was after all still a private sector of agriculture, the administrative control of the state over the organization was such that at least theoretically it could exercise strict control over a large part of the production in this sector.

This kind of intervention was, however, not contrary to the immediate monetary interests of the small producers, inasmuch as the production directives generally affected crops which were much in demand and whose prices were formed freely at least in part.[14]

3. Administered Farms

Between 1961 and 1962 a certain number of small, and particularly of medium-sized farm units, were abandoned by their owners. A part of these were simply incorporated into the different existing kinds of state farms, while another part, even though nationalized, was given over to private administration. This explains the name of these enterprises: "administered farms"[15] (it being understood that they were managed by the private sector). This was an original management formula which was justified by two factors.

In the first place, the farm units thus placed under the administration of the private sector were relatively small, fragmented and sometimes distant from the state farms. Under these conditions, it would have been difficult to manage them in the same fashion as the state farms, given the cost of running the administrative apparatus which directed every social-

---

[14] These free markets were allowed to function only in the countryside. Elsewhere, the prices fixed by the state buying organizations, even if their relationships were not always satisfactory, were usually remunerative.

[15] *Fincas administradas.*

ist enterprise. A first factor which determined that these units were handed over to the private sector for their management, was thus the difficulty of physically integrating these plots of land in the state sector.

The second factor was of an experimental nature. The non-integration of these dispersed farm units into the state sector was also the result of a desire to experiment, without any dogma, with the possibility of organizing small farm units and to compare their results with those of other state units which, according to the orthodox theory, were large in size. Furthermore, by having these farms managed by individual peasants, an experimental answer was to be given to the polemical issue which developed between those who thought that the "peasants" were better qualified to run farms than the "administrators," and those who believed the contrary.

The administered farms, whose number varied greatly and which in 1963 represented approximately 170,000 hectares, were managed from the beginning by a board of directors and a manager selected from among the basic nuclei of the regional ANAP. Later, as their number increased, it became necessary to organize a system of control and coordination. Thus within the administrative structures of ANAP a hierarchical and centralized substructure arose which was concerned with the management of these farms.

In 1963, when the second agrarian reform took place, these administered farms disappeared and were integrated into the state farms, at the level of the *agrupaciones*. There were two reasons for this:

· With the incorporation of private units of over five *caballerías* in size into the state sector, the technical reasons (their small size, their fragmentation and dispersion) for the creation of these administered farms disappeared, because very often, after the second agrarian reform, they found themselves physically located within the area of the newly nationalized enterprises;

· The experiment of having small units administered by "peasants" appeared to be negative; their results were no better than those of the large state farms.

In fact, inasmuch as the functioning of the administered

farms was managed through administrative structures similar to those of other state farms, that is to say, in a strongly hierarchical and centralized fashion, the experiment did not really allow the economic potential of these units to come to the fore. At best, it was able to demonstrate the weaknesses inherent in all strongly centralized management systems.

4. The Cooperative Sector

One of the political roles assigned to ANAP was the formation of a socialist conscience among the small peasants. Particularly, the Association was charged with the diffusion of socialist ideas concerning the form of agricultural exploitation considered as most efficient: the agricultural production cooperative.

Thus, in 1961 a statute of "Agricultural and Cattle-Raising Societies"[16] was adopted, which is the legal framework within which real cooperative production units were to function. These must be formed by small farmers who voluntarily contribute their land and their means of production in order to work in common. The revolutionary government has always been very careful in this field, and it does not wish to accelerate the process of collectivization, recognizing the need to turn this sector into an example in order to guarantee the efficiency of future cooperative agriculture.

Consequently, the cooperative sector is still very limited to this day. Its development is very slow; the state, as a matter of fact, holds it back rather than stimulates it. In 1963, there were 230 "Agricultural and Cattle-Raising Societies," all of them very small, almost family groups. They covered about 17,000 hectares, of which 7,000 were contributed by the members and 10,000 by the state. In 1966 there were 270 cooperatives, covering about 20,000 hectares. These production cooperatives work along the same lines as cooperatives that one can find in any capitalist country. There is no direct intervention in their administration or management. At most,

[16] *Sociedad Agropecuaria.*

the production plans of each cooperative are supervised by ANAP in the same fashion as those of the private peasants. An important part of the produce may be marketed on the free market. Profits from sales to the state remain entirely in the hands of the cooperators, who are nevertheless obliged to invest a certain part every year. All questions relating to material supplies and production plans are handled with ANAP.

Let us also point out that other kinds of cooperatives were created with private farmers: particularly 537 credit and service cooperatives with about fifty thousand members.

Cuban agriculture, both the state and the private sectors, has thus always been characterized, in large measure, by strong administrative centralization and a rather strict compartmentalization into different sectors.

13

REPORT ON THE SUGAR HARVEST*

Fidel Castro

I would like to begin by explaining how the plan for the ten million tons came about.

Ever since we opened trade relations with the Soviet Union, following the aggression of the United States which deprived us of our sugar quota, the USSR purchased the sugar which had been shut out of the U.S. market.

The first sugar it purchased was paid for at more or less the going price on the international market.

As you know, part of our sugar is sold on what is known as the free market, and another part is sold through trade agreements with different countries. Sugar prices are subject to fluctuation, but usually the prices stipulated in the trade agreements are higher than those of the free market. A large part of the world's sugar is marketed through trade agreements.

Our country needed oil, a whole series of raw materials, foodstuffs and equipment, and there was no place to get them other than the Soviet Union.

As a result, our imports from the USSR grew considerably, while our paying ability was limited. The amount of sugar we could sell it was limited, as also were some other products we sold it following the U.S. blockade.

Sugar was the most important product we exported, followed by certain amounts of minerals, small quantities of tobacco, etc. Sugar, nickel, small quantities of tobacco and rum were the basic export items of our country, the key lines.

As a result of conditions created by the Yankee blockade,

* Speech delivered on May 20, 1970. Translated by the Cuban Government. Reprinted from *Ediciones COR* (Havana), May 20, 1970, pp. 23–45.

it was very difficult for us to make purchases in other markets. We faced not only foreign exchange difficulties, but practical difficulties even when we had the foreign exchange.

We began purchasing a great number of items that were necessary for our economy from the socialist camp—and especially from the Soviet Union.

As a result of this and the needs of a developing country— we might even say of a disorganized country, as every country in the first stage of a revolutionary process is disorganized —our trade deficit with the Soviet Union grew larger with every passing year. And, since our import needs were growing and would continue to grow, because the development of the country required it—both to raise the standard of living even a little every year and to develop the economy of the country —studies on the development of our economy clearly indicated that imports would grow but that exports could not grow. Because, in addition to sugar, the nickel we exported to the Soviet Union was limited. This was because the capacity of our mining industry was limited. The equipment for mining and processing nickel is terribly expensive, and large investments are necessary over the years. Many years must be spent in research and planning, as well, before this equipment can be put into production.

Our other export items were also limited. There was only one item whose exports to the Soviet Union could be increased: sugar.

As a result of this, we proposed a long-term sugar export agreement to the Soviet Union, an agreement which would help meet the growing needs presented by our economy—and especially by our development.

Sugar was practically the only product whose export we could increase rapidly. First, because there was a certain amount of underutilized industrial capacity. Second, because there were many sugar mills which could increase their production with relatively small investments in new equipment— some of them, for example, had the equipment to handle more cane, but bottlenecks (which could be eliminated through relatively small investments in new equipment) kept production from rising. Moreover, we could lengthen the harvest period.

The original development plans of the Revolution called for exporting three million tons of sugar to the Soviet Union at a price of four cents a pound. This would be more or less 88 pesos a ton, and it would mean sugar exports of 264 million pesos.

When our import needs were studied, we saw that the gap between our imports and exports would widen with every passing year. If we limited our exports—even though three million tons was considered quite a substantial figure—the going market price being four cents more or less, it would have been practically impossible to establish any solid basis for the import increase which the country needed.

We therefore proposed a long-term agreement to the Soviet Union based on our possibilities for increasing sugar production.

As a result of the acceptance by the Soviet Government of the proposals made by Cuba, it was decided to gradually increase exports until the figure of five million tons of sugar was reached. The price was also upped, from 4 to 6.11 cents a pound.

The plans called for the value of our exports to increase from 264 to 672 million pesos.

The initial plan of three million tons of sugar to the USSR was part of a larger plan calling for a future production level of seven or seven and a half million tons of sugar a year.

With exports of five million tons at 6.11 cents a pound, the value of our exports would be increased by 408 million pesos.

We must say that the needs of a country are so great that even this huge increase was barely enough to enable us to establish trade relations which would meet our development needs.

We must take into account that our country uses up five million tons of fuel alone every year. Then there were the new electric plants, factories, equipment, raw materials and even foodstuffs to import, because we import large quantities of food from the Soviet Union—mainly cereals, and, of these, mainly wheat.

This was the reason, the need, for making a great plan for increasing our sugar exports. It was not the result of a whim or the desire to set ourselves difficult goals or obtain glory by producing ten million tons of sugar; rather, it was the result of a real need. And, also, it was the only possibility our country had, the only way through which—by taking full advantage of the land, increasing productivity per unit area, making full use of existing capacity, lengthening the harvest period and installing some new equipment—we could obtain a 400-million-peso increase in our exports.

This is the economic basis, the foundation for the plan of the ten million tons.

The proposed figure of three million tons was based on an overall production of seven or seven and a half million tons a year; when five million became the amount in question, it was necessary to increase production to about ten million tons —because the Soviet market was not the only one opened to us: there were other markets throughout the socialist camp— and our sugar exports increased. We had to meet the commitments we had assumed in the trade agreement we had made with the Soviet Union, which was very favorable to us; we had to meet the commitments we had undertaken in trade agreements with other socialist countries; and we had to meet our export commitments to the free market area and, also, our internal sugar consumption needs, which practically tripled. This is the origin of ten million tons.

And some people doubted that there were enough markets for the ten million tons. It wasn't a problem of markets. The problem facing our country ever since it began large-scale trade relations with the socialist camp—in spite of the blockade, in spite of the blockade!—has been one of production, not markets. Our country has enough markets for any amount of sugar it can produce.

This was the reason for our plan to increase sugar production to the 10-million-ton mark.

This required a program of gradual production increases, year by year; it also called for an investment program.

Of course, the ten million tons was to have been the culmination. Before that, we would have to produce 6, 7, 8 and

9 million tons, progressively. And in 1964, 1965, 1966, 1967 and 1968 the expected increases in sugar production did not take place—for various reasons. In some cases it was because of drought, and in others, lack of resources and also, shall we say, basically a lack of ability to organize and administer all those activities in order to obtain the expected increases.

In 1963 we had the smallest harvest in our history: 3,882,-000 metric tons. In 1964, 4,474,000. In 1965—it was the largest of this period—6,156,000. In 1966, 4,537,000. With the droughts, the harvest went up and down. In 1967, 6,236,000; in 1968, 5,164,000; and in 1969 it dropped to 4,459,000.

In 1968 we should have produced eight million tons and in 1969, nine million. All gradually.

In 1966, at the end of 1966—which had been a year with a very small harvest, of only 4,537,000 metric tons—a meeting of all the sectors of agriculture, industry and the Government was held to work out a serious plan, a peak-capacity plan, for increasing sugar production in the agricultural field so as to wind up with the 10-million-ton harvest and recover in two years the increases which should have been taking place over a six-year period.

At that moment our country had the prospect of having more resources made available to it. At the meeting, which was held on November 26 and 27, 1966, it was foreseen that in 1967 we still wouldn't be able to make great increases in the planting, because we lacked bulldozers. We had purchased some new equipment, but it wouldn't arrive until 1967. But in 1968—so very near 1970—we would have the resources and means for the planting, and, if we hadn't reached our goals for the other years—and, as it turned out, we were far from reaching them—we would have to make a supreme effort to reach our goal for 1970. Meanwhile, a program for mill expansion was developing along with this plan.

The agricultural—rather than the industrial—side of the process had always been considered the limiting factor in production. Actually, more sugar was not produced because there was a shortage of cane—not because there was any lack of mill capacity. That is, raw material for the harvest was lacking. Moreover, the milling equipment was under-utilized every year, even though the plans for winding up in 1970 with a 10-million-ton harvest were already under way.

The meeting which I mentioned was held in Santa Clara and was broadly representative. Shorthand notes were taken of all those long reports and analyses for use in making a precise study to determine exactly how much land had to be planted to cane; the expected yields; and the area, mill by mill—because there were some mills with surplus capacity and insufficient land, and others with plenty of land but little industrial capacity. In short, it was necessary to make the industrial and agricultural sides of the process mesh so that enough cane for the ten million tons would be available in 1970.

At the meeting the figures for the acreage that would have to be planted, the amount of cane needed for the 10-million-ton harvest in each province and the expected yields were all worked out. The meeting was detailed and all-encompassing.

This meeting was the takeoff point for the whole program that followed. Some very interesting things were reported at these sessions. There was a series of very interesting discussions on cane types. But the most important thing—what I want to bring out here—is the figures for planting and production that were agreed upon for the 1970, the 10-million-ton, harvest.

Over three and a half million acres were to be planted. The program went as follows; Oriente Province was to have 547.5 million cwt. of cane, with an approximate yield of 12.70 percent, to produce 3,196,000 metric tons of sugar. Camagüey was to have 499.875 million cwt. of cane, with a yield of 12, to produce 2,750,000 metric tons of sugar. Las Villas was to have 386 million cwt. of cane, with a yield of 12.54, to produce 2,225,000 metric tons. Matanzas was to have 180.5 million cwt. of cane, with a sugar yield of 11.90, to produce 987,000 metric tons. Havana, including the four mills which were transferred to its jurisdiction from that of Pinar del Río and which were to continue operating according to the plans assigned to them in Santa Clara, was to have 126.25 million cwt., with a sugar yield of 12, to produce

697,000 tons. Pinar del Río, not counting the mills which were removed from its jurisdiction, was to have 30 million cwt., with a sugar yield of 12, to produce 167,000 metric tons of sugar. This made a grand total of 10,027,000 metric tons of sugar.

Now, how were the sugar yields determined? A lot was said at the meeting about the agricultural side of the process, the cane yield. The sugar yield estimates were made by practically taking into account the historical yields. In part the historical yields and in part the yields of the capitalist period, taking two things into account: that the harvest would be a bit longer—in a long harvest it is difficult to get high yields—and that almost all the cane of the capitalist period was of types that are now obsolete as far as cane production and sugar yields go. The new types have been spreading rapidly.

The yield indicated for Oriente was 12.70, which was the same as that obtained in the capitalist harvest of 1952.

The capitalist harvest of 1952 was the largest one; that was the last year after the war in which there was an unrestricted harvest. It was the year of the coup d'etat, and after the men responsible for the March 10 coup took power, they announced it would be the last year of a free harvest. So the capitalists tried to cut every last stalk of cane. It is said that in some cases they even altered the figures, since the quotas they would receive in the future were to be based on the amount of sugar they produced that year. And that was when they produced their famous harvest of 7,298,000 metric tons of sugar, 96° basis, which was the largest one they ever turned out. And afterwards they even had to store 2 million tons of that sugar.

But we will consider these figures valid as far as the volume of total production goes.

Data on production and yields has been collected, province by province. And that year, with types of cane inferior to those we have today, they obtained a yield of 12.70 in the mills of Oriente Province. And that was set as the yield this year for Oriente.

Camagüey had a yield of 12.26 that year. However, it was assigned an approximate yield of 12. Only two provinces were assigned yields above those they had obtained in the 1952 harvest.

For example, the average nationwide sugar yield had been estimated roughly at 12.30 on that occasion.

I have been making a detailed study of all the data on each of the other provinces, and I have found that, although the nationwide yield was 12.30, some of the provinces historically—as a result of local climate and soil characteristics—should have yields above 12.30, while others will fall below it.

And we find that only two provinces. . . . Las Villas, whose sugar yield in the 1952 harvest was 11.98, was assigned a yield of 12.54. This was determined on the basis of the province's record in recent years.

On the other hand, Matanzas' recent record had been much lower. Whereas in 1952 it had had a yield of 12.17, the yield figure set in the Santa Clara meeting was 11.90—that is, lower than the 1952 yield.

In 1952 Havana Province had obtained a yield of 11.75. The figure set for the 1970 harvest was higher, 12 percent. This was determined on the basis of the province's record in recent years.

Therefore, two provinces should have had sugar yields higher than they had had in 1952: Las Villas and Havana.

One of the provinces, Oriente, should have had a similar yield, while the others—Camagüey, Matanzas and Pinar del Río—were expected to have lower yields than those they obtained in 1952.

Therefore, the sugar yield figures established in the Santa Clara meeting were not unreasonably high, as they accorded with what had been obtained with cane of lower quality.

As a matter of fact, the question of sugar yield was not a matter of great concern at that time, as we knew the excellent yield that could be obtained from the new cane varieties. Almost all of the cane that was being planted was of the new strains which already had been replacing the varieties grown during the capitalist era.

The largest capitalist harvest showed an average nationwide sugar yield of 12.25—or, to be more exact, 12.258; almost 12.26. The 1970 harvest, with higher-yield varieties of cane, was expected to show a yield of 12.30, broken down by province as indicated above.

Now, then, let's look at other figures, which correspond to the beginning of the harvest.

I forgot to mention that the total amount of cane needed for the 10-million-ton harvest was set at 1770.25 million cwt. in the Santa Clara meeting; 1770.25 million cwt. of cane.

Needless to say, we worked toward having a much larger supply of cane available, as it wouldn't be logical to limit our program to a bare minimum.

For this reason, we adopted the policy that in the provinces where there was some excess industrial capacity we would create a reserve supply of cane just in case some other province didn't meet its goal.

For example, that policy was adopted for the provinces of Havana and Matanzas. The problem of the limited amount of available land in these two provinces was the subject of much discussion in the Santa Clara meeting. The old argument that all of the land was already under cultivation, that there was neither water enough nor enough available land, was trotted out all over again.

But after that meeting we got busy, tried to look into all the possibilities that existed for increasing the supply of cane in Havana and Matanzas, as these two provinces otherwise would not make full use of their industrial capacities. And so an effort was made to create an additional supply of cane, over and above the planned amount, so as to produce more sugar.

The fact is that all the provinces were instructed not to limit their cane-planting programs to just the bare minimum, but rather to strive for overshooting their respective goals, set on the basis of the amounts needed for the 1970 harvest.

When the harvest was begun . . . There was a preliminary stage in the summer, and later, toward the end of October, the massive stage began.

In the meeting at the Chaplin Theatre we figured, according to estimates, on 1875 million cwt. of cane. This was the estimated amount of cane available for the harvest including what had been harvested last summer. A total of 45 million cwt. had been cut during that period. That period of early harvesting was necessary mainly in order to meet commitments the country had made to deliver specified amounts of sugar before the end of the year. That is the reason for that period of early harvesting.

In the meeting in the Chaplin Theatre we pointed out:

"We need 1825 million cwt. of sugarcane, with a yield of 11.75, in order to reach the ten million tons.

"According to existing estimates, the net amount of sugarcane is 1875 million cwt.

"We are aiming at a physical yield of 11.75. This will be approximately 11.90 to 11.95, on the basis of a polarization of 96, which is the historical figure—I should have said 'historical basis'—used in our country, and throughout the world, to measure sugar tonnage."

Then I added: "This means that our country has enough sugarcane on hand to produce 10.3 or 10.4 million tons of sugar," on the basis of the estimated 1875 million cwt. of cane, with a yield of 11.95, 96 basis, which was below what had been programmed in Santa Clara.

The truth of the matter is that we began the harvest assuming that there was an excess supply of sugarcane.

Notwithstanding this, the problem of the sugar yield was given great attention in that meeting, as in instructions, publications and other media and in my subsequent appearance on TV. I would like to read some of the principal paragraphs in which these points were mentioned at the Chaplin meeting.

I said, "A factor that contributes to a high sugar yield and counteracts the effects of a long—and, in some cases, early—harvest is the makeup of the sugarcane plant. In no previous year, in no previous harvest, has our country had such high-quality sugarcane, of both the early and intermediate-maturing types. Most of the sugarcane was of the 2878 variety —almost 80 percent was of that variety, which is a late-maturing type. On many occasions the need to cut this type of cane during the early months had an adverse effect on the sugar yield.

"However, by now the amount of sugarcane of the 2878

variety has been considerably reduced, and more than 50 percent of the existing sugarcane is of an early- or intermediate-maturing type." I could have added, "and of higher sugar yield."

We pointed out a number of factors which were very important for the harvest, and said, "With regard to the cutting of the sugarcane, a factor of primary importance is the cutting schedule. That means that all the sugarcane—of different varieties and different ages—must be cut according to schedule at each mill.

"Another point, of equal importance, a decisive point for the success of the harvest, is the question of the freshness of the cane, of the time that elapses between the cutting and the grinding of the cane.

"Everybody—all the workers, all the people—has heard that if the cut sugarcane lies around for days before reaching the sugar mill it suffers a loss in both weight and yield. We have heard this many, many times. However, it is quite possible that the vast majority of us do not know the full extent of the adverse effect such a delay may have on the sugar yield." And we pointed out some data taken from a study in Camagüey.

And I continued, "Thus, if the quantity of cane needed to produce ten million tons of sugar if brought to the mill within, say, 48 hours of being cut reaches the mills seven days after being cut, it would produce only approximately eight million tons of sugar.

"Just look at the difference: between an average of the two days and an average of seven days, the same cane needed to produce ten million tons of sugar would produce only eight million tons. This is not counting the inconveniences caused the industrial process by cane that takes too long to reach the mill, the problems of sugar inversion, which creates and multiplies the difficulties in the process.

"Therefore, it is important for everybody to know these figures and to recognize the decisive importance of bringing fresh cane to the mills and coordinating the effort and the work, organizing it and directing it so that we act in strict accord with these principles related to the time which elapses between the cutting and the grinding of the cane.

"At the same time, there are still many problems in the countryside—for example, the problem of the cane that is left on the ground after being cut, which at times amounts to as much as 5, 8 or 10 percent of the cane.

"Five percent, in a harvest of ten million tons, means enough sugarcane to produce half a million tons of sugar."

Later on we said, "None of these factors can be disregarded, none of these factors can be overlooked, because the amount of cane that is left on the ground or is dropped along the way to the mill can represent as much as a million tons of sugar.

"Thus, strict compliance with the standards established for cutting and loading cane also has a great influence on the sugar-making process."

Thus, from the very beginning, emphasis was placed on all those factors that might have anything to do with the sugar yield from the standpoint of the cutting of the cane, the cutting program, the freshness of the cane, the various strains, etc.

That is, we tried to combat and overcome every possible deficiency that might have an adverse effect on the sugar yield. Not so much attention was paid to the recovery problems in the sugar mills, because this had never been the problem. . . . In former years, good yields had been obtained in the sugar mills even without a cane-cutting program, without fresh cane, without any of these measures—measures which had never before been as much emphasized as they were for this harvest of 1970.

In the first months of the harvest—November and December—the sugar mills that were in operation were mainly those of Havana and Matanzas Provinces, and their yields were above the estimate for that date; the influence of the new strains of sugarcane was being felt.

The cutting of early-maturing cane was begun in practically every canefield in Havana Province on October 28.

Nevertheless, as soon as we noticed that some of the mills had low yields for one reason or another, we took measures to stop those mills. In other words, this was a policy aimed at keeping the sugar yields high from the very beginning, a policy that became more and more evident as time went by.

In December, Comrade Guillermo, in Oriente Province, informed us of the complications that were arising with regard to the new machinery in that province. He reported that the situation was complicated, that the installation of the new machinery was behind schedule and that this would consequently lead to problems with the harvest.

We went to Oriente Province, where we held a meeting with a great many of the comrades to analyze all the problems thoroughly. Comrade Almeida also went, and, with him, the comrades from industrial investments. An analysis was made of the situation, which, as early as December, was beginning to become complicated. At that time we had not yet thought of the possibilities for hauling cane in trucks, but there already were a number of mills that were going to end operations very late as a result of the delays that had occurred in December.

The Guiteras, Menéndez and Argelia Libre Sugar Mills had some cane accumulated as a result of the new machinery installed in previous years. Moreover, these sugar mills were the ones with the most surplus cane, where industrial problems were beginning to have an adverse effect on the harvest.

We began to adopt measures in that province as early as in December.

An analysis was made of every critical situation in every mill in that province. Decisions were made, because we saw clearly that we were going to have to deal with a harvest running into the rainy season, since the Guiteras and other mills would end their harvest in July. Therefore, the thing to do was to prepare ourselves from that moment on to carry on the harvest in the rainy season.

We began by analyzing the situation in the Manatí Sugar Mill—all the cane available, all the measures to be adopted, the topographical problems presented by the zone. . . . The Antonio Guiteras was scheduled to grind 51.75 million cwt. of cane.

The Guiteras had already milled 2.09 million cwt. of cane, with 49.75 million cwt. remaining to be ground as of December 4. The mill's daily grinding capacity as of December

15 was 115,000 cwt., as a result of the delay in new installations. From January 15 to 30 this would increase to 165,000; from February on, to 215,000, and, even with this schedule, as much as 7.5 million cwt. of cane would remain to be ground by July 30.

That is when we decided to look for means of transportation, to find railroad ties and build some 25 miles of railroad, so that the surplus cane could be hauled to other mills to be ground. The variant of the trucks had not come up yet. In other words, this meant, at best, a deficit of approximately 7.5 million cwt. of cane remaining to be ground, which would have to be hauled to other mills.

The same thing can be said about the Jesús Menéndez, Perú and Urbano Noris Sugar Mills. An analysis was made of the situation with regard to the new installations and the measures to be adopted. It was decided to call a halt on all road construction work on highways and mountain roads that was not directly related to the harvest, all the road-building equipment was concentrated on the building of roads for hauling cane in that province. This concentration of building equipment included the equipment which was getting ready to start the building of several dams. Several brigades were left to complete the building of the Sabanilla Dam, in Nipe, but the other dam construction brigades, with all their equipment, were given new work, one of them in the rice project and two on canefield roads. Thus, as early as December, measures were being taken to insure a constant supply of cane to the mills.

This was at the beginning of December. Things continued the same through the middle of the month: the mills in the province had three million cwt. of cane scheduled for grinding in December, but this was impossible to carry out, due to the problems of industrial delays. In fact, this even obliged us to put several mills in operation ahead of schedule, since deliveries of sugar had to be made, and the giant sugar mills were not grinding up to capacity.

The situation remained unchanged in January, and, therefore, things were getting worse. The railroad line in the Guiteras Sugar Mills was insufficient to handle the problem. Now it was not a matter of 7.5 million cwt. but almost 17.5 million cwt. of cane left over, and no solution was in sight. It was precisely on account of the complex situation in the Guiteras Sugar Mill that the idea of the trucks came up as a possible solution. In other words, we didn't have to depend on the railroad line, since the trucks allowed for more flexibility and could haul cane to some sugar mills—such as the Rio Cauto—which ended their operations early but with which it was impossible to make connection via railroad.

Then we went back to Oriente Province and made a study of the situation. We found similar problems in Camagüey and Las Villas, especially in connection with the sugar yield. It was obvious that if that pace kept up, with such yield. . . . We were concerned about two aspects of the sugar yield: first, and at that moment, because it was below its level, and, second because if all that cane was ground in July it would result in a lower yield.

An estimate was made of the amount of cane that remained and we came to the conclusion that it was necessary to reach a reasonable yield from that cane if we were to make the ten million tons. And also, of course, that if that yield continued and we had to depend on mills remaining in operation into August and September—because the Guiteras Sugar Mill wouldn't finish before September, despite the railroad line—it would be impossible to obtain the yield necessary for the ten million tons, which mean that the battle of the ten million tons would already be lost by the halfway mark. It was then that a considerable number of measures were adopted, especially with regard to Oriente Province.

I have forgotten to mention that, in order to speed up completion of installations in the sugar mills—the ones where there were delays—we decided to call upon the Communist Brigade of Cienfuegos—our best industrial construction brigade—and the entire Brigade was sent to Oriente.

This decision was adopted that same day, December 4, so that the members of the Communist Brigade, with their high level of awareness, work spirit and skill, would give the work of installation a real boost as a measure to help guarantee that those mills would grind all the cane they should grind.

Following that trip we made our television report on the situation.

At the time, even the estimate of available cane—1875 million cwt.—had been increased. Why? Because it had been raining in Camagüey and Las Villas—and even Oriente had heavy rain in January—but the rains were having an adverse effect on the sugar yield and this was one of the factors that were having a bearing on the problem.

Naturally, rain might also lead to an increase in the amount of available cane. Therefore, it was evident, according to the existing estimates, that there was a possibility of securing the ten million tons as long as, above all, we tried for high yields. And, of course, we decided on the intermill hauling of cane to avoid having to grind cane in July and have the yields drop in the final stage. A whole program was drawn up in keeping with the historical yield curve: several sugar mills that were ahead of schedule, that would have ended their harvest in mid-April, were stopped, and all the measures that were broadly explained on that occasion were adopted.

Additional measures were adopted later, since the situation was such and such at a specified moment and then became more complicated later. A decision was taken at the end of January or beginning of February based on the estimate that a certain mill would increase its grinding capacity by mid-February, but by mid-February, it remained the same, and the same in April and at the end of April. And so, every new delay in starting up new capacity obliged us to adopt new measures, new maneuvers.

On that occasion, we reported on the situation of the harvest, in which the strategy was aimed mainly at trying for a high sugar yield.

We explained at that time: "In the first place, difficulties in the harvest have shown up mainly in the provinces of Oriente, Las Villas and Camagüey. In the rest of the provinces —that is, Matanzas, Havana and Pinar del Río—the harvest is going well.

"In some provinces—Camagüey, for example—the problem is not in the daily grinding. The grinding in Camagüey Province has been going along satisfactorily. In Camagüey the main problem lies in some sugar mills which we may describe as critical and in their comparatively low sugar yields. I say 'comparatively low' because the sugar yield in Camagüey is more or less close to the province's historical yield. However, compared with the yields in Havana, Matanzas and Pinar del Río, this yield is low. In other words, while these provinces are attaining yields that are higher than their historical yield curve, Camagüey is not.

"In Las Villas Province, the yield is quite good, but there are problems with regard to the amount of cane being ground —and, above all, problems concerning several critical sugar mills.

"The greatest difficulties are concentrated in Oriente Province. These are related to the rate of grinding, in the first place, and, to a certain extent, to sugar yields.

"The harvest is an activity that is going on in 152 different places in the country. Abstract figures—that is, overall figures —are only of relative value. To evaluate an overall figure, it is necessary to break it down into its component parts for each of the points where the harvest is taking place.

"What does this mean? It means that one day the grinding rate may be a little low but if on that day the mills that have a surplus of cane but also have problems grind to capacity, even though the overall grinding figure may be a little low, this is not of major concern. There may even be a high rate of grinding in general in spite of the fact that the so-called critical mills have a relatively low grinding rate. In such a case, even though in its overall aspect the harvest is going along well in that province, its problems in reality are greater.

"However, there are mills with cane surpluses that do have industrial problems. These are the really critical mills, since those mills that are operating well can be speeded up to the maximum in grinding, thus saving time and solving the problem. But the mills with cane surpluses and industrial problems constitute a somewhat more complicated problem."

Then we spoke of how the harvest was progressing in the province from the standpoint of human effort, from the manpower standpoint:

"Let us go first into the problem in Oriente Province, since it is the most complicated.

"We have seen that 2.25 million cwt. and occasionally 2.5 million cwt. of cane were being ground in Oriente Province, and it became imperative that a higher grinding rate be attained in the province to carry out its harvest successfully. There were many who asked themselves what the problem was—whether it was a question of manpower, industrial difficulties or organization; why the yield in Oriente Province was not up to the plan; if there was a good cutting program; if fresh cane was being milled; and if the harvest was well organized or not.

"In order to investigate the problem of Oriente Province personally, we went to that province and spent nearly two weeks there. We had been there before, in December, getting an idea of the problems, such as delays with the new equipment in the mills, and adopting a series of measures to accelerate the completion of industrial installations.

"On this occasion we were able to pinpoint, with absolute objectivity, the fundamental problem in Oriente Province. Thus far it has not been a question of manpower or fresh or days-old cane delivered to the mills. It does not lie in any of these points.

"As for the spirit of the workers in Oriente Province it is simply magnificent. The work spirit of the cadres in the province appears to be very good.

"The cane is being ground in keeping with a program and it is being ground fresh.

"There is good organization in the harvest.

"Now, then, problem number one in Oriente is the new industrial equipment. That is something that is clearly evident.

"So that you may understand this, we must say that important expansion work was done in 20 mills in Oriente Province, out of a total of 39 mills."

I explained the situation of the mills, how much they would have to grind, the problem they faced, the percentage they had milled as of that moment—all of which was summarized in a paragraph reading: "Therefore, the main problem in Oriente is that those mills that were supposed to have a capacity of 2,918,750 cwt. really have a capacity at this moment of 2,305,500 cwt. Of these 20 mills, 16—the most important ones —that should have a capacity of 2,668,250 cwt. in reality have a capacity of 2,054,500 cwt., and have ground at 61.56 percent capacity."

The mills with no new industrial equipment had ground at 74.07 percent capacity.

Therefore, theoretically speaking, those 20 mills should have had a capacity of 2,918,750 cwt. Theoretically speaking, they had a capacity of 2,305,500 cwt., and in reality they were grinding at a little over 50 percent of that theoretical capacity. It was useless to talk of over two million. It was necessary to calculate 61.56 percent of 2,305,500 cwt. and that comes to less than one and a half million.

That was problem number one.

We explained the reasons for the delays and we said that some of the mill tandems had arrived late.

And, in fact, still more must be said: Some of the new equipment for mills in Oriente Province still hasn't arrived in this country, for reasons of course beyond our control. But the fact remains that some equipment for those mills still hasn't arrived.

Then we said, "The second problem in Oriente Province: the sugar yield is a long way from the goal that had been set by the comrades in that province.

"There are two things to be said about this. In our opinion the sugar yield goals set by Oriente were overly ambitious." That is, the sugar yield goals set were very high.

"For example, they had planned to reach a yield of 13.56 by the first ten days of February. After taking a series of measures, they have reached a yield of 11.56." That is, far removed from the estimated figure; however, as high as the estimate was, the actual results were too low.

And we pointed out something that was unquestionable: at that moment, it was clearly evident that Oriente Province would not be able to meet its goal of 3,196,000 metric tons of sugar, but that a real effort must be made to reach the three-million-ton mark.

We said, "In Oriente we aspire to an aggregate yield of

13.3 from what remained to be ground as of February 1. This is below what had been estimated for the mills in Oriente but perfectly in accord with the historical average yield and the quality of the cane."

Therefore, we cut down on the yield they had programmed and estimated that the cane remaining to be ground could reach a yield of 13.3 from February on, in order to reach the three-million-ton mark.

The yield in Las Villas had to reach 12.5 from February on. And the same for Camagüey.

Even so, this implied failure to meet the programmed production goal in Oriente and in Camagüey, even with a sugar yield of 12.5. We expected to compensate this by a possible overfulfillment of goals in the provinces of Las Villas, Matanzas and Havana. At that moment the possibility existed of making up for the deficit in Oriente and Camagüey. But it was imperative that reasonably high yields be obtained from the cane that remained if we were to reach the ten million tons of sugar.

At the time of our February 9 television appearance, we were ahead of the largest capitalist sugar harvest—the largest harvest!—by 1,860,000 metric tons.

As of February 1, our mills had ground a total of 635 million cwt. of cane. According to estimates there were still almost 1250 million cwt. to be ground. 1250 million! Therefore, every possibility existed in February for reaching the 10-million-ton mark if a serious effort was made, and, of course, this included all the intermill hauling of cane and a battle for a high sugar yield.

Thus, on that occasion, a study was made of all the problems; they were made public, and, in addition, every pertinent measure was adopted.

Those teams from state agencies which had managed sugar mills in Havana Province with the highest degree of efficiency as well as teams of economists were sent to Oriente Province. A mobilization of every available resource was also made toward Camagüey. A great number of resources were brought into play to build roads in Camagüey and Oriente.

There was also the matter of obtaining the trucks needed

for the intermill hauling of cane in Oriente, Camagüey and Las Villas. A total of 519 new Zil-130 trucks have been sent to Oriente since then to be employed in intermill hauling of cane. Some rebuilt trucks were also sent. In all, some 800 trucks—including some from Army reserves in Oriente Province—were put into the effort to overcome the difficulties there.

A request was made of the University of Havana to send the greatest possible number of engineers and students from the School of Technology to the Guiteras and Jesús Menéndez Sugar Mills. The Ministry of the Sugar Industry was asked to concentrate the largest possible number of technicians in the Argelia Libre Sugar Mill, which had to reach a daily grinding rate of 233,750 cwt. of cane.

All possible measures were taken on that occasion.

In talks with the provinces, the Party, the regions and with everybody, great emphasis was placed on the battle for the sugar yield. From that moment the battle of the yield became the battle for the ten million tons. If we lost the former, we would undoubtedly lose the latter.

If we look at the situation of the yield at that time we can see that it began to respond.

All the mills which were stopped because their harvests were ahead of schedule started up again with a yield increase of 2 or 3 percentage points. All, without exception! The results were notable.

But we began noticing a series of problems which we hadn't commented on on February 9. We had referred to the yield being below its historical average and the grinding problems in Oriente. We saw that the mills with large installations of new machinery were holding things up because they reduced the grinding rate, and because they were going to lengthen the harvest and affect the yield by obliging us to grind cane in June and July that could have been ground in February, March and April when the yield was at its highest level.

We still hadn't discovered another thing: that the mills with large installations of new machinery not only were grinding less but had a lower sugar yield from the cane they were grinding—as much as 2 or 3 percentage points less. It was discovered then.

How was it discovered? Or how did it become plainly evident that they were not getting all the sugar they could from the cane? With the intermill hauling! The intermill hauling of cane began. For example, the cane of the Cristino Naranjo Mill was sent to the Arquímedes Colina Mill. And what became evident? The Cristino Naranjo was one of the mills that should have been grinding 100,000 cwt. of cane per day but wasn't even grinding 50,000, and even so it had to be stopped in order to finish the installation of new machinery. This mill and the Maceo had to grind 200,000 cwt. between them, and it was expected that they would be at peak capacity in February. Neither ever passed the 50,000 cwt. mark.

But what happened with the 50,000 they were grinding? Gross yield: Cristino Naranjo on February 28, 10.24; Arquímedes Colina, 13.4. And the Arquímedes Colina was grinding the same cane as the Cristino Naranjo. Just one day? No! The 27th: Cristino Naranjo, 10.54; Arquímedes Colina, 12.43. Cristino Naranjo on the 26th—10.53; Arquímedes Colina, 13.16. And so on.

The same cane ground at the Arquímedes Colina was producing almost 3 percentage points more sugar than at the Cristino Naranjo.

So a new and more serious problem became evident then: the mills with new installations were not only grinding less but had a lower sugar yield from the cane they were grinding.

This caused serious concern. We decided to transfer cane from the Cristino Naranjo not only to the Arquímedes Colina but to the América Libre as well. Why? Because América Libre has its cane growing on high ground and gives high yields into June. We decided to take cane from the Cristino and the Maceo to the América and the López Peña. That is, new intermill hauling, in view of the new problems, to solve not only the problem of the low grinding rate of those mills, but of the low yield as well.

If on this map there are 50 arrows indicating the first intermill hauling plan, I want you to know that if all the hauling that has been done were indicated on the map there would be 300 arrows. Why? They represent new solutions to new problems and difficulties. It has been a tremendous struggle.

Then, we waited to see how the yield would act. The first increase took place in Camagüey. It went from a yield of over 10 to over 11, an important increase. After all the measures that were taken, the yield increased 1 percentage point in a few days. This was very encouraging in the month of February.

So Camagüey's leap took place in February. By the 23rd they had 11.16, and by the 28th, 11.50. And I can assure you—I won't waste too much time on this—that the yield in Camagüey increased 1 percentage point in practically a week.

Of course 11.50 was far below the required yield. However, we could reasonably hope for it to increase in March.

The weather was doubtful. There was no rain during February in Oriente. The weather improved. After January, not another drop of rain fell. It kept raining, however, in Camagüey and in Las Villas. In some areas there was an excess of rain, in others strong drought; in some areas of Oriente, Jebabo and other spots, the cane became very dry.

So the yield didn't behave as it should have, but the total amount of cane was still in doubt, precisely because of the rains in Camagüey and Las Villas. And the yield was above average in the areas where cane was being cut.

In general, the new cane areas were giving a reasonably high yield.

The benefits obtained by the intermill hauling declined steadily in March. The possibilities of producing the ten million were being progressively reduced, but we still had some reserves: cane which had been planted in June, July and August 1969, cane which at a given moment could be cut to make up for a deficit of 200,000 or 300,000 tons.

But it was becoming steadily clearer that the production of sugar was not up to the required level, especially in the months of February, March and April, and the yield was more than one percentage point lower than what it had to be. This would naturally have its cumulative effect.

The yield in February, March and April led to a 500,000-ton drop in the production of sugar.

Together with this, a deficit in the estimated amount of available cane turned up in late April. The deficit turned up

in Oriente, and in Havana Province, where we had counted
upon a cane reserve.

Periodic estimates were made, and in April estimates were
made of the cane that would be available in early May in order
to definitely determine the situation in view of the problem
of production affected by a low sugar yield.

A bit further on, I am going to show you figures on the
yield obtained in 1952 and one or two other items of interest.
But I want to point out that we called a first meeting here in
Havana at the beginning of May.

We had followed a policy of doing everything possible so
that no comrade, no provincial leader would have to come to
Havana, and we visited all the provinces, knowing that the
battle had to be won in the provinces, where thousands of
details have to be taken care of, thousands of problems have
to be solved. We were in constant contact with them to help
with problems related to the intermill hauling and any other
difficulty.

But early in May, when the data on existing cane was available, we decided to hold a meeting here in Havana. Comrades from all the provinces and from the manufacturing
branch of the sugar industry were present.

At this meeting it became evident that a reduction of over
25 million cwt. of cane had to be made for Oriente, that
Camagüey had more or less the amount expected, Las Villas
had to be reduced by about 20 million cwt., Matanzas by
about 5 million cwt. and Havana by about 25 million cwt.
Of course, the problem of Havana was already known, but
the reductions for Oriente and Las Villas, some for Matanzas
and some additional for Havana became known at that time.

That situation removed all hope of making the 10-million-
ton harvest, considering the amount of cane that was lacking
and the sugar yield, even if we resorted to cutting our reserve
early-plant cane. There was no longer any reason for making
use of the reserves, since, even then, we wouldn't have made
the ten million tons.

In our earlier television appearance we pointed out a detail which I believe to be important—something which has
always concerned us a great deal. . . .

On that occasion, on February 9, we said, "We have a double problem to attend: the rate of grinding and the sugar yield. In our opinion, the problem of the yield is now of first importance. Why? If we were to minimize the importance of the yield and devote all our efforts to grinding all the available cane, we would run the risk of waging a battle doomed to failure. We must wage a battle with full guarantees from first to last in order to be certain of success."

Therefore, we maintained the principle that the ten million tons were to be defended to the end.

In fact, we thought we could finally decide whether or not it would be possible to make the ten million tons on the basis of available cane and rainfall, and depending upon the sugar yield's remaining as it was or dropping for the cane we'd have to grind in June, the cane that we had left untouched on high ground where both the historic yield curve and the local climate would be in our favor.

That is, a great effort was made to grind all the cane from low-lying fields early, to grind all the cane where there were problems in connection with the historical yield, so as to maintain the possibility of the ten million tons until the very end.

We were deeply worried that, as a result of this phenomenon of the sugar yield, we would find, around the halfway mark of the harvest, that it was possible to establish, mathematically, that the ten million tons were out of our reach, because then we would have to tackle the rest of the task, at its most difficult stage, without the hope of the ten million tons.

And it goes without saying that our position from the very beginning—from the very beginning!—was that if the estimates at any time showed that we would not be able to reach the ten million tons we would immediately report this to the people, because not doing so, keeping alive the illusion of the ten million tons in order to get the workers to work with a maximum degree of enthusiasm would not be moral or honest or in accord with the revolutionary principles that should be maintained or the methods to be followed with the people. This was the position we adopted from the very beginning.

It must be said that we really did not think that the hope of making the ten million tons would be discarded quite so abruptly and at such an early date. Neither was it at the half-way mark of the harvest. If we hadn't taken all the measures that were taken in February, the hope of making the ten million tons would already have been discarded by the middle of March. In fact, those measures made it possible for us to hope, until early in May, that we might still reach the ten million. Once the April results were in, and in view of the sharp drop in the estimated amount of available cane in some areas, plus the consequences of the low average yield from January on, the possibility of making the ten million tons had gone over the brink.

Now, then, as I told you in February, we were ahead of the capitalists' largest harvest by 1,860,000 metric tons.

What happened in the capitalists' largest harvest? What was their grinding capacity? It was in the months of February, March and April that it became evident that our grinding capacity for 1970 was below that of the capitalists, for all the reasons we have pointed out, derived mainly from problems in our mills.

Thus we see that in 1952, in the month of March, the capitalists ground 314.75 million cwt. of cane—a daily average of 10,162,500—with a daily sugar production average of 58,600 metric tons.

We, although ahead of them by 1,860,000 metric tons due to having started our harvest much earlier, had ground 270.5 million cwt. of cane—a daily grinding average of 8.725 million cwt. and a daily sugar production average of 48,460 metric tons: a difference of 1,437,000 cwt. less in cane ground and 10,230 metric tons less in sugar produced, per day. In addition to a lower grinding rate, the effect of the lower sugar yield was also being felt.

In other words, we were waging our battle for the ten million tons with a grinding capacity almost 1.5 million cwt. of cane below that of the capitalists in 1952. That was the real situation.

Thus, in February, March and April our mills were grinding cane and making the sugar harvest with almost 1.5 million cwt. less capacity. Because a province like Oriente, that had to grind between 3.25 and 3.5 million cwt. wasn't even grinding 2.5 million. The same thing was happening, although on a lesser scale, in Camagüey. In reality, our expansion program was aimed at giving us a daily grinding of no less than 10.5 million cwt. and, actually, our capacity was 1.75 million below that.

Why do I say "actually"? Because, often the problem did not lie directly in the fact that not enough cane was being ground. What very often happened was this: In Oriente Province, for instance, all those giant sugar mills had all the necessary manpower, trucks, cane loaders, everything, waiting for the mills to reach their scheduled level of grinding capacity. The result? Constant breakdowns and stops. Therefore, in order not to have an accumulation of cut cane lying on the ground, it was necessary time and again to paralyze 40,000 or 50,000 workers. Farmers mobilized from the mountains of Baracoa, from the Sierra Maestra, from all over, who had gone to those canefields moved by tremendous enthusiasm, were asked to stop cutting. And this had a tremendous demoralizing effect.

Since the cane couldn't be accumulated in advance, the day that a giant sugar mill was operating well it didn't have enough cane to grind.

Moreover, since it was precisely in those sugar mills that the critical problem existed, it was there that all the resources had been concentrated. At times a mill that was grinding more or less at a good pace, that had no industrial problems, lacked resources while all the resources were concentrated in mills that had problems. As a result, in March we told the comrades in the province to cut down on the grinding norms. That is, if their theoretical capacity was 250,000 cwt. it was suggested that they consider it as being 187,000 cwt. and assign manpower for a capacity of 187,000 cwt. instead of for 250,-000. We'd say, "In the Argelia Libre Sugar Mill, instead of figuring on a work force for a capacity of 225,000 cwt., make it for a capacity of 150,000 cwt." These were suggestions we made for a number of sugar mills that had new installation kinks, so that the surplus manpower could be utilized in other mills that were operating without any trouble. Because the work stoppages had a really demoralizing effect on the work force made up of farmers and workers who had responded to the mobilization with enormous enthusiasm.

So the fact is that we've been making the 10-million-ton harvest with a daily grinding capacity almost 1.5 million cwt. below that of the capitalists when they made their giant 7,298,000-ton harvest, and 1.75 million cwt. under our programmed capacity.

Every day we were grinding less than they, and every cwt. of cane we ground less would have to be ground later. Much of the cane that was being processed in those sugar mills was yielding less sugar than it should, even though this was not the only problem. Because the sugar yield was affected even in mills with no new equipment. There are other problems which had an adverse effect on the sugar yield.

The mills with new installations had trouble with both grinding and sugar yield.

But those weren't the only factors. While we had 20 mills in Oriente with new machinery and all 20 of them were giving us headaches, the other mills, in which no expansion work had been done, did not receive all of the attention or all of the maintenance required.

This happened in Oriente Province and it happened in other provinces, in Las Villas Province. The capitalists produced 7,298,000 tons with an average sugar yield of 12.25. This was in 1952, when 90 percent of the cane was of the POJ 2878 variety. And today the POJ 2878 constitutes a minority in our overall cane area. We have much better varieties of cane.

Where is the proof of this, gentlemen? The proof can be found in a mill I'm going to cite as an example.

Here we have, for example, the México Sugar Mill, in Colón, on February 28. Barbados 43-62 type cane. Yield, 13.58. February 27, 13.53; February 26, 13.50; February 25, 13.48.

That is a well-managed, well-maintained mill, grinding good cane.

As early as February 19, a yield of 13.49.

Let's look for an even earlier date. Already by February

14, the yield was 13.02. Comfortably ahead of the historical yield curve, grinding cane of the 43-62 variety. Practically throughout the period from February to May, the mill's gross yield has been 13.5 percent.

You look at the Caracas Sugar Mill, in Las Villas, and find the gross yield: March 8, 13.80; March 10, 13.63; March 13, 14.27; March 16, 14.45; March 19, 14.47; March 22, 14.44; March 31, 14.24. This mill has had a yield of 14 from as early as the first two weeks in March, and now, in the middle of May, its yield is practically the same. You will find the same situation in a series of well-managed, well-maintained mills that are grinding cane of the new varieties. These mills have even reached a high yield when grinding inferior cane.

Three factors have made their influence felt in the low yield: number one, the new equipment; number two, maintenance, which was not up to par in many mills; and number three—and to tell the truth, it's an open question whether this is really factor number three or the principal factor—inefficient managing of the mills.

Naturally, our sugar mills are now 18 years older than they were in 1952. They are carrying the weight of an additional 18 years. But we are of the opinion that age is not the fundamental factor, since all those mills such as the Caracas are of the same age and have a much higher sugar yield than they had in the time of capitalism.

In other words, even an old mill that has good maintenance and good management, with a good variety of cane, will reach whatever sugar yield level is desired. Now, then, a good number of mills that were grinding the same cane, even without new machinery, were getting a yield of 14; others got 12 and others 11. An endless number of examples of this type. We received the daily report, and, besides, these reports have been published day after day. The newspaper has been announcing not only the sugar yield per province—the planned yield, the actual yield and so on—but I asked GRANMA to publish the yield, mill by mill, every day.

Therefore, there has been no lack of publicity at any moment with regard to the problems. Everybody could see what was happening, what serious problems we were encountering in the harvest, because our mills have not, even for one day, ever ground as much as ten million cwt. of cane. And the same thing applies to the sugar yield.

Nevertheless, a number of mills prove that mills that are managed well and given adequate maintenance can get a yield as high as 13.5 and 14, grinding the new varieties of cane, during February, March, April and even May.

If our mills in general had behaved this way I'm sure that we would have had more than enough cane to make the ten million tons. No question about that.

What does this mean? It means that there is something that has deteriorated more than the mills themselves, and that is management, the operation, the direction of the mills, as a result of the fact that many of the older workers have been retiring.

A good number of the old workers delayed their retirement until after the 1970 harvest, giving a demonstration of their spirit of self-sacrifice despite their 50 years in the sugar industry—so that they could help in this harvest. But we have not carried out an adequate program of renovation and training of new personnel.

And it is our responsibility to do this. Since we have never had industrial problems, because our problems had always been due, not to lack of mill capacity, but rather to lack of cane, we were faced with the fact that the main problem came from the least expected quarter.

In other words, we neglected the industrial side, and that is the side that laid bare all its problems to us in 1970.

Some of the problems were quite logical: the matter of the new installations; all new equipment, adjustments—as I explained on that other occasion—cause a lot of problems. But the question of the managing of the mills was of decisive importance.

Running a sugar mill is not as easy as running a streetcar or a bicycle. It's a complex matter; it includes mechanical and chemical aspects that require extreme care. And one of the questions that should be given tremendous emphasis now is the industrial aspect, both in maintenance and training of personnel to operate the mills.

For their record harvest of 1952, the capitalists ground 1294.25 million cwt. of cane. They produced 7,298,000 tons of sugar, with an average yield of 12.25. Eighty percent of the cane ground was of the POJ 2878 variety.

By the time we had produced 7,305,000 tons of sugar, plus an additional 50,000 in process—if I remember correctly, on May 15—we had ground a total of 1476 million cwt. of cane, with an average sugar yield of 10.85. 10.85! In other words, we had used 181.75 million cwt. more of cane to produce the same amount of sugar as the capitalists.

With a yield equal to that of the capitalists we would have produced 8,314,000 metric tons of sugar—some 950,000 tons over what we had actually produced.

As of yesterday, we had ground some 1503 million cwt. of cane. With a yield such as the one mentioned in Santa Clara —a yield which was not at all exaggerated, considering the new varieties of cane—which was 12.30, we would have produced, as of now, 8,499,724 metric tons of sugar with those 1503 million cwt. of cane. And we have now 7,456,000, plus some 50,000 in process.

That is, we have some 990,000 metric tons less than we would have had if we had obtained the yield that was programmed in Santa Clara.

A 10-million-ton harvest, with a gross sugar yield of 12 percent, would call for approximately 1810 million cwt. of cane. A gross yield of 11 percent would call for 2000 million cwt.

And, by now, the aggregate yield for the harvest of 1970 is approximately 10.85. It may possibly be 10.87. And with a gross yield of 11 percent you need 2000 million cwt. of cane!

It must be said that, even if we had had 2000 million cwt. of cane, it would have been impossible to produce the ten million tons, because this would have required grinding that cane in July, August and September, with a sugar yield of five or six percent. Therefore, it would have been impossible to make the ten million tons even with 2000 million cwt. of cane available. And, of course, we don't have 2000 million cwt. of cane.

Of course, in many places and at many mills, problems

resulting from an incorrect cane-cutting program or from cane left lying in the field too long before delivery to the mill have had an adverse effect on the sugar yield. But these have not been decisive factors. What was really cause for concern was that the same type of cane, cut by the same people, with the same degree of freshness, would yield two and a half percentage points more in one mill than in another.

This is what made us realize to what extent the question of operation was having an adverse effect on the yield. And we have dozens of such examples here.

A series of mills grinding the same type of cane but with a noticeable difference in the yield obtained.

Now, then, what performance did we get from the agricultural program?

As I said before, according to the Santa Clara plan, we needed 1770.25 million cwt. of cane. Following the last analysis made in this month's meeting—which revealed how much cane we had left and the deficits in the estimates made at the beginning of the harvest—we realized that the situation was as follows. . . . We made our analysis on May 7.

Oriente Province had 502.75 million cwt. of cane, and according to the program of Santa Clara, it needed 547.5 million. Therefore, there was a deficit of 44.75 million cwt.

Camagüey had 467 million cwt. and a programmed 499.875 million cwt. A deficit of 32.875 million cwt.

Las Villas, with a planned 386 million cwt., had 429.25 million cwt. An excess of 43.25 million cwt.

Matanzas, which should have had 180.5 million cwt., had 205 million. 24.5 million cwt. over.

Havana, including the four sugar mills from Pinar del Río, should have had 126.25 million cwt. and had 159.75 million. 33.5 million over.

And Pinar del Río, which should have had 30 million cwt., had 29.5 million cwt. A 500,000-cwt. deficit.

We made an effort to overreach the program in Matanzas, Havana and Las Villas. And there was a time when the estimate for Las Villas was 450 million cwt. Then there came a period in which the cane in the zone of Cienfuegos, where the bulk of the cane was, began to dry up and, as a result, this led to a cutdown on the estimate.

I must point out that one of the ways in which the mills with new equipment problems had an adverse effect on the yield was not only by not grinding cane at the best possible time, but also because they made it possible for some of the cane to dry up and lose in both weight and sugar yield. This is what happened in several mills, one of them the Perú Sugar Mill, which is located on lands that for a good part still lack irrigation, and much of its cane that should have been cut in February, March and April is now dried up.

When we study the sugar yield picture and see the yield at the Perú Sugar Mill, we see a yield of a little over nine, a little over ten. Why? Because tens of millions of cwt. of cane that should have been cut in February, March and April have not been cut yet. And this has led to the cane drying up as a result of a long dry season. This is a third aspect that has had an adverse effect on the sugar yield.

Thus, according to the study made on May 7, the total amount of available cane is 1793.25 million cwt. The Santa Clara program called for 1770.25 million. Therefore, there are 23 million cwt. more of cane available than what was programmed on that occasion, when we counted on a sugar yield equal to that of the capitalists in 1952, when the new varieties of cane were still unknown.

As of yesterday, the total amount of cane ground was 1503.025 million cwt. According to the study made on May 7, close to 290.25 million cwt. remain to be ground as of now—a land area of over 650,000 acres. We have produced 7.5 million tons of sugar.

Fortunately, a great part of this cane is located on high land. The canefields of the América and the Nicaragua Mills and others. . . . The Nicaragua's sugar yield in June is as high as 13.

Therefore, this cane is located in zones that allow the reasonable hope of getting a good yield from it. This means 290.25 million cwt. of cane available, if there is no change. It may be a little more or a little less.

Therefore, 117.5 million cwt. remain to be ground in

Oriente Province. That was the figure as of 7:00 p.m. yesterday.

Camagüey, 96.75 million; Las Villas, 61.5 million; Matanzas, 12.5 million; Havana, .25 million; and Pinar del Río, 1.75 million.

A total of approximately 290.25 million cwt. of cane. It might be a little more or a little less. There is also a reserve supply of new-plant cane, planted in June and July, that could be ground in this harvest if it should be desirable to do so. That is the amount of cane remaining to be ground as of now.

Therefore, it is evident that although the cane supply should have been in excess of 1793.25 million cwt.—and we strived to surpass that figure so as to have a surplus—actually we had almost 25 million cwt. more than the planned amount.

One should not lose sight of the fact that achieving that large an increase in our supply of cane—which was achieved not over a period of several years, but in just 18 months' time—increasing the country's cane production from an average of barely over one thousand million cwt. to more than 1750 million cwt. has been an outstanding achievement. We can't feel satisfied over the effort made, because we feel that we actually had the possibility of reaching a larger supply of cane. We had the possibility of reaching 1925 million and even 1950 million, considering the resources at our disposal. An earnest effort was made and all of the nation's resources were directed toward that end; we programmed the work, the use of machines and all other possible resources. And the fact is that we barely went over the planned 1770.25 million. We should have had an additional 150 to 175 million.

But we repeat that even if we had had a cane supply of 2000 million cwt. and begun the harvest on October 28 and wound it up in August, we wouldn't have reached the 10-million mark because of the all-important problem of having to mill that much cane with a grinding capacity of 1,750,000 cwt. less than what we needed and the tremendous adverse effect on sugar yield of the new installations with their operational and maintenance problems. No matter how large the supply of cane, it is impossible to reach the 10-million mark in sugar production unless the basic factor of adequate sugar yield is present.

Milling all of our supply of cane, 1793.25 million cwt., will give us at least a million metric tons less than the mark: at least a million metric tons less. Our harvest will end up in the neighborhood of nine million, give or take a little. Whether we reach that figure or not depends on how good a job we do from now on. That is the situation at this moment: our reaching nine million depends on how good a job we do now. And I should add that the goal is going to be rather difficult to attain.

We should strive to reach that mark, we should put forth a most earnest effort to reach it, and with the remaining supply of cane available, we can, theoretically, attain it. That's theoretically, and we'll see in actual practice if we can reach the figure with the supply of cane we have left. A small error in the estimate of available cane will affect production results. And so we are going to strive to reach the 9-million mark, but with the limited amount of cane, as I have just explained, plus a possible reserve supply. But we must consider adverse developments: the dry season might be longer than usual, the yield might or might not hold, and so on.

All kinds of measures, all possible measures are being taken to that end.

And so, we have lost the battle of the ten million because of the problem of the sugar yield. I must say that we could have produced a little more sugar, for example, in the province of Havana, if we had started the harvest somewhat later —from 50,000 to 100,000 metric tons more. Why? Because we started from an estimate of available cane that turned out to be too high. We therefore started the harvest on October 28, but if we had started 15 to 20 days later we could have wound up toward the end of May or early in June and we would have had a somewhat larger supply of cane available and the sugar yield would have been higher. That means that the harvest in Havana Province started a little too early. Another factor—but the degree of its effect is rather difficult to determine—was the stormy weather we had in February, with winds of about 65 miles per hour, that lasted

24 hours. The damage done by the wind in some canefields where I cut cane was considerable.

In my opinion, the damage done by that storm has been underestimated, as I also believe the damage done by the 55-day dry spell to the cane planted in November and December of 1968 was underestimated. Another thing that was underestimated is the fact that in a long and early-started harvest the cane supply cannot be estimated on the same basis as in a normal harvest.

Thus we can see that an additional 7.5 million cwt. of cane could have been obtained in this province and this would have given us up to 100,000 metric tons more sugar. But this is not a decisive factor.

Oriente Province's shortcoming is not so much due to an insufficient supply of cane as it is to the low sugar yield of the cane. This low yield is the basic cause for the province's failure to meet its goal, resulting in a deficit of 600,000 to 700,000 metric tons of sugar. Nonfulfillment of the province's production goal is due in good part to low sugar yield, and the yield, in turn, was adversely affected by the province's industrial problems.

All these problems have a definite influence on the cadres, on the people who are working in the harvest, as they cause a feeling of discouragement which, of course, must be overcome.

We must point out something which is basic in this problem of the ten million, and that is that the people aren't the ones who have lost the battle for the ten million. We can say with absolute certainty that the people didn't lose the battle. If we can't say the battle was won—because we can't say the battle of the ten million was won—we can say that the people didn't lose the battle of the ten million. We—we alone—are the ones who have lost the battle. The administrative apparatus and the leaders of the Revolution are the ones who lost the battle. The people have more than measured up to the ten million—and to eleven million, as well. We are the ones who haven't measured up to the ten million. And I think we must say this as a matter of elementary justice, because it is the plain truth.

The battle of the ten million wasn't lost in the last year,

or in the last two years: we lost it in the last four years, and we lost it in an area where we hadn't expected to lose, because it had never been the main problem.

That is, our ignorance of the problems of the sugar industry kept us from realizing as soon as was necessary, detecting as soon as necessary, the different types of problems of a subjective nature, of skilled workers, and other problems, so as to take necessary measures in time. Even if we had had 2000 million cwt. of cane, we could not have reached the ten million under those conditions.

I can also tell you that there were matters which affected the industrial problem, independent of anybody's wishes. But we and nobody else are the ones who have lost the battle. The battle of the ten million had become a symbol, a battle, a lot of things.

But the people were capable of ten, of eleven, of doing whatever was necessary, there is no doubt about this, and bear no responsibility for the setback suffered.

Now then: yesterday we analyzed two problems: the magnitude of the effort made by the people; the magnitude of the effort of the nation, the achievements obtained. To explain it with data that indicates the magnitude, the extent of the effort. . . . Why do we say that it is a record which will probably never again be equalled, that we ourselves will never again match? Because, having started from the base of being the world's most important sugar producer with no close rivals, and being the world's most important sugar producer with mills 18 years older than in the capitalist period, and with some 1,250,000 cwt. less in daily grinding capacity and with all the new equipment undergoing installation and adjustment, an impressive increase has been achieved, which gives a full idea of the people's effort.

This doesn't mean we won't be producing similar amounts of sugar. I'm talking about the percentage increase which was obtained. Next year we will have more cane in some of the provinces because of the planting which is under way. Oriente will have more; Havana, more; Matanzas, the same; Las Villas and Camagüey, less, because the planting program is behind schedule in those provinces. We can turn out the same amount of sugar, with a good harvest, with 150 million cwt. less of cane next year. With 150 million cwt. of cane less we can turn out the same amount of sugar as this year. Because in 1971 we won't be able to talk about a leap, because conditions are complex.

We have the subjective problems to be overcome in the sugar industry. We will have to be a bit patient before trying another leap. I think that the next time we won't say it, we'll just do it. Of course, the ten million will be surpassed in the future, but it will be done gradually.

Because the possibilities of the 4,300,000 acres of land devoted to cane, flat land where machines can be used, where the cane doesn't compete with any other crop, can provide for much more than ten million metric tons of sugar, given the present level of agricultural technology. But before this we must solve the problem of mechanization of the harvest once and for all.

But I want to give an idea. If we produce eight million, how does it compare with previous harvests, with capitalist harvests—the last ten capitalist years and the past ten socialist years?

We had three harvests which passed six million: one in 1961 which almost reached seven. The average in the last ten years of capitalist harvests was 5,521,000 metric tons. The average of the socialist harvests in the past ten years was 5,261,000 metric tons. This has been the average in the past ten years.

Now then: producing eight million and comparing it with the largest capitalist harvest—with the disadvantages we have already mentioned—eight million means 702,000 metric tons more than the biggest capitalist harvest, which was 7,298,000 metric tons. That is, ten percent more than the biggest capitalist harvest.

To explain this I'm going to use two figures: eight and nine, and tell what they mean.

Compared with the average of the last ten years of capitalism—which, as I said, was 5,521,000—producing eight million would put us 2,479,000 metric tons of sugar above the average of the last ten capitalist years. That is, 44.9 percent more than the average produced by the capitalists in their last ten years.

Now, comparing it with our socialist production of the past ten years, gives us 2,739,000 metric tons more than the average of the last ten harvests of the Revolution—a 52-percent increase.

Compared with last year's production, it is 3,541,000 metric tons more than last year, when production was 4,459,000 metric tons. That is, a 79 percent increase over last year's production; 52 percent above our average and 79 percent above our last year's production.

Compared with the smallest harvest of the Revolution: it is 4,118,000 above the smallest we had—which was 3,882,-000. That is, a 106-percent increase over our smallest harvest.

That is with eight million. Now the figures with nine—if we produce nine million.

Compared with the largest capitalist harvest, a harvest of nine million would be 1,702,000 metric tons greater. That is, 23.32 percent greater: 3,439,000 metric tons greater than the average of their last ten years, which, as we said, was 5,521,-000 metric tons. That is, 63.01 percent greater than the average of the last ten capitalist years.

If we turn out nine, it will be 23.32 percent greater than the largest harvest and 63.01 percent greater than the average for the last ten capitalist years.

Now, comparing it with our socialist harvests, 3,739,000 metric tons more than the average of the past ten socialist harvests, which was 5,261,000 metric tons. That is, 71.07 percent, and 4,541,000 metric tons more than last year, which was 4,459,000. That is an increase of 101.83 percent.

Now, if we produced nine million and compared it with our smallest harvest, it would be 5,118,000 metric tons more than the 1963 harvest. This would be 131.83 percent more than the smallest harvest of the Revolution.

This is why we said that if the FAO statistics are checked, if any other data sources are checked, as far as net percentage goes, such an increase in sugar production is unknown.

We can rest assured that this is a real Olympic record—the record, not the harvest—because we said we didn't want a silver medal. But as far as record production increase goes, it is of such magnitude, starting from where we started, with the industry we had—now 18 years older—with new installations playing an unfavorable role in production for the moment and with almost 1.5 million cwt. less of daily grinding capacity, in those conditions. . . . What is more, in other conditions, under the best possible conditions, these figures will surely never again be found in any manual, statistical report or archive.

And that is precisely the situation. That is why we said an unprecedented record had been established. Production will grow year by year, but it can never again grow with such magnitude. And it was a case of trying to achieve in a period of 18 months what wasn't done in five or six years, what couldn't be done in a period of five or six years.

The effort was emphasized to such an extent that it became a symbol and took on international standing.

These are the figures if we produce eight or if we produce nine million.

We should strive for the highest production possible—not only because of the honor involved. From the economic point of view, it is indispensable to grind up to the last stalks of cane and get the highest possible sugar yield from them!

But these figures are not for us. We aren't going to console ourselves with them. We have pointed them out for the people's benefit, so that they can gauge the results of their work, of their effort, and so that they will know they have set a record increase in agricultural production—because this forms part of our overall agricultural production—which no one will ever surpass. In our opinion, at least, it is very, very unlikely. Let us hope someone is able to equal it—even more, overcome it! Let us hope one of the underdeveloped countries, where needs are so great, is one day able to accomplish this!

These are the facts and figures with eight and nine million. If we produce 8.8 or 8.9, well, it will be a little less than with nine million.

Of course, right now counting the sugar in process there is a bit over 7.5 million. Yesterday there was. . . . At this moment, there should be about 7.53, 7.54, including the sugar in process. And about June 10, more or less, we shall reach eight million, although we have a hurricane nearby with winds up to 100 miles per hour, threatening the area from Pinar del Río to Las Villas. It's not very convenient, but, well, it's one of those things.

Now observe how the mill expansion work was done.

New equipment with a value of 55 million pesos was installed in Camagüey Province. This was 32.5 percent of the nationwide total of new investment in sugar mills.

The amount spent in Oriente for industrial installations in sugar mills was 68 million pesos, or 40.2 percent of the total. The two provinces together account for 123 million pesos, or 72.7 percent of the nationwide total. This constitutes our best proof. We find that the provinces where most expansion of mill capacity was done are the provinces where there is a deficit of somewhat more than a million metric tons of sugar; that is, basically in the provinces where 72.7 percent of mill expansion work was carried out.

Of course, the new installations are there for future harvests. They have proved a headache in the current harvest, but they are an investment that should begin to pay off from now on. Naturally, once all the bugs and kinks are ironed out and they are running smoothly, it will be as in the case of the Panama Sugar Mill, which was a terrible headache last year but has operated well this year. It is a pity that the good results won't be obtained until 1971, whereas we needed to achieve the 10-million-mark this year.

What measures have we taken? We have been trying to send all available reinforcements to Oriente Province. Having practically finished the harvest in Havana Province, we are moving its skilled manpower and technical resources to Oriente Province, toward the zone where the Nicaragua, Fernando de Dios, López Peña and Guatemala Sugar Mills are located, a zone where the sugar yield curve historically stays very high in the month of June. A total of 18,000 workers are being moved from Havana to that zone.

There are 14 road-building brigades from Havana Province working there now. A total of 10,000 to 11,000 crack canecutters, cane-loader operators, truck drivers and construction workers specialized in building canecutters' camps. In sum, these workers constitute a support force made up of advance-guard, hardworking and aggressive people and we believe that this is a fine opportunity to broaden the ranks of the party, drawing new members from among those who are going to take part in and give support to the work to be done in that part of Oriente Province, making it possible for Oriente to con-centrate its efforts on the cane belt of the Guiteras Sugar Mill while the people from Havana give a boost to the work in the cane belt in the Banes area.

It is of decisive importance to cut the 117.5 million cwt. of cane remaining in Oriente Province and extract every ounce of sugar from them.

It is possible to overreach the 8-million-ton sugar produc-tion mark by a wide margin just with the cane remaining in Oriente Province.

And the remaining cane supply in Camagüey, Las Villas and Matanzas will go to add to the eight million.

Therefore, we can overshoot the eight million by a good margin just with the remaining cane supply in Oriente Prov-ince. But it has to be cut and every ounce of sugar extracted from it.

I was forgetting to mention that many sugar mill workers from Havana Province are also going to reinforce the personnel of Oriente's mills. This is one of the measures that is being taken.

As we said last night, the province of Camagüey is putting forth an outstanding effort at this moment, making the biggest contribution to production of all the provinces. Comrade Almeida and Comrade Acevedo, with the comrades from the Armed Forces, are giving a hand in that province and provid-ing together with the Youth Column and the Suárez Gayol Column and the technological institutes' students, a decisive boost to the harvest work there.

That's a good example of what an organized and well-disciplined force can do. The province is milling 2.25 million cwt. of cane a day, and we might add that it is being done with outstanding regularity.

This is to say that we are fully confident that the forces working in Camagüey will wage their battle without letup to completion.

There are still the amounts corresponding to Matanzas and Las Villas.

We are now entering a stage that is somewhat harder, not withstanding the fact that we have been taking measures since December. We have been building roads at the rate of 50 miles a day. This means that 2500 to 3000 miles have been built in 90 days, 90 days!

I imagine that, for example, in a country as large as Brazil— from 50 to 80 times the size of Cuba, let's say, 70 times the size of Cuba—some 3000 miles of roads are built in three years. Here we have built 2500 to 3000 miles in three months. This will give an idea of the power, of the resources this country has now and also the spirit with which the road builders are now working so as to help out the task of the sugar harvest. The road builders have been building roads at a rate that is two or three times their normal rate. The road builders have been putting forth a tremendous effort as a contribution to the 10-million-ton harvest. The amount of work being done these days—in terms of volume of earth moved and miles of road completed—is simply incredible!

The measures that have been taken include cutting first those areas that are low-lying, leaving the areas of high ground for last. Consequently, we can reasonably expect to obtain a good sugar yield from the cane still to be milled in this harvest.

What should the harvest be called now? Should it be called the 9-, the 8-, or the 10-million-ton harvest? We should continue to call it the 10-million-ton harvest. Our maintaining the 10-million goal, including the date for attaining it and the harvest calendar, will serve as a yardstick to measure what we have done, how far we have advanced and what we have failed to accomplish. That's how it should be. We should continue to call it. . . . We have to call it by some name. Christenings are sometimes important. Anyway, we should go on calling it the 10-million-ton harvest. . . .

But we must pay attention to the needs posed by development. Very often. . . . For example, this is the principle we uphold: if we create a research center in the western part of the country, we should also create one for Las Villas, Camagüey and Oriente. Why? Because, if there is no technological and scientific development, the regions that don't have the benefit of a research center will always remain underdeveloped.

We have enormous resources in Oriente. It is the province with the most sugarcane and highest sugar yield—due to its local climate, clearer skies, more hours of sunshine, dry weather during the harvest time, which makes it possible, with irrigation, to obtain higher sugar yields (the higher the drier the weather during the harvest, within certain limits)—and enormous amounts of mineral resources. The world's largest nickel reserves are in Oriente Province.

Oriente has 33.8 percent of the nation's population—that is, 2,847,000, almost three million, people—and the province's area is 14,132 square miles, almost 33 percent of the country's land area.

Oriente is the province with the largest number of children; it has the highest birth rate, especially in the mountain areas. There you'll find the largest number of children in this country, and that constitutes an enormous resource for the future of the nation. However, the material base for education—teachers and resources—needed there is enormous. The number of children is terrific there. How much could be accomplished in that province—and the Revolution is duty-bound to develop it, from the standpoint of its human and natural resources, not as a question of doing justice to a province, but rather as a matter of national interest. . . . And, as the nation builds links with the rest of the world, this would be of international value, as well. Oriente's mineral, agricultural, water and other resources must be developed. . . .

14

THE PROBLEM OF UNDERDEVELOPMENT*

Fidel Castro

The world is divided into developed and "underdeveloped" countries. The euphemism "developing" is also used for these countries; in the language of international organizations they are called developing countries. And we would like to call attention to some data that may help our masses understand the problem of Cuba within the context of the present world situation. . . .

Many of the developed countries initiated their development more than a hundred years ago. They developed slowly and, in many instances, with the aid of the resources of their colonies, which were mercilessly plundered, and with resources taken from the sweat of their masses, who were incredibly exploited. Written testimony is available of all of these; there are chapters written by Marx and Engels concerning the plight of the working class in England: workers who labored fifteen or sixteen hours each day, and children under ten years of age who worked full time under the worst conditions. In other words, the resources enabling those countries to accumulate capital to invest and on which development was based were taken from the backs of the workers.

Industry was mainly developed in Europe, the United States, and Canada in such a way that today these countries with developed economies have an extraordinary head start in relation to the underdeveloped nations, which they exploited yesterday and which they exploit today in many ways, directly or indirectly.

* Editors' translation and excerpts of Fidel Castro's speech delivered on March 13, 1968.

Let us look at the figures for the gross products of the developed countries—what their production was in 1960 and what it is expected to be in 1975. The United States, with a population of 180 million persons, had a gross national product of $446,100 million. This was the gross national product of the U.S. economy in 1960, and in 1975 it should reach $865,400 million. Western Europe had a gross product of $394,659 million in 1960 with a population of 353 million inhabitants. It is estimated that in 1975 the figure will be $750,748 million for a population of 402 million. In 1960 Japan had a gross national product of $55,604 million for a population of 93 million inhabitants, and in 1975 it is estimated that the figure will increase to $138,350 million for a population of 106 million persons. Canada had a GNP of $31,530 million with a population of 17 million in 1960; it is estimated that in 1975 the figure will be $63,527 million for a population of 23 million inhabitants.

These are the figures for the major developed capitalist countries of the world. . . . All these countries—the United States, the Western European countries, Japan, and Canada—had a total gross national product of $927,893 million in 1960, and in 1975 it is estimated they will have $1,818,025 million. That is almost $2 billion. The Spanish billion, at least in my time, was a million millions; I believe the U.S. billion is a thousand millions; here I am talking about Spanish billions.

And what was Latin America's gross product in 1960? It was $61,750 million for a population of 204 million. That is, $61,750 million in all of Latin America as compared to $446,100 million in the United States. According to optimistic estimates, which probably will not be borne out, in 1975 Latin America will have a gross product of $117,800 million for a population of 299 million inhabitants. . . .

In 1960 all the countries of the underdeveloped world produced a total of $159,520 million for a population of 1,294 million. That is, all the underdeveloped world together produced a third of what the United States produced and less than half of what Western Europe produced. And it is estimated that this will reach $301,000 million in 1975. That is, in 1975 the countries of the underdeveloped world, all together, will have a gross product much lower than the United States' gross product for 1960.

The entire underdeveloped world, now with 1,294 million inhabitants, will reach 1,853 million by 1975. Thus the developed world produced twelve times as much per capita in 1960 as the underdeveloped world, and in 1975 this per capita production will be fourteen times as great.

The developed world will increase its production by almost a billion while its population will only increase by some 122 million. In other words, 122 million new inhabitants, but $890,000 million increase in production. Meanwhile, the underdeveloped countries will increase population by about 559 million, but their total production will increase by only $142,000 million.

Thus from 1960 to 1975, in developed countries, production as an average will increase by $7,300 a year for every additional inhabitant, while in the underdeveloped world the increase for each new inhabitant will be $250 a year. For each new birth in the developed countries production will increase twenty-nine times as much as it will for each new birth in the underdeveloped countries.

Translated into available income this means the following: the per capita available income in the United States in 1960 was $1,762; in 1975 it will be $2,564. That is an increase of $802.

Canada in 1960 had an average income of $1,296; in 1975 it will be $1,981, an increase of $685. France in 1960: $1,078; in 1975: $1,848, an increase of $760. Britain in 1960: $1,087; in 1975: $1,620, an increase of $533. Italy in 1960: $960; in 1975: $1,733, an increase of $773. Japan in 1960: $393; in 1975: $860, an increase of $467.

To take the underdeveloped countries as a whole: the underdeveloped world's available per capita income in 1960 ranged from $70 to $85, while in 1975 it will range from $90 to $110. . . . If in 1960 the average increase, or rather the per capita available income in the United States, for example, was twenty-two times as much as that of the underdeveloped countries, in 1975 it will be twenty-five times larger.

The imbalance—that is, the deficit in the balance of payments between the underdeveloped nations and the developed capitalist countries in world trade—was $4,640 million in 1960, and it will be $10,500 million in 1970 and $18,900 million in 1975.

We must add to this incredible situation of poverty the profits repatriated from investments, that is, the amount drained off by consortiums and monopolies must first be subtracted from the profits that would have accrued to the underdeveloped countries. And there is still an even more subtle—although very evident—method of exploitation: the fact that the developed world imposes its own conditions upon the underdeveloped world. The prices paid for the products of the underdeveloped countries are ever lower, while the manufactured goods of the developed world are sold at ever higher prices. It is estimated that tea, for example, will drop some 6 percent in price by 1975; wool, 6 percent; cotton, 6 percent; cacao, 9 percent; skins and hides, 9 percent; jute fiber, 14 percent; rubber, 32 percent.

This is the situation. Does it have any solution? Is there a way out? How was the situation created? Can any underdeveloped country repeat today the history of those countries when they began their industrialization? If not, why not? What are the major obstacles? One factor, no doubt, is population increase.

Let us look at just how the population of the world is increasing. In 1967 the population of the world increased by 70 million persons. It will reach a total of 3,500 million in 1968. In 1968 there will be 118 million births and 49 million deaths. At this rate of population increase, by the year 2,000 the world will have 7,000 million inhabitants. And for many of you, especially the students, the year 2,000 is not so far away. . . .

And what is the situation in Latin America? Let us look at what the United States Demographic Office states in information received on March 10:

The Demographic Office today predicted that within thirty-two years the population of Latin America will increase by 157 percent, the highest rate of increase in the world. The present population of this region, some 268 million, will increase to 690 million by the end of the century. In contrast, the population of North America and the Soviet Union will increase by 42 percent and that of Europe by just 25 percent.

That is, Europe, whose population of 353 million produced some $400,000 million in 1960, will increase its population by 25 percent in thirty-two years. At the same time, Latin America, whose population of 204 million inhabitants produced a total of $61,750 million in 1960—that is, less than one sixth as much as Europe—will have a population of 690 million in thirty-two years. . . .

What was the rate of population growth when England began its industrial development? It was 0.6 percent a year. At that time plagues, diseases, and epidemics still provided a sort of natural balance. Plagues appeared and wiped out large segments of the population. Modern medicine was then non-existent.

So the rate of population growth was as follows then: England, 0.6 percent; France, 0.4 percent; Belgium, 0.7 percent; Germany, 0.8 percent; and Italy, 0.8 percent.

With an 0.7 percent increase in population it would take fifty years to grow 40 percent.

During the first sixty to one hundred years of their development those countries achieved only a 1 percent increase in gross product per person each year. That is, then they had four times greater available per capita income than that of a person living in an underdeveloped country today. That is to say that once they had reached a level four times higher than that of any underdeveloped country today, they raised, or rather a raise occurred—since this was not the product of specific planning but rather the result of a prevailing reality— of 12 percent in the amount of gross product invested in economic development.

Now, that is the story of how development began, what the population increase was, what percentage of the gross product was invested, what percentage of growth they reached, and how much they grew from sixty to one hundred years.

On the other hand, if a country's population grows at the rate of 2.2 percent yearly, in fifty years it will be tripled. Thus, while the population of the developed countries in the beginning of their development increased by 40 percent in fifty years—or could have increased by that percentage—the countries that are underdeveloped today, or any underdeveloped country that increases its population by 2.2 percent, will triple its entire population in fifty years and will need to invest no less than 12 percent of the gross product to compensate for the population growth.

Consequently, while the countries that we were talking about compensated for the population growth by investing 6 percent and increased production by 1 percent yearly, an underdeveloped country with a 2.2 percent population growth rate at present needs to invest double that amount to compensate for the population increase, without augmenting its annual per capita production.

If such a country wants to increase its gross product per capita by 1 percent, it must invest no less than 16 percent of its gross national product. Thus, a country with a 2.2 percent rate of growth, investing 16 percent of its gross product, will compensate for the population increase, and its production will grow by 1 percent annually. In eighty years that country would double its income, and that income is today ten times less per capita than Europe's, and twenty times lower than that of the United States.

In order to increase the per capita gross product by 2 percent, a country whose population grows by 2.2 percent each year should invest 20 percent of its gross national product in economic development.

But none of those developed countries reached an investment of 20 percent until its income was already five or six times as high as the present income of the underdeveloped countries. . . .

Latin America, with a 3.2 percent population growth rate, would need to invest 25 percent of its gross national product in order to achieve a 2 percent annual per capita increase in its gross product. It would need to invest 25 percent of its GNP, which it does not invest, nor can it invest, nor under the prevailing political conditions will it ever be able to invest. Even with an incomparably higher per capita income no currently developed country ever invested such amounts. . . .

In countries with a 2.2 percent population growth rate and a low average life expectancy, more than 30 percent of the population is under ten years of age and cannot participate in production. So that is another factor related to this enormous yearly increase. In the underdeveloped countries more than 30 percent of the population is under ten years of age, while in the developed countries the percentage fluctuates between 15 and 18 percent. This means that the rich countries, which have more available income, have less population under ten years of age—about half of the same population category as the poor country with a very low per capita income. The percentage of the population under ten years of age in an underdeveloped country is double that of a developed country.

In the developed countries, per capita food production increases nearly 2 percent a year, the slow increase of their population notwithstanding; with all their technology, the developed countries achieve an increase of 2 percent. In Latin America as a whole, with a population growth of over 3 percent, the per capita food production in 1961 was 2 percent lower than what it had been prior to the Second World War. . . .

What factors that facilitated development when those countries were developing in the past obstruct development today? We have already discussed the problem of population. Another factor is modern technology, which involves an investment much higher than that of an earlier period. In the times of the first machinery with low technical requirements, low cost, and low levels of investment, men who had practical experience would invent certain machines. The necessary investment per active worker—that is, investment in machinery required to keep a worker active—was equivalent to a worker's salary for five to eight months at that time. The necessary financial investment was the same as that earned by a worker in five or eight months.

Today, in order to build an industrial plant with modern technology in an underdeveloped country, it is necessary to invest in machinery the equivalent of a worker's salary for 350 months—that is, for thirty years. Therefore, for example, any of the cement factories we have, or the nitrogenous fertilizer plant in Cienfuegos, will cost more than $40 million in foreign exchange alone, and in all, more than $60 million, and will employ fewer than a thousand workers. Naturally, this fertilizer cannot be produced in any other manner if it is to be done efficiently. Otherwise it means wasting fuel, wasting all sorts of things. . . . The complexity of modern technology demands an enormous investment—that is, sixty times as much as was needed when the Industrial Revolution began in those industrialized countries.

Another problem: almost all the rudimentary machines with which the Industrial Revolution began could be produced in the country, so that England and France imported approximately 1.5 percent of the machinery they used. They imported only 1.5 percent.

The underdeveloped countries, given the technical complexity of modern machines, have to import close to 90 percent of the machinery needed. It is obvious that there is a difference between manufacturing a carriage and a locomotive. . . .

Today, when an underdeveloped country needs an industrial plant, it must import machines at a high cost because those machines are costly, and the equipment costs the country sixty times more than it used to cost per worker employed. And not only that: technical complexity demands skilled labor and specialists who must be trained over a long period of time, and the training programs are also costly.

These are not all the problems. Not at all. But I am pointing out some that serve as examples to explain the great and unavoidable difficulties that the underdeveloped countries have to face.

There is another issue that has to be taken into account. Many underdeveloped countries have sectors of the popula-

'tion devoted to many unproductive activities, such as bureaucratic and commercial activities, so that a very high percentage of the population and the resources are invested in those activities.

Those are the objective problems and difficulties. Now, let us consider the subjective ones: the social system, the political regime, the feudal exploitation of the land, strong-arm oligarchical governments imposed from abroad by imperialism and neocolonialism, the control of the economy by imperialist monopolies which sack the natural resources, even the technical resources. And one of the most serious problems is illiteracy. In 1950 90 percent of the underdeveloped countries had an illiteracy rate of more than 50 percent. . . .

Cuba is a country that began its economic development after the Revolution. The average rate at which the population of Cuba has been growing in the past five years is 2.3 percent annually. This rate is three or four times as great as the rate of the industrial countries when they began to industrialize.

In 1953 36.3 percent of the population was under fifteen years of age. In 1967 37.9 percent is under fifteen. In 1953 the percentage of the population over sixty years was 6.9 percent. In 1967, due to an increase in life expectancy, 7.2 percent of the population was over sixty. Perhaps these increases appear small, from 36.3 to 37.9 percent and from 6.9 to 7.2 percent. But let us consider how this affects the percentage of the population that is actively working. Taking fifteen and sixty as the age limits for active work, the change in the age structure represents some 226,000 fewer persons doing active work in 1967 than if the age structure had been the same as it was in 1953. If we had the same age structure we had in 1953—36.3 percent under fifteen and 6.9 percent over sixty —we would now have 226,000 more persons between the ages of fifteen and sixty. The increased birth rate, on the one hand, and, on the other, greater life expectancy, mean that we have 200,000 fewer people in the active work age bracket.

By 1970, according to present estimates, the population will reach 8,349,000. There will be 1,214,000 persons under five years of age; 1,125,000 from the ages of five to nine; 916,000 from the ages of ten to fourteen. In all, there will be 3,255,000 persons under fifteen—in other words, 39 percent of Cuba's total population. Think how production will need to be increased, milk production, food production, the production of every single item, for a population whose youth sector is increasing.

With an annual population growth rate of 2.3 percent and with almost 40 percent of the population made up of persons under fifteen years of age, the effort our people must make is considerable. Just to meet the population increase alone we must invest no less than 12 percent of the available gross national product. And to attain a 1 percent production growth rate, and double our income in eighty years, we must use at least 16 percent of the gross national product. If the economy is to develop at a rate of no less than 5 percent of the gross per capita product per year we must invest 30 percent of the available gross national product. And this effort has to be made primarily by half of the population, excluding children and persons over sixty years of age.

Naturally these are only some of the indexes. This does not mean that it all happens in an absolutely exact mathematical way. It all depends on what fields are selected for investment. We have many more possibilities in agriculture, because this is a natural resource available to us. It is a matter of climate. Furthermore, the same level of technology is not required for the development of agriculture as for the growth of a steel industry. Nor does it require the same amount of investment. Clearly, some fields require greater or lesser investments than others. But I wish merely to present an idea, and this is the only way to explain how a country develops, what obstacles are involved, the significance of population growth and its influence on development—an idea of the size of investments that must be made. Investing in development necessarily implies not consuming all that we might consume. We have a good example: our foreign exchange.

If we spend it all on consumer goods and nothing on a single machine, irrigation equipment, or machinery to build drainage systems or water conservation projects, what will follow is quite clear. We would eat today, but it is very certain that we would not be able to eat next year, and as time passed there would be progressively less food. Progressively less! With a growing population and greater dependency on climatic factors, on imponderables of every kind. The picture is clear.

How have our investments increased during these years? In 1962 state investments were $607.6 million; in 1963 $716.8 million; in 1964 $794.9 million; in 1965 $827.1 million; in 1966 $909.8 million; in 1967 $979.0 million; and in 1968 state investments are expected to reach $1,240 million. In 1967, including state capital investments and others, such as the increase in our cattle reserves, and the increase in inventories, the nation was able to devote 27.1 percent of the available gross national product to investments. This is including national resources and those capable of being obtained abroad.

In other words, with foreign credit we can buy bulldozers or powdered milk. Credit means that payments must be made later on. And those who have had occasion to stroll along Havana's Malecón Drive know how much equipment is entering this country. Moreover, this is not the most important factor. What is the work yield of equipment coming to Cuba today that is put to use by organized brigades, with military discipline and optimum maintenance? It is incomparably greater than at any other time.

In 1968 we will invest approximately 31 percent of the available gross national product. We believe that no other underdeveloped country today is doing anything like this—not even remotely! . . .

We have been making great efforts. The nation has made enormous investments in education, in universities, in educational programs. It does not matter if the fruits of these tremendous efforts, which began from practically nothing with the literacy campaign, cannot yet be seen. We must point out that no value has been assigned to voluntary work in these investment figures—that is, all voluntary work done is in addition to the figures already cited. All those hundreds of thousands of people who have been mobilized at one moment or another to fill bags for coffee seedlings, to plant, those who are working from one end of the island to the other in similar mobilizations, all the efforts they make, and all the trees they plant, are in addition to this 31 percent of the gross national product invested in economic development. And our people will someday see the results of this effort with great satisfaction and will be extremely proud of what they are now doing. . . .

15

REPORT ON THE CUBAN ECONOMY*

Fidel Castro

Today we are going to talk about our problems and difficulties, our setbacks rather than our successes, and we would like to make a series of analyses, even though we realize that a forum of this type is hardly the ideal place for either cold analysis or figures.

I don't usually come to events such as this loaded down with papers. However, this time I had no alternative but to bring some papers with me, since there are a lot of data and figures.

Let's express the essence of our difficulties in the simplest possible terms.

Above all, we want the people to be informed. We want the people to understand. We want the people to gird themselves for battle. This is because our problems will not be solved by means of miracles performed by individuals or even by groups of individuals. Only the people can perform miracles.

So that you will better understand what I am going to explain, I would like to give you some data:

In 1958, on the eve of the triumph of the Revolution, Cuba's population was 6,547,000. In 1970 it is estimated that the population will reach a figure of approximately 8,256,000. Our population has increased. We will know the exact figure after the census that is going to be made within a few weeks has been finished; this will be made very carefully to include everybody—that is, everybody but those who want to stop being a part of this conglomerate.

For them, it will be the dolce vita and the consumer society.

---

* Speech delivered on July 26, 1970. The present version is an official Cuban Government translation.

We will stay with other things that are harder but more honorable and worthy. Though in the social order the real harshness of life is the lot only of cowards.

As I said before, our population has registered an increase of 1,709,000, of whom 844,000 are minors under working age and 188,000 are men and women over working age. Out of that 1,709,000, there are 1,032,000—that is, 60 percent—who are either under 17 or over working age—women over 55 and men over 60. In other words, 60 percent who do not participate in production.

Not counting those who are studying or are physically or socially disabled, the net increase in labor resources in these last 12 years has been 580,000. On the other hand, the needs of the economy for its new economic and social activities and the replacement of those who have reached retirement age call for 1,200,000 people.

What with our new labor resources and the number of unemployed that existed before the Revolution, we have been partly—only partly—able to meet our growing manpower needs.

Of course, at the beginning, in 1958, there were 686,000 unemployed. A large number of them are working today; others have reached an age that no longer makes them fit for work; and there remain 75,000 who, neither housewives, students nor disabled, simply do not work. There are 75,000 of them.

These are the figures showing our population growth along these years and the makeup of the population.

According to estimates, how will things stand between 1970 and 1975? The situation will be even more serious. It is estimated that between 1970 and 1975 there will be a population increase of 660,000. Of these 660,000, the increase in minors—that is, the increase in those under working age—will be 280,-000, the increase in people over working age will be 108,000 and the increase in people of working age will be 275,000. Thus, not counting those who will have to study and others who, for various other reasons, will not work, there will be a net increase in our labor resources of 167,000 people in the next five years.

Therefore, our problem in connection with manpower and the makeup of the population will continue to worsen in the next five years and will only begin to improve toward the end of the decade, close to 1980. It is estimated that the population increase between 1975 and 1980 will be 828,000. The increase in those under working age will be 160,000, the increase in those over working age will be 121,000, the increase in those of working age will be 550,000 and the net increase in our labor resources between 1975 and 1980 will be 535,000.

This is what the trend will be for the next five years, and—I repeat—it will begin to improve from 1975 to 1980.

Now, then, this population makeup—this happens not only in our country but also in other countries that have experienced a population explosion, which means almost all of the underdeveloped countries—means that only 32 percent of the population is engaged in activities related to our economy. That is, less than a third of the population is engaged in furnishing goods or services. And that third includes those who are furnishing services that constitute investments for the future, such as public health services and education, and those engaged in services that are absolutely necessary to the defense of the Revolution and the homeland.

We must know these figures, first of all, in order to be fully aware of the situation, so we will know some of the obstacles that must be overcome.

I would like to point out that some of the services have increased, as a result of this population makeup and also as a result of elementary measures of justice that the Revolution had to adopt—measures which, in our opinion, could not be postponed. Social security, first of all.

A total of 379,842 retirement and survivors' pensions have been granted since the triumph of the Revolution. That is, in the revolutionary process, a total of 379,842 people have had their right to these benefits recognized and these allotments have been paid to them.

In addition, a total of 193,260 survivors and retired people—most of whom had received pensions as low as under ten pesos a month—have had their allotment increased to a minimum of 60 pesos a month.

The outlay for social security services increased from 114.7 million pesos in 1958 to 320 million in 1970.

Public health services: In 1958 there were 8209 workers in public health services. In 1969 the number increased to 87,646—87,646! Outlay for public health services, which in 1958 was 22.7 million pesos, increased to 236.1 million in 1969.

Outlay in education or in general services in education: In 1958 there were 936,723 people enrolled in schools throughout the country. A total of 2,239,464 enrolled in the 1969–70 school year—1,560,193 of them in primary education.

In 1958 there were 23,648 workers in public education. In 1969 the figure rose to 127,526.

The number of scholarships—15,698 in 1958—is now 277,505. This figure does not include the children in day-care centers and semiboarding schools.

In 1958 the outlay for public education was 77 million pesos. This figure rose to 290.6 million in 1969.

The number of beneficiaries of social security—that is, those who received new pensions and retirements—public health workers, workers in education and scholarship students amount to no fewer than 900,000 in 1970. And, if we add the men engaged in the defense of our country, the figure goes over 1,100,000.

Outlay for social security, public health and education—three sectors—which was 213.8 million pesos in 1958, amounts to no less than 850 million for 1970. If we add the outlay for defense to these three sectors, the total comes close to 1200 million pesos a year.

I wanted to give comparative figures in pesos as well as comparative figures in people.

The average number of double rations distributed among industrial workers and workers in services, scholarship students, those in day-care centers and semiboarding schools, people mobilized for agricultural work and the sugar harvest, hospital patients and combatants of the Ministry of the Revolutionary Armed Forces and the Ministry of the Interior amounted to approximately 2,250,000 per day.

Needless to say, such services must continue to increase. Suffice it to say that the number of working women increased from 194,000 in 1958 to close to 600,000 in 1970—which, naturally, creates new, extensive needs for not only children's day-care centers but also semiboarding schools.

At the same time, notwithstanding the number of people working in education mentioned here and our expenditures for education, we must say that those needs are still far from being fully met—in both quantity and quality. There are still many cases of pupils who attend school only half a day, as a result of shortages of teachers and classrooms.

We will need 7000 new primary school teachers a year from 1970 to 1975. Seven thousand new teachers must be graduated every year! Some of them will go to meet outstanding needs, another part will replace those who must retire because of old age and the rest will constitute increases in both quantity and quality. Consequently, we need 35,000 new teachers in the next five years. For the same reasons, we will need 4000 new junior high school teachers every year through 1975.

One thousand eight hundred new senior high school teachers will be needed every year. This means that we need to graduate—but this does not mean that we are going to graduate them, because, unfortunately, we can't do this yet—12,800 new primary and junior and senior high school teachers every year—an aggregate of 64,000 in five years.

I believe that anyone can understand the significance that the solution or our failure to solve this problem has for this country. I believe that anyone can understand what a country will become or not become if it solves or fails to solve the problem of education. And the problem has to be solved in the conditions that I have explained to you, and all those resources have to be obtained from a population whose age makeup is worsening, with 32 percent—a percentage that will not grow in the near future—of the population producing all the resources.

By way of comparison, suffice it to say that the industrialized countries of Europe, including the socialist countries, with incomparably higher labor productivity, with much greater development of their productive forces, employ, or employed in the decade just past, approximately 45 percent of their total population. We are employing and will have to employ—not only for development, not only for providing for all of our unsatisfied needs, not only for our increasing needs—only 32 percent of the population. And, as we succeed in employing more women, more and more needs in the form of schools, day-care centers, semiboarding schools and the like will arise.

Under the Urban Reform Law, 268,089 families have been made home owners and do not have to pay any kind of rent; the value of that real estate is estimated at 3500 million pesos. In the same way, more than 100,000 families in rural areas who before the Revolution had to pay rent for their land have received the lifetime use of that land absolutely free.

The increase in the number of retired workers, free educational services and medical care and the essential services of the nation's defense, together with the savings in connection with home and land rentals, have caused the amount of money and savings accounts in the hands of the people to shoot up to 3000 million pesos.

A price policy to compensate for this imbalance—this will help us and also those abroad who are interested in such things to understand the reason for rationing—would have been nothing short of a ruthless sacrifice of those sectors of the population with the least income. This is quite plain: a price policy aimed at evening up the total amount of goods and services that the people have to purchase—the things that are distributed free of charge are not taken into consideration in this—on the one hand, and money, on the other, would have been nothing less than a ruthless sacrifice of that part of the population with the lowest income.

That policy could be employed in connection with luxury and nonessential goods and services, but never for necessities. This is how we feel about this problem, and we believe that the people feel the same way.

Devaluation—or rather, the exchange of the currency,

which was done in the early years—is a correct measure when applied against the bourgeoisie, but it would be despicable if enacted against the workers' savings. This is how we feel about it, and we believe the people feel the same way.

This is just one of the complex problems of our economy that we must solve.

Now, then, how are these problems, such as the population makeup and the increase in essential and necessary services, translated . . . ? Because I don't believe there is a single person who doubts how essential it was to grant old-age pensions to men and women who had been exploited all their lives. What kind of a people would this be if it selfishly failed to repair such an injustice; what kind of a people would this be if it remained unmoved by the plight of cane-cutters who, after laboring for 30 long years, ended up with a pension of only seven pesos a month?

I don't believe there is a single Cuban who has the slightest doubt about the effort that has been made in connection with the health of the people, to remedy the tragic conditions in which millions of people in this country lived, where scores of thousands of families witnessed the death of their young ones—this could be figured mathematically—and I don't believe that anybody, much less any of those who have had an opportunity to travel in the interior of the country, has the slightest doubt as to the absolute necessity of the medical services provided by the Revolution, whatever their price. On the contrary, every time the people discuss this problem, they express the wish to have a polyclinic of such and such a size in the place where they live, or to have a doctor where they work or live, or at least to have one on duty during the night. We must say that, of the thousands of sailors in our merchant marine who traverse the oceans of the world and the thousands of fishermen in our fishing fleet, very few are on ships which we have been able to supply with a doctor to attend cases of accident and urgent sickness. To tell the truth, we are far from having taken care of that need.

We don't believe there is a single Cuban who has any doubts about the essential and dramatic need of lifting this country out of the state of illiteracy and semi-illiteracy in which it finds itself. If 30 percent of us were illiterates, 95 percent of us were semi-illiterates. And we'll still be paying the price of that illiteracy and semi-illiteracy for many years to come. We can see this; we have occasion to see this every time we find comrades in posts of leadership, in factories and other activities who, though full of the best intentions in the world, in many instances don't have more than a sixth-grade education.

We don't know of anybody who, when discussing education, has told us that we should have made less of an effort in education, granted fewer scholarships, offered fewer jobs to teachers and built fewer schools. What we do find all the time throughout the country are thousands upon thousands of persons who say that such and such a school is too small, that it is overcrowded, that a larger one should be built, that a double session has to be established, that a dining room should be provided. There are thousands upon thousands who say we need more and better teachers, more books and more school supplies, and there are towns where the people want to have junior and senior high schools. Moreover, there is a demand for more and more scholarships. This is because already no fewer than 60,000 pupils are being graduated from the sixth grade every year, and in the near future, if we succeed in winning the battle of education, no fewer than 150,000 should be graduated every year.

And I ask myself if the future of the children of this nation is only to reach the sixth grade, if the future of this people in the midst of a world that is undergoing a technological revolution at a terrific pace can be any future at all with a sixth-grade education as an average. Today a sixth-grade education is practically equivalent to illiteracy.

Therefore, despite all our outlays and efforts, what we find today is a tremendous demand for new outlays and new efforts.

And I don't believe there is a single Cuban—we don't believe there is a single revolutionary—who thinks that this country should have folded its arms in the face of that most powerful imperialist enemy 90 miles from our shores, an enemy that did not hesitate to use all means and weapons to destroy our Revolution. I don't believe there is a single Cuban who thinks that, in the face of this enemy's actions, in the face of every threat and danger, our people should have remained unarmed and defenseless. On the contrary, the vast majority of the people have learned how to use weapons, as they have realized that the number of permanent cadres and men would not suffice for the defense of the country if that enemy attacked. In that essential task of the Revolution it has been necessary to employ hundreds of thousands of men—we can say hundreds of thousands, though the number may be under 300,000—and scores of thousands of cadres. It is true that, just like our students, they take part in tasks of production in critical periods—that is, in periods of peak manpower demands in the countryside, as during the sugar harvest—but it is also true that, to the extent that our technological and high school students have spent long months cutting cane, we'll have to wait more years to have the technicians we need so urgently. And, to the extent that our soldiers have had to spend months in the canefields, we have had to sacrifice their combat preparation in case of war. Unfortunately, given the low level of our productive forces and our labor productivity, we'll have to continue doing this.

These are realities imposed on us by the Revolution itself. However, we are not mentioning them as excuses and pretexts or as an explanation or the only explanation of our problems. We mention them simply as facts to serve as the basis for an overall evaluation.

To all this we must add one more reality—one that weighs rather heavily—which is our own inefficiency, our inefficiency in the general work of the Revolution.

What does this conflict among the various needs posed by development result in? If we want to build a plant such as the one in Cienfuegos, with a capacity to produce half a million tons of nitrogenized fertilizers per year—fertilizers we are now importing, since what we produce here is not actually made here but is rather mixed of various elements we import—we will have to invest more than 40 million dollars.

And the same thing is true of every other industrial plant and every item of machinery and equipment this country imports.

The conflicts stemming from the various needs posed by

development, together with the supply of those essential resources, considering the age makeup of our population, plus the unquestionable inefficiency of all of us. . . .

We have just finished waging a heroic battle, a battle that can truly be called heroic. The heroes of that battle are represented here. The people were the heroes of that battle, the battle for the ten million tons, both in the planting and in the harvesting. And enough cane was cut to produce practically ten million tons, enough to have resulted in ten million tons if the industrial side of the sugar-making process had held up its end.

The people were heroes—not only in fulfilling that task, but even more so in deciding to cut every last stalk of cane, even when they knew that the ten million tons would not be reached. And the people followed through on that. There is still a little cane left in Oriente Province, but we decided that it was no longer reasonable, from any point of view, to continue cutting after July 23.

Of course, we achieved a large increase in sugar production: more than four million tons over what was produced last year. This is a production increase that is a true record, one that will be really difficult to surpass—this doesn't mean that someday we won't produce more sugar but it will be difficult to achieve such an increase in production again—especially if we consider what we have said about the age makeup of the population and the shortage of manpower, because there have been not only quantitative increases in our needs but also qualitative changes, as well, because, in the past, hundreds of thousands of Cubans in our countryside had to work from 15 to 17 hours a day cutting cane with a machete and loading it by hand, hauling it in ox-drawn carts, starting in the wee hours of the morning. Only by working no less than 15 hours a day could they complete the task.

And today there are no Cubans in our fields who, except in cases of trying to reach a goal or fulfill a pledge, as a matter of honor—such as these comrades here, these Heroes of Labor. . . . The reasons why our workers put forth extraordinary efforts are not the same as in the past, when they were spurred by hunger and death, for now they are motivated by their sense of honor.

The unquestionable fact is that the former motivations are not, nor could they in any way be, parameters of work. Neither could the Revolution simply say to the people of Cuba: "Continue working 16 and 17 hours a day while the country attains development." Even if it were theoretically possible to keep that up, from the political point of view it would be entirely advisable to send any government official who tried to put such a measure into practice to the insane asylum.

Let us not forget that in the beginning we were just a rebellious people, emotionally revolutionary, but very confused regarding political and social problems, and thoroughly indoctrinated by imperialist newspapers, magazines, films, books and other media.

Let us not forget it and we affirm it, not with any feeling of shame, but rather with pride. And as proof of what a people is capable of achieving, as proof of the possibilities of a revolution, we must say that in 1959 the majority of our people weren't even anti-imperialists. There was no class consciousness. Only class instinct, which isn't the same.

It is necessary to recall that the first years were the years of great political and ideological battles between the capitalist road and the socialist road, between the proletarian path and the bourgeois path, and the task facing the small revolutionary vanguard was above all to gain the awareness of the masses.

No one spoke of production then—the capitalists were the ones concerned with production—nor of data or statistics or structures. The problem was the needs accumulated as a result of unemployment, exploitation, abuse and injustice of all sorts.

The battle against the enemies of the Revolution was waged in daily events and on the ideological battlefield.

So there have been not only quantitative but also qualitative changes in the needs. And we must continue to carry out tasks like that of the harvest and still in conditions of manual labor. In these years many life-long canecutters retired, and many other Cubans who had formerly worked 15 or 16 hours a day shifted to other activities. And nobody was going to stop them. Nobody could stop them. No revolution could tell a man: "You are doomed to spend the rest of your life in this work, without hope of learning to operate a machine or of working at something else."

And these tasks are carried out today, not by those who in the past had to do them in order to avoid dying of hunger, but in their great majority by workers from industry and other services, students and soldiers.

And we said that in these new conditions the tensions become evident, and in these conditions we waged the heroic battle. But we were unable to wage the simultaneous battle.

This term was much used before the 10-million-ton harvest, and while the cane for the 10-million-harvest was being planted. It referred to our need to carry out that indispensable effort that, as we explained on one occasion, was required not as a sports activity but for basic needs of the economy, for our development, to overcome and climb out of our poverty.

Let us not forget that in spite of everything during these years we have had an unfavorable foreign trade balance, mainly with the Soviet Union. Let us not forget that we must import more than five million tons of fuel, a product we must import because oil exploration and discovery and putting oil wells into operation requires detailed study which can't be carried out from one day to the next. We are a country without coal, and practically without hydraulic energy. Our rivers are small and best adapted, under the conditions of our climate and other circumstances, to irrigation.

We import all the energy for the lights we use, for every lathe that moves, for every machine and motor of every kind. This energy replaces man in all kinds of activities; it powers cane-conditioning-centers, moves machines, satisfies essential needs.

We have never found a single citizen who says: "Why so much light? Why not reduce the light?" But rather citizens who say: "There is no electricity; we want more electricity; we need power plants; we need this and that, we need machinery, we need transportation; we don't have this and we don't have that."

And even so, we import more then five million tons per year plus the wheat we consume and the raw materials we use in many of our industries and the machinery we need. And we have been investing somewhat more than we have produced.

I repeat that we were incapable of waging what we called the simultaneous battle.

And actually, the heroic effort to increase production, to raise our purchasing power, resulted in imbalances in the economy, in diminished production in other sectors and, in short, in an increase in our difficulties.

Of course the enemy insisted that the 10-million-ton sugar harvest would lead to some of these problems. It was our duty to do everything possible to avoid it. And actually we haven't been capable of doing so.

Our enemies say we have problems, and in this our enemies are right. Our enemies say we have problems, and in reality our enemies are right. They say there is discontent, and in reality our enemies are right. They say there is irritation, and in reality our enemies are right.

As you see, we aren't afraid to admit it when our enemies are right.

But I'm going to give more data. This that I have here is not a speech. No sir, it is not a speech. This data is part of a highly secret economic report. What I have here is not a speech but the secrets of the economy, one of those things that are written and discussed in secret so that the enemy won't learn of them. Here we have them. We aren't revealing them for the benefit of the enemy. We couldn't care less about the enemy. And if the enemy makes use of some of the things we say and causes us deep shame, let us welcome it! The embarrassment will be welcome if we know how to turn this shame into strength, if we know how to turn the shame into a will to work, if we know how to turn the shame to dignity and if we know how to turn it into morale!

Here are the secrets for the people.

To analyze the problems by sectors, in the agricultural field we explained the problems of the sugarcane, the sugar produced and the records that have been established.

In rice planting, there has in reality been a considerable increase in the area under cultivation, increases in production; but we are a long way from being able to be satisfied yet, both in quantity and in quality with the advance of our rice plans.

In pastureland, as of June 15 some 92,300 acres had been planted, equal practically to the amount planted throughout 1969. There are almost 175,600 acres in preparation, so we can say that this year's planting should top the 330,000-acre mark, which will reverse the decreasing trend in the amount of available pastureland that we have been feeling in the last few years.

Meat. Deliveries of cattle on the hoof to the Meat Enterprise have been similar to those of 1969. Average weights have been low. Thousands of head: 485. That is, in 1968 there were 485,000 head; in 1969, 466,000; the trend in 1970 indicates the figure will also be around the 466,000 mark. In thousands of tons: in 1968 it was 154,000; in 1969, 143,000, and this year is expected to be about 145,000.

Average weight. In 1968: 697 pounds per head; in 1969: 675 pounds per head; in 1970: 682 pounds per head.

The shortage of fattened cattle and problems of transportation have produced distribution delays in the provinces of Oriente, Matanzas and Havana.

And that is not all. The effort made in regard to pasturelands, which as we stated, is on the increase, is not enough. A tremendous effort must be made to increase the number of calves born; likewise, a tremendous effort must be made to create pasturelands for regular grazing and for cattle fattening, for unless such an effort is made the result may very well be a reduction in the herds—because in a growing population it is imperative not only that every cow, or as many cows as possible, give birth to a calf, that the maximum number of calves reach maturity, but that all reach maximum weight in the least possible time. Otherwise the consequences may be that a cattle population that increases as a result of the non-sacrifice of cows may have to be reduced to avoid cutting levels of meat consumption. And, of course, every effort, every possible effort, must be made to avoid this!

Fresh milk output from January through May is 71.3 million quarts, 25 percent decrease compared to the same period in 1969, which was 95.1 million quarts.

This output drop occurs in both state-owned and privately-owned sectors, but is relatively greater in the latter. This decrease is a result of the limited number of installations and of nonreplacement of dairies which were taken out of production, such as the old palm-thatched dairies.

Our milk potentials are not being fully exploited due to a lack of installed capacity.

Therefore, the milk problem is no longer a matter of the number of cows and heifers with potential milk-producing capacity, but rather a problem of installations for handling milk output.

This output decrease has made necessary a notable increase in powdered milk imports from the freely-convertible-currency area in order to meet consumer demand within the established limitations.

These imports, for 1970, amount to 56,000 tons, at a cost of close to 12 million dollars. Similar imports are planned for 1971. Imports of saltless butter also result from this decrease in milk output.

Fishing. Although the fishing plan for the first half of the year was only 78 percent fulfilled, this represented approximately 8000 tons over the catch for the same period in 1969.

Cement. The amount of available cement as of July is slightly over that for 1969, and 23 percent less than the figure for the same period in 1968 due to difficulties in the transportation of sand and movement of the finished product.

Steel bars. Deliveries as of June were 38 percent under the figure for 1969 due to lack of transportation. On June 30 there were approximately 25,000 tons in the yards of the Antillana de Acero steel works. Nearly 60 percent of the first semester's production is lying still there in the steel plant's yard.

Fertilizers. This refers to the fertilizer that is mixed here. The production plan shows a 32 percent delay, that is, 130,000 tons, originated mainly by limitations in transportation of the finished product.

Farm machinery. Deliveries to the agricultural sector included in the national farm machinery production plan have been fulfilled only by eight percent as of May.

Nickel. According to the plan, exports of this product represent 217.8 million pesos in 1970. As of July, the plants in Nicaro and Moa have fulfilled 96 percent of their plan for the first half of the year. Therefore, there has been no problem in general in nickel production. There are no problems, either, in regard to fuels and lubricants, that is, in the refining industry. That sector is meeting its plan.

Electric power. Electric power output as of May was approximately 11 percent above that for the same period last year; at the same time, there was a high increase of roughly 17 percent in maximum demand.

In other words, electric power production has increased by 11 percent while the demand has grown by 17 percent.

The existing deficit in relation to maximum demand results in power interruptions—which will tend to become more frequent—caused by a shortage in the manpower needed for maintenance service and delays in the installations of new generating capacity.

The manpower shortage has an adverse effect on the laying of powerlines and the construction of power substations. The installation of the 220-kilowatt Renté-Nuevitas powerline to Holguin does not look as if it will be concluded by the end of the year, as had been planned. In other words, it may take a few months longer.

Rayon. In view of the critical manpower situation it has been necessary to cut down production plans, a measure which has principally affected the manufacture of tires. Reconditioning of the plant will be begun shortly for completion this year.

This plant, which is very important to our economy, the base for the production of tires which, in turn, are essential in such a critical sector as transportation, is facing a special kind of problem: contamination of the environment by sulfocarbon, as a result of the chemicals utilized in the plant.

What was the picture in the past? In the past, contamination was three times as high as it is today. Nowadays, the contamination has been cut down to one third. However, the owners and managers of that plant kept quiet about the harmful effects of sulfocarbon upon the workers' health. And yet many people wanted to work there, and considered the work a good, well-remunerated job. Today there is no secret about the contamination, because a revolutionary management cannot deceive the workers. Efforts were made to reduce the degree of contamination, and it was cut down to one third. But it is not easy to keep workers on the job even by rationalizing working conditions, which is feasible, by not prolonging the stay of workers in the plant beyond an established number of hours, rotating them from one department to the other and other measures. That is the plant that is allotted the best food and the largest amount of food in our country. So the difficulties there do not stem from mobilization to the harvest but rather from this special problem. And investments of more than one million pesos are being made in imports to totally eliminate the phenomenon of contamination by sulfocarbon. But the fact remains that this phenomenon has had an adverse effect on an important plant.

Paper and cardboard. Production has been affected in the amount of 5900 with regard to the plan by limitations in the supply of bagasse and by delayed reception of imports of aluminum sulfate and caustic soda. The fulfillment of this year's plan depends on the transportation of 30,000 tons of bagasse from Camagüey to the paper manufacturing plant of Damuji and the arrival of the caustic soda. In turn, difficulties in the transportation of products from the paper manufacturing plants to corrugating plants have led to nonfulfillment in the plan for the production of cardboard boxes—which, in turn, has an adverse effect on the production of condensed milk, beverages, paint, pharmaceutical products, etc.

Bottles. Production has been affected by manpower problems, and by difficulties in the transportation of raw materials to the various plants and of removal of the finished product. Imports of some two million dollars in convertible currency have been made to make up for insufficient production of medicine bottles. Larger imports are foreseen for 1971.

Tires and batteries. The tire production plan will fall short by 216,000 units, that is 50 percent of the plan. Of these 150,-

000 are tires for passenger cars. Deliveries to the shipping agency for light cargo transportation will also suffer. This is due to the reduced supply of rayon cord which, in turn, stems from problems in the rayon plant in Matanzas. In addition, irregularities in the arrival of imported raw materials have obliged us to make changes in the formulas to the detriment of the finished product.

Naturally, not all the tires used in our country have ever been produced here by any means. Large numbers are imported. But the adverse effects on the production of tires are felt.

The production of batteries is also 33 percent—approximately 16,000 units—below the aggregate plans as a result of delays in the delivery of lead oxide and casings. The low percentage in the recovery of casings, and the bad condition of these casings as a result of excessive use and the bad condition of the equipment has also had an adverse effect on the fulfillment of the plan.

Leather footwear. The plan for this year was scaled down from 15.6 to 13.9 million pairs. As of May, production had fallen short by approximately a million pairs, due to delays in the start-up operation of a new factory in Manzanillo, absenteeism and mobilizations for agricultural work. Some 400,000 pairs of work shoes and boots are included in this production lag. Moreover, there has been a deterioration in the quality of this footwear, due to changes in the technological process and the time needed for the curing of the hides.

Together with this, it should be pointed out that the factory that is turning out plastic footwear is nearly in full production, and no fewer than ten million pairs will be manufactured within the next 12 months. This will be a considerable aid in supplying the demand for women's and children's shoes. Such is not the case with men's work shoes or with closed shoes, because the material being worked with is still impermeable. There is a type of material being analyzed, called polyurethane, of which closed shoes can be made, and its technology is already being studied.

These machines were acquired and installed in a very short time. They are run by 300 workers—the overwhelming majority of whom are women—and these 300 workers will produce some 12 million pairs of shoes a year. In Santiago de Cuba the foundations are being laid for a similar plant. So that, while 600 workers—the majority of whom are women—in four shifts . . . because it must be pointed out that this plant already has, on a test basis, due to its great productivity, a shift system according to which the women who work the midnight shift are only required to work five hours. The longest shift is seven hours; the shortest, five; and there are two six-hour shifts. That is, there are two six-hour shifts, one five-hour shift and one seven-hour shift. Six hundred workers—almost all of them women—with these machines and this chemical product will produce 24 million pairs of shoes a year. At present, all types of footwear considered, some 19,-000 workers produce between 18 and 19 million pairs. This is perhaps indicative of the way—the only way—to solve the problems to which we have already referred.

Fabrics and garments. As of June, there was a production lag of 16.3 million square meters, due principally to a labor shortage, which was aggravated by mobilizations for agricultural work. This implies an adverse effect on the supply of textiles for personal and domestic use, which, in turn, caused delays in garment manufacture, and resulted in a reduction in direct distribution to the population. The delays in garment manufacture are mainly in children's school clothes, men's underwear, sheets, pillowcases and dresswear.

Toothpaste. 11% of the production plan has not been met, mainly due to a lack of aluminum tubes, because of the mobilization of workers to agricultural work.

Soaps and detergents. There is a 32% lag in the production plan, due to transportation problems abroad with raw materials such as dodecilbenzene and delays in the shipment of caustic soda.

There has also been a delay in the production plan for soaps, due to delays in shipments of raw materials and a lack of transportation facilities abroad for purchases made in the capitalist market.

Bread and crackers. In Havana bread production is 6% below plan for the first semester of this year and 2% below the first semester of 1969. This is due to absenteeism, breakages in the bakeries and power shortages. Cracker production has been affected primarily due to mobilizations for agricultural work.

Consumer levels. The following increases in distribution have been recorded: rice: the quota was raised to six pounds per person per month throughout the nation for home consumption in April and for state agencies in January; fresh fish: the supply to the population was increased in April; eggs: there was an indirect consumer increase.

Nevertheless, there has been a considerable restriction and decrease in other consumer goods: root and other vegetables, fresh fruits and fruit preserves.

Meat and poultry. Consumer levels have been restricted, due to certain priorities, and, furthermore, there have been delays in distribution to the population, due to transportation problems.

Beans and edible fats. There has been a slowdown in distribution, due to delays in imports, difficulties at the ports and internal transportation difficulties. Soft drinks: there has been a decrease in the supply, due to a shortage of bottles. Beer and alcoholic beverages, there has been a decrease in the supply, because of a slowdown in bottle return, due to limitations in the consumer network and the accumulation for the July festivities.

Cigars and cigarettes. An increase in the demand and a shortage of tobacco have been responsible for the rationing of these products.

There have also been difficulties in the distribution of industrial products such as detergent, toothpaste, textiles and clothes of all types, including underwear.

The following were the most important difficulties caused by internal transportation problems: delays in receiving trains with cattle from Camagüey and Las Villas, which resulted in a loss of weight in the cattle; nonfulfillment of the lard distribution plan and nonfulfillment of the plan for milk bottles to the provinces. Practically all the beer, milk and other bottles which are not imported are produced in the western part of the country; as is all the nonimported cloth; this re-

REPORT ON THE CUBAN ECONOMY 337

quires shipping all this material east. Bottles for all the beer made in Oriente are produced in the western part of the country, in Havana.

Industrial goods pile up in the provincial warehouse of the Ministry of Domestic Trade in Havana; the plan for transportation of raw materials used for soaps and detergents, as well as the finished product, was not fulfilled, the transportation of silica sand for the production of cement and bottles, the transportation of steel bars, the transportation of fodder for the animals on state farms and the transportation of bagasse for the paper factories in Las Villas were insufficient, there was a work stoppage in the nail factory in Santiago de Cuba due to a lack in the transportation of raw materials; and the national fertilizer production plan was not met because of low extraction of the finished product. There was a 36-percent drop in the number of railroad passengers, compared with 1969 in the January–May period, caused by the transfer of locomotives to the sugar harvest and the withdrawal of coaches from circulation due to lack of spare parts.

We have outlined the main difficulties in agriculture and industry. And the list, of course, is not complete.

There are also serious difficulties—which have been growing worse for some time—in certain services to the population, such as laundries. They are part of the limitations we have discussed here, and there are others we haven't mentioned.

This statistical outline contains only a part of the cause. We must say that inefficiency, the subjective factor, is partly to blame for these problems.

There are objective difficulties. Some of them have been pointed out. But we aren't here to discuss the objective difficulties. We must discuss the concrete problem, and man must contribute what nature or our means and resources have not been able to provide. It depends on man. Men are playing a key role here and especially the men in leadership positions.

We are going to begin, in the first place, by pointing out the responsibility which all of us, and I in particular, have for these problems. I am in no way trying to pin the blame on anyone not in the revolutionary leadership and myself. Unfortunately, this self-criticism cannot be accompanied by other logical solutions. It would be better to tell the people to look for somebody else. It would be better, but it would be hypocritical on our part.

I believe that we, the leaders of this Revolution, have cost the people too much in our process of learning. And, unfortunately, our problem—not when it is a case of the Revolution; the people can replace us whenever they wish—right now if you so desire! One of our most difficult problems—and we are paying for it dearly—is our heritage of ignorance.

When we spoke of illiterates we didn't include ourselves among the illiterates, or even among the semiliterates. We could best be classified as ignorant. And we were ignorant—almost without exception (and I, of course, am not the exception)—all of us. The problem is even worse. Signs of illiteracy or semiliteracy can be found in many men in positions of responsibility.

Foreign trade. In our foreign commerce we are faced with a non-fulfillment of export and import plans due to the following: delays in contracts; difficulties in securing ships to move our import and export cargo; a critical situation in loading and unloading at the ports.

The aforementioned has been responsible for the following: problems in the transportation of equipment coming from Europe; delays in the importation of raw materials and foodstuffs; ships delayed in port. Market difficulties in the convertible currency area with regard to the buying of wood pulp continue to affect the production of containers. That is, even with ready cash wood pulp is difficult to obtain. Although purchases for 1971 and 1972 have been authorized, we have yet to find the necessary supply.

Situation at ports of entry and internal transportation. The volume of dry cargo handled in our ports from January to April is 20 percent over the corresponding period for 1969. The number of ships in our ports is increasing and this situation will become more pronounced in the present month of July when 450 thousand tons of cargo are expected—a greater volume than in previous months. From March to the present moment the accumulation of cargo in our ports has increased from 100,000 to 140,000 tons on the average.

The mechanization program now being carried out should have a favorable influence on the solution of operational difficulties. Special attention must be given to the buying, building and reconditioning of barges and tugs to ensure the shipments of sugar and molasses contemplated in export plans for 1971. To this must be added dredging, reconditioning and building of important port facilities.

Internal transportation. Difficulties have been encountered in highways as well as railroad transportation. These difficulties have been determined partly by the priority given to the transportation of sugarcane and by-products, and partly by a lack of spare parts. The result has been a decrease in the number of available vehicles which has led to operational problems and seriously interfered with economic activities during the period.

From January to April of this year there was a 26% increase over the corresponding period last year in the volume of freight hauled by rail. During this period 60 locomotives (27% of the total number) were used for the transportation of cane. In transportation by truck the main difficulties have been due to the lack of spare parts and the high level of absenteeism, which has been one of the highest in recent years. And one of our most serious problems is the one we face when we go looking for the man to fit the job.

A few days ago, gathered in Céspedes Park in Santiago de Cuba, after having visited several factories one by one and having talked with thousands of people, we discussed the problems of each and every one of the industries in detail.

There was a 50,000-ton drop in the production of the Titán Cement Factory because its storage areas were full, while in the city of Santiago de Cuba—as in the other cities of the countries—there was a tremendous demand for cement to repair homes.

There was a 6000-ton drop in the production of the flour mill—a factory which had been enlarged—because the flour which had been produced wasn't removed and the factory had to shut down, which meant that a town might be left without bread, for lack of flour. And we had the wheat to produce the flour, and the workers and machines. The harvest wasn't to blame; the harvest resulted in some problems, but not all. I am giving you a few examples.

With the best of intentions, a concentration of transportation was carried out which proved to be excessive. These plants had to depend on an operative base.

There were problems in the cement industry with quarry equipment. We spent hours talking with the equipment operators about a series of specifications, calling on their experience and hearing their ideas so that, given the resources which will enter the country this year and those already available. . . . All the complementary equipment, plus a surplus to put the factory at peak capacity is on its way to the Titán Factory. Quarries require excess capacity, since an attempt to save can result in underutilization of the investment of millions of pesos in the industry and the work of hundreds of workers. . . .

In many industries we detected the following problems: lack of lathes, lack of work tools, lack of measuring instruments.

It's curious but microinvestments are what our country needs most at this moment, microinvestmental investments in lathes for maintenance in industrial shops, work tools that are lacking in almost all industries, and measuring instruments.

How did we find the spirit of the workers in Santiago de Cuba? Knowing their many needs—because if transportation affected distribution anywhere, it affected it in Oriente, and especially in Santiago—their main concern was production. And only later in the discussion did they raise any other problems! And sometimes we were the ones who had to bring up the other problems!

And sometimes we saw workers with torn clothes, or shoes —we have seen this—because these problems of quality . . . It wasn't so much the quantity as the quality of the footwear: the introduction of a new method of production which hadn't been sufficiently grasped, such as those rubber soles which led to their breaking. And the canecutters in Oriente and other areas know very well how a sole can fall off after five or 10 days.

And when quality is affected, what is the point of making 30 million pairs of shoes, if it doesn't solve the problem?

The problem of footwear was seriously affected by the decline in quality.

And workers with torn shoes and clothes were asking for lathes, machine tools and measuring instruments—more concerned about this than with their other problems. Even in spite of the bad food supply, they were more concerned with the factory and production than with food. And this is really impressive! This is a real lesson for us! This is a living confirmation in reality of the proletariat and what it is capable of. The industrial proletariat is the truly revolutionary class, the most potentially revolutionary class.

What a practical lesson in Marxism-Leninism! We began as revolutionaries not in a factory, which would have been a great help for all of us. We began as revolutionaries through the study of theory, the intellectual road, the road of thought. And it would have helped all of us if we had come from the factories and known more about them, because it is there that the really revolutionary spirit of which Marx and Lenin spoke is to be found.

And that's the spirit of the great majority! The few lumpen elements that may still exist—most of them recent arrivals in the plant—the absentees, they are of no importance. And sometimes conditions are such that the amazing thing is not that there are absentees, but rather that there are some who do come to work. And the spirit, the sense of duty that inspires those who go to work; and the scorn they feel for the lazy, those who are resting on their oars.

Go to any factory and ask the workers what should be done about the lazy ones, the ones who don't work. If you don't watch out, they'll go so far as to demand that they be shot. If you don't watch out, they'll demand just that! But, naturally, they will not go that far. Not that they lack the desire to do it, but they realize that the thing to do is to reeducate those people through work.

Thus, we came face to face with these problems, most of

which have a solution. And we must say that we are to blame
for a large part of these problems and that, simply as a result
of a lack of capacity. . . .

We—I began to explain an idea to you—were holding a
conversation with some people from Santiago de Cuba in
the city's park following a three-day visit. We were talking
about these problems with them, and we asked the people
there, "Do you know of someone who is efficient whom we
could entrust with some of these tasks?" That is what we
asked the people, because the tragic thing, one of the many
tragic things in our country—and this should not, by any
means, constitute a reason for resigning ourselves to putting
up with this tragedy—is our lack of cadres, of men with a high
enough level of training and intelligence who are capable of
carrying out the complex tasks of production.

These tasks are apparently easy. Most of the time we make
the mistake of minimizing the difficulties, of minimizing the
complexity of the problems. And we have seen this happen
to a number of well-trained comrades, comrades well known
to us for their iron will and their desire to do a good job—
we've had these experiences—and we have seen them, in a
specific task, going through what is practically an apprentice-
ship that lasts one, two or even three years before they begin
to do an efficient job.

If only we could solve our problems by simply replacing
these men! We have to make changes. There is no question
about the fact that many comrades have worn themselves out,
have "burned themselves out," as they say. There are some
who have had to pay for the errors committed by others, because sometimes the error points to somebody who simply
cannot do anything to solve the problem.

For example, we found that, in spite of the tremendous demand for housing and for repairs to houses everywhere—
and especially in Santiago de Cuba—the comrades in the districts of the local administration and the Party don't even have
a truck or a concrete mixer with which to face such demands.

As I said before, the cement factory there would stop operating. And, while the cement plant just outside Santiago

de Cuba was shut down, Santiago was suffering from a cement shortage.

It was established that a certain percentage of the cement production be earmarked for Santiago and, in addition, that whatever amount of cement that the state agencies—due to problems in transportation or plan nonfulfillment—weren't going to take away would be delivered to the city. This is easy, for the same trucks that are used for the hauling of the raw material from the quarries can be used to deliver the cement to Santiago. And there is one problem: once the cement is taken out of the silos and put into bags it cannot remain in the bags for more than three months. That is why, when the silos are full, we can't just say, "Let's pack the cement in bags for storage."

These comrades were shown how to solve the problem, since, for any repair work, they are dependent on an operational base of trucks—which they didn't have.

You cannot hold a man responsible for anything unless he is in a position where he can decide things, or else we appoint a man from the Party, we give him a job involving responsibility, and what we do is turn his job into a man-killer. He becomes a wailing wall, a poor man on whose lap everybody and his brother dumps his problems.

There are lists of houses to be delivered. There are lists, yes, but no houses. There are very few of them, or a plan for house building hasn't been completed. Thus, a worker who has headed the list for a year and a half and still has no house—and this has happened in Santiago—even loses all hopes of ever getting one.

As we talked with the women comrades of the beer and malt beverage brewery and the bottling plant in Santiago, we realized that nine out of ten women—nine out of ten!—mentioned the housing shortage as one of the most pressing problems. The women felt this more than the men did.

This was something similar to the problem as to whether malt beverage or beer should be served at the workers' dining room. The women, logically, said malt beverage, while the men, also logically, said beer.

In the analysis of recreation centers. . . . What happened

in Santiago? Every single bar was closed because of the cane harvest. The result was a kind of prohibition. As a result, the people started to make rotgut and mix it with other things, and they came up with some sort of product.

Really, we don't feel that was necessary, and it should teach us a good lesson. Because what has here been suggested and what we have been saying since the revolutionary offensive is that it is no crime to have a beer or some other alcoholic beverage; what we were against were those dark, dingy joints where having a drink or anything was a big mystery. The Revolution is not against drinking as such.

And that was done. And it is being analyzed.

We have asked the comrade in charge of this matter to analyze the question of recreation centers to decide on which days they should be open. And the workers should be consulted in the analysis of this matter. Even there we found different opinions: whether it should be two days or four days a week. And some workers said that their free day didn't fall on a Saturday or Sunday; it came on a Thursday or Friday or some such day. And the women had a different opinion than the men.

Once we took a poll on this question, and that's the way it turned out. So this time I told them: "Don't rush, find out what they think and why."

I was witness to an argument, an analysis carried out among men and women. One man, a vanguard worker whose opinion I asked, stood up and spoke. He said that a real worker, a conscientious worker, would be on time for work no matter what he did on his day off, even if he finished at 5:00 in the morning. He said that he had been working there at the factory and had gone to bed at 5:00 in the morning and had been back again at 8:00.

One woman had already said that the men would be absent from work.

Another woman said that there was no labor problem but that some men would leave half their salary at home and drink the other half.

Well, that was the problem. And I told them to study everything carefully so as to come up with a rational solution to the problem of the recreation centers, because the workers want them—especially those workers with great work spirit, workers who have spent up to eight months cutting cane, as many workers from Havana have done.

Often men with no authority to make decisions are the ones who have to confront the problems.

On the other hand, some people believe that problems can be solved miraculously, that it is just a matter of replacing certain individuals.

I was saying that it has been necessary to remove some ministers and that it will be necessary to make some other changes. But sometimes it occurs to me with a certain sadness that there might be some confusion when the masses think that the problem can be solved simply by replacing individuals. And sometimes people say, "If they take this one out and put that one in. . . ." And there are a tremendous number of government organizers and disorganizers and soothsayers.

But, of course, politics is not a game.

We must make changes, because, logically, there are comrades who have worn themselves out; they have run out of energy and are no longer able to handle the responsibility they have on their shoulders. And we must make changes. But what I want to say is that it would be a fraud and we would be guilty of demagoguery, of unforgivable deception of the people, if we tried to make them believe that our problems are problems of individuals, if we tried to conceal the root of the matter, if we didn't come right out and say that it isn't a problem of an individual, group of individuals or even teams. We believe this is a problem of the whole people! And we sincerely believe that the only way we can solve the problems we have today is by all working together—all of us—from the men in the highest positions of responsibility in the Party and state right on down to those in the most humble industrial plant and not just those in leadership positions there.

On this trip we discussed a series of ideas with the Minister of Labor. We said that we were still somewhat underdeveloped in the field of industrial administration; we explained why a factory of the people, which belongs to all the people, doesn't even belong to its workers. A worker wouldn't gain anything by being the owner of a cement factory together with his group, absolutely nothing at all. We have never shared that opinion.

We have seen the love the workers have for their factory —this is something else again—and believe it would be a good idea to link the workers' everyday life—even their family problems, vacations and birthdays, lots of things—to the job. The workers' affection for the factory would be strengthened if it were extended to tie in their families with their work. Some vacation plans have already been organized along these lines.

Some of the factories quite a ways out from Santiago were assigned some of the buses that are being put together here in a shop which has greatly increased its productivity. The shop is assembling about four medium-sized buses a day. We gave some of these buses to the factories so the workers would use them at certain hours of the day. If a shift at a power plant or oil refinery winds up late at night and the workers have to try to catch a bus at a time when there are fewer buses on the streets, logically, the factory's buses could be used to take the workers to their destination. These same buses can be used when the vacation period comes around, to take the workers and their families to the beach or other recreation areas.

The problem of housing distribution can be handled through the factories, as well. And the workers should be the ones to make the decisions. They, better than anyone else, know which worker needs a home most, or if he has a home. . . . He should speak about it. This problem should never be solved through administrative channels.

In the same vein, we told the comrades in Santiago de Cuba whom we have assigned the cement, trucks and electric concrete mixers that we couldn't solve that problem by looking for a labor force we don't have. Urgent problems such as that of housing can only be solved with the aid of the masses!

Why? We have already explained the manpower problems we have and our problems with important industrial installations, schools, hospitals and new factories.

Among other things, over 100 jobs involving the installation of the equipment that is already here must be done. We could add that the installation of plants that are already here must be completed before we bring in new ones. Before we bring in new plants, we must first have all the already established ones operating at full capacity. Before we purchase new plants, we must purchase lathes for maintenance shops; tools; gauging equipment; and, occasionally, even a motor—these are what we call microinvestments—in order to get all those plants operating at 100-percent capacity, first of all—and, if possible, at 110-percent—and raise the workers' productivity. We must also install all the equipment whose installation is still pending.

Suppose this crash program makes it impossible to organize the brigade needed to solve the problem of repairs. . . . What did we tell the people in a number of towns? In Caney, for instance, they said to us, "We don't have a barbershop or a store." And we said, "If we supply you with the materials, will you take care of the construction end?" The answer was, "We'll do it." The same thing happened in Matáguá, in Las Villas Province, and in Quiñones. We got the people together, and now they're even going to build a polyclinic. Right away a bricklayer pops up from somewhere, and then another, and then still another.

They're even going to build a 30-bed polyclinic! They want a polyclinic? Then, let them have the prefabricated sections and the equipment with which to do the job, and they'll take care of the construction. Because the main problem is to find 10 or 20 workers to build a house, anywhere. This problem of housing should be handled by the masses—repairs in some cases, construction in others.

And we used to say to our comrades, "Whenever there is repair work to be done, never decide what's to be done by yourselves; let the neighbors decide, for only they have the right to decide, with their spirit of equity and justice, who needs the repairs the most." Because, even though the decision may rest on the administration, it is subordinate to a series of contradictions and opinions and even subject to the danger of favoritism.

Let us conserve our men, let us protect our cadres from this danger and let's make it a point that it will be the neighbors who will make the decisions. And if the neighbors make a mistake, they are allowed to make mistakes. It may be hard, but it's their decision. If the workers in a factory err on deciding on a problem of that type, it is hard, but it's the people's decision.

Take the problem of plant management. Last time we spoke of the work of the Party, of how we had to revive the work of the mass organizations and give them a broader field. But that is not enough. New problems come up, and we must delve deeper into the matter. We don't believe that the problems of managing a plant should fall exclusively to the manager. It would really be worthwhile to begin introducing a number of new ideas. There should be a manager, naturally —for there must always be someone accountable—but we must begin to establish a collective body in the management of each plant. A collective body! It should be headed by one man, but it should also be made up of representatives of the advance workers' movement, the Young Communist League, the Party and the women's front—if such a front can be organized within the plant. We must remember that, in a factory, we cannot appoint the Party Secretary to the post of manager— there are certain things on which we must have a clear understanding—nor can we appoint the manager as Party Secretary. This is because, if he devoted his time to the task of production, he wouldn't have time for anything else. The plant works with machines that handle material, and the Party works with men, handles men. The Party's raw material are the workers, and the management's raw material is just that—material. It could be iron or any other material. Each shop has its own laws, and that shop must be attended to; somebody must always be concerned about it. These tasks must not be confused, and the Party should not be held responsible for the management of the plant. The Party's responsibility should be an indirect rather than a direct one. It is the Party that must immediately call the attention of the superior administrative body to any deficiency, any error of an administrative nature, but the Party should never tell the manager what to do. The functions of the head of the Party nucleus and those of the manager—or, rather, of administration—should be clearly defined.

Why should a manager have to be absolutely in charge? Why shouldn't we begin to introduce representatives of the factory's workers into its management? Why not have confidence? Why not put our trust in that tremendous proletarian spirit of men who, at times in torn shoes and clothes, nevertheless keep up production?

And we'll have to work seriously on the problem of industrial efficiency, based mainly on labor productivity.

There can be the case of two factories, in one of which the workers seem to have attained higher productivity, due to the fact that that plant is better equipped technologically and its work force is more highly trained, while another factory, working under different conditions and apparently with a lower productivity per man, may be putting forth a greater effort.

Why do we mention these problems to our workers? Because there is something that is real and crystal-clear: Arithmetically speaking, the account does not jibe nor can it jibe. Those figures we mentioned in connection with our population growth, the age structure, the basic services that cannot be curtailed except at the cost of paying a terrible price for it in the future. Nonetheless, with all our inefficiency, we must solve those problems that we mentioned. . . . We must win the battle against inefficiency! We must win the battle against those difficulties!

An effort of a subjective character—we were saying—has to be made by all the people.

These days it has been satisfying to see the people enjoying themselves. They certainly have earned it. We wouldn't want any worker's vacation to be spoiled by this analysis we are making here. We wouldn't want that at all. At the same time, we are very aware of the fact that there can be no rest for us. Those of us who have major responsibilities cannot take a rest.

To tell the truth, we have wished for the 8th or the 10th—when all activities will be resumed—to arrive. Deep down in our innermost feelings we have wished for the day when we'll begin tackling those problems. This is not the first time we have had to face our realities.

The comrades here have given me a certificate for something that I don't think is important at all. We actually cut the amount of cane the certificate says we have cut. But there are other comrades who went to the canefields at the cost of much greater sacrifice than we did. Our Comrade President also worked in the canefields many times, often despite health problems. This is not to say that our Comrade President's health is not good, but many times he went to the canefields while suffering from backache. Of course, we know of a great many other comrades who went to cut cane even being ill. Having cut the amount of cane we cut carries no special merit —it rather served as a diversion. Perhaps the hardest thing for us about cane cutting is not the physical work but having to do it while thinking about so many problems. During the first few days the hardest thing was to keep from thinking about the problems until we began to more or less control our thoughts.

The fact is that we would have liked to cut a little more cane than we did. We had had the illusion—as it were—that we would work four hours daily in the canefields all through the harvest, that we could live the utopia of dividing our time between mental and physical work, which is a most healthful thing. As you can see, our pace was good, but as of January 9 the thing came to a stop. As a matter of fact, we hadn't given any thought to the idea of winning a certificate. We rather thought of the scores of thousands of men who were making the effort and we had wished to share somehow the effort they were making. That's why we had wished—had had the illusion, if you wish—to cut cane all harvest long. But then the problems began to appear; the problems of low sugar yield, transportation and those connected with the mills. Then began a truly anguishing battle that went on day after day without letup: the battle of the sugar harvest in the face of a reality that was becoming increasingly evident.

In reality we have some debts pending with irony, with the illusion we have indulged in at times. We have some debts pending with our needs. We have debts pending with poverty. We have debts pending with underdevelopment. And we have debts unpaid with the suffering of the people: every time we hear a mother say that she has twelve children sleeping in one room, that the children suffer from asthma, that they suffer from this and that. Every time we see people suffering and asking for help, when we face the realities of life, we wish we were a magician and pull the solutions out of a hat. But this country faces the reality that we need a million new homes before all families can live in a decent house, one million!

And how much is needed to build a million dwellings! How much sand, cement and other building materials!

We have been enlarging our plant capacities to that end. We mentioned the Titán cement plant, but we must also mention the one in Mariel; we have to finish building the Siguaney plant and the one in Nuevitas. We must finish those plants any way we can and begin to produce cement at the earliest possible time, supplying them with everything they need, including an adequate work force. And if we don't have enough workers to build houses, if we have the necessary building materials we can work with the people's participation in many places and in others with the brigades that put up prefabricated dwellings. . . . The problem of productivity in home building has to be solved through those brigades. For some months now we have been working on the organization of the construction sector and we have seen all the problems having to do with equipment, industrial plants and everything else, including the kind of technology needed. This holds the only solution to the problem of building productivity, because if we were to employ scores of thousands of masons to lay bricks we still couldn't solve the problem. The people who are to live in those new homes could in many instances and with the necessary technical supervision take part in the work of building and thus help solve the problem.

But as we have said, we feel these realities and the need to overcome them very deeply, and we have a debt with these realities. This is the reason behind our impatience to renew work on a normal basis.

It will be necessary to take a series of measures in the leadership of our Party in order to, starting from above, solve some structural problems.

And it is no longer possible to direct social production with just a Council of Ministers. There are many agencies. Why? Because social production today depends on society's administration of its resources.

In the past, industries, schools and hospitals were often run by private owners. Today this is not the case. In the past, all a citizen expected from the state was that it build post offices or telegraph stations. He didn't dream of the state's solving his housing problem or any of his other problems. Today the citizen feels that the state should solve the problems. And he is right. This is a really collective mentality, a socialist mentality. Today everything is expected from the administrative apparatus, and especially from the political apparatus that represents it. Today it is not possible to depend on individual effort and means as was the case in the past.

The fact that today the people expect everything is in keeping with the socialist awareness the Revolution has created in the people. Any inefficiency in a service—I am not referring to those problems which cannot be solved by man but those which are within his power to solve and are delayed and left unsolved—can affect thousands of people.

Today it is impossible to direct and coordinate this entire apparatus. We must create a political structure to coordinate the different sectors of social production. For example, some comrades are already at work coordinating the activities of the Ministry of Domestic Trade, the National Institute of the Tourist Industry, the Food Industry and Light Industry—those sectors most related to consumption and to the people directly. Other comrades are at work coordinating different sectors of the construction industry. Groups of not more than seven or nine comrades—the number needed, but not too many—are coordinating the different sectors. For example, from the data we mentioned, the need to coordinate the activities of the Armed Forces Ministry, Ministry of Labor, Ministry of Education and Ministry of the Interior, can be easily understood, because these sectors draw their manpower from the same source. We must carefully coordinate and conciliate all the interests of the country through the activities of each one of them and the way in which they draw their manpower. We believe this is a fundamental and immediate task in our country. And this front will have to support and coordinate all these activities.

We must also add that nobody here is going to solve a problem if he doesn't obtain the cooperation of others. Seeing only one's own sector is inadmissible and absurd! More than a crime it is a stupidity! In a society where the means of production are collective, lack of coordination is stupid. Thus the need for coordinating different sectors and linking them to a coordinating team at the highest level.

In our opinion, our Central Committee should not only have a Political Bureau but also a Bureau of Social Production, a political instrument of the Party to coordinate the activities of the different administrative branches. We must obtain the highest possible efficiency in that coordination and in planning.

How can we solve this contradiction between our overwhelming needs and the situation reflected by the data I read at the outset on our population growth, on the growth of our labor force and the demand for manpower? How are we going to manage from now until 1975 and then from 1975 to 1980? We just don't have any other alternative but to solve the problem and we must solve it! There is no other way out. Will we solve it? Yes. I am absolutely convinced that when a people wants to solve a problem it will solve it! I am absolutely convinced!

It is not a case of coming here to promise that we will solve the problem tomorrow. It is a matter of conscience in every worker in the country, in every one with the slightest responsibility. A universal and profound matter of conscience to rationalize our effort and optimize our effort. We must beat our brains out with the difficulties as a whole and with the concrete problems as well; we must beat our brains out to obtain maximum and optimal utilization of every machine, every gram of raw material and every minute of man's work.

It isn't a case of working more and more extra hours in a

mechanical way. No! This has already been talked about: optimum utilization of working hours, the exception being when circumstances of a very urgent nature justify it, but only as an exception and when it is clear and evident that there is something to be gained, not just to pile up hours or to meet a goal. Things done mechanically are useless, absolutely worthless. We must realize once and for all that doing things mechanically doesn't solve anything. Very often we fall into doing meaningless things.

Our problem requires the general awareness of all the people, of how to optimize the very last machine, the last gram of raw material and the last atom of energy correctly and to the highest possible degree. We must use our heads to solve the problems. If the 10-million-ton sugar harvest was a problem of brawn, what we now have before us is a problem of brains.

And if the general level of our men still isn't very high and if the people of today are different from the people of 20 or 30 years hence as far as knowledge goes, this people of today must make the use of intelligence, a sense of responsibility and concern for problems a vital affair. It is a matter of exhaustive utilization of the intelligence and sense of responsibility of each and every one of the workers of this country.

The road is hard. Yes. More difficult than it had seemed. Yes, imperialist gentlemen: building socialism is hard. But Karl Marx himself believed socialism would be a natural result of a technologically highly advanced society. But in today's world, given the presence of industrialized imperialist powers, countries such as ours have no other alternative—to overcome their cultural and technical backwardness—than socialism. But what is socialism? Socialism is the possibility of utilizing natural and human resources in an optimum way for the benefit of the people. What is socialism? It is the elimination of the contradiction between the development of productive forces and the relations of production.

Today industry, raw materials, natural resources, factories, machines and all kinds of equipment belong to the whole nation. These resources can and should be at the service of all the people. If we don't make the best use of those machines and equipment, of those resources, it isn't because the capitalists and imperialists prevent us from doing so; it isn't because we are prevented by the proprietors who owned factories—and would just as soon have produced milk products as poison, cheese or marihuana to make money. The owners of factories couldn't have cared less about the use to which their products would be put. Here, each product and each service is produced with the needs of man, of the people, in mind.

If we don't make the best use of our resources it isn't because anyone keeps us from doing so—it is because we don't know how to, don't wish to or cannot. That is why we must know how to use our resources optimally, we must wish to use our resources optimally, and we must be able to use them optimally by simply drawing on the reserves of willpower, morale, intelligence and determination of the people, who have demonstrated that they possess those virtues; they have demonstrated it!

If there is something here that is not open to question, it is the people's spirit. This is a people with a revolutionary spirit; this is a people with an internationalist spirit!

We are not offering magic solutions here. We have stated the problems facing us and we have said that only the people, only with the people—and the people's awareness of our problem, the people's information, the determination and will of the people—can those problems be overcome.

When we tried to take the Moncada Garrison by storm 17 years ago it wasn't to win a war with a thousand men but rather to begin a war and wage it with the people and win it with the support of the people. When, years later, we came back with a group of expeditionists, it wasn't with the idea of winning a war with a handful of men. We hadn't yet received the marvellous experiences and lessons we have received from the people during all these years, but we knew that that war could only be won with the people. And it was waged and won with the people!

When this Revolution, only 90 miles distant from the ferocious and powerful empire, decided to be free and sovereign and challenged the imperialists, got ready to face all difficulties and started on a truly revolutionary road—not the path of the capitalists and imperialist monopolies, but rather a people's path, a path of workers, of peasants, a path of justice—many said that that was entirely impossible because of such factors as cultural, political and ideological influence and the like. But we believed that the battle could be won with the people—and it was waged with the people and won with the people!

We aren't after power or honor! What is power good for if we are unable to win the battle against poverty, ignorance and all those things? And power. What is power? Or any power? It is the people's will aimed at a given goal, marching down a single road, united in a single spirit! It is the simple and indestructible power of the people. That is really power! And that is the power we are interested in!

None of us as individual men, nor our glories or honors, is of any interest or value. If we have an atom of value, that atom of value will be through our service to an idea, a cause, linked to the people.

Men are of flesh and blood, incredibly fragile. It is true that we are as nothing. We are only something in relation to this or that task.

And we will always be ever more conscientiously at the service of this cause.

All that remains to be said in the name of our Party, our leadership and in the name of my own sentiments, in view of the attitude, confidence and reaction of the people, is thank you very much.

Patria o Muerte!
Venceremos!

B. LABOR AND REVOLUTION

INTRODUCTION

General Characteristics of Labor

The Cuban proletariat never developed uniformly. Prior to the Revolution a small segment, primarily industrial, banking, railway, and public utility employees, enjoyed the fruits of progressive legislation, pocketed good salaries, worked under adequate conditions, and benefited from social security programs. They experienced relative comfort and received preferential treatment over those in other occupations. They had higher wages, were better organized, and worked mainly in urban centers.[1]

A large portion of the working people, however, suffered from low pay, lacked elementary protection, and were constantly threatened with unemployment. In 1953 (when the last population census was made) 2,059,659 workers constituted the Cuban labor force. The lucky ones with employment numbered 1,788,266, while 271,393 persons were unemployed most of the year. Of the available work force, 51.4% of the workers had jobs for less than ten weeks; 11.4% labored between ten and forty-nine weeks; and only 37.2% were employed the whole year.[2] Several years later conditions had not improved.

In 1956–1957, when the island had the highest income per capita in its republican history, the labor force consisted of 2,204,000 workers. There were, however, only 1,539,000 employed, 150,000 underemployed, and 361,000 totally un-

[1] The unfair wage and social security benefits have been studied by Carmelo Mesa-Lago, *Planificación de la seguridad social: Análisis especial de la problemática cubana,* Havana, 1960.

[2] Cuba, Oficina Nacional de los Censos Demográficos y Electoral, *Censos de Población, Viviendas y Electoral, 1953,* Havana, 1955.

employed. To the latter figure should be added 154,000 persons who worked without pay, and who for all practical purposes could also be considered unemployed. Thus, at the height of the sugar harvest, and during one of the nation's richest years, there were 615,000 men and women (30.2% of the labor available) suffering the pangs of starvation due to unemployment, underemployment, and simple exploitation without remuneration.[3]

With the ascension to power of a revolutionary government, the problem of unemployment rapidly took precedence. The policies of the new regime were aimed at increasing salaries, the standard of living, pensions for the poor, and creating new jobs for those at the bottom of the social pyramid. Such aims soon won the wholehearted backing of the lower classes, which became one of the essential pillars of the Revolution.

By 1962 rural unemployment disappeared from the countryside as peasants and farm workers began to work on state farms, migrate to the cities, join the armed forces, or find better opportunities in the tertiary sector of the economy.[4] By 1970 full employment had been achieved, although close to 75,000 persons still refuse to work.[5] Many of those who were unemployed or underemployed in the past have retired, found new jobs, or have been subsidized by the state in one form or another.[6]

Underemployment, theoretically abolished, still remains. Until recently, on the state farms people worked five hours and got paid for eight. In the sugar industry 77% of the labor force is seasonally employed, and in tobacco production 47% work only half of the year but get paid twelve months a year. The same phenomenon can be found in services, administration, and management, where of every 1,000 workers, 960

---

[3] Cuba, Consejo Nacional de Economía, *El Empleo, el Sub-empleo, y el Desempleo en Cuba,* Havana, 1958.

[4] Today a large percentage of the former sugar cane cutters work for the Ministry of the Interior.

[5] Fidel Castro, July 26, 1970, speech. In this volume.

[6] Until 1969, a large portion of the sugar cane workers were forced to take paid vacations lasting two or three months, because there was nothing for them to do. See *Granma* (Havana), June 13, 1969, p. 2.

are employed the whole year and the rest, while getting paid, undergo training to function in other sectors of the economy.[7]

Today Cuba has a shortage of manpower, especially in agriculture. This is due to far-reaching changes in the economic structure which provide better opportunities for the rural population than ever before, the creation of more jobs, the migration to the cities, the inefficient utilization of the work day,[8] and the low productivity of workers.[9]

Since output per worker has been lower than planned, administrators have tried to meet their production quotas by hiring more workers, thus bringing about further labor shortages. There are, then, more job openings than there are able-bodied men and women entering the labor force.

In 1967 there were 11,981 new job openings, but 24,622 remained unfilled. The following year the demand rose to 341,027, but only 188,086 people entered the labor market. Presently, it is estimated that the economy could rapidly absorb close to 450,000 new workers.

To solve the manpower shortage in the countryside, where the problem is most acute, the Revolution has mobilized the urban population to the rural areas through volunteer labor, which by 1967 represented from 8 to 12% of the total labor force. The success of this measure and its significance in saving wages is open to debate.[10] It is clear, however, that because of a lack of motivation, experience, or knowledge, the cost of production in the volunteer brigades often has been higher than the value of the items produced.

[7] *Granma* (Havana), April 1, 1969, p. 2.
[8] In 1968 a study of ninety-nine work centers showed that the loss in man-hours represented a potential manpower reserve of 87,554 workers. Those same places of work had requested during the same period 35,855 laborers. If their workdays had been used efficiently they would have had an excess of 51,699 workers.
[9] When the request for labor is analyzed we find that in 1967 job openings due to vacancies (from illness, death, retirement, military service, and exile) accounted for 41% (29% in 1968), while 59% were the result of new jobs (64% in 1968). Furthermore, 65% of the demand comes from the primary and secondary sectors. *Granma* (Havana), March 31, 1969, p. 2.
[10] See the essay by Carmelo Mesa-Lago in this volume.

TABLE 1

Economically Active Population by Provinces, 1953 and 1970

	1953 *(State and Private)*	1970 *(State only)*
1. Pinar del Río	150,648	106,000
2. Havana	607,487	640,000
3. Matanzas	125,895	125,000
4. Las Villas	348,554	272,000
5. Camagüey	220,393	243,000
6. Oriente	519,289	496,000
7. Isla de Pinos	——	13,000
	1,972,266[11]	1,895,000[12]

The distribution of the active labor force by province over the years has shown marked differences in some regions and insignificant changes in others.[13] The foremost factor to keep in mind, though, is that while close to 379,000 persons have retired from 1959 to 1970, only 580,000 people have gone into the labor force in the same period, when the country required one and a half million new workers. Today this drastic labor scarcity is felt in every section of the economy and now for every new worker the ranks of the nonproductive increase by three.

Income Distribution

Although the means of production are collectively owned in Cuba today, a wage-earning class still exists. Within this class differences of income can be found, but it is extremely difficult to ascertain what percentage of the national income of the island is received by a specific sector of the working population. This is so because very little data is available.

[11] Includes those receiving payment for their work as well as those who were not remunerated. Source, *Censo de la República de Cuba*, Havana, 1953; and July 31, 1970, speech by the Cuban Minister of Labor.
[12] There are also 400,000 private farmers and military personnel not included in this table.
[13] Of the available male labor force, 69% are actively working. The percentage is 22 for women.

Nonetheless, when pre-revolutionary years are compared with the last eleven years of the Revolution, significant shifts in wages can be noted. Thus, real incomes notably increased from the elimination of unemployment, and today almost everyone has a guaranteed annual wage. (Political enemies of the regime are the exceptions.) More important, the average worker's salary has gone up. In 1958 it was about 1,000 pesos yearly, and in 1970 it amounted to 1,560 pesos (inflation not considered). Especially striking is that the highest percentage increase is in the sectors traditionally paid the lowest salaries. This change is apparent in the national salary fund, which was 1,407 million pesos in 1958,[14] and 2,942 million in 1968. At the same time, pensions increased from 105.4 million to 253.3 million. Salaries of sugar workers climbed from 272.1 million in 1958 to 481 million in 1968.[15]

In 1958 insurance pensions covered only 60% of all the employed persons. There were no health insurance programs as such, and only a few workers received unemployment compensation. Five years later, the privileges enjoyed by a small fraction of workers were suspended,[16] but social security, illness, and other benefits were extended to the entire economically active population.

A social security law was established on March 27, 1963, giving illness benefits to all workers. The plan provided for cash payment, medical care for the entire period required for recovery of health, up to one year, or retirement (if incapacitated). The law stated that the sick worker could collect 40% of his salary if hospitalized, and 50% if staying at home. In 1964 vanguard workers were paid 100% of their salaries in case of illness or accident.[17]

On July 26, 1968, Fidel Castro disclosed a Government plan by which workers giving up overtime pay were to receive in return payment of their entire salary in case of ill-

---

[14] Banco Nacional de Cuba, *Memoria,* Havana, 1959.

[15] Report of the Cuban Revolutionary Government to the International Labor Organization at Geneva, June 1969, pp. 13–15.

[16] Pensions awarded under the former provisions had been maintained by the revolutionary regime at their former net rate. See Revolutionary Law No. 1100 of March 27, 1963.

[17] Clearly a material reward for "morally oriented men."

ness or retirement. Two months later, on October 22, a social
security law came into effect giving full salaries to workers in
case of illness, maternity, old age, or death (in the latter case
the widow would receive the payment). But to qualify one
had to demonstrate "a Communist work attitude." The requirements for such status were: 1) renunciation of payment for overtime labor, 2) forty-four hours or more labor
per week, 3) no unauthorized absences from work, 4) exceed
the work quotas, and 5) be an active participant in volunteer
work. In 1969 only about 6% of the workers met those
conditions.[18]

Considerable gaps in earning power still remain as a consequence of a system of salary scales established in 1963. There
are large differences in income due to the fixed wage rates
for three occupational sectors (divided into eight separate
grades). In 1965, for example, agricultural workers received
wages ranging from 63 to 153 pesos, while non-agricultural
workers and administrative personnel earned from 85 to 264
pesos, and executive/technical workers were paid from 302
to over 930 pesos per month.

TABLE 2

Wage Rates and Labor Distribution (1965)[19]

Type of Work	Percentage of Labor Force	Wage Range (in pesos)
1. Agriculture	42	63–153
2. Non-agriculture and administrative	53	85–264
3. Executive and skilled	5	302–938

By 1968 the minimum wage was set at 85 pesos a month,
but salary differences continued. It should be noted that the
Revolution respected the high wages paid to highly produc-

---

[18] This law contradicts Cuba's self-proclaimed insistence on the superiority of moral incentives. Monetary benefits are simply renounced
in time; instead of getting material rewards now, the workers get them
in the future.
[19] Carmelo Mesa-Lago, *The Labor Sector and Socialist Distribution
in Cuba,* New York: Praeger, 1968, pp. 94–101.

tive industrial units when salaries were frozen in 1961. Thus, in some plants where labor unions were strong, wages have remained high, while other work centers, doing exactly the same sort of labor, receive less.

Monthly wages are remarkably different, as Table 3 shows.

TABLE 3

Monthly Income of Selected Occupations, 1968

Occupation	Median Monthly Wage (in pesos)
Supreme Court Judge	900
University Professor	750
Cabinet Minister	700
Lower Court Judge	500
Electric Power Worker	254
Government Functionary	200–250
Petroleum Worker	250
Foreign Trade	189
Army Sergeant	185
Wholesale Trade	184
Fishing	180
Chemical Worker	169
Construction	166
Beverages	161
Mining	161
Metallurgy	160
Food Industry	158
Agricultural Services	156
Textile Worker	151
Restaurant Worker	147
Retail Trade	128
Rural School Teacher	120
Livestock Worker	104
Forestry	103
Warehouse Worker	100
Unskilled Worker	100–120
Cane Cutter	96
Minimum Wage	85
Minimum Old Age Pension	60
Youth in Compulsory Military Service[20]	7

[20] The information in this table has been derived from Eduardo Novoa, "Cuba hoy," *Punto Final* (Santiago, Chile), July 30, 1968, pp. 10–16; Maurice Zeitlin, "Inside Cuba: Workers and Revolution," *Ramparts,*

When we compare the minimum wage earned by many agricultural workers with the maximum salary of technicians, a ratio of 1 to 10.5 is attained. For every peso earned by a young man serving his military service (room and board provided), a cabinet minister earns 100, and a Supreme Court judge 149. To these monetary differences should be added the non-monetary bonuses of the top income groups, that is, the fringe benefits and privileges accumulated by a politico-bureaucratic elite. The elite receive good apartments or houses, travel abroad, expense accounts, banquets, meals at expensive restaurants, free cars and drivers, and visits to resorts, to mention just a few.[21] In 1969, for example, when the Cuban people were undergoing extreme austerity, the revolutionary government bought 1,500 new Alfa Romeo sedans for the party bureaucrats.[22] This outright manifestation of privilege aroused the most profound indignation among the masses.[23]

In spite of the above it should be kept in mind that only personal or sectoral income differences have been considered, and that often those gaps are more formal than real. Monthly wage figures do not express the reality of social wages, that is, society today offers many free social services to the population, such as education, health care, hospitalization, medicines, and sports.[24] Once those benefits are noted, wage differences, although large, might not be as meaningful.

Discrepancies between the urban and rural areas have been reduced. Yet in 1968 Havana, with 27% of the population, received 38% of the national income, consumed 35% of the goods, and had 49% of the nation's commercial services. The Havana worker, as a rule, is much better off than his counterpart in other urban centers or the countryside.

March 1970, p. 11; The Economist Intelligence Unit, *Quarterly Economic Review* (London), 1970, supplement, p. 3; and various broadcasts of Radio Habana Cuba (1968–1970).

[21] Adolfo Gilly, "Inside the Cuban Revolution," *Monthly Review*, October 1964; and Rene Dumont, *Cuba: Est-il Socialiste?*, Paris: Editions du Seuil, 1970.

[22] *The Wall Street Journal*, August 28, 1970, p. 6; *Jeune Afrique* (Paris), March 31, 1970.

[23] Fidel Castro, August 22, 1970, speech. *Granma* (Havana), August 30, 1970, p. 4.

[24] See the section on social development in this volume.

The wage policy of the Revolution is based on the ideal of eliminating income differences. In practice, however, the Government refuses to equalize wages overnight by reducing the salaries of those at the top, because it would alienate the much needed managers and technicians. Instead, equality will be achieved by a gradual process of narrowing the income gap. Presently the Government emphasizes the increment of the salaries of those at the bottom of the wage scale. On July 24, 1968, Castro outlined this aspect:

> The road of communism must pass through the process of egalitarianism, but we want to establish it from the bottom up. As production increases, as the nation's wealth is increased, we shall begin to raise the standard of living of all those at the lowest levels, of those who earn less and receive less. With the increase of our wealth, and starting from the bottom up, we will establish egalitarianism.

Equality and money, the revolutionaries maintain, are in direct conflict. That is why they believe that in the final analysis the real problem is not to equalize salaries or emphasize the distribution of income, but to do away with money altogether. Such a goal would be accomplished by ultimately giving all items and services free to the people, making money unnecessary.

Productivity

Despite inequality in income and property, real income, for most workers, has increased. But this has had unexpected consequences. Since production did not increase at the same rate as wages, soon there was more money than there were goods on the market, creating a generalized scarcity of consumer goods. Hence, in 1962 rationing began while productivity progressively declined in the agricultural sector.[25]

[25] After 1962 wages were reduced in many sectors, but the salary reduction did not keep pace with the decline in production. Therefore, wages still surpassed the amount of available goods.

TABLE 4

Agricultural and Food Production in Cuba, 1952–1969

(1952–1956 = 100)[26]

	Agricultural Production		Food Production	
	Total	Per Capita	Total	Per Capita
1952	121	127	123	129
1953	97	99	97	99
1954	95	95	94	94
1955	92	90	91	89
1956	95	91	95	91
1957	108	101	108	101
1958	107	98	108	99
1959	112	101	112	101
1960	114	101	113	100
1961	122	106	122	106
1963	86	72	85	71
1964	93	75	93	75
1965	112	89	114	90
1966	94	72	93	72
1967	115	88	116	88
1968	106	79	107	80
1969	99	73	99	73

Total agricultural output declined 23% from 1961 (when socialist planning commenced) to 1969. Still more significant, per capita food production in 1969 was 28% lower than in 1959, and agricultural production per capita also declined 28% from 1959 to 1969. In this respect, Cuba has moved backward, although dramatic advances have occurred in other sectors, namely, in nickel, electric power, milk, fish, eggs, and beef (as shown in Table 5).

The persistent economic difficulties and oscillations in production are closely related to a dramatic decline in productivity, which is surpassed only by the growth of tardiness, negligence, and absenteeism in the labor force.

What are the reasons for work absenteeism and for the low output of workers? Are these matters related in any way to the achievement of social and job security? Do sickness

[26] United Nations, FAO, *Monthly Bulletin of Agricultural Economics and Statistics,* July–August 1970, pp. 14–17.

TABLE 5

Economic Improvements: 1959–1969

	Nickel[27]	Electricity[28]	Milk[29]	Fish[30]	Eggs[31]	Beef[32]
1959	17.8	—	—	28.2	318.0	200.0
1960	14.5	2.1	—	31.2	429.0	170.0
1961	18.1	2.0	—	30.5	434.0	174.6
1962	24.9	2.2	219.4	35.0	530.0	196.3
1963	21.6	2.3	217.1	36.5	483.0	143.0
1964	24.0	2.4	225.0	37.1	309.0	170.0
1965	29.1	2.5	231.0	40.9	920.0	309.9
1966	27.8	2.7	329.0	44.4	1,019.0	326.3
1967	34.9	3.0	324.0	65.9	1,165.0	324.1
1968	—	3.2	302.1	66.0	1,191.0	369.3
1969	—	—	—	78.1	—	—

benefits, wages, or age affect work in an adverse fashion? These and many other questions are difficult to answer. This is primarily due to the lack of data necessary for a coherent and exhaustive analysis. Hence, only trends and generalizations can be presented at this point.

Fidel Castro has contended that many Cubans share cultural values from the Spanish colonial period which are antithetical to manual or productive labor. According to this notion, to work is something shameful and degrading.[33] Other suggestions seem more satisfactory since they look at the issues more concretely.

A case in point is the manner in which manual labor and low productivity in agriculture have been linked. On March 13, 1969, Castro asserted that a definite relationship existed

[27] Thousands of metric tons. *Bohemia* (Havana), January 2, 1969, p. 21.
[28] Billions of kilowatts. *Bohemia* (Havana), April 11, 1969, pp. 22–29.
[29] Billions of liters. Cuba, Dirección Central de Estadística, *Compendio estadístico de Cuba,* Havana, 1969.
[30] Thousands of metric tons. *Bohemia* (Havana), June 19, 1970, p. 38.
[31] Millions of units. *Bohemia* (Havana), October 17, 1969, pp. 52–56; and Carmelo Mesa-Lago, "Availability and Reliability of Statistics in Socialist Cuba," *Latin American Research Review,* Summer 1969, Table 3, p. 56.
[32] Thousands of metric tons. Same as footnote 29.
[33] November 4, 1969, speech. See *Ediciones COR* (Havana), No. 16, 1969.

between the routine of simple, monotonous work and production problems. However, no data were provided.[34] Months later, making no mention of the discipline necessary for an effective labor force, he declared that Cuba did not have "work habits" because the country did not have a developed industry. According to Fidel:

Industrial production contributes much to disciplining workers due to the productive processes inherent in such activity. A country with very few industries, with an immense majority of its population of peasant background, accustomed to start working at one hour today and at another hour tomorrow, waiting for rain, cannot develop work habits.[35]

On various occasions the revolutionary authorities have tied age or work experience to productivity. In August 1969 the Cuban Labor Minister stated that young men and women entering the labor force lacked discipline and revolutionary consciousness, and as a result, production had declined. Moreover, he added that the "heterogeneous composition of the labor force accounts for the fact that while the number of vanguard workers increases, absenteeism, the wasting of the workday, negligence, and other acts of labor indiscipline proliferate and become more acute."[36] Education also seems to play a part. Reports have shown that many workers refuse to use machines and prefer the old, traditional methods of labor. Their anti-machine attitude stems from their lack of technical and educational development.[37]

On the other hand, the Revolutionary Orientation Commission of the Cuban Communist Party has admitted that since 1961 wages have surpassed the amount of available goods.[38] Under such conditions the proletariat recognized that there was no need to labor for an entire month, since one

---

[34] *Granma* (Havana), March 16, 1969, pp. 2–5.
[35] November 4, 1969, speech, *op. cit.*
[36] Jorge Risquet, "La disciplina laboral es la condición indispensable para la victoria," *Bohemia* (Havana), August 15, 1969, pp. 70–71.
[37] Jorge Risquet's speech of July 31, 1970. See *Foreign Broadcasts Information Service* (Washington), August 4–7, 1970.
[38] *Granma* (Havana), October 30, 1969, p. 2.

could earn enough money to buy all those items rationed by working only fifteen or twenty days.

Unrealized purchasing power was experienced by the Cuban working population two years after the revolutionaries assumed power. In 1961 the more productivity fell, the more absenteeism increased. In desperation the government attempted to put an end to such problems by instituting a program that would put into concrete form the enthusiasm of the masses.

Socialist emulation began. This was a system by which the workers were urged to compete with one another and with other work centers in order to produce more, while material rewards were mixed with honorific titles and recognitions ("vanguard worker," "hero of production," etc.). The important factor was to raise productivity at a minimum cost. Ernesto Guevara defined the setup as a "weapon by which production is increased and the consciousness of the masses improved."[39]

Organized socialist emulation started in April 1962, but at the end of the year only 9% of the entire labor force was reported as participating in the competition. Various changes soon occurred and by 1964 the emulation system was more severe and strict, limiting to a large degree proletarian initiative.[40] On October 13, 1964, an important official of the government stated:

Very few workers truly participate in the emulation campaign. . . . To the emulation assemblies go only 20% of the workers. . . . Sometimes it is reported that 92% of the workers are taking part in emulation, but the truth is quite the opposite. Fraternal competition has not taken root in the masses.[41]

Why? Because the laborers are not permitted to present their opinions. "The workers have to remain silent," the same official noted, while government officials make the decisions to which the proletariat can only say, "Fine, I agree."

[39] *Obra Revolucionaria* (Havana), No. 5, 1963.
[40] *El trabajo en Cuba Socialista,* Miami: Ed. FORDC, 1965.
[41] *Hoy* (Havana), October 18, 1964.

By mid-1962 absenteeism reached extraordinary proportions, so coercive measures were introduced. On August 27, 1962, a scheme of graduated punishments (ranging from salary reductions to job transfers) was announced to the workers.[42] The expected results were hardly adequate, as people expressed their dislike for such a unilateral step imposed from above. Nonetheless, by 1964 the government initiated new measures attempting to curtail labor indiscipline and improve productivity. Output standards were established by a system of norms and quotas. Each worker had to meet specific production levels in order to receive his full salary. If the quota was not fulfilled, salaries were reduced proportionately. On the other hand, if the quota was met with ease, higher ones were introduced at each workplace.

More often than not the norms were unjust and impossible to carry out since they were decided arbitrarily without the participation of the proletariat. Rather than ensuring production, the norms ensured only discontent among the workers.

But since the problem remained, new pressures were decreed. On October 3, 1964, the "Law of Labor Justice" spelled out what was to be considered undisciplined bahavior at work. The following were major offenses: 1) failure to meet work quotas or time schedules, 2) unjustified absences, 3) damage to tools or negligence, 4) disrespect for superiors, fellow workers, or visitors. Sanctions varied from public admonition at a workers' assembly to reduction of wages and imprisonment in extreme cases.[43]

The law is not directly administered by the workers themselves, but by work councils. The councils are composed of five workers who must meet four requirements. First, they must have a "socialist attitude" toward work; second, they must be disciplined; third, absentees are not allowed to be members; and fourth, the member could not have been sanctioned previously by a labor justice organ. In other words, one must be totally identified with the state. They could be

---

[42] Cuban Economic Research Project, *Labor Conditions in Communist Cuba*, Coral Gables: University of Miami Press, 1963, pp. 44–49.

[43] Carmelo Mesa-Lago and Roberto Hernandez, *La Nueva Ley de Justicia Laboral*, Miami: Agencia de Informaciones Periodísticas, 1964.

replaced at any time by the Ministry of Labor. The workers, the Cubans believed, now had the progressive right of coercing themselves.

The implacable crisis continued. In 1965–1966 a shift from coercion[44] started to take shape as the need for the formation of a revolutionary socialist consciousness was accentuated. An awareness of the need for hard work moved forward in the priority list of the revolutionary regime. Everyone had to be immersed in the understanding that a country could move away from underdevelopment only by hard work.

On August 29, 1966, Fidel Castro, speaking to the Cuban Confederation of Workers, discussed the causes behind productivity's decline and the high absenteeism. His approach was principally concerned with structural reasons. His thought went as follows.

The method by which capitalism assured production— namely the threat of unemployment, demotion, reduction of wages, and starvation if work was not done properly—has been abolished by the Revolution. The disappearance of the whole capitalist system forcing men and women to work a maximum number of hours with extreme intensity means, simply, the relaxation of a series of pressures that had forced people to work in the past. Job security, the eradication of unemployment, and higher salaries made the old system obsolete, yet a new method of motivating the people or making work exciting did not appear right away. Thus, each worker did not become conscious, from one day to the next, of his social responsibilities to the nation. Instead discipline slackened and the intensity of work was reduced, bringing about drops in production. The old instruments used by capitalism have not been replaced by a revolutionary consciousness throughout the working class. Work is not yet perceived as the means to enrich the country, to benefit all.[45]

Persuasion and proselytism began to be emphasized as a means by which the people were to understand the need for hard work, for a heroic effort and discipline in order to build

---

[44] Although coercive measures were not abolished and still practiced.
[45] Fidel Castro, August 29, 1966, speech.

a strong and developed economy. To create revolutionary consciousness became the new goal. Economic development, in the minds of the revolutionaries, was to emerge from that awareness, which was to be based in moral incentives. At first, from the mass rallies and the all-pervading enthusiasm of the Cubans, it seemed as if the thesis was correct. But soon it was clear that revolutionary fervor was not manifested in a collective effort of revolutionary construction. This was made quite clear on May 7, 1968, when the official organ of the Cuban Communist Party editorially urged labor officials to start a campaign of vigilance over the workers to foster labor discipline, which "had failed to emerge spontaneously." If persuasion failed, the editorial added, then "moral and social sanctions" had to be applied.[46]

Two months later, Fidel disclosed that a "revolutionary attitude toward work" did not exist among most of the people.[47] The Cubans, he said, were ready to die for the Revolution, to fight for it, but not ready to work in its behalf. Between 1966 and 1967 the national average of productive work, on a daily basis, per worker was four hours.[48] And in 1967 agricultural workers labored less than eight hours a day on the average.[49] Persuasion, as the authorities conceived it, failing, the regime opted for the progressive militarization of the economy, one of the most extreme forms of labor coercion.

The arguments for the militarization approach were, to some extent, sophisticated. The major proponent of the militarization thesis has been Armando Hart, organizational secretary of the Cuban Communist Party.

Whenever a comparison is made between habitual workers in agriculture and personnel in the armed forces, Hart maintains, the productivity levels of the military are much higher than those of civilians. Hart credits the military superiority to its command structure, defining the duties and responsi-

[46] *Granma* (Havana), May 7, 1968.

[47] Fidel Castro, July 5, 1968, speech.

[48] K. S. Karol, *Guerrillas in Power*, New York: Hill & Wang, 1970, p. 426.

[49] FAO, *Report of the International Symposium on Industrial Development*, New York, 1967, p. 106.

bilities of those below. The agricultural workers lack a structure of command. Neither do they have a system of vigorous discipline, including harsh punishments for disobedience or poor performance, nor do they have well-defined responsibilities. Thus, he concludes that only when the military model is introduced to agricultural production will there be improvements.[50]

The argument *appears* well founded. Wherever the labor force is dispersed, unorganized, and unskilled, production has shown little or no progress and absenteeism has climbed. Good examples are to be found in tobacco, sugar, and coffee production.[51] On the other hand, when the labor force has been skilled, highly concentrated, well-organized, and with good leadership and clearly established control procedures, concrete improvements have followed. That is why, on one occasion, Armando Hart stated that "socialism in Cuba necessarily requires a concentration of workers," which he considered an essential condition for all other mechanisms affecting production to function in the correct manner.[52]

In 1968 the policy of militarization started in the agricultural sector. Military personnel were placed at every important administrative and managerial position throughout the island, especially at the provincial and regional levels of sugar production. A large percentage of the labor force was organized as military units waging a war in the belief that such a model would create discipline in the working class.[53]

A year later it was clear that the efforts to raise productivity were disappointing. In a report of early August 1969, the Labor Minister conceded that at the same time that a vanguard with "Communist consciousness" was growing and developing, there was a rear guard flourishing and expanding a capitalist mentality.[54] Henceforth, on August 29, 1969, while Cuba was going through its militarization stage, the

[50] *Granma* (Havana), May 25, 1969, pp. 3–4; July 20, 1969, p. 10.
[51] Small private farmers account for the production of 100% of cacao, 23% of sugar, 85% of coffee, 90% of tobacco, 40% of cattle, and 40% of vegetables in 1970.
[52] *Juventud Rebelde* (Havana), October 26, 1969, pp. 2–4.
[53] *Granma* (Havana), November 16, 1969, pp. 2–4.
[54] *Bohemia* (Havana), August 5, 1969, pp. 70–71.

regime decreed a measure to exert a more direct control over workers. The step, known as Law No. 225, which was not publicly debated, made it mandatory for all workers to have a work force control card in which their productivity, background, political views, and employment history are recorded. The card is necessary to obtain or change a job and to receive a salary.[55] Moreover, a worker wishing to transfer employment needs the permission of a regional office of the Labor Ministry. Thus, the law restricts the free mobility of the labor force. Changing employment without permission is a crime.

Also, management is required to keep exhaustive administrative files, in chronological order, on the life and job history of each worker, including merits and demerits. Whether a laborer receives social security benefits or a salary raise depends on what his work record shows, as written by government-appointed officials.[56] And every six months at each workplace the performance of workers is publicly examined, and workers are counseled, praised, or criticized. In the latter case penalties are set.

Still, in May 1970 Castro acknowledged to the Cuban people something they had known for some time: Cuba still had very many economic problems. The militarized model had not brought about the hoped-for solution; instead, productivity remained low and labor indiscipline high.[57]

A month later the Cuban Confederation of Labor called on the proletariat to work overtime without pay and reasserted its commitment to deal with "the weaknesses in behavior that still persist in the working class." Neither were they going to quit the "struggle against labor indiscipline, absenteeism, wasted workdays, and cultural-technical backwardness."[58] The statement revealed that meetings were to be held in the forthcoming weeks to evaluate "the merits and demerits" in the performance of each worker, aspects which were to be included in the labor dossiers.

The following day, June 30, 1970, the Commission of Rev-

[55] *Radio Habana Cuba*, September 23, 1969.
[56] *Granma* (Havana), October 17, 1969, p. 3.
[57] New York *Times*, June 1, 1970.
[58] *Granma* (Havana), June 29, 1970.

olutionary Orientation of the Central Committee of the Communist Party urged that a campaign of self-criticism be undertaken by students, workers, and peasants in order to overcome their weaknesses. The Commission asked the workers to labor more and better, be disciplined, and eradicate absenteeism. The peasants, on the other hand, had "to eliminate greed, individualism, and speculation [with agricultural goods] and fulfill production plans."[59]

On July 26, 1970, Castro disclosed Cuba's critical economic problems and shifted the responsibilities to the lower level of the revolutionary leadership. Although he did not concede that militarization had failed to improve production, he implied that the regime was searching for a new solution. Days later the Minister of Labor attributed difficulties to low productivity and labor indiscipline.[60] By August 1970 work absences on a daily basis ranged from 100,000 to 400,000, or approximately 20% of the work force.[61]

The regimented labor force had been organized from above along military lines at the national, regional, and provincial levels, following hierarchical relations. Under such a scheme civilians were treated as second-class citizens. Workers were transferred from one workplace to another, from one activity to another, without any consideration for their views on the matter. Although well organized, the workers showed their opposition by not laboring as they were instructed.

The Cuban government at first considered the problem as the logical consequence of a transitional period, and later changed to the view that low productivity and high work absences seemed to be related to organizational weaknesses. Now it has discovered that the root of the matter is subjective in character—the human factor.

In an interview with Chilean reporters on July 31, 1970, Fidel Castro indicated that in the struggle to conquer underdevelopment Cuba had to "overcome the subjective factors

---

[59] *Granma* (Havana), July 5, 1970.

[60] In 1970 worker productivity, on the average, amounted to $1,350 or about 400 pesos less than the average annual wages. See *Foreign Broadcasts Information Service* (Washington), August 4–7, 1970.

[61] *Granma* (Havana), September 20, 1970, p. 9.

preventing a more rapid pace."[62] He added that Cuba was beginning a new era, battling against "subjective errors" and searching for efficiency at all levels (such as putting an end to leaking roofs). Speaking to the Cuban Federation of Women on August 23, Castro returned to the same theme:

> We must win the battle *within ourselves*. Changes can be brought about in the quality of our work, the efficiency of our organization, and the efficiency in the general effort of the entire people. Where we can improve, where we can bring about a change in quality is in the subjective factor, in the human factor.[63]

Two weeks later Fidel stated that the Revolution was faced with "an endless number of problems." Some were "objective" in nature, relating to very bad and inadequate working conditions,[64] but they could not be solved rapidly. Instead, workers were told to labor more, despite difficulties, and to make possible, sometime in the future, the solution of those conditions. The solution, then, has to be subjective; but here the Revolution faces problems too. According to Castro, many people have not internalized the spirit of socialism and altruism. Neither have they made the commitment to work as a good in itself, to produce rather than consume, and to deny oneself through rigorous discipline for the benefit of the nation. The essential reason for this, according to Castro, is that:

> Some people without morals and without a sense of their social duty today take the liberty of scorning their work, remain idle, let the weight of the productive effort fall on the shoulders of others, cheat, and do a million and one other things. . . . Perhaps our greatest idealism lies in having believed that a society that had barely begun to live in a world that for thousands of years had lived under

[62] *El Siglo* (Chile), August 8, 1970, p. 3.
[63] *Granma* (Havana), August 30, 1970, pp. 2–6. Emphasis added.
[64] The Cuban Confederation of Labor in August 1970 declared that absentee workers were the consequence of very bad working conditions, transportation problems, inefficient organization of work, and lack of adequate treatment of workers.

the law of "an eye for an eye, and a tooth for a tooth," the law of the survival of the fittest, of egoism and deceit, the law of exploitation, could, all of a sudden, be turned into a society in which everybody behaved in an ethical, moral way.[65]

Right afterward all work centers in the country held a number of workers' assemblies aimed at working out new methods to eradicate absences from work and augment productivity. The mood of the meetings was outlined by Castro when he stated that he was sure that there were "some people who, as a result of our economic situation, require a certain amount of coercion to get them to go to work."[66] Not surprisingly, a series of severe and drastic measures to strengthen labor discipline, drafted by the Labor Ministry and the trade union leadership, was presented to the workers.[67]

These measures now in effect restore the system of work quotas without material incentives, update the record of workers' performance, define in detail the proletariat's responsibilities, and declare that anyone between the ages of seventeen and sixty, if physically and mentally fit, has the "social duty to work." Temporary absentees will not be permitted to buy durable goods, their homes will not be repaired, new or better housing will be denied, and their vacations will be suspended. Further, they can be excluded from social benefits such as the use of beaches, free education, and hospitalization. Furthermore, these absentees will not be able to eat at the inexpensive workers' dining rooms,[68] and they can also be deprived of their ration cards because "those

[65] *Granma* (Havana), September 20, 1970.
[66] *Granma* (Havana), September 9, 1970.
[67] The preamble to the law against absenteeism and "loafers" was written in 1968, but a law was not decreed then, according to the Cuban Labor Minister, because certain prerequisites had to be fulfilled first if the law was to be effective at all. The prerequisites were: 1) total eradication of the private sector, excepting small farms, making it impossible for anyone to hide whether he worked or not; 2) the creating of personal records on every worker established in 1969; and 3) a census of the population in order to have exact information on the manpower by regions, zones, and street blocks. *Granma* (Havana), September 20, 1970, pp. 10–12.
[68] *Radio Rebelde* (Havana), September 9, 1970.

who do not work do not have the right to eat."[69] In the case of "incorrigible absentees," their salaries will be completely suspended[70] and the offenders transferred to special prison farms.

To add a humiliating dimension, absentees will be paid at specific times and locations. Moreover, propaganda will be employed to make their names known at work and in their neighborhoods in the belief that this will help the people "know those who maintain a negative and harmful attitude toward the economic development of our whole society."[71]

To preach socialist morality constantly, to denounce the residues of the capitalist past, or to enact a complex set of disciplinary measures is not sufficient to create labor discipline and a socialist man. Furthermore, it is naïve—although ideologically appealing—to think that education and the abolition of material incentives in an economically underdeveloped society of scarcity can create a socialist and revolutionary outlook toward work. The Cubans disagree with the argument that "it is necessary *first* to see the withering away of money economy through the production of an abundance of goods and services, before the psychological and cultural revolution can fully manifest itself, and a new socialist consciousness bloom."[72] Cuban revolutionary authorities think that socialist consciousness must precede abundance.

A problem whose existence has only recently been acknowledged is still to be dealt with by the revolutionary regime. It is becoming increasingly more important to resolve the high degree of social tension found between the labor force and the various state bureaucrats. The strained relationship between the two arise from several factors: not only does the Cuban working class have no decision-making power, but also channels are lacking for redressing its grievances or for controlling the production process.[73] Their views are not even con-

---

[69] *Radio Rebelde* (Havana), September 11, 1970.

[70] Their families could receive social security checks. See *Granma* (Havana), September 20, 1970.

[71] *Radio Rebelde* (Havana), September 10, 1970.

[72] Ernst Mandel, *Marxist Economic Theory*, New York: Monthly Review Press, 1968, Vol. 2, p. 655.

[73] Lionel Martin, "The Search," *Direct from Cuba* (Havana), September 30, 1970.

sidered when economic plans are made, output standards drawn, wage scales set, discipline established, or workplaces managed. There are no institutions available to criticize, to present a different position, or to change specific policies or procedures.

More often than not, workers are urged to make greater efforts or to intensify their labor, but almost never are they asked for an opinion.[74] In a society allegedly functioning in the interests of the masses, such behavior is a bad joke, aggravated even more by the impositions from above and by the arbitrary abuse of power by bureaucrats and revolutionary leaders.

The Cuban worker, despite the socialization of the economy, is still alienated from his labor. He feels that he owns neither the means of production nor the products of his own labor. He is not the master of his working conditions, and there is no rapport between him and his superiors. The Minister of Labor, on July 31, 1970, revealed this when he stated:

> Theoretically, the administrator represents the interests of the worker and peasant state, the interests of all the people. That is all fine and good. Now, the administrator may be making one mistake after the other, and this happens every day everywhere. . . . The workers see this and feel resigned. They can do nothing about it. In many cases the way is closed for them to do anything against the administrator.[75]

In the same speech it was noted that the rule is for administrators and managers to be the representatives of the Communist Party at the same work center. Although they allegedly represent the vanguard of the proletariat, these people are quite insensitive to the problems of the masses. When a worker has a complaint against the administration, he can go to the Communist Party nucleus, but in most cases the party leader and the administrator are the same person. Then, "there is nowhere a worker can take his problem."[76]

[74] Jorge Risquet, July 31, 1970, speech, *Foreign Broadcasts Information Service* (Washington), August 4–7, 1970.

[75] *Ibid.*

[76] *Ibid.*

A description of the state's administrators has been provided by Fidel Castro. On September 2, 1970, he said that they "do not look at all like the rest of the workers," and are "absolutely insensitive and lazy," having the opposite of a proletarian spirit. They also have an "anti-worker outlook" that scorns the thinking of the working class. Castro further referred to the "preferential treatment" accorded to the administrative personnel and some political leaders who get better housing and consumer goods right before the eyes of the masses. Such matters caused, he said, "tremendous damage" to the authority and prestige of the Revolution.

Steps to eradicate corruption are in the making, and a major rectification drive to get workers and the economic and political cadres closer together has begun. The Revolution has recently announced its interest in the "democratization" of the labor movement in order to reach higher levels of efficiency. Criticisms have been aired about having underestimated the role of the proletariat in the development of the economy. Democratization, then, will mean the setting aside of bureaucratic and administrative methods and their replacement by mass methods.

> The formulas of a revolutionary process can never be administrative formulas. Administrative procedures could reach a given efficiency but can never go beyond it. . . . No administrative formulas can solve problems that are only susceptible to mass solution.[77]

Rather than trying to bring forth the control, vigilance, militancy, and mass energy necessary to overcome difficulties from above by bureaucratic methods, the workers will be trusted with doing so from below. Moreover, democratization will involve collective management.[78]

[77] Fidel Castro, August 23, 1970, speech.
[78] Collective management should not be confused with workers' self-management. Under collective management a workplace will have one person appointed by the state to preside over production, but he will be aided by a collective body made up of representatives from the trade union, the Communist Party, the Young Communists, and the women's front. In this scheme the collective body can give advice but cannot handle administrative decisions. The right to decide still rests with the manager or administrator.

On November 9, 1970, a major reorganization of the *lower* echelons of the Cuban Confederation of Workers began.[79] The workers, through secret ballot elections, chose new officers of trade union locals. Supervised by representatives of the state-run labor organization, the working class, by December 2, constituted 26,427 new locals with 117,625 officials. Eighty-seven percent of the elected personnel were new at these tasks, while the rest were "re-elected."[80] How many of the new officials really represent the interests of the working class? The answer can only be provided sometime in the future. Nonetheless, the so-called democratization drive of the labor movement has not brought about any significant change in attitude on the part of the workers.

The official organ of the Cuban Communist Party, on November 21, 1970, disclosed that the head of the state-run propaganda apparatus had stressed the importance of "fighting enemy ideology, negligence, deficiencies, vices, and errors; and to diminish absenteeism and increase efficiency and productivity." The same source indicated that the Cuban workers preferred material to moral incentives, and were still motivated by individualism.[81] And as early as December 7, Fidel Castro pointed out that the 1971 sugar harvest, which began in late November, was behind schedule.[82] He added that the establishment of a socialist community of interests was far from accomplished due to a lack of commitment by those who ought to know better.[83] Such a reaction by the working class is not surprising. Nothing has really changed. The free election of local officials does not appear likely to bring about true and meaningful socialist democ-

[79] The officials at the top of the organization are not yet freely chosen by the rank and file, although some of the personnel have been changed recently.

[80] In Havana 40% of the old officials managed to continue in office. *Radio Liberación* (Havana), December 2, 1970; *Radio Rebelde* (Havana), December 3, 1970.

[81] Several weeks before, a large number of workers demanded a raise in wages, to which the Labor Minister replied: "What has priority today is not the increase of salaries, but the increment of productivity." *Radio Liberación* (Havana), October 4, 1970.

[82] *Diario las Américas* (Miami), December 10, 1970, p. 1.

[83] *Diario las Américas* (Miami), December 9, 1970, p. 1; and *Radio Habana Cuba*, December 7, 1970.

racy. The Cubans laboring in factories, farms, and other
activities are well aware of this.

A truly serious democratization of the Revolution cannot
take place and grow under a system still relying on centralization of decisions and a militarized model for economic
development. Military discipline seems incompatible with
more freedom for the masses and more initiative on their
part, unless democratization is defined as the application of
discipline from below instead of from above.[84] Fidel himself
seems to view it in such a manner:

> We are going to trust our workers and hold trade union
> elections in all locals. . . . They will be absolutely free,
> and the workers will choose the candidates. The workers
> will elect their leaders. . . . If the worker has really been
> elected by a majority vote of all his comrades, he will have
> authority. He will not be a nobody who has been placed
> there by decree. He will have the moral authority of his
> election, and *when the Revolution establishes a line, he
> will go all out to defend and fight for that line.*[85]

In other words, the representatives of the workers might
be freely chosen, instead of appointed, but their function is to
carry out orders issued by state authorities or the party. Union
officials have to identify themselves with the decisions of the
revolutionary leadership and press the workers for their implementation because, supposedly, a unity of interests exists between labor and the state. No room for conflict or differences
between the two is allowed, as if implementation by the workers and decision making by another sector were always compatible or identical.

The revolutionary substitute for capitalism's reliance on
selfishness cannot be coercive decrees nor militarization, but
the concrete practice of decentralization and socialist democracy. To continue to adhere to the concept of the trade union
as a "transmission belt" to implement party directives in the

[84] Democratization has been defined in such terms. See Armando Hart,
"We Must Wage a Relentless Struggle," *Granma* (Havana), September
28, 1969.
[85] *Granma* (Havana), September 20, 1970, pp. 2–9. Emphasis added.

economic sector is an obstacle to meaningful democratization. Socialist democracy, to be real, requires that revolutionary initiative and power be found in the hands of the people and not be the monopoly of a group which sometimes lacks revolutionary convictions. The state should be the instrument of the masses and not the other way around.

16

ECONOMIC SIGNIFICANCE OF UNPAID LABOR IN SOCIALIST CUBA*

Carmelo Mesa-Lago

Forced labor has played a significant role in traditional societies. It has existed in Egypt, China, Rome, and other centers of ancient civilization. Some societies in transition have resorted to *corvée* as a political-economic tool to stimulate economic development. The Soviet Union, during the Stalinist period, is a well-known example. In socialist countries, unpaid labor has been used also as an educational tool in the construction of the so-called communist society. Cuba is a new socialist country which has relied heavily on the use of various types of unpaid labor. This experience has unusual validity because the Cuban revolution is a source of inspiration to several other developing countries.

At the end of 1966, UNESCO held in Havana its first International Seminar on Leisure Time and Recreation. In his opening address to the seminar Antonio Núñez Jiménez, chairman of the Cuban Academy of Sciences, stated:

In Cuba, since the Revolution took place, leisure time is a social value used in the national reconstruction, both in the economic and ideological fields. . . . In our effort to

* Reprinted with permission from *Industrial and Labor Relations Review*, Vol. 22, No. 3, April 1969, pp. 339–357. Copyright © 1969 by Cornell University. All rights reserved.

Carmelo Mesa-Lago is assistant professor of economics and acting director of the Center for Latin American Studies, University of Pittsburgh. He wishes to thank Professors James O. Morris and Duncan M. MacIntyre, New York State School of Industrial and Labor Relations, Cornell University, and Professor José Moreno, Department of Sociology, University of Pittsburgh, for many helpful suggestions on the form and content of this article.—EDITOR raise production and productivity, hundreds of thousands of persons have been mobilized to perform numerous [unpaid] tasks, such as the arduous jobs of cutting cane or picking coffee. All these tasks have been fulfilled during the leisure time of the people.[1]

Who are these persons mobilized in Cuba? How is their labor utilized? Why has this nation relied heavily on unpaid labor? What is the real contribution of such labor input to the economy? Hopefully this article will provide some answers to these questions. After a brief description of the various types of unpaid labor, an analysis will be made of the economic advantages and disadvantages of the system. In the conclusion, the significance of unpaid labor to Cuba's economy will be evaluated.

Types of Unpaid Labor

Five types of unpaid labor may be distinguished in Cuba: (1) work performed by employed workers outside of regular working time, (2) work done by unemployed women, (3) work performed by students as a method of socialist education, (4) work accomplished by politico-administrative prisoners as a means of "social rehabilitation," and (5) work included as part of the compulsory military service. Table 1 summarizes the characteristics of the various types of unpaid labor.

Unpaid labor performed by employed male and female workers is usually called "voluntary work." It is performed beyond the regular working hours, whether at the work site or any other place, in behalf of the state and commonly without pay.[2] Voluntary work may be accomplished in four different ways: as overtime hours subsequent to the regular workday; on weekends, especially on Sundays; during the

[1] Antonio Núñez Jiménez, "Discurso de Apertura del Seminario Internacional de la UNESCO sobre Tiempo Libre y Recreación," *El Mundo* (Havana), Dec. 7, 1966, p. 7.

[2] "Reglamento para la Organización de la Emulación," *Gaceta Oficial*, May 21, 1964, p. 450.

TABLE 1

Summary of the Characteristics of the Five Types of Unpaid Labor in Cuba, 1967

Typology	Employed Workers	Nonemployed Women	Performer		
			Students	Military Recruits	Prisoners
Age bracket	18–65	—	Grammar school (g.s.): 6–12 Secondary school (s.s.): 12–16	17–45	—
Approximate number in man-years	60,000 to 70,000	5,000 to 10,000	g.s. unknown s.s. 18,000 to 23,000	84,000 to 120,000	20,000 to 75,000
Recruiter	Managements, trade unions	Federation of Cuban Women	Schools, UJC,* student unions	Military-service offices	Revolutionary courts & penitentiaries
Degrees of compulsion	Exhortations, pressures, "compromises," emulation, legislation	Exhortations, pressures	Curricular or extra-curricular duty	Forced	Forced

	Short term: yearly targets Long term: 1–6 months	Often, the harvest period	g.s. unknown s.s. 6 weeks	1–3 years	Depending on penalties
Length of commitment	Short term: yearly targets Long term: 1–6 months	Often, the harvest period	g.s. unknown s.s. 6 weeks	1–3 years	Depending on penalties
Place of work	Short term: work site Long term: agricultural fields	Commonly in agricultural fields	g.s. area close to school s.s. stage farms and factories	UMAP† camps, agricultural fields	Forced-labor camps, penitentiaries, agricultural fields
Benefits granted by the state	Short term: social security Long term: leave of absence, lodging & board, social security	Sometimes lodging & board	g.s. none s.s. lodging & board	Lodging, board, clothing, $7 per month, education	Lodging, board, clothing
Administrative direction	Secretariat of Voluntary Labor of the CTC‡	Federation of Cuban Women	Ministry of Education	Ministry of Armed Forces	Ministry of Interior

* Communist Youth League.
† Military Units to Aid Production.
‡ Confederation of Cuban Workers.

annual paid-vacation time; or for a continuous period of several months, during leave of absence from a regular job. The last is generally known as "long-term" voluntary work; workers abandon their regular jobs from one to six months to work mainly in agriculture. Because such workers use a leave of absence, they are paid their regular (i.e., industrial) wages. Their companions who remain on the urban job site must maintain production levels by carrying out the duties of those mobilized.

Fragmentary information suggests that the number of voluntary workers (measured in man-years) rose from 15,000 in 1962 to 70,000 in 1967, and that the number continues to grow. The tasks performed by the voluntary work force are varied: planting and cutting sugar cane; picking coffee, cotton, vegetables and fruits; harvesting rice; planting trees; weeding and fertilizing fields; repairing damage caused by hurricanes; building construction; and almost any kind of industrial and service work.

With the exception of those on leave of absence, voluntary workers receive neither wages nor other kinds of pay. Long-term voluntary workers are provided with lodging and board as well as tools. Since 1963, voluntary workers suffering occupational accidents have been credited, for benefit purposes, with the time spent performing unpaid labor. Long-term voluntary workers on leave of absence are also credited with this time of service for retirement pensions.[3]

Early in the revolution, unpaid labor was donated on a spontaneous basis, but since 1962 voluntary workers have been recruited because of pressure from trade unions and the managers of state enterprises and have been organized in battalions and brigades under Communist party guidance. The state has regulated the performance of unpaid labor by introducing several measures: criticism among voluntary workers, annual contracts binding the workers to achieve a determined number of unpaid hours of labor, management and trade union checks on the amount and quality of the labor done, weekly reports by the battalions on their own

[3] "Ley de Seguridad Social," Law No. 1,100, March 27, 1963, *Gaceta Oficial,* May 24, 1963, pp. 17–23.

performance and that of others, inspection teams to keep discipline and discover flaws, and penalties for disciplinary violations of the state regulations.[4]

Since the Federation of Cuban Women (FMC) was formed in 1960, tens of thousands of Cuban females, particularly those doing housework, have been recruited by that organization as unpaid laborers in the cane, cotton, rice, and coffee fields. There are no accurate data on the number of women annually donating unpaid work, but a 1967 estimate, based on scattered information, of from 5,000 to 10,000 man-years seems reasonable. Women do not receive wages, and because they often perform their agricultural tasks close to their homes, lodging and board facilities are reduced to a minimum.

In mid-1962, students began to perform unpaid labor during vacation time, in coffee, cotton, and rice plantations. Recruitment was mainly done through exhortations by the student unions, the Communist Youth League (UJC) and the school boards.[5] In mid-1964, the system was made compulsory by a decree of the Ministry of Education. Subject to the legislation are youngsters from six to fifteen years of age, enrolled in elementary and secondary schools, between first and ninth grades. One type of unpaid labor (titled "productive") is performed by from 150,000 to 180,000 secondary-school students on state farms and factories, on weekends and during school vacations. In the case of agricultural work, students generally remain at the work site for a period of from one to six weeks. Another type of unpaid labor (titled "socially useful") involves 1,280,000 primary-school children and is aimed to suppress differences between physical and intellectual work as well as to inculcate in the children a sense of obligation to society. Toward the end of 1965, the Ministry of

[4] Regulations of voluntary labor are contained in "Reglamento para la Organización de la Emulación Socialista," *Gaceta Oficial*, Feb. 7, 1963, and May 21, 1964, pp. 447–459; "Communicado Conjunto del Trabajo Voluntario," *Nuestra Industria*, Vol. 4, No. 11 (November 1964), pp. 41–43; "Declaración de Principios y Estatutos de la CTC," *El Mundo*, July 6, 1966, p. 6; and Alfredo Núñez Pascual, "Trabajo Voluntario en la Próxima Zafra," *El Mundo*, Sept. 23, 1966, p. 4.

[5] CMQ Radio, July 23, 1962 and Aug. 21, 1964.

Education also ordered university students to participate in unpaid labor for a period of from three to six weeks a year. Students performing unpaid labor are provided food and shelter when mobilized away from their homes.[6]

Unpaid labor is used as a punishment for two classes of convicted persons: state employees and functionaries guilty of errors or transgressions committed during the performance of their functions; and political prisoners, i.e., people imprisoned for opposing the government. In both cases, forced labor has two goals: "rehabilitation" or "reeducation" of those convicted and the performance of a productive task. Political crimes are judged by the revolutionary courts while administrative faults are under the jurisdiction of the Administrative Disciplinary Commission (CODIAD). The management of labor camps is entrusted to the Ministry of the Interior.[7] According to Prime Minister Castro, in 1964–1965, there were from 15,000 to 20,000 political prisoners in Cuba, although other sources give figures ranging from 50,000 to 75,000.[8] The number of convicted state officials is unknown but is presumed to be small. Tasks to be performed by those convicted include cultivation of rice, planting trees, extraction of minerals, etc. Prisoners receive food, shelter, and clothing.

The desire to bring a large number of "vagrants" (i.e., idle youngsters, jobless bourgeoisie, etc.) into production was allegedly a main reason for establishing compulsory military service in 1963. Included are males between the ages of sixteen and forty-five, who are obligated to serve a period of three years. Recruits are divided into two categories, i.e., those

[6] Resolution of the Ministry of Education, *El Mundo*, May 27, 1964; Regulations of the National Education Council, Apr. 5, 1965; Resolution of the Ministry of Education, Dec. 7, 1965; and Fidel Castro, "Discurso en la Clausura del Encuentro Nacional de Monitores," *El Mundo*, Sept. 18, 1966, pp. 5–8.

[7] "Reglamento del Centro de Rehabilitación de Uvero Quemado," *Nuestra Industria*, Vol. 2, No. 3 (March 1962), p. 44; *ibid.*, Vol. 4, No. 2 (February 1964), pp. 75–76; *ibid.*, Vol. 4, No. 9 (September 1964), pp. 69–71; *Bohemia* (Havana), Oct. 22, 1964; and Fidel Castro, "Tercera Plenaria Nacional de la FMC en Isla de Pinos," *Obra Revolucionaria*, No. 4–5 (March 1965), pp. 12–14.

[8] Fidel Castro interview with Richard Eder, *New York Times*, July 6, 1964, p. 12; and Castro interview with Lee Lockwood, *Playboy*, January 1967, p. 74. See also *Time*, Oct. 8, 1965, p. 39.

"not politically integrated" and those "free of suspicion." Those in the former group enter the so-called Military Units to Aid Production (UMAP) and are employed in agricultural work throughout their service period. Recruits free of suspicion are under a training regime which combines military instruction and productive work.[9]

The number of recruits is unknown. The Minister of the Armed Forces (FAR), charged with the administration of the military service, said in 1963 that 1.5 million persons were covered although only a selection of youngsters between seventeen and twenty-two years old would be drafted initially. The author has estimated, based on official data released in 1963, that 84,000 persons were enrolled in military service at the end of 1966.[10] In 1968, however, the Prime Minister asserted that the compulsory military system embraced practically every young man within the military age bracket.[11] Hence, the previous estimate seems conservative. Recruits receive food, shelter, and clothing, plus a monthly allowance of seven pesos ($7).[12]

When unpaid workers are totaled, it appears that by 1967 from 200,000 to 300,000 man-years of unpaid labor were employed in the Cuban economy. These figures may be measured against the 1967 labor force of some 2.5 million workers. Unpaid labor thus represented from 8 to 12 percent of the regular labor force. The man-year contribution from the several types of unpaid labor was as follows: 60,000 to 70,000 from employed workers; 5,000 to 10,000 from women;

[9] Fidel Castro, *Hoy* (Havana), Mar. 14, 1963; Raúl Castro, *Hoy*, Nov. 13, 1963; Law No. 1,129, Nov. 26, 1963; and Regulations of the Ministry of Armed Forces, Nov. 29, 1963, *Hoy*, Nov. 29, 1963.

[10] Raúl Castro announced in 1963 that in the first three years of military service $60.5 million would be saved as the result of multiplying the annual wage of each former soldier or militiaman ($819.40) times the total number of recruits at the end of the third year. Therefore X = 60,500,000 ÷ 819.40 = 84,000 recruits.

[11] Fidel Castro, "Speech at the Commemoration of the Defeat of Yankee Imperialism at Playa Girón," *Granma* (Weekly Review [W.R.]), Apr. 28, 1968, p. 2.

[12] Prior to 1959, the Cuban peso was at par with the U. S. dollar. After the revolution the Cuban government officially claimed the parity of the peso with the dollar although in the black market the peso has been exchanged for $0.10 to $0.30. This paper assumes parity in the exchange; the $ stands for pesos.

18,000 to 23,000 from secondary school students; 84,000 to 120,000 from military recruits; and 20,000 to 75,000 from prisoners. What has been the contribution of this large unpaid labor force to the Cuban society and economy?

Significance of Unpaid Labor

There is no unanimity among Cuban leaders on whether the principal advantage of unpaid labor is ideological or whether it is economic. The so-called old communists, former members of the prerevolutionary Communist party who are committed to the Soviet line, often accept (although with serious reservations) unpaid labor as an economic tool for development purposes.[13] The new communists, those thrown up by the revolution, stress the ideological side. However, the stand of this group often is ambiguous, as two statements by the late "Che" Guevara illustrate:

> Voluntary work should not be looked at for its economic importance or for its present value to the state. Ultimately, voluntary work is the element that most actively develops the workers' conscience, preparing the road to a new society.
>
> In the history of the Ministry of Industry, only once has the whole production plan been fulfilled on schedule. This was in July 1964 when we arranged a labor mobilization to meet the goals and everyone put in voluntary work.[14]

For those who stress ideology, unpaid labor is crucial in the process of building a communist man who will be cleansed eventually of selfish tendencies. Thus, gratuitous labor must be organized systematically to permeate all stages of life. Unpaid labor begins in childhood during grammar school and continues into adolescence in secondary school. Children be-

[13] For example see *Hoy*, Mar. 30, 1964, and Mirta Aguirre, "Lenin: Burocratismo y Trabajo Comunista," *Cuba Socialista*, Vol. 6, No. 57 (May 1966), pp. 149–155.
[14] Ceremony during which certificates of communist work were awarded to unpaid workers, broadcast by CMQ Radio, Aug. 15, 1964.

tween six and sixteen are exposed to rural life and taught the importance of manual labor in society. Special care is taken to combine intellectual education and physical work. The transitional stage, adolescence into adulthood, occurs during military service. Youngsters between sixteen and twenty-two are trained both in warfare and useful work. By collecting idle teenagers and bringing them into the work force, compulsory military service prevents the development of a "parasitical class" incompatible with a socialist society. At any age, but especially among employed workers, unpaid labor aims to reduce differences between town and country, industry and agriculture, intellectual work and manual work. The use of unpaid female workers is the first step toward incorporating women into the labor force and toward elimination of sex discrimination.

Pathological deviations from the socialist pattern must be corrected through rehabilitation, a process in which work plays a key role. Bureaucrats committing serious administrative errors and bourgeois elements rebelling against the socialist legal system are condemned to forced labor designed to reeducate them according to communist principles.

If unpaid labor is judged according to these educational and sociological perspectives, it may be worthwhile because of its long-run effects in achieving some consensus in society. Granting that this may be true, this article stresses the more pragmatic and immediate advantages of unpaid labor. Two economic aspects of unpaid labor are important: the provision of manpower to cope with labor shortages in agriculture and the generation of wage savings to reduce inflation.

A Palliative to the Agricultural Labor Shortage

Unpaid labor is the most important means of solving the most grave structural problem in the Cuban economy, i.e., the mismatch between a labor shortage in agriculture and a labor surplus in the tertiary sector concentrated in the cities.[15]

[15] A detailed treatment of this subject is offered by Carmelo Mesa-Lago, "Unemployment in Socialist Countries: Soviet Union, East Europe,

The early years of the revolution witnessed an exodus of unemployed and underemployed workers from rural areas to the cities, mainly Havana and Santiago. Many of the immigrants were absorbed by the rebel army, educational institutions, the bureaucracy, various mass organizations, and construction. Unemployment and underemployment were aggravated by reductions in employment in the industrial and trade sectors due to nationalization, consolidation of enterprises, and obstacles posed to foreign trade. With the elimination of private building activity, and with a decline in government construction due to lack of building materials, construction employment received a serious blow. A large part of the surplus labor force continued to receive its previous wage instead of being laid off. This combination of excess labor and state subsidy negatively affected labor productivity. Initially, the new socialist government hoped to absorb the labor surplus through industrialization. However, geopolitical considerations induced the socialist bloc to shift the emphasis in economic aid to Cuba from industry to agriculture. Facing hypertrophy in the tertiary sector and a low rate of employment growth in the secondary sector, the only outlet for the labor surplus was the primary sector, that is, agriculture.

While this phenomenon was taking place in the urban areas, the agricultural sector was undergoing a radical transformation. Part of the former labor surplus disappeared through migration, while other workers found stable, fairly well-paid jobs on the state farms which, by the mid-1960's, embraced 70 percent of the total arable land in Cuba. Encouraged by job stability, salaried workers at the state farms slackened their efforts. The small farmer and the self-employed worker were trapped by the lack of economic incentives, i.e., their obligations to meet state delivery quotas at low prices and the general scarcity of manufactured goods available for purchase. They typically reduced their efforts to a minimum in order to receive just enough income to buy the few goods available in the market. (Most essential con-

China and Cuba" (Ph.D. dissertation, New York State School of Industrial and Labor Relations, Cornell University, 1968), pp. 415–480.

sumer goods were rationed in 1962, and the list of rationed items has been growing.) The result was the appearance of an artificial labor shortage in agriculture. Unpaid labor became the main device for coping with this problem.

Unpaid labor is recruited mainly from urban areas and from jobs where labor surplus is more acute. It also must be remembered that a significant number of surplus workers are not laid off, i.e., they continue to receive their former wages without making a positive work contribution to the economy. Their productivity can be characterized as negative. A large number of these workers are mobilized for unpaid labor, particularly in the sugar harvest. Havana and Oriente provinces furnish about two thirds of the unpaid labor force, as shown in Table 2.

TABLE 2

Distribution by Province of Unpaid (Employed) Workers in the 1965 and 1966 Sugar Harvests

Provinces	1965		1966	
	Number of Unpaid Workers	Percentage Distribution	Number of Unpaid Workers	Percentage Distribution
Pinar del Río	1,638	2.8	2,220	3.1
Havana	27,000	46.8	31,740	44.5
Matanzas	1,956	3.4	3,500	4.9
Las Villas	4,000	6.9	7,200	10.1
Camagüey	4,500	7.8	4,446	6.2
Oriente	18,655	32.3	22,208	31.2
Totals	57,749	100.0	71,314	100.0

Source: Hoy, Jan. 8, 1965; Radio Progreso, Feb. 8 and 12, and Dec. 7, 1965; and Radio Rebelde, Mar. 1, 1966.

It should be noted that the sectors furnishing voluntary workers are mainly those suffering from disguised unemployment. In the 1967 sugar harvest, one third of all voluntary workers came from the service sector, particularly from administration and trade, while another third was recruited from construction workers.[16] This explains, in part, why important declines in output have not occurred in the sectors which provide voluntary workers for the sugar crop. Increased effort by those remaining at the work site has been enough to cope with the problem.

The migration of surplus rural labor, temporarily and partially absorbed by the cities at the cost of lowered productivity, now has been reversed. However, most surplus urban workers do not have experience in agricultural tasks, as do most youngsters who migrated from the countryside to the cities early in the revolution.

The heavy cost of the rebel army and the militia has stimulated their transformation into a compulsory military service, which is not only cheaper but also provides a disciplined, mobile labor force. The military service conscripts the unemployed and urban "vagrants" and sends them to work in agriculture. High educational costs and shortages engendered by the exodus of youth from the countryside are partly offset by the unpaid labor performed by students. Excessive employment in the service sector, in the state bureaucracy, and in mass organizations is partially siphoned off by unpaid labor. However, the inherent economic irrationality of the system induces a series of maladjustments.

Criticisms of the System

Cuban officials and foreign experts committed to socialist ideals have explained and criticized this situation. René Dumont, a French agronomist invited on three occasions by the Cuban government as an advisor, reported that several crops —the 1962 cotton harvest, for example—were lost because of the artificial labor shortage. After discussing the inefficiency of unpaid labor, he conceded that to use it was still better than to lose the crops. He then pointed to the core of the problem:

[16] *El Mundo,* Sept. 10, 1966, pp. 1 and 5.

"It would be desirable to rectify the economic and structural errors that have caused this situation."[17]

At the Twelfth Congress of the Confederation of Cuban Workers (CTC) held in 1966, Miguel Martín, the new secretary general, complained that the effective work day (for paid workers) at the state farms was four hours, instead of the legal eight hours. This situation was nourished by trade union leaders who were "the first ones in giving such a bad example." Then Martín revealed that "unpaid labor was used to fulfill the output targets and thus cover [management's and their employees'] deficiencies."[18] In the closing speech of the CTC Congress, Prime Minister Castro elaborated on the subject:

> [Managers] try to solve all their problems through the use of unpaid labor. . . . Voluntary workers, students, and females must not fill the vacuum left by laziness. . . . Often, they are employed to fill out the shift of agricultural laborers that only work three or four hours per day. . . . Prisoners have been used for this purpose also. [Everybody] seeks the easier solution instead of attacking the problem at its roots.[19]

The main obstacle in solving the problem at its roots seems to be poor implementation of output standards (work quotas) in the agricultural sector. According to the Vice-Minister of the Agrarian Reform Institute, Raúl Curbelo, the employed agricultural labor force is only half utilized, and therefore its productivity is extremely low. Output standards have not corrected this situation. Because of this, there is an artificial labor shortage in the countryside which reaches a spring peak of 140,000 workers. A solution would be to hire extra, skilled manpower at current wage rates. But skilled manpower is not available, mainly because of artificial full employment and lack of economic incentives. In addition, if needed manpower

[17] René Dumont, *Cuba, Socialisme et Développement* (Paris: Editions du Seuil, 1964), p. 82.

[18] Miguel Martín, "Informe Central al XII Congreso de la CTC," *El Mundo*, Aug. 26, 1966, pp. 5–7.

[19] Fidel Castro, "Discurso de Clausura del XII Congreso de la CTC," *El Mundo*, Aug. 30, 1966, pp. 5–9.

were hired at current wage rates, production costs would rise significantly. Hence, the answer to the dilemma has been to utilize unpaid labor.[20]

Harvest mechanization, particularly of sugar cane, is not an easy solution to the labor shortage. Initially, Soviet combines were used in Cuba but they broke down, there were not enough spare parts, unlevel terrain was a serious obstacle, and the machines cut the cane in an inefficient manner with considerable waste. Cuban-built machines now are in experimental use. According to official sources, tests of such combines have been positive, but the machines still need to be improved considerably. The government hopes to have a "good number" of such combines by the 1970's, although this will mean that one fifth of the sugar mills will have to be shut down because their location in mountainous regions means that combines cannot be used.[21]

Late in 1966, the Minister of Labor, Basilio Rodríguez, tried to eliminate the need for unpaid labor by enforcing output standards.[22] He was not successful, and early in 1967, he was removed from office. The new Minister, Captain Jorge Risquet, is approaching the problem differently. Instead of applying output standards to individual employees or relying exclusively on unpaid labor at peaks in the labor shortage, he is trying to inject into the rigid agricultural labor market a considerable number of excess workers from the cities. An agricultural mobilization of youngsters working in the service sector started in January 1967. CTC and UJC recruiters came to urban work sites, and managers were advised not to pose obstacles. By mid-1968, 40,000 youngsters had been recruited and sent off to work for three years in agriculture.[23]

---

[20] Raúl Curbelo, quoted by Alfredo Núñez Pascual, "Mas Productividad en el Trabajo Agrícola," *El Mundo,* Sept. 20, 1966, p. 4; and Alfredo Núñez Pascual, "Señalan Tareas en el Sector Agrícola," *El Mundo,* Sept. 21, 1966, p. 4.

[21] Fidel Castro, "Speech in Commemoration of the Anniversary of the April 9 Strike," *Granma,* Apr. 14, 1968, p. 3.

[22] Basilio Rodríguez, quoted by Alfredo Núñez Pascual, "Ampliar la Norma en las Tares Agrícolas," *El Mundo,* Nov. 8, 1966, p. 4.

[23] "Statements of Young People Off to Jobs in Agriculture," *Granma,* Jan. 15, 1967, pp. 1 and 15; *El Mundo,* Jan. 24, 1967, p. 1; and "The Battle of Agriculture . . . ," *Granma,* May 5, 1968, p. 1.

The labor mobilization for agriculture has been accelerated since March 1968, when Prime Minister Castro launched "The Revolutionary Offensive" against such "residues of capitalism" as selfishness, parasitism, bureaucracy, and individualism and in support of self-sacrifice, strict discipline, hard work, collectivism, and greater stimulation of productive efforts concentrated in agriculture.[24] If the agricultural mobilization is successful, then short-term unpaid labor will be reduced substantially and replaced by more institutionalized, long-term types of labor. This would solve most of the problems linked with the mobilization of unpaid workers.

Wage Savings

From a theoretical viewpoint, unpaid labor permits raising production levels without altering labor costs since the state siphons off wages which otherwise would go to the workers. Thus, unpaid labor may operate as a deflationary device, if it creates goods and services whose value is greater than the operative costs. Some of the disadvantages of unpaid labor (to be discussed later) raise serious questions about its profitability.

Table 3 is an attempt to compute the value of wages saved through unpaid labor for the period 1962–1967. Data on unpaid labor performed by employed workers are relatively abundant but scarce for the other types of workers. In addition, the various types of unpaid labor are often mixed or combined, and detailed disaggregated data are not available. Due to space limitations, it is neither possible to explain in detail all the computations made nor to give all sources used. An explanation of the methodology used to compute the figures in Table 3 is given in the appendix.

The data in Table 3 are admittedly speculative, but in making his estimates, the author has used highly conservative figures. In the industrial sector, only wages saved at a few branches have been included. Potential wages saved by gram-

[24] "The Revolutionary Offensive," *Granma*, Mar. 31, 1968, p. 2.

TABLE 3

Estimated Value of Wage Savings from Unpaid Labor, 1962–1967
(in million pesos)

Performers	1962	1963	1964	1965	1966	1967
Employed workers						
Sugar[a]	9.0	12.0	15.0	20.1	30.8	37.8
Industry[b]	1.0	1.5	1.6	n.a.	n.a.	n.a.
Other sectors[c]	3.0	4.0	2.0	n.a.	n.a.	n.a.
Women[d]	1.5	1.7	2.5	n.a.	n.a.	n.a.
Students[e]	1.5	1.5	5.5	10.0*	10.0*	10.0*
Prisoners[f]	n.a.	n.a.	5.0†	5.0†	5.0†	10.0†
Military recruits[g]	n.a.	n.a.	10.0	20.0	30.0	40.0
Totals	16.0	20.7	41.6	55.1	75.8	97.8

* Includes unpaid work performed by secondary-school students only. If unpaid labor by grammar-school students had been added, figures would have been increased substantially.

† Based on official figures of the number of prisoners. If the higher number of prisoners given by non-official sources had been used, figures would have been increased by as much as 7 times for 1964–1966 and 3 times for 1967.

n.a. = not available.

Sources: [a] Resolution of the Labor Ministry regulating wages of sugar workers, in *El Mundo,* Jan. 11 and Dec. 23, 1963, Feb. 10 and Dec. 3, 1964, and Nov. 4, 1966. Data on the length of the sugar crop as well as on number of and yield from unpaid workers, from *Hoy,* Jan. 7 and Dec. 14, 1963, Apr. 8, May 12, June 6, July 1, and Oct. 3–9, 1964, Jan. 8 and 28, 1965; *El Mundo,* Jan. 11, 1963, July 5, 1964, Dec. 6, 1965, and Sept. 10 and Nov. 22, 1966; and *Trabajo,* Vol. 4, No. 22 (December 1963), pp. 63–67. Additional information from Radio Progreso, CMQ Radio, Radio Havana, and Radio Rebelde.

[b] "Un Trabajo Comunista," *Nuestra Industria,* Vol. 4, No. 2 (February 1964), pp. 46–49; Ernesto Guevara, "Discurso en el Acto de Entrega de Certificados de Trabajo Voluntario Comunista," Aug. 15, 1964. Minimum industrial wage from "Bases para la Organización de los Salarios y Sueldos de los Trabajadores," *Suplemento de la Revista Trabajo,* June 10, 1963, p. 9.

[c] Work on plantation of tubers, fruit and pine trees, as well as harvest of rice and vegetables, and repair of damage inflicted by hurricanes, from numerous radio broadcasts, and reports in *El Mundo, Hoy,* and *Granma.* Minimum agricultural wage from Israel Talavera and Juan Herrera, "La Organización del Trabajo y el Salario en la Agricultura," *Cuba Socialista,* Vol. 5, No. 45–46 (May–June 1965), p. 70.

[d] Mainly work on cotton harvest, from *Hoy,* June 21, 1963; Vilma Espín, Radio Progreso, Nov. 15 and 16, 1964; various radio broadcasts

mar school students have been excluded. A significant downward bias factor in the calculations (except for most work done at the sugar harvest) results from the arbitrary use of the lowest rates in the corresponding wage scale, despite the fact that skilled workers ranked higher in the scale certainly have performed unpaid labor. A compensating factor for such underestimation may arise from the fact that unpaid workers often are not able to fulfill the minimum yield (output target) to which the minimum wage rate is attached. Finally, a check with the scarce official figures on wages saved through voluntary work alone (for example, $13 million, both in 1962 and 1963) seems to confirm the author's estimates.[25]

The wages saved through unpaid labor apparently exceeded $300 million in the period 1962–1967; the annual average saving was more than $50 million, 1.4 percent of the yearly average of Cuba's national income during this period, i.e., $3,550 million.[26]

In 1964, a Communist party publication explained the measures taken by the government to withdraw $70 million annually to fight inflation. After referring to increases in official prices and encouraging saving accounts among work-

---

monitored during December 1964 and January 1965; and *El Mundo,* Jan. 27, 1967.

[e] Work in coffee, rice, and cotton harvests from Carlos Rafael Rodríguez, Radio Progreso, July 23, 1962; Radio Progreso, Nov. 4 and 6, and Dec. 4 and 28, 1963, Jan. 1 and 20, May 6, and August 2, 1964; "Información Pública Sobre la Zafra Cafetalera," broadcast by CMBF-TV, July 14, 1964 and CMQ Radio, Sept. 4, 1964. Compulsory unpaid labor from Resolution of the Ministry of Education, in *El Mundo,* May 27, 1964; *El Mundo,* May 31 and Sept. 18, 1966; and *Granma,* Jan. 8, 1967.

[f] Number of prisoners from *New York Times,* July 6, 1964, p. 12; *Playboy,* January 1967, p. 74; and *Time,* Oct. 8, 1965, p. 39. Work schedule and other data from *Nuestra Industria,* Vol. 4, No. 2 (February 1964), pp. 75–76; and *Bohemia,* Oct. 22, 1964.

[g] Number of recruits computed by the author based on Raúl Castro, *Hoy,* Nov. 13, 1963. Other data from Law and Regulations of Compulsory Military Service in *Hoy,* Nov. 29, 1963.

[25] Reports from the CTC's National Secretariat of Voluntary Work, *El Mundo,* Jan. 12, 1963, and Radio Progreso, Feb. 11, 1964.

[26] National income figures mainly from U. N. *Statistical Yearbook 1966* (New York, 1967), p. 551; and U. N. *Monthly Bulletin of Statistics,* Vol. 22, No. 6 (June 1968), p. 178.

ers, the article mentioned "the establishment of the military service which saves 40 million pesos per year" and wages saved through unpaid labor as two important anti-inflationary devices.[27]

Low Productivity of Unpaid Workers

The preceding sections suggest that the use of unpaid labor has been beneficial to the Cuban economy, but other factors cast some doubt on whether the ultimate result has been positive or negative. Three problems must be analyzed: the low productivity of unpaid workers, the negative impact of this kind of labor upon sugar production, and the effects of unpaid labor upon other sectors of the economy.

Blas Roca, member of the General Secretariat of the Cuban Communist party, has said this about the unprofitability of unpaid labor:

> It suffers from the deficiencies flowing from the lack of expertness and low productivity of these workers, and the high costs and inconveniences provoked by this kind of labor. . . . Forced labor is not profitable from an economic viewpoint because it is not very productive. Only truly-free and fairly-paid labor can reach high output targets and productivity.[28]

To evaluate Roca's statement, it is necessary to introduce a distinction between unpaid labor performed by skilled workers at their work sites and that performed by workers without expertise in the type of work done. When a worker puts in unpaid overtime in his regular job he is creating net product, even though he may perform the task with less enthusiasm than during paid hours. Net product also could be created through forced labor from prisoners and military recruits who would have to be state-supported in any event. However,

---

[27] Partido Unido de la Revolución Socialista, *Aclaraciones* (La Habana: Imprenta Nacional, 1964), p. 48.

[28] Blas Roca, "El Trabajo Libre y el Servicio Militar," *Hoy*, Apr. 16, p. 2, and Apr. 18, 1964, p. 2.

when a worker is moved away from his customary job site to do unpaid labor for which he lacks skill or experience, his real output must be measured in relation to his real costs. (In the case of underemployed workers doing unpaid labor, the question is whether his output in the unpaid job minus his operational costs is greater than his output in the previous job minus his costs there.)

The labor productivity of skilled labor is higher than that of unskilled, unpaid workers. Dumont reported that in the 1962 coffee harvest, 41,300 unpaid workers (most of them students) picked only 7.8 percent of the total crop. The students' productivity was equal to one seventh that of an average paid worker and as low as one twelfth that of an outstanding coffee picker.[29] As Table 4 shows, two years later the situation had improved considerably. The unpaid labor force had increased almost threefold, but the productivity gains were much higher because 58 percent of that year's harvest was gathered by the students. Still, the productivity ratio between an unpaid, unskilled student and a paid, skilled coffee picker was disproportionate, less than one to five. In addition, the expenses of lodging, boarding, and transporting the students absorbed a sizeable share of the value created by their work.

For the 1962–1965 sugar harvest, unpaid workers usually

TABLE 4

Comparison of the Productivity of Unpaid Students and Paid Workers in the 1964 Coffee Harvest

Pickers	Number	Grain Gathered (tons)	Average Yield per Picker (lbs.)	Crop Value (million pesos)	Labor Productivity (pesos per picker)
Unpaid students	110,000	25,000	450	23.5	213.63
Paid workers	15,000	17,500	2,400	16.5	1,100.00
Totals	125,000	42,500	Ratio 1:5.3	40.0	

Source: Based on "Información Pública Sobre la Zafra Cafetalera," broadcast by CMBF-TV, July 14, 1964, and CMQ Radio, Sept. 4, 1964.

[29] Dumont, *op. cit.*, p. 82.

cut less than one ton of sugar cane per day while the daily
average for skilled cutters was two or three times higher. Due
to the large-scale utilization of unpaid labor, production efficiency (measured in daily average output) in the 1967 sugar
harvest was 22 percent below that of the 1957 harvest.[30]

A second negative aspect of unpaid labor, as acknowledged
by the Minister of the Sugar Industry, Orlando Borrego, is
that untrained workers may cause waste or damage. According to this official, some unpaid cane cutters left the pinnacle
and the leaves—which contain no sugar—on the cane. Later
these were ground at the mill with resultant waste. Others cut
cane too high, wasting the lower section of the plant which
has the highest sugar content. As a result, the plant grows
weak and short in the next season because it develops "air
roots" and loses strength. The Minister also reported that a
significant amount of sugar cane was dropped either at the
cutting or loading stage and abandoned in the fields. Finally,
when the sugar crop was over, unskilled weed cleaners damaged the cane buds.[31] In the coffee harvest, unskilled students often picked unripe beans or harmed coffee plants.

A third problem involves transportation and maintenance
expenses. Although short-term voluntary workers earn no
wages, sometimes their transportation, lodging, and food expenses are higher than the wages saved. The former secretary general of the CTC has stated that "some of the weekend
volunteers measure their productivity by their fatigue. But
many of them would not consider their jobs done if we explained clearly to them the relationship between their real productivity and the cost of transporting them to their work."[32]

Workers doing unpaid labor on leave of absence earn regular wages from the enterprise to which they belong while
working in the sugar fields or on other crops. Their urban
wages are usually higher than those currently earned by the
rural workers who reach greater productivity than the volunteers. The poor performance of the latter—who often boast

[30] Data for 1957 comes from Cuban Economic Research Project, *A
Study on Cuba* (Coral Gables: The University of Miami Press, 1965);
data for 1967 from Radio Havana.
[31] Orlando Borrego, "Esta Zafra Será Superior," *El Mundo,* Dec. 6,
1966, p. 5. See also Dumont, *op. cit.,* p. 81.
[32] Lázaro Peña, *La Tarde* (Havana), Sept. 3, 1962.

that they are performing a patriotic task—irritates the regular paid workers and induces protests from them.[33] In 1963, Prime Minister Castro complained that skilled workers with a daily productivity of $10 were being pulled out of their jobs and set to do unpaid labor in agriculture with a daily productivity of $1.50.[34] The Minister of the Armed Forces gave an example of such irrational behavior in the 1963 coffee harvest:

> One brigade composed of 14 electrical workers gathered 553 cans of coffee beans. At a wage rate of $0.55 per can they saved the amount of $304. However, the operational costs of this brigade, in terms of wages paid by the power enterprise, lodging and board, and other expenses were as high as $5,795. Therefore, the nation had a net loss of $4,491, due to the unpaid labor of this brigade.[35]

The number of occupational accidents among unskilled, unpaid workers cutting cane or cleaning weeds in the sugar fields has increased considerably.[36] This is a fourth negative factor. Urban workers not accustomed to arduous agricultural work often collapse or suffer heat strokes. Industrial workers can also faint when overtime hours are prolonged. Several such cases have been reported by the government, among them that of a worker who had accumulated 1,742 hours of unpaid labor with a work schedule of 16 hours a day—including Sundays—and who had suffered a serious accident which damaged his spine.[37]

To improve productivity among unpaid workers the government has introduced numerous control measures which have been noted in this article. Output targets (work quotas) were put into operation in 1964: "General output targets for each brigade and specific daily quotas for each cane cutter have been fixed in order to squeeze the maximum effort from

[33] Dumont, op. cit., pp. 81–82.
[34] Fidel Castro, Revolución (Havana), Oct. 22, 1963.
[35] Raúl Castro, Revolución, Nov. 13, 1963.
[36] For more details see Carmelo Mesa-Lago, The Labor Sector and Socialist Distribution in Cuba (New York: Praeger and The Hoover Institution, 1968), pp. 170–174.
[37] "Un Trabajo Comunista," Nuestra Industria, No. 8, August 1965, p. 58.

the volunteers."[38] This measure, in turn, induced an increase in occupational accidents. For work on the 1967 sugar crop, unpaid workers were selected from those who in previous years had reached a two ton daily average of cane cut and who had observed discipline in the fields. Training courses were given to the heads of cutting brigades to increase collective output and to reduce waste and accidents. In 1968, the party newspaper reported that groups of unpaid workers had been trained and organized into special brigades to do a certain kind of job such as construction, trailblazing, or sanitation.[39]

Negative Effects Upon Sugar Production

According to a report released by the National Commission of Economic Research of the Schools of Revolutionary Indoctrination, low productivity among unpaid laborers made it necessary to lengthen the sugar-crop period. This induced waste and raised costs. Prior to the revolution, the sugar season usually began in mid-January and ended in April. Now work starts in November and ends in June or July. In 1966, the Economics School of the University of Havana directed an investigation of the economic consequences of this policy. According to its findings, cane contains a lower percentage of sugar during the months from November to January, increases during February and March, and finally, begins to decline in April. A large amount of sugar is lost every year because tons of cane are cut from November to January and from April to July.[40]

Sugar mills now operate for longer periods of time, not only because the season lasts longer, but also due to the ir-

[38] "Voluntarios para la V Zafra del Pueblo," *Hoy,* Nov. 11, 1964, p. 1.
[39] Rigoberto Fernández, *El Mundo,* Nov. 26, 1966, p. 7; "Selección de Macheteros," *El Mundo,* Nov. 12, 1966, p. 1; and "Editorial" and "A los Trabajadores," *Granma,* Mar. 31, 1968, pp. 1 and 3.
[40] Alfredo Núñez Pascual, "Mayores Costos por Problemas del Corte," *El Mundo,* Nov. 18, 1966, p. 4; Alfredo Núñez Pascual, "Factores a Tener en Cuenta para la Zafra," *El Mundo,* Nov. 25, 1966, p. 4; and Borrego, *loc. cit.,* p. 5. For a divergent viewpoint see Edward Boorstein, *The Economic Transformation of Cuba* (New York: Monthly Review Press, 1968), pp. 206–207.

regular supply of cane cut by unstable, unsk
workers. Higher grinding costs result from larger
fuel and labor, and wear on the equipment is greater.
in 1963, when utilization of unpaid workers was much low
than in subsequent years, the grinding period at Cuba's biggest sugar mill was twice as long as normal. In that year, the
cost of the 250 lb. sack of sugar rose by $0.85.[41]

In 1968, due to difficulties with the Soviet supply of oil, the
Cuban government began a campaign to save fuel in the
sugar harvest, putting emphasis on a steadier flow of cane to
the mills, increasing the use of oil substitutes such as bagasse
and firewood, and putting more reliance on the transportation of cane by ox cart.[42]

Effects Upon Other Sectors of the Economy

It is a matter of speculation whether the annual withdrawal
of thousands of workers from other sectors of the Cuban
economy to do unpaid agricultural labor on a six-month basis
has resulted in lowered production in these other sectors. The
Cuban government alleges that output has not suffered. In
1963, for instance, "official certificates" from state enterprises
showed that industrial production had not fallen due to the
absence of workers cutting cane in the countryside.[43]

The method used to maintain output levels has been to
pressure the remaining industrial workers for greater effort.
In 1964, meetings were held at the factories to approve "collective compromises" by which workers promised that they
would not permit drops in output. As time passed, the system
became better organized. For the 1967 sugar crop, the CTC
required all workers "to fill the vacuum left by the volunteers
so to avoid a decline in output." The final decision was "to
demand four hours of unpaid overtime" from all workers who

[41] Alfredo Núñez Pascual, "Hay que Abastecer a Cabalidad el Ingenio,"
El Mundo, Nov. 11, 1966, p. 4.
[42] "The 1967–68 Cuban Harvest . . . ," *Economic Intelligence Report:
Cuba* (Miami), Vol. 1, No. 3 (Feb. 29, 1968), pp. 1–2; and "Abreast of
the Harvest," *Economic Intelligence Report: Cuba* (Miami), Vol. 1,
No. 4 (Apr. 19, 1968), p. 3.
[43] *Trabajo,* Vol. 4, No. 22 (Dec. 1963), p. 67.

D LABOR

407

In addition, unpaid females recruited
⁚ome of the manpower needed to fill
Havana province, 4,000 unskilled fe-
ccupied vacant jobs in transportation,
icturing.[44]

ned that the government has been able to
maintain production levels in the economic sectors
affected by labor depletion, the question of the economic ra-
tionality of unpaid labor remains. Skilled laborers have been
withdrawn to do work in which they lack expertise. In turn,
unskilled laborers have been obtained to help fill the vacuum
left by those mobilized for work in the agricultural sector.

With regard to students doing unpaid work, Dumont
pointed out in 1963 that the main loss was that of study time.
According to Seers, the price paid has been a lowering of the
quality of future professional employees. In 1966, Prime Minister Castro asserted that unpaid labor performed by students
was an evil due to its negative effect on the educational development of the country.[45] In spite of these complaints, unpaid labor performed by students is still fitted into the academic year.

Conclusions

Unpaid labor in socialist Cuba is supplied by employed
workers, nonemployed women, students, prisoners, and military recruits. The exact number of people engaged in unpaid
labor is unknown, but the author estimates that the equivalent
of approximately 200,000 to 300,000 man-years were provided in 1967, or from 8 to 12 percent of the regular labor
force, although a much larger number of individuals was in-

[44] *Hoy,* Nov. 11, 1964; "Llamamiento de la CTC," *El Mundo,* Nov. 22,
1966, pp. 1–5; Alfredo Núñez Pascual, "Buenos Resultados de la Zafra,"
El Mundo, Dec. 2, 1966, p. 4; "Ocupan Federadas Plazas de Obreros,"
El Mundo, Jan. 27, 1967, p. 7; and *Granma,* Feb. 21, 1967.
[45] Dumont, *op. cit.,* pp. 70 and 82; Dudley Seers *et al., Cuba: The
Economic and Social Revolution* (Chapel Hill, N.C.: The University of
North Carolina Press, 1964), p. 6; and Castro, "Discurso de Clausura en
el XII Congreso de la CTC," p. 6.

volved. The state sometimes provides board and lodging and pays other expenses of unpaid labor.

Unpaid labor may serve educational and sociological objectives, i.e., it may build up "the communist man" by reducing discriminatory practices allegedly produced by capitalism and based on location, sex, and type of work. Despite its potential value as an ideological tool, two economic factors seem to have stimulated the initiation of the system in Cuba. The most important factor is the artificial labor shortage in agriculture caused by migration to the cities of part of the rural unemployed and by the reduction of the full potential of effort and the consequent low productivity of the remaining agricultural workers, due to poor economic incentives. Optimal solutions to the artificial labor shortage include mechanizing agriculture, increasing the productivity of the employed rural labor force, or training the existing urban surplus and pointing it toward agricultural employment. But these are complex, long-term types of solutions while unpaid labor has provided an easy, expedient way to cope with the labor shortage.

Another factor influencing the utilization of unpaid labor has been the desire to reduce current inflation through wage savings—filling the labor vacuum with unpaid workers. During 1962–1967 the total wages saved through unpaid labor exceeded 300 million pesos, an annual average of more than 50 million pesos. The latter figure represents approximately 1.4 percent of the estimated annual average of the Cuban national income for this period.

Despite their economic value as manpower-supply and wage-saving devices, some kinds of unpaid labor have had negative effects on sugar production and other sectors of the economy. This is due to the low productivity of unskilled, unpaid laborers, their high operative costs, and the economic dislocation and waste caused by their utilization. Nevertheless, the total product contributed by Cuba's unpaid labor seems to be greater than its operational costs plus its alternative costs, therefore resulting in net product. This conclusion should be analyzed in more detail.

The premise is that net product always occurs when the total product resulting from the use of unpaid labor is greater than the real costs involved in its utilization. Net product may result in each of the following three cases:

1. When unpaid workers are already fully or partially employed and unpaid labor is done at the work site, net product always results from overtime, weekend work, and vacation work because there are neither operational costs involved (i.e., maintenance, transportation) nor damage inflicted on production. This is the typical case of unpaid labor done by employed workers at the jobsite. In this case net product is always equal to total product.

2. When unpaid workers are not already employed, net product results if the output created by them is greater than their operational costs. This is the case of military recruits, prisoners, females, and students whose output must be balanced with their transportation and maintenance expenses, plus the potential damage which they may inflict on the production process because of their lack of skills. Despite some contradictory reports, the overall trend seems to be that the use of these kinds of unpaid labor is beneficial to the Cuban economy. The best reason supporting this assumption is their continued utilization by the state.

3. When unpaid workers are already employed, either fully or partially, and unpaid labor is of a different nature than their regular job, net product results if the total output created by them, at the new place of work, is greater than their operational costs plus the potential costs induced by their absence from their original job. This is the case of unpaid workers, often underemployed at the work site, who are recruited to perform agricultural work. Another way to approach the problem is to check whether net product generated by these workers at the unpaid job is greater than their former net product at the work site.

Alternative opportunity costs in the latter case appear to be almost negligible for two reasons: the relatively small contribution of this excess labor to the sectors from which they departed, and the extra unpaid labor required from the remaining employees at the work site to offset the deficit of labor experienced by these sectors. With regard to operational costs, the situation is not as clear, but the continuing use of long-term unpaid workers suggests that costs incurred by them are smaller than total product generated by them. In any event, the government is trying to reduce such operational costs through the following measures: selection of unpaid workers according to their previous unpaid-labor performance, organization of training courses for the heads of brigades, training of special brigades to do a given type of job, and strict regulation of unpaid labor including the imposition of output standards. Even more significant is the fact that as time passes, formal organization of unpaid labor—akin to military organization—is emerging, and the long-term types of unpaid labor are gaining in use over the short-term type. Through such a process the state seeks to eliminate the negative effects of some kinds of unpaid labor, thereby strengthening the net contribution of unpaid labor to the Cuban economy.

The final conclusion is that the total product created by all kinds of unpaid labor is greater than its operational and alternative costs, therefore resulting in net product. Improved organization seems to have resulted in a rising net product. Lack of data, due to Cuban secrecy on the subject, impedes quantification of this net product, but the author hopes that in the future better statistical information will permit further research.

Appendix

Wage-savings computations in Table 3 are chiefly based on the equation $UW = (n.t.w) - m$, where "UW" stands for the total value of unpaid wages in pesos, "n" for the number of unpaid workers, "t" for the time spent in unpaid labor, "w" for the wage rate applicable, and "m" for maintenance expenses, when deductible. Several variations in the application of this formula have been introduced in relation to the various types of unpaid labor.

In computing unpaid labor performed by women and students in cotton harvests (as well as in most other agricultural work), "w" stands for the minimum hourly rate established by the wage scale for agricultural laborers ($0.36), while for unpaid labor in industry, the hourly minimum for nonagricultural laborers ($0.48) has been used. In unpaid labor performed in the sugar harvest, "w" results by adjusting the legal rate for a fixed yield of chopped sugar to the average yield actually reached by unpaid workers. For instance, in 1963, the minimum wage rate for cane cutters chopping less than 1.5 tons of cane was $1.98 per each 1.25 tons. Since unpaid cane cutters chopped a daily average of one ton, the average minimum wage saved daily from each unpaid worker was $1.56.

The number of unpaid workers (n) is occasionally given by official sources, as in the case of the sugar harvest or in work performed by women or secondary-school students. More often "n" has been computed by the author from scattered data. For instance, in the case of military recruits, "n" has been equated to 28,000 men in 1964, 56,000 in 1965, 84,000 in 1966, and 120,000 in 1967.

Time spent in unpaid labor (t) has been taken from official sources in the case of secondary-school students or employed workers in the sugar harvest. These sources often give the annual number of unpaid hours worked (that is, n.t), in, for example, the industrial sector. In computing unpaid labor performed by prisoners and military recruits, a regular work schedule (eight hours daily) has been assumed although scattered information suggests that such workers put in a longer day. Lack of information about time spent in unpaid labor by grammar-school students precludes any calculation of wage savings from them. However, for illustrative purposes, if each of these students had donated fifteen unpaid hours of work per year (secondary-school students commonly donate 288 hours), wages saved annually would have been close to $7 million.

The maintenance costs (m) of unpaid labor include board and lodging, monthly allowances ($7 for military recruits), and clothing in some cases. Transportation, wages of workers with leave of absence, and other expenses have been excluded. Maintenance costs in varying proportions have been subtracted from wage savings derived from unpaid labor performed by military recruits and prisoners as well as employees and students working on a long-term basis.

17

THE PROBLEM OF ABSENTEEISM*

The Revolutionary Orientation Commission

A treatment of this topic is quite complicated and will require more extensive and detailed analyses, but we are going to present here some ideas on the problem that seem useful to us.

Che described absenteeism as one of the most subtle and obscure enemies of the Revolution, when he pointed out that this did not mean that every absentee was a counterrevolutionary and that there are those who missed work unjustifiably but did not cease feeling that they were revolutionaries because of that.

We have the impression that considerable progress has recently been made in clarifying this problem, in analyzing its causes and the methods to be used against it. There is also a greater concern about absenteeism, although, of course, the evil persists and is causing us serious harm every day.

There is no political and administrative leader who is not inclined to fight in one way or another against absenteeism. The "guerrilla drive" has also shaken many consciences. The workers are increasing their awareness of this problem. What do we lack?

We lack a complete understanding, to its fullest extent, of what is meant by the fact that the struggle against absenteeism is above all a political and ideological struggle and that it requires an effort of organization and production control.

Of course, we are talking about the great mass of men, not about exceptional and incorrigible cases, which always occur.

This means that we have to go deeply into the causes of absenteeism, that we cannot be simplistic, because it is a com-

* *Granma* (Havana), October 30, 1969, p. 2.

plicated phenomenon and it is not solved by "tightening down" only at the bottom.

Why is there absenteeism? It would be necessary to say, essentially, that it is because we have broken—and very well broken—with the mechanisms of capitalist society, and we have not developed sufficiently the mechanisms peculiar to the new society, which must replace them.

Absenteeism was inconceivable in capitalism and that was not owing to any virtue of the bourgeois. It was the whip of hunger, the fear of unemployment, the meagerness of the income and the insecurity, which forced an observance of the existing labor discipline. There was also the army of unemployed, ten or twenty men behind each job, as a factor of organization. That whole brutal situation came tumbling down with the Revolution. Unemployment disappeared and the mechanism of the wage, the key instrument of capitalism, has ceased governing.

Today the worker usually earns much more than before and everyone in his family who wants to work or has capabilities works. He also receives numerous social services that have been organized by the Revolution in a truly Communist manner. The worker's wage, owing to the present limitations of production, is not a real wage, since the mass of goods in circulation on which to spend it completely does not exist. Every worker knows that he would have enough to live on what is paid him for fifteen or twenty days of work a month.

The wage has ceased to be the motivator and organizer of production, which is a historical victory of the Revolution, and in our conception we do not seek to restore these functions, but rather entirely to the contrary. We shall develop production, but we shall do it, we are already doing it, on other bases.

Now, transcendental implications are derived from this fact, because, when any possibility of coercion on the basis of needs for subsistence or a threat of unemployment has been eliminated, when men have been liberated from that slavery, it is only possible to demand more and better work on the basis of a sense of responsibility, of social duty and revolutionary awareness. This is our problem that we are addressing to free men!

Therefore, in our society there is not and there cannot be an efficient, capable work of administrative leadership if there is no connection with mass work, discussion, reasoning, political and ideological education of the workers.

The success of a socialist enterprise, which transforms it into a Communist collective, lies in the fact that the producer sees in the product of his labor his own creative work and he sees this as an important part in the building of the new society.

Therefore, we have to struggle to reach every man with the organization of the revolutionary forces, with our Party, and we must carry to the last worker information, analysis and requirements in his work.

There is still a long way to go for the new values to prevail entirely over the individual attitude of each worker. The struggle against absenteeism is part of that process.

The struggle against absenteeism cannot be a drive for one or two months. It has to be part of the plan of the administration, the Party and the worker movement. In this plan, the first thing is to raise the organization of work and to increase the requirement and administrative controls.

In some places of work, we have still found criteria like the following, when we held discussions with absentees:

"Well, I do not know what mess this is that has come about because I do not come to work for a few days if, after all, they do not pay me when I do not come."

With the explanation that while he did not come to work, the rest of society continued to work for him—the physician, the teacher who is educating his children, the baker—a decrease in absenteeism was achieved.

We have seen a whole series of methods for disciplining absentees and we can say that the ones that have really produced results are the ones that have been based on political, personal discussion with the workers by commissions composed of comrades from the administration, the Party, the youth organization and the worker movement.

It is necessary to know how to perform this work.

It is necessary to approach those who incur absenteeism sometimes through their own working companions, through their friends.

It is necessary to bring the most persistent cases up for personal political discussion, with an analysis of their errors and by pointing out to them a just revolutionary requirement.

Simultaneously, it is necessary to raise the general orientation of the workers, to strengthen control measures, to increase requirements in quality, to fight against sloppy work and to explain time and again the importance of that work to the country's economy and life.

It is necessary to make effective use of revolutionary propaganda and the Historic Dates Competition as mobilization factors.

It is necessary to pay attention to the social problems and the needs of the workers, to solve what can be solved immediately and to explain the reasons for which specific problems cannot be solved.

By experience we know that when all this work is performed, absenteeism drops to the minimum. Does it disappear completely? No. A small group of incorrigibles, of people unaware and unresponsive to every revolutionary call, may always remain.

But now, after performance of a mass political and ideological work, we shall have the authority and the morality to adopt any energetic measures that may be necessary. What is most important is the understanding and the support of the workers, in order to be able to do this.

Now indeed it will be possible to call a general assembly to summon the absentees by name, because the mass will back up and strengthen their awareness by virtue of this example-giving measure. And if a still more energetic measure is necessary, it will be discussed with the masses and it will be taken with the masses.

All this is what is meant by the fact that the struggle against absenteeism is essentially a political and ideological struggle. Bureaucratic methods, capitalist methods, do not give results.

This is the course, if we want to combat absenteeism and to combat it well.

18

WORKERS' DOSSIERS LAW*

Law 1225, which establishes the Labor Dossier and Work Force Control Card, reads as follows:

I, Osvaldo Dorticós Torrado, President of the Republic of Cuba, let it be known: that the Council of Ministers has agreed, and I have ratified the following:

Whereas: The accelerated development of our economy demands the most logical use of available human resources, through correct planning, distribution, and redistribution of the labor force.

Whereas: The preparation of trained workers, and of technical and administrative cadres, on a large scale, is a necessity for our economic development.

Whereas: It is essential that we implement the means for optimum utilization of the labor force, as well as for the proper selection of personnel, with a view toward the training and promotion of cadres, based upon the evaluation of the work merits that have been accumulated, technical or professional qualifications, physical aptitude and cultural level, background data that is also useful to the Social Security administration for purposes of pension and retirement transactions.

Whereas: The foregoing requires the establishment of a uniform procedure whereby there is a systematic notation of the data, background, and employment history of each worker actively employed, by means of his personnel file.

Whereas: The enforcement of the initial controls established by the Revolutionary Government, with regard to employment policy and the labor force, has made it possible to attain sufficient levels of organization and experience to institute a single system that will provide for an adequate cen-

* *Granma* (Havana), September 1, 1969, p. 3.

sus, as well as an understanding of, and control and statistical data on, the available labor force.

Whereas: By virtue of the faculties with which it is endowed, the Council of Ministers resolves to decree the following:

Law Number 1225

Article 1. The "Labor File" and the "Work Force Control Card" are established, as a compulsory measure, for all the workers in the country, whatever be their activity.

Article 2. The "Labor File" is to be comprised of the orderly, chronological accumulation of all data and background information on the life and job history of the employee. The "Work Force Control Card" is to be drawn up for each "Labor File" that is established, and must contain the necessary description and items to identify and locate both the worker and his dossier.

Article 3. The administrations of the country's work centers shall be required to establish the "Labor File" and "Work Force Control Card" on each of the workers on active duty at their centers, as well as to keep the file up to date with the pertinent notations.

Article 4. The "Labor File" shall constitute a basis for the Social Security administration to initiate transactions for granting pensions and retirement.

Article 5. The initiation of the "Labor File" and the preparation of the "Work Force Control Card" on new employees shall be the responsibility of the administrations of work centers.

Article 6. The administrations of work centers shall, at the times and places indicated at the convenience of the Ministry of Labor, render an account of the changes that have occurred in the "Labor Files" for which they are responsible.

Article 7. The administrations of work centers may not discharge a new employee, whether to transfer him to another center or to refer him to the Regional Delegation of the Ministry of Labor, without having first received or initiated, as the case may be, the "Labor File" and set up the "Work Force Control Card" on the employee in question.

Article 8. The agencies of the National Bank of Cuba shall, henceforth, issue salary funds only to work centers whose salary accounts they handle, on the basis of the total amounts covered for their plans. The salaries of workers who are on probation shall be paid by the bank agencies herein described, upon presentation of the "letter of introduction" of the employee in question, by the respective work centers. Similarly, the salaries of employees who are temporarily assigned to a work center different from the one with which they are affiliated may be paid by the banking agency which handles the account of the work center where they are actually employed, by means of a request submitted for that purpose.

Article 9. When a worker resigns permanently from a work center, the administration must send the Regional Delegation of the Ministry of Labor, through the bank agency involved, his "Labor File" and notification of the individual's resignation.

Temporary Measure

The administrations of the country's work centers shall initiate the "Labor File" and draw up the "Work Force Control Card" on all of their employees on active duty within the time limit set for this purpose by the Ministry of Labor.

Final Orders

First: Anyone guilty of falsification, loss, or total or partial destruction of the Labor File and Work Force Control Card shall be charged with a criminal offense, and referred to the proper judicial authorities for issuance of a penalty.

Second: The Ministry of Labor shall be required to decree the enforcement of this Law, establishing the necessary coordination with the National Bank of Cuba, with both entities responsible for issuing the necessary resolutions and instructions to carry out the terms of this Law.

Third: Hereby repealed are any legal and regulatory measures contrary to the enforcement of the terms of this Law, which shall go into effect as of the date of its publication in the Official Gazette of the Republic.

Therefore: I order that this Law be obeyed and executed in all its terms.

Given, in the Palace of the Revolution, Havana, 29 August 1969.

> Osvaldo Dorticós Torrado.
> Fidel Castro Ruz, Prime Minister.
> Captain Jorge Risquet Valdés, Minister of Labor.

Part IV

++

SOCIAL DEVELOPMENT

INTRODUCTION

Despite the different political interpretations and the economic difficulties of the Revolution, social development has been one of its fundamental achievements. The formerly exclusive resorts of the wealthy have opened their doors to everyone. Recreation centers and their facilities, such as all sports, are free. Rents and utilities have been lowered. Public telephones are free, books are either inexpensive or distributed without charge. Institutional racism has terminated and, with time, women are gaining true equality. Modern communal child care centers, which are free, proliferate throughout towns and villages. Housing rentals have been reduced by more than 50%, but the greatest progress has taken place in education and health. The educational revolution, which is an attempt to destroy the old values of a selfish and money-oriented society, is methodically studied by Nelson P. Valdés. The essay by Ricardo Leyva on the health of the Cubans represents a major contribution to the understanding of the Revolution because of its description of the entire sector and the wealth of statistical information.

19

THE RADICAL TRANSFORMATION
OF CUBAN EDUCATION*

Nelson P. Valdés

Introduction

The educational situation of Cuba has undergone profound transformation. Before the revolutionaries attained power, education reflected the depressing and backward outlook of authorities who did not seem much interested in developing the human resources of the country. The cultural development of the masses, however, has been one of the major concerns of the regime since 1959.

In order to understand the advances and radical changes that have occurred in the educational structure of Cuba, it is necessary to compare and examine the state of education prior to the Revolution and after it.

The State of Education Before the Revolution

The pre-revolutionary years of Cuban education present a concrete example of a country having the potential for educational growth, but hindered by a lack of leadership and structural obstacles.

When education trends are considered in Cuban history it is clear that from the turn of the century to the mid-1950's a steady decline in the percentages of illiteracy had taken

* This is an original article, written especially for this volume.

place.[1] In 1899 43.8% of the Cuban people did not know how to read or write. Forty-four years later 28.6% of the population was illiterate. By 1953 the illiteracy rate in the island was 23.6%. Nonetheless, at the same time that percentages presented a downward trend, the absolute number of illiterates in Cuba increased. Thus, in 1899 there were 690,565, and half a century later there were 1,032,849; that is, an increment of over 342,000.

Furthermore, national averages failed to disclose the uneven cultural development within the country. The picture of illiteracy by province was as follows:

Illiteracy by Province, 1953

Province	Percent (over 10 years of age)
Pinar del Río	30.8
Havana	9.2
Matanzas	19.2
Las Villas	24.8
Camagüey	27.3
Oriente	35.3
Average	23.6

Thus, Havana, where the administrative apparatus was concentrated, displayed an amazingly low number of illiterates. The regions that were the backbone of the economy, such as Oriente province, on the other hand, showed a regional average above the national figure.

Differences could be found not just between provinces, but within them. These differences were rooted in the great contrast between the urban and rural areas. Illiteracy in the rural sector was almost twice the national average, amounting to 41.7%, while the urban areas showed only 11.6% illiteracy.

Children between the ages of six and nine accounted for 558,000 persons, but 385,000, that is, 84%, were illiterate. The percentage of illiterates among the population in the six-to-fourteen age brackets in the urban areas was between

[1] All the data that follow have been compiled from Cuban censuses, unless otherwise indicated.

44.5% in Havana and 81.2% in Oriente province. The figures for the rural areas are not surprising:

Province	Percent
Pinar del Río	76.5
Havana	64.1
Matanzas	72.2
Las Villas	78.7
Camagüey	77.5
Oriente	89.5

Literacy figures, however, do not provide an entirely accurate picture of the state of Cuban education prior to the radical changes brought about by the Revolution. A much more useful index of educational development is the percentage of the total population enrolled in primary, secondary, and higher education. In relation to its total population in 1923, Cuba had *more* primary students enrolled than thirty years later. In the mid 1950's Cuba occupied the seventeenth place in primary school enrollment in all of Latin America, since the rate of growth of primary education was 50% lower than that of the population growth in the same period.

By 1958 approximately 49% of the Cuban children of primary school age (six–fourteen years) had no education, while the Latin American average was 36%.[2] Only 24.2% of the total population of fifteen years and over ever went to school. Close to 75% of the Cubans were either illiterate or had failed to complete primary school.

Furthermore, in 1953, of the total population of the island, 52% never managed to go beyond the third grade, and 44% had between a fourth and eleventh grade education, while only 3% of the Cuban people had schooling ranging from the twelfth grade to three years of college. Only 1% of the Cubans ever finished four years of higher education and less than half of that percentage acquired a university degree.[3]

[2] In the rural areas children of school age in 1959 numbered 782,000, but there were classrooms with a capacity for 279,000 pupils.

[3] United Nations, *Compendium of Social Statistics,* New York, 1963, p. 314.

But even those with a higher education reflected the imbalance of the society. Most university graduates tended to be in the fields of humanities, law, or medicine, while agriculture and industry suffered from a lack of highly trained personnel. Moreover, the state of the rural schools was absolutely outrageous. In a study made by the University of Las Villas in 1959, it was discovered that 96.2% of all schools in the province had just one classroom, but in that classroom students ranging from the first to the sixth grade met at the same time and were taught by one teacher. On the average there were thirty-eight students per classroom, but only twenty desks. Eighty percent of the schools were made out of wood, while 45% had thatched roofs, 86% lacked bathrooms, and running water could be found in only 3% of the schools. The average number of textbooks per student was one, although approximately fifteen different subjects were taught.[4]

The Early Educational Outlook of the Revolution

The educational structure that the revolutionary regime inherited from the past was archaic and restricted the cultural potential of the Cuban people. So as soon as the revolutionaries gained power they began to carry out a thorough and radical change of the whole system. Their program was based on the conviction that education was the inalienable right of every human being, a necessary condition to attain integral fulfillment. Further, the democratization of education was considered a just measure that would end inequality, and the revolutionaries were also convinced that there was a close relationship between economic development and education. To invest in schools and human improvement seemed one of the most rapid ways of moving away from underdevelopment.

In mid-1961 all private schools were nationalized and edu-

[4] Samuel Feijoó, "Situación de la escuela rural cubana," *Revolución* (Havana), November 5, 1959, p. 2; and by the same author, "Libros en la escuela rural cubana," *Revolución* (Havana), November 9, 1959, p. 18. See also: Various authors, *La Educación Rural en Las Villas*, Santa Clara: Universidad Central de Las Villas, 1959.

cation became free. Educational opportunities were made
available to all Cuban citizens who were able and willing to
study, regardless of sex, race, or socioeconomic background.
But availability and opportunity, the Cuban regime realized,
were not entirely similar. A massive drive had to be launched
to teach many thousands to read and write.

The Literacy Campaign

"A person cannot feel like a human being or call himself
such until he knows how to read and write," wrote José Martí
in the late nineteenth century.[5] The view was shared by most
people in the island when the campaign to eradicate illiteracy
started.

Since April 1959, 817 literacy centers had been in operation, and by the end of 1959 they had a total of 2,751 teachers and more than 16,000 students.[6] Nineteen sixty-one was
entitled the "Education Year," and it was the year in which
an all-out effort was made virtually to eliminate illiteracy in
Cuba. Perhaps it was this program which was one of the most
spectacular of all of the educational reforms carried out by
the Castro government.

The dependence of Cuban development plans on skilled,
informed labor had become increasingly clear, and with it
the need for adult education. The desire to bring the whole
population, peasant and worker, of low education as of
high, within the full strategy of political-social economic
development added a further urgency for stressing the program of adult literacy. Both produced the Campaign of
1961.[7]

The main aim of the Year of Education was to make all

[5] José Martí, *Obras completas,* Havana, 1964, Vol. 19, p. 136.
[6] Ministry of National Education of Cuba, "Cuba: Educational Developments in 1959–1960," *International Yearbook of Education,* XXII
(1960), p. 131.
[7] Dudley Seers, ed., *Cuba: The Economic and Social Revolution,*
Chapel Hill, University of North Carolina Press, 1964, p. 191.

persons over fourteen literate and to do the same for those under that age who had had no chance for schooling. This was to be done with individual instruction provided by the *alfabetizadores* (adult volunteers) and *brigadistas* (mobile student volunteer brigades). To take care of finance, technique, publicity, and publications, a National Literacy Commission was created.

The first step of the Literacy Campaign was to locate and register all illiterates. At the end of the census, on August 30, 1961, 929,207 illiterates had been located. Already in April 1961 the first group of *brigadistas*, which would ultimately number 105,664, had been sent into the field. Many of these student volunteers had only a primary education themselves. Rural areas were the primary area of operation for the *brigadistas*.

Characteristics of the "Brigadista" Teaching Force, 1961
(In Thousands)

School Background	Female	Male	Total
Primary School	28.1	27.1	55.2
Secondary Basic	17.4	16.0	33.4
Pre-University	2.1	2.4	4.5
Teacher Training	1.7	0.3	2.0
Commercial College	1.8	1.0	2.8
University and School Teachers	2.1	0.6	2.7
Other	1.8	3.3	5.1
	55.0	50.7	105.7

The *alfabetizadores,* consisting of 126,069 "people's teachers" and 33,960 professional teachers, were meanwhile teaching those illiterates in the towns that were close to them. They taught reading and writing in convenient hours which did not interfere with their regular work commitments.

The Second National Congress of Education was convened on August 30, 1961, and it was decided that the *brigadistas* needed assistance. Thus the *Patria o Muerte* Brigade was dispatched to give them help. This group was composed of 13,-

882 workers who were given paid leaves of absence from their jobs so that they could help in the campaign.[8]

Official results were announced on December 21, 1961, and of the 929,207 illiterates located, 707,212 were made literate, leaving only 221,995 unsuccessfully taught.[9] This brought the illiteracy rate down to 3.9% in a single year.[10]

Literacy and Illiteracy Levels

Year	Literacy		Illiteracy	
	Total	Percent	Total	Percent
1899	882,232	56.20	690,565	43.80
1953	3,343,680	76.40	1,032,849	23.60
1961	5,964,000	84.45	929,207	15.55*
1962	6,777,000	96.10	221,995	3.90

* Estimated. *Source:* U. S. Department of War. *Census of Cuba,* Washington, 1900; Armando Hart, *Informe,* Havana, 1961; UNESCO, *Report on the Methods and Means Utilized in Cuba to Eliminate Illiteracy,* 1965.

The percentages of illiteracy by provinces were notably reduced, although Camagüey, Oriente, and Pinar del Río continued to have a rate above the national average. And while in 1953 Oriente had the highest illiteracy rate, it was surpassed by late 1961 by Camagüey province (which in 1953 was the third largest in illiteracy). In 1953 four provinces had rates of illiteracy above the national figure; by 1962 only three provinces were found in that category. In order of accomplishments, Oriente province was at the forefront in eradicating the largest percentage of illiteracy, followed by Pinar del Río, Camagüey, Las Villas, Matanzas, and lastly Havana.

Although the fundamental purpose of the Literacy Cam-

[8] *Ibid.,* p. 194. Total number of teachers was 279,575.

[9] Included would be 25,000 Haitian immigrants in Camagüey and Oriente provinces who did not know Spanish; senile individuals; those mentally incapacitated, and some people who simply refused to cooperate. *Verde Olivo* (Havana), August 16, 1968, pp. 40–43.

[10] Proceedings of UNESCO General Conference, 14th Session, 1966, p. 498.

Literacy and Illiteracy Percentages by Provinces
(over 10 years of age)

Province	Literacy		Illiteracy	
	1953	1962	1953	1962
Pinar del Río	69.2	94.9	30.8	5.1
Havana	90.8	97.6	9.2	1.4
Matanzas	80.8	96.8	19.2	3.2
Las Villas	75.2	96.1	24.8	3.9
Camagüey	72.7	94.5	27.3	5.5
Oriente	64.7	94.8	35.3	5.2
Average	76.4	96.1	23.6	3.9

paign was to teach as many people as possible to read and write, there was another factor to keep in mind, that is, the revolutionary government's desire to enable teachers, students, and workers who participated in the campaign to obtain a better understanding of the Revolution, its causes, goals, and ideals. Most certainly, many of the *brigadistas* reported that they thought that they had learned more than their students.[11]

Popularization of Adult Elementary Education

When the Literacy Campaign ended, a program to elevate the educational level of workers and farmers began, and primary and secondary schooling was offered in farms, factories, offices, and night schools. First, courses in self-improvement, by which a third-grade education could be obtained, were made available to more than 500,000 adults. Then, follow-up courses enabling students to get through the sixth grade were opened. Those graduating could later enroll in the Worker-Farmer Education programs to complete secondary education.[12] With that preparation they could continue their education by going into vocational school or the university.

[11] *Granma* (Havana), January 12, 1969, p. 6.
[12] Armando Hart, "Educational Progress in New Cuba," *Political Affairs,* May 1963, p. 39.

Total Adult Enrollment

Year	Students (in thousands)
1958–59	27
1961–62	70
1962–63	492
1963–64	479
1964–65	839
1965–66	434
1966–67	413
1967–68	425

Source: UNESCO, *International Yearbook of Education*, Geneva, 1959–1969.

In the Worker-Farmer Education program the rates of enrollment were also high, showing a definite desire on the part of the Cuban labor force to improve themselves. In 1962–1963 the number of students was 468,000 with 44.5% in attendance. In 1964 attendance climbed to 66% while enrollment went up to 818,000.

Educating the workers and farmers is not easy since teaching hours must be adjusted to fit the work schedule of the students. Hence, since 1965 three different calendars have been created for the rural, mountain, and urban areas. The rural school year begins in June and ends in December; in other words, classes begin with the end of the sugar harvest and terminate when the harvest starts. In the mountains classes have been adapted to the coffee harvest. Thus, classes begin in January and the sessions conclude in October. In the urban areas classes are held from September to July.

Enrollment in Rural and Mountain Areas of Farmers

	1965	1966	1967
Rural Zones	160,666	173,898	200,708
Mountain Zones	46,450	36,680	35,755
Total	207,116	210,578	236,463

Most of the teachers in Worker-Farmer Education are not professionals. The majority, due to the shortage of teaching staff, are young men and women who have little education themselves but much interest, enthusiasm, and revolutionary spirit. In 1966, for instance, instruction was done by 21,696 amateur teachers and 8,899 professionals.[13] Close to 1.7 million adults reached the fifth-grade level from 1962 to 1967,[14] while 365,720 completed the sixth grade by 1968.[15]

If basic secondary courses were passed (as they were by 578,444 adults in 1968)[16] the workers and peasants could register in the Worker-Farmer Preparatory Faculties of the universities, or go into technical and vocational education. The Worker-Farmer Faculties were created in 1964 with branches in cities and towns where adults receive crash courses that prepare them for entrance to the universities. To register in these classes one must be a member of a trade union, the Ministry of Education, mass organizations, or the military. Classes are adjusted to work shifts. So far, by 1968, approximately 1,400 graduates from this program went into higher education.[17]

Surplus personnel in enterprises, labor centers, and state farms also are sent to school by the revolutionary government to receive training in order to keep up "with the demands of the country's economic development and with the better distribution of the labor force."[18] The students do not relinquish their salaries but study full time.

Schools for the advancement of women, it should be added, are an important aspect of adult education. These schools provide a one-year course, as well as accommodations for thousands of farm girls and women from isolated

[13] Leo Huberman and Paul M. Sweezy, *Socialism in Cuba,* New York, Monthly Review Press, 1969, p. 29.

[14] Oscar F. Rego, "Mas de 100 años de lucha en la educación," *Bohemia* (Havana), January 2, 1969, p. 110.

[15] *Granma* (Havana), January 20, 1969, p. 2.

[16] Gerald H. Read, "The Cuban Revolutionary Offensive in Education," *Comparative Education Review,* June 1970, p. 142.

[17] *Granma* (Havana), November 20, 1968, p. 1.

[18] *Bulletin of the International Bureau of Education* (Geneva), No. 156, 1965, p. 147.

regions of the country.[19] They are taught dressmaking and hygiene, as well as how to run centers for child care, and other activities.[20]

Regular Elementary and Intermediate Education

The Cuban system of education is divided into four stages: six years of primary schooling, three of secondary, three of pre-university or vocational, and varying time periods of university training. At present, only the elementary stage is compulsory; however, it is planned that sometime in the near future compulsory education will cover secondary schools.

When the revolutionaries started to rule they discovered

Primary Education Enrollment

Year	Total
1955–56	728,087
1956–57	746,880
1958–59*	717,417
1959–60*	1,092,264
1960–61	1,231,700
1961–62	1,590,000
1962–63	1,205,702
1963–64	1,280,664
1964–65	1,323,925
1965–66	1,321,768
1966–67	1,353,899
1967–68	1,391,147
1968–69	1,460,000
1969–70	1,560,193

* Private sector excluded.

Source: UNESCO, *International Yearbook of Education,* Geneva, 1959–1969. Slightly different figures appear in another UNESCO publication. See: UNESCO, *Statistical Yearbook,* 1968.

[19] *Bulletin of the International Bureau of Education* (Geneva), No. 163, 1967, p. 90. The schools run by the Federation of Cuban Women house the students in more than three hundred mansions where the wealthy once lived.

[20] Hilda Perera, "Women in a New Social Context in Cuba," *International Journal of Adult and Youth Education,* Vol. XIV, 1962, p. 144.

that 49% of the children between the ages of five and twelve were not going to school. But it was vital that as many children as possible receive an education. Thereafter, special attention was paid to this phenomenon in order to bolster enrollment. From 1959 to 1970 enrollment rapidly climbed, doubling the number of children attending classes. Students in primary schools in 1969 represented some 80% of the total number of young people receiving regular (full-time) education.

The majority of children in elementary schools receive a general type of instruction. The curriculum comprises five main learning areas: 1) language arts and expression (language, spelling, drawing, music, manual arts), 2) mathematics (arithmetic, elementary geometry), 3) social studies (geography, history, civics), 4) natural science (elementary zoology, botany, physics, chemistry, astronomy, physical geography), and 5) health and safety (elementary anatomy, physiology, hygiene, first aid, camping, physical education).

School children are not allowed much leisure. The primary school year, which in 1957–1958 consisted of 36 weeks of 5 days each and represented 810 hours of school attendance, was increased in 1964 to 40 weeks of 6 days each, or 1,080 hours in the urban areas and 900 hours in the countryside.[21] Homework assignments vary from one to three hours daily.

Polytechnical education was introduced in 1965. In a report to the United Nations this education was described as the method by which children "from the outset in the primary schools" learn the scientific principles underlying all subjects and "acquaint themselves with the handling of tools and machines so as to acquire the abilities, habits, and dexterity, and communist attitude toward work which are important to society today."[22]

Students are required to devote school time to three types of work: educational, productive, and socially useful. The pupils take care of the school, its surroundings, the local com-

[21] UNESCO, *International Yearbook of Education*, Geneva, 1963, p. 109.
[22] UNESCO, *International Yearbook of Education*, Geneva, 1966, p. 104.

munity; they plant trees, work in garden plots, raise animals, study wood- and metal-working, sewing, handicrafts, and much else. Visits are made to factories and farms, political discussions of speeches by revolutionary leaders are held, and "works of revolutionary content" by theater groups portrayed.[23]

Upon completion of the general studies in elementary school, students are urged to continue their education. This systematic call on the part of the revolutionary government is aimed at finding the manpower that is to be trained en masse, as technical cadres, in order to overcome underdevelopment. The problem, however, is far from solved, although steps have been taken in the right direction.

Student enrollment in secondary education, which in 1958 showed a total enrollment in public schools of 63,526, had tripled by 1968.

Public Secondary Enrollment

Year	Total
1956–57	57,401
1958–59	63,526
1959–60	59,582
1960–61	89,754
1961–62	109,324
1962–63	123,118
1963–64	137,930
1964–65	135,745
1965–66	148,991
1966–67	170,285
1967–68	177,087

Source: UNESCO, *International Yearbook of Education*, Geneva, 1959–1968.

Yet, on the average, only one out of every seven students in elementary school in the last ten years has managed to enter high school.[24] This reduction of students as the level of edu-

[23] *Granma* (Havana), November 18, 1968, p. 6.
[24] Percentage distribution of enrollment in the mid-1960's was as follows: 90.6% in primary, 8.1% secondary, 1.3% higher education. See

cation increases is well illustrated by the year 1967. In that year, regular enrollment by grades in primary and secondary schools was as follows:

Student Enrollment by Levels

Level	Students (in thousands)
PRIMARY	
1st grade	341
2nd grade	254
3rd grade	217
4th grade	205
5th grade	155
6th grade	99
graduates	66
BASIC SECONDARY	
1st year	60
2nd year	50
3rd year	36
graduates	15
PRE-UNIVERSITY	
1st year	16
2nd year	9
3rd year	8
graduates	4

Source: Verde Olivo (Havana), December 17, 1967, pp. 6–9.

The secondary student, as a rule, takes courses in history, Spanish, geography, biology, chemistry, mathematics, physics, polytechnical instruction, and agricultural-livestock production. The humanities play a very minor role.

Since 1965 agricultural plots and workshops have been worked by these students. Two years later a policy of appreciably shortening the secondary-education cycle was announced. The tenth grade has been incorporated into the seventh, eighth, and ninth grades.[25] The obvious intention is

Betty Cabezas, *América Latina, una y múltiple*, Barcelona, 1968, Table 67.
[25] UNESCO, *International Yearbook of Education*, Geneva, 1968, p. 124.

to reduce the number of years of full-time intermediate schooling while compressing the curriculum into a more unified cycle. This compression and acceleration of secondary training has gone hand-in-hand with the reduction of time spent in examinations and the tightening of control over class hours, permitting students to spend more time in self-study and productive labor.[26]

With respect to exams the Revolution has followed the traditional approach, placing extreme emphasis on grades.[27] Examinations of full-time students at elementary and intermediate schools are national. The tests are prepared by the Ministry of Education and given on specific dates. Qualifications to take a test are 100% attendance, completed classwork, and a mark of B in no less than 50% of the work done in class. Passing grade is above 70 points. Those failing more than two subjects in a year are not promoted and most take those classes again. In the courses already passed, students are required to work as teaching assistants in their own grade or in lower ones.[28]

Students finishing basic secondary schooling can also enter technical schools where skills ranging from fishing to agriculture are taught. This vocational training, begun in 1962, at first required the direct participation of other governmental agencies, due to its widespread differentiation. But in time more specialized vocational schools, under the supervision of the Ministry of Education, have been opened.

Throughout the years the number of pupils at these vocational schools has increased, although the rate has not been as rapid as in other sectors of education. And it should be noted that the rate of graduates is not very high either. From 1964 to 1969 a total of 6,140 persons successfully concluded their studies.[29] In other words, only one out of every nine persons who enrolled in 1964 graduated five years later.

---

[26] *Granma* (Havana), September 8, 1969, p. 5.
[27] There are some exceptional cases. In 1968 the Vento School of Monitors in Havana, because of its excellent record, eliminated examinations. *Juventud Rebelde* (Havana), January 20, 1969, p. 2.
[28] *Granma* (Havana), June 20, 1969, pp. 4–5; September 8, 1969, p. 5.
[29] *Granma* (Havana), October 26, 1969, p. 4.

Nonetheless, almost six thousand new agricultural technicians have been added to the economy.[30]

Technical Education Enrollment

Year	Students
1959–60	21,254
1960–61	26,023
1962–63	63,011
1964–65	52,667
1965–66	40,541
1966–67	46,376
1967–68	46,732

Source: UNESCO, *International Yearbook of Education*, Geneva, 1959–1968.

Higher Education

University education has undergone reorganization. The traditional autonomy has terminated, and the institutions have been under the direct control of the government since the early years of the regime.[31]

New departments and majors have been created. Greater emphasis is now placed on technology and exact sciences instead of the traditional studies in humanities and law.

Percentage of Students by Departments

	1956–57	1968–69
Sciences	7.9	11.3
Technology	10.3	28.4
Medicine	22.0	24.8
Agriculture	4.3	11.9
Humanities	32.0	5.8

Source: *Granma* (Havana), January 20, 1969, p. 2.

[30] *Ediciones COR* (Havana), No. 14, 1969, p. 25.
[31] For a discussion of this process, see Jaime Sucklicki, *University Students and Revolution in Cuba, 1920–1968*, Coral Gables: University of Miami Press, 1969, pp. 105–135.

Higher Education Enrollment

Year	Students
1955–56	24,273
1958–59	25,514
1959–60	19,450
1960–61	17,726
1961–62	19,152
1962–63	17,522
1963–64	22,128
1964–65	26,934
1965–66	30,536
1966–67	33,704
1967–68	35,046
1968–69	35,490

Source: UNESCO, *International Yearbook of Education,* Geneva, 1959–1968.

The reason for the slow rate of increase in university enrollment is twofold. First, the number of persons graduating from high school is still quite small, and significant changes may only take place sometime in the future. Secondly, the Castro government has not followed an open-door admission policy. The requirements for enrollment include the completion of high school, passing of an entrance examination, a personal interview, concrete proof of revolutionary attitude, and in some cases, a letter of recommendation from a mass organization.[32]

Financing the Educational Revolution

Educational expansion, regarded as essential to the achievement of the economic, social, and political objectives of the new society, has been costly.

Since 1961, when private schools were nationalized, all the funds for the educational system have originated with the state. Appropriations for education during 1958 amounted to

[32] Jaime Sucklicki, *University Students and Revolution in Cuba, 1920–1968,* Coral Gables: University of Miami Press, 1969, p. 124.

77 million pesos. A year later the revolutionary government raised the education budget to 90 million pesos. Thereafter, appropriations for education progressively climbed. From 1961 to 1969 the Cubans spent, on the average, about 275 million pesos yearly in education, or four times as much as ten years before.[33]

By 1967 educational costs accounted for 18.8% of the national budget. The main items given priority were the quantitative development of primary and secondary classrooms. Thereafter many classrooms were built, particularly in the rural areas. Thus, from 7,567 primary public schools in 1958, Cuba went to 14,726 by 1969,[34] and from 171 secondary public schools to 416 in the same period. Vocational schools increased from 73 to 127.[35]

State Education Budget

Year	Total (millions of pesos)
1958	77
1959	90
1961	128
1962	270
1963	283
1964	285
1965	294
1966	303
1967	332
1968	283
1969	290

Source: UNESCO, *International Yearbook of Education*, Geneva, 1959–1968; and Fidel Castro, July 26, 1970, speech.

[33] This of course does not take into consideration what was spent on private education in the 1950's, nor the change in the value of money.
[34] *Bohemia* (Havana), July 24, 1970, p. 27.
[35] Carmelo Mesa-Lago, "Availability and Reliability of Statistics in Socialist Cuba," *Latin American Research Review*, Vol. IV, No. 1, p. 74. It should be noted that to some extent the *real* increment in public schools was not solely the consequence of the building of more classrooms and the transformation of some military barracks into schools, but also the result of the takeover by the state of private schools.

Allocations have been made over the years for the construction of libraries, laboratories, shops, and the publication of new teaching materials.

Finally, it should be noted that since 1961 education has been free and students have been given all the books and school material they need. This is one of the most notable and positive accomplishments of the Revolution: no person is prevented from studying due to the lack of economic resources.[36]

The broad scholarship program maintained by the state is also noteworthy. Since 1962 room, board, clothes, shoes, medical care, recreation, and a monthly allowance have been provided for a larger number of students. In twelve years, the number of scholarships has multiplied eighteen times.

State Scholarships

Year	Total
1958	15,698
1962	71,258
1965	127,490
1966	164,131
1967	240,000
1970	277,505

All scholarship recipients must live in boarding houses,[37] attend class daily, follow teaching discipline, and maintain a high academic average. Further, the *becados* can leave the boarding homes only on Sundays, they must be loyal to the Revolution, and study at least twenty hours every week.[38]

The philosophy of financial assistance to loyal revolutionaries has been outlined by Fidel Castro. On September 28, 1967, he said:

Let no one ask me for an office job, because I will never in all my life give office jobs to anyone. Ask us to help

[36] One should add, at the same time, that some people are sometimes prevented from education due to their *political* viewpoints.

[37] The homes of some of the (formerly) rich families who left Cuba have been converted into boarding homes.

[38] *Juventud Rebelde* (Havana), February 9, 1966, p. 1.

you become a technician, and we will make you a technician, as we have done with tens of thousands of young workers. We will care for your wife and your children five years, seven years, ten years if necessary, and without charging a cent, without asking interest for it.[39]

Two months later a decree[40] was issued granting a non-repayable subsidy to the "workers who meet the requirements for their enrollment in any university course." Such a measure allowed many workers who had graduated from their secondary classes in 1966 the possibility of continuing education if they met the necessary requirements. Those requirements were: 1) to be excused from work obligations by the administration of the work center, 2) to elect a career considered urgent for the development of the country, and 3) to have the correct educational and moral (i.e., political) background. Once accepted by the university the worker receives a subsidy according to his salary and he must live in a boarding house, close to the university, until he concludes his studies. By March 1970 there were 2,816 workers benefiting from the program.[41]

Despite these positive measures the educational system in Cuba is still plagued with difficulties.

Teacher Shortage

One of the problems faced by the Revolution has been the acute shortage of teachers. This has been the consequence of two different factors. On the one hand, the unprecedented growth of the student population absorbed the available supply of primary and secondary teachers. On the other, the flight of the professional class, particularly after 1960, drained the educational resources of the country. Although professionals, semiprofessionals, and the managerial sector constituted 9.2% of the total Cuban population in 1953, they represented

[39] Fidel Castro, September 28, 1967, speech.
[40] *Granma* (Havana), November 30, 1967, p. 6.
[41] *Granma* (Havana), March 15, 1970, p. 9.

32.8% of the Cuban émigré community from 1959 to 1966.[42] Moreover, a recent study of the exiles has shown that while in 1953 only 1% of the people in the island had four years of college or more, the percentage among the exiles was 12.5%. And while only 4% of the Cubans had more than a high school education in 1953, among the exiles the percentage was 36.[43]

Faced with such a problem, the revolutionary authorities were forced to put into practice emergency measures. Students with upper secondary background were trained rapidly (in a few weeks) to teach elementary courses in the rural areas. Many women with an elementary education were given the job of teaching at nursery schools. At the same time, non-certified instructors, called popular teachers, coming primarily from the ranks of those who participated in the 1961 literacy drive and not having over a sixth-grade schooling, went through crash courses to teach at the first levels of elementary school. The popular teachers received in-service training every Saturday and a forty-five-day course during vacation for a period of four years, after which they were considered fully qualified teachers.[44] By 1969 close to 60% of all grammar school instructors originated from this group.

At the secondary level the teaching personnel has been comprised of student monitors, university students, and qualified teachers. In 1967 there were 36,000 student monitors employed at this level. Needless to say, while a quantitative increase in the number of teachers has been produced, the quality of the teaching personnel quite often leaves much to be desired. An American educator who studied the problem states:

These stopgaps, while filling the critical demand, have not

[42] José Ignacio Rasco, "Sociología del Exilio," paper presented at the "Primera Reunión de Estudios Cubanos" (Washington, April 2–6, 1969).
[43] The figures for the exiles cover the years 1959 to 1962. The percentages, moreover, were arrived at from random samples (1,085 persons constituted the roster sample). See Richard R. Fagen, Richard A. Brody, and Thomas J. O'Leary, *Cubans in Exile,* Stanford: Stanford University Press, 1968, p. 19.
[44] UNESCO, *International Yearbook of Education,* Geneva, 1964.

been and will not be without serious failings. Under such conditions, it is difficult, if not next to impossible, to expect minimally trained personnel to perform with the same sensitivity and intelligence as experienced teachers.[45]

From 1958 to 1970 the number of primary school teachers grew by 30,541, but many of the instructors lacked the necessary qualifications. Nonetheless, although the shortage of trained teachers is still serious, advances have been made.[46] Presently, 45% of elementary teachers are in the rural areas.

Qualified primary instructors, who reside in boarding schools throughout the island, now study for five years in order to obtain the equivalent of a normal school education. They, like all other students, are nationally supervised and follow similar programs of studies. Each province presently has its education plan, and those who desire to go into teaching are trained in their own province where they will ultimately teach. In this manner, the government believes, students will become well acquainted with the social, cultural, and economic characteristics of the region. Student teachers

Teaching Personnel

Year	Primary	Secondary	Higher
1958–59	17,355*	2,580*	1,046
1959–60	24,443*	3,612*	992
1960–61	30,824	4,200	1,482
1961–62	33,916	6,500	1,987
1962–63	36,822	7,380	2,620
1963–64	37,843	8,064	2,835
1964–65	38,473	8,467	3,032
1965–66	41,922	9,552	4,151
1966–67	43,256	10,196	4,499
1967–68	46,910	11,276	——

* Private sector excluded.
Source: UNESCO, International Yearbook of Education, Geneva, 1959–1968; Bohemia (Havana), May 22, 1970, pp. 24–26.

[45] Marvin Leiner, "Cuba's Schools, Ten Years Later," Saturday Review, October 17, 1970, p. 60.
[46] The Makarenko Institute for primary teachers, from 1962 to 1969, graduated 6,205. Granma (Havana), August 10, 1969, p. 7.

in this education plan in 1969 serviced 8% of the entire primary school enrollment (118,000 students).

The number of secondary school teachers has nearly quadrupled in ten years, while university faculties have tripled. Both are trained at the pedagogical departments of the three Cuban universities.

All teachers, at all levels, are encouraged to go through a continual process of self-improvement. This includes studies in pedagogy, specialization on a given field, and the use of the most modern methods in the classroom. Promotions and the renewal of contracts depend, to some extent, on fulfilling such requirements, although security of employment for all teachers is guaranteed by law. The main causes for dismissal are non-fulfillment of duties, professional incompetence, and acting against the "stability of the nation."

In 1958 there were 23,648 persons working in public schools. By 1969 the figure had risen to 127,526. Nonetheless a shortage persists. On July 26, 1970, Fidel Castro stated that the quantity and quality of teachers remained low, adding:

There are still many cases of pupils who attend school only half a day, as a result of shortages of teachers and classrooms. We will need 7,000 primary school teachers a year from 1970 to 1975. Seven thousand new teachers must be graduated every year! Some of them will go to meet the outstanding needs, another part will replace those who must retire because of old age, and the rest will constitute increases in both quantity and quality. Consequently, we need 35,000 new teachers in the next five years. For the same reasons, we will need 4,000 new junior high school teachers every year through 1975. One thousand eight hundred new senior high school teachers will be needed every year. This means that we need to graduate—but this does not mean that we are going to graduate them, because, unfortunately, we cannot do this yet—12,800 new primary and junior and senior high school teachers every year—an aggregate of 64,000 in five years.[47]

[47] Fidel Castro, July 26, 1970, speech. *Granma* (Havana), August 2, 1970, p. 2.

It has been admitted that the shortage of classrooms, schools, teachers, and books will not be remedied "until 1980."[48]

Quality of Education and Other Shortcomings

Much remains to be done about the quality of education. Teachers are very often poorly trained and lacking the time to improve.[49] A former Minister of Education has said that teachers are generally employed as active participants in a multitude of social tasks which prevent them from "studying, improving themselves, preparing their classes, and getting a minimum amount of rest." The teaching personnel are so overworked that many lack the "proper degree of emotional balance, sufficient mental clarity and strength" required for pedagogical work.[50] The government, aware of this issue, only hopes that one day things will change for the better.[51]

More schools are needed, many could be improved, and more material made available. Teaching methods, on the other hand, could be modernized, allowing greater possibilities of creative self-expression, independence, and freedom, instead of encouraging uniformity in students and manipulation on the part of teachers.

Discipline is a major problem. In the elementary and secondary schools teachers are very young and inexperienced, and quite often they do not receive any cooperation from the students.[52] Instead of teaching they have a terrible time

[48] José Llanusa, speech at the First National Plenum of Student Brigades, September 1968.

[49] The massive use of television and radio, to some extent, has ameliorated this by making available to a large audience highly skilled professional teachers who use the latest educational methods. This procedure began in 1968 with seventy-two hours of formal classes every week on television.

[50] José Llanusa, "Our Teachers," *Granma* (Havana), July 6, 1969, p. 6.

[51] *Granma* (Havana), July 26, 1970, p. 10.

[52] *Granma* (Havana), August 23, 1970, p. 5.

trying to discipline their young charges. They must also contend with cheating, laziness, and lack of attendance.[53]

It is estimated that there are 400,000 individuals between the ages of six and sixteen not attending school, including 200,000 between the ages of twelve and fifteen.[54] In Camagüey province they number over 15,000.[55] In Oriente province, the region with the lowest scholastic level on the island, it was reported in late 1970 that 80,000 youths (thirteen to sixteen in age) did not work or study.[56] To this must be added the large number of students repeating their grades. In 1968–1969 more than 700,000 students at the elementary and secondary levels had to repeat the equivalent of more than two years of studies.[57] Almost one out of every three children between the first and sixth grade fails to be promoted at the end of the school year, and approximately 12% of those in secondary education go through the same process.[58] In Las Villas 31% of all students in primary schools in 1969–1970 failed the entire year,[59] while in Matanzas the percentage was 29 (in 1963–1964 it reached 44%).[60] And to complicate matters even more, there frequently remains a lack of clear understanding as to the importance of technological and other educational training. Thus, in Oriente province only 24,000 workers and farmers are enrolled in schools operating at their work centers, although capacity exceeds the 44,000 mark.[61]

[53] In 1967 school officials reported that in 1958 elementary and secondary school attendance was 60.8% of the enrolled, and that about 85% attended classes in 1966. Months later, however, lack of attendance was still considered a problem by the official organ of the Communist Party. See *Bohemia* (Havana), December 29, 1967, pp. 24–27, 29; and *Granma* (Havana), April 14, 1968, p. 8.

[54] *Granma* (Havana), January 20, 1969, p. 2.

[55] *Bohemia* (Havana), July 31, 1970, pp. 22, 23.

[56] *Granma* (Havana), October 25, 1970, p. 4. Some workshop schools have been opened for these people.

[57] *Granma* (Havana), January 20, 1969, p. 2.

[58] *El Mundo* (Havana), January 7, 1969, pp. 2–3.

[59] *Granma* (Havana), September 16, 1970, p. 3.

[60] *Granma* (Havana), March 2, 1970, p. 3.

[61] *Granma* (Havana), October 25, 1970, p. 4.

Education and the New Man

Education in Cuba serves the needs and goals of the society. Those ends, defined by the revolutionary government in a coherent fashion since 1965, are closely connected with the building of a Communist society. Hence, schools throughout the country have the fundamental function of implanting in students the knowledge, skills, allegiances, and value orientations required to attain that end.

The formation of the New Man—a person with scientific and technical knowledge—a humanist culture, and a mentality that identifies personal and community interests as one and the same are the avowed aims of the Cuban educational system.[62] Education is entrusted "with the delicate function of forming new generations, of forming the new man for the new society we are building."[63] The schools are also expected to raise upright and law-abiding citizens who are absolutely devoted to revolutionary leaders, the security of the state, and the goals of the Revolution. The present generation of students is conceived as bringing forth a new type of individual, a person fully committed to equality, brotherhood, and solidarity, devoid of selfishness and with no need for material incentives, a human being ready to sacrifice and constantly filled with heroism, abnegation, and enthusiasm.[64]

In Cuban revolutionary pedagogy, theory and practice are closely combined. Education and economic development are considered parts of a similar process. To overcome underdevelopment it is imperative to produce skilled workers, technicians, scientists, and researchers, but this large contingent of manpower cannot be divorced from production;

[62] José A. Aguilera, "Una revolución educacional en la Cuba revolucionaria," in *Cuba: una revolución en marcha,* Paris: Ediciones Ruedo Ibérico, 1967, pp. 266–278.

[63] *Juventud Rebelde* (Havana), April 29, 1968, p. 1.

[64] These ideas can be found in most of Castro's speeches since 1965–1966. A summary of what the New Man should be like can be found in "The Aim of Ideological Work," *Granma* (Havana), March 2, 1969, p. 2.

rather students must engage directly in the efforts of economic development. Thus, knowledge starts with practice.[65]

Since the early 1960's the principle of combining education and productive labor has been followed. This idea is not uniquely Marxist.[66] In the nineteenth century José Martí, a liberal humanist, wrote of a future system of schools in the island in which "behind every school there will be an agricultural field."[67]

Education and work have been coordinated in two different ways. On the one hand, the workers and peasants have elevated their intellectual standard, and have gone through a process of intellectualization. On the other, the educated have been proletarianized by participating in production. These two processes have the aim of eventually doing away with the distinction between intellectual and physical work, and forming men and women who are manual and intellectual workers at the same time.

The process of intellectualization of workers by the campaigns to end illiteracy and universalize an elementary education among the masses has been analyzed already, but the process of proletarianization of the educated remains to be considered. The thinking behind this procedure has been well outlined by a Cuban education official:

Work is a powerful instrument to provide our youth with a rigorous moral and ideological foundation. Through work character is educated, will power is strengthened, creative ability is channeled, and the basis for conscious discipline is created. . . . Through productive labor, students and teachers learn that in the society we are constructing, a society of workers, work constitutes the most precious value of man. Also, students and teachers realize the worth of production. Work in agriculture modifies the

[65] The phrase originates with Mao Tse-tung. See his *Selected Works*, London, 1954, Vol. 2, p. 292.

[66] Fidel Castro, "El trabajo ha de ser el gran pedagogo de la juventud," *Obra Revolucionaria* (Havana), No. 31, 1964. A similar position to that of the Cubans has been developed by the Chinese. See Chang-tu Hu, "Recent Trends in Chinese Education," *International Review of Education*, Vol. 10, No. 1, 1964, pp. 12–21.

[67] Carlos A. Martínez, *Código martiano*, Havana, 1943, pp. 282–285.

consumer mentality which characterizes capitalist society, because in a socialist society the men that are formed have a mentality geared to the production of wealth. Moreover, students and teachers acquire a strong agricultural orientation with scientific and technical foundations, which is very important for the economic development of our country. . . . Although this plan was not conceived for economic reasons, but as a pedagogical tool, it has also helped to solve our production problems.[68]

It was not until 1964 that productive labor became a central task of the educational revolution. That year was the first implementation of the experiment of taking students and teachers for an extended period of time to work in agriculture (the School to the Country Plan).[69] Twenty thousand secondary pupils of both sexes participated. The following year the plan became national in scope and 160,000 students and their instructors spent forty-five days of the school year on state farms. By October 1968 participation at the secondary, vocational, and university levels was massive, and the time was lengthened to sixty days. Work was done in the morning and classes held in the afternoon, followed by political discussions, recreation, sports, and cultural activities.[70]

Agricultural and factory work is performed also by students with a low scholastic background (ages thirteen to sixteen) who already have been sent to special workshop schools. There they receive a junior high training and learn special skills. The students go to class four hours a day and work four hours more, six days a week.[71] Day nurseries labor in "symbolic agricultural workdays" too,[72] while elementary pupils work two hours daily at some productive task.

The university has also been incorporated into the country's development. Biology, chemistry, economics, hydraulics,

[68] Oscar F. Rego, "La Escuela al Campo," *Bohemia* (Havana), January 31, 1969, pp. 24–26.
[69] *Bulletin of the International Bureau of Education* (Geneva), No. 160, 1966, p. 145; *Bohemia* (Havana), January 2, 1969, p. 111.
[70] *Granma* (Havana), December 16, 1969, p. 4.
[71] *Granma* (Havana), January 4, 1970, p. 11.
[72] *Granma* (Havana), July 6, 1969, p. 1.

and engineering students since the mid-1960's have aided in carrying out economic plans. For months these future technicians work in factories, on farms, and assist in the building of dams, roads, or hill terracing. They are entrusted with coffee and citrus plantations or the analysis of soils. Political science students, for instance, work in sugar mills, involving themselves with analyses of what factors contribute to greater productivity or labor absenteeism. Some faculties (like engineering) have begun to move away from the campus entirely. Fidel Castro, commenting on this phenomenon, said on March 13, 1969:

> These first experiments in moving universities from their traditional seats, which convert a mountain-work project into a university classroom and the physical planning room of an administrative office into an architecture classroom, are examples showing how it will be possible gradually to create university classrooms in all work centers as more and more instructors and more highly qualified personnel become available in these centers. These examples show the process through which the present university will gradually disappear. . . . The old idea of the classic university will wither away.[73]

In the future Castro believes that practically every factory, farm, and hospital will have the appropriate facilities to do the research and higher studies now done in institutions of higher learning.[74] Furthermore, once universities are decentralized, higher education is to be universalized, since the monopoly over science and technology by a minority in a communist society is inconceivable. The universalization of universities, hence, will be the culmination of the revolution in education which began with putting an end to illiteracy. Educational stratification will no longer exist and cultural equality will be a reality.[75]

[73] For the entire speech see *Granma* (Havana), March 16, 1969, pp. 2–5.

[74] The revolutionaries have never discussed what will occur in advanced studies in economics, law, humanities, or history in this scheme.

[75] Carlos Amat, Francisco Varona, et al., *La Universidad y el desarrollo*, paper presented at the IXth Latin American Sociology Convention

The experience of mobilizing students and teachers to the countryside to aid production and improve the cultural character of the community (mainly by eliminating residual illiteracy) has been the basis for the progressive and permanent transfer of secondary schools to the rural areas. In the near future all high schools will be found in the countryside, and none in the urban areas.[76] Students will be in boarding schools, under strict discipline, and will be able to see their relatives only on weekends.

Presently a program is under way to place all students in semiboarding or boarding schools where they will get everything free (food, clothes, shoes, room, medical and dental care, etc.). Boarding schools were created in the rural areas in 1966 for all the students entering sixth grade. The following year all those in the fifth grade were also grouped in boarding establishments in the countryside.

At the secondary level and in agricultural and industrial institutes, in the near future, the same principle will be followed. The revolutionary regime envisions this move as the educational units that will produce the first generation of real communists.[77] On June 28, 1967, a model of the forthcoming boarding units was opened at San Andrés, in Pinar del Río province. It has been described in the following manner by the regime:

This school has been organized on a new concept of the life and education of boys in a boarding school. In it, use is made of new teaching methods, and of connection between the school, the family, and the work of parents. The teacher is an educator, an instructor, and a guide who shares fully the life of the students, their daily routine, their sports and their cultural and recreational activities.[78]

(Mexico City), December 1969. See also "Universalización de la Universidad," OCLAE (Havana), July 1969, pp. 13–16.

[76] *Bohemia* (Havana), December 13, 1968, supp. p. 14.

[77] *Granma* (Havana), December 21, 1969, p. 8.

[78] Report of the Cuban Government to the XXXth Session of the International Conference on Public Education, 1968. The assistant director of the San Andrés complex in 1968 was merely twenty years old, and the mathematics teacher seventeen.

It is from this program that the New Man is to emerge. The boarding schools have a communal system of living and the students' lives are totally organized under the guidance of instructors. In this fashion a spirit of brotherhood, cooperation, egalitarianism, and solidarity is fostered and no opportunities are allowed for anyone to go astray or acquire bad habits. In these schools everyone is discouraged from egotistical views, private property is played down, and a new conception of labor is encouraged. Work becomes a pleasurable and ennobling activity, not a sacrifice or duty.[79]

The new boarding schools, with individual, collective, and guided studies for its pupils, will usually have a library, an assembly hall, dining room, kitchen, pantry, barbershop, infirmary, and dormitory.[80] These schools also will serve as the core around which factories and farms will be built and a sort of communism in microcosm will flourish. In 1969 one out of every nine regular students was already in boarding school.[81]

This model of mini-communism, however, requires well-disciplined cadres.[82] And recently, the armed forces, an authoritarian institution, have begun playing a very important function in introducing discipline into the educational system.

The Militarization of Education

At first, the Revolutionary Armed Forces (FAR) was simply concerned with operating its own academies and schools. This was a period (1959–1962) when thirty-seven military barracks were converted into public (civilian) schools and most Cubans, including the revolutionary leaders, were "allergic to military matters."[83] But with the consolidation of

[79] Fidel Castro, "A Revolutionary Believes in Man," *Granma* (Havana), February 5, 1967, pp. 1–7.

[80] *Granma* (Havana), March 2, 1969, p. 7.

[81] See the section "Financing the Educational Revolution" in this essay.

[82] This model basically resembles the theory of guerrilla war. Communism (like the acquisition of power) is to be reached once the pockets of communist strongholds (like guerrilla *focos*) expand throughout the whole nation, bringing about a radical rupture with the past.

[83] *Granma* (Havana), March 16, 1969, p. 7.

military structures and the growing sophistication of military equipment it became necessary to open new schools[84] and introduce compulsory military service (late 1963). Thereafter, the influence of the military in the educational system began to grow.

In 1964 the FAR and the Education Ministry commenced discussions as to the form in which military training was to be introduced in the nation's schools in order to inculcate the habits of courtesy, precision, and respect for and loyalty to constituted authority.[85] An article in the official organ of the armed forces considered the introduction of militarism in the school a most positive development, "the ideal of the most outstanding educators of mankind."[86]

By 1966 military instruction became part of the curriculum in some secondary schools, while "circles of military interest" began to spread throughout the country's classrooms.[87] In 1969 military training from the secondary level on became compulsory for boys and girls, on the grounds that military knowledge aided the integral development of students and was part of the obligation to bear arms for the country and to defend the Revolution.[88] Those students studying in high school are not called upon to carry out active duty. On completion of their studies the time spent on military training in school is counted as active military service (with the exception of those who drop out).[89]

Parallel with the introduction of military training into all schools (except elementary) in 1968, all twenty-three agricultural and livestock technological institutes were placed under the direct supervision and control of the military.[90] A Cuban periodical described the phenomenon as follows:

For a number of months, the technological schools have

[84] There are four types of military schools in Cuba: officers, technical, advanced, and cadet schools.

[85] *Granma* (Havana), December 24, 1968, p. 3.

[86] *Verde Olivo* (Havana), November 10, 1969, pp. 35–36.

[87] *Verde Olivo* (Havana), September 28, 1969, pp. 8, 10.

[88] *Granma* (Havana), December 16, 1969, p. 4; and *Radio Habana Cuba,* February 4, 1970.

[89] *Granma* (Havana), September 29, 1970, p. 6.

[90] Gerald H. Read, "The Cuban Revolutionary Offensive in Education," *Comparative Education Review,* June 1970, pp. 139–140.

been operating like military camps. The students behave like what they are: real soldiers. . . . Whenever a new class starts, the freshmen have to reorganize their lives, they must submit to military discipline.[91]

In January 1970 the Minister of Education informed his audience that in the very near future all agricultural, industrial, and pre-university schools were "to come under the direction of the vice-minister of technological training of the Ministry of the Armed Forces."[92] Six months later Major Belarmino Castilla (military vice-minister of technological training) became Minister of Education, instead of taking charge of those sectors of the education system.[93] In the following month Major José Fernández, who had played a key role in setting up military schools in Cuba, became the second most important official of the Education Ministry, providing another concrete proof of the definitive control of that sector by the military.[94]

The militarization of education is a most serious and disquieting development. One must wonder whether the Cubans are unable to draw the line between Spartan-like militarism and communism because of the apparent egalitarianism, discipline, and action orientation of the former.[95] The preaching of obedience and uniformity, however didactically carried out, seems an impossible means of developing truly new men and women.

Conclusion

The changes that have occurred in Cuban education since 1959 have been positive in many respects. Children no longer

[91] *Verde Olivo* (Havana), December 29, 1968, pp. 24–25.
[92] *Granma* (Havana), January 26, 1970, p. 4.
[93] *Diario de las Américas* (Miami), July 7, 1970, p. 1.
[94] *Granma* (Havana), August 23, 1970, p. 1.
[95] The Cuban Government makes a point of not differentiating the military from the people at large. In their view the armed forces "represent the best of our people . . . and offer the most outstanding example of firmness, generosity, integrity, and creativity." *Radio Habana Cuba* (Havana), September 1, 1970, 8:30 P.M.

roam the streets. In Cuba the state provides a free education —including lunch and materials—for every child of school age, while in the rest of Latin America 22 million children have no schools. Elementary education is compulsory. Workers and peasants have an educational opportunity unprecedented in Cuban history. Scholarships are widely available. The universalization of education and the mobilization of the entire population has been extremely efficient.

There are factors which, owing to the initial backwardness of the nation, could not be overcome immediately. The great leap forward in education, from a numerical standpoint, has been impressive, but has exacted a heavy toll in quality. Many of the teachers, themselves students, are young and inexperienced. The lack of personnel, materials, and schools is part of the general scarcity found in any underdeveloped country. In the long run, the drive toward mass education should prove useful in improving the economy of the country.

Certainly there is more room for experimentation in educational methods. And the combination of work and education remains an open question. It takes an enormous amount of planning and coordination to ensure that education does not suffer and that the work of students and teachers is really productive. Will there be a large rate of dropouts once students begin to see themselves as workers and realize that education might not bring personal advancement? The answer will be negative *only* if the Revolution succeeds in creating a new set of values, allegiance to work, country, revolution— a real cultural revolution in the hearts and minds of the Cuban people.

20

HEALTH AND REVOLUTION IN CUBA*

Ricardo Leyva

Introduction

The assumption of power by the Cuban revolutionary government on January 1, 1959, found dramatic economic, social, and cultural differences and inequalities between the urban and the rural regions. The towns, despite the pockets of poverty within them, monopolized national income, consumption, nutrition, education, comfort, and health. Meanwhile the rural population, under the heavy burden of misery, remained powerless, forgotten, and backward in every respect.[1] It was the classical pattern so common to the Third World: internal colonialism,[2] that is, the exploitation of the countryside by the urban areas which controlled the institutional framework of the country and prevented rural workers and peasants from benefiting from the product of their own labor. The rural people produced the wealth of the country, but only the city folk profited from the effort.

If justice and equality were to become a reality, it was absolutely necessary to put an end to the degradation and want of a large segment of the people. Thorough social and economic changes had to be instituted to assure the progress of the nation and the health of its citizens. The sanitary prob-

---

* This is an original article, written especially for this volume.

[1] Dudley Seers, ed., *Cuba: The Economic and Social Revolution,* Chapel Hill: University of North Carolina Press, 1964; and Lowry Nelson, *Rural Cuba,* Minneapolis: The University of Minnesota Press, 1950.

[2] The phenomenon has been systematically discussed by Pablo González Casanova, "Internal Colonialism and National Development," in Irving L. Horowitz et al., *Latin American Radicalism,* New York: Vintage, 1969, pp. 118–139.

lems, conditions, and changes that have occurred before and after the ouster of the Batista regime are the fundamental concerns of this paper.

The Sanitary Environment

The health of a people is not solely related to the availability of hospitals, physicians, or medicine. Any attempt to consider the frequency of sickness or death must look at the social milieu in which men, women, and children live in order to discover whether the environment is conducive to the growth and development of a healthy population. The income, diet, and housing conditions of a family determine to a large degree the preponderance of disease.

1. Earnings and Diet

In Cuba the poor, as a rule, were sicker than the rich. They had more children and a shorter life expectancy. These differences were directly connected to income differentials. The affluent could pay to be healthy; they could eat more and see medical personnel often. The poor, on the other hand, were medical indigents, people who suffered from malnutrition and could not finance their own health. Concrete evidence demonstrates these assertions.

In 1956 the Catholic University Association made a survey of the agricultural workers (40% of the country's population) in Cuba's 126 municipalities. The report states:

The inquiry had three principal aims: to make, for the first time in Cuba, a detailed, accurate, statistical study of the living conditions of agricultural workers, which may serve as a firm base for analyzing economic and social problems and finding solutions to them; to give our members in the cities an opportunity to become aware of the reality of our countryside and learn its difficulties. And, last but not least, to be able to affirm, with certain knowledge and proof ready at hand, that the Cuban peasants find themselves in the no man's land between abandonment and helplessness, thanks to national egoism, and that our nation cannot aspire to true progress as long as it does not give proper attention to our countryside.

The city of Havana is enjoying an epoch of extraordinary prosperity, while the countryside, and especially the agricultural workers, must live under almost unbelievable conditions of stagnation, misery, and hopelessness.[3]

In 1956 there were 350,000 agricultural workers with 2.1 million dependents who had a total annual income of 190 million pesos. In other words, 34% of the total population received only 10% of the national income.[4] Moreover, a family of six had an annual income of 548.75 pesos,[5] or a monthly per capita figure of 7.60 pesos. More than 50% of the families had yearly incomes below 500 pesos, and only 7.2% earned over 1,000 pesos yearly.

Sixty-nine percent of earnings were spent on food, that is, 10% more than in 1934. This was a consequence of a 194% increase in salaries from 1934 to 1956, compared to a 228% rise in the price of food. Thus, in 1956 the rural families spent more money on food while eating less than they had twenty years earlier.[6]

In 1956 a family of six could spend only seventeen cents per person to feed each member.[7] It is not surprising then that malnutrition was widespread (91% in the countryside) and the average weight of the agricultural worker was sixteen pounds below the theoretical average, and the height was much less than that of the average Cuban.[8]

[3] Melchor W. Gaston, Oscar A. Echeverría, and René de la Huerta, *Por qué Reforma Agraria,* Havana: Agrupación Católica Universitaria, 1957, p. 6.

[4] *Ibid.*

[5] In the work edited by Dudley Seers the erroneous figure of 590.75 pesos is given.

[6] Foreign Policy Association, *Problems of the New Cuba,* New York, 1935, pp. 79–86.

[7] *Por qué Reforma Agraria,* p. 60.

[8] *Ibid.,* p. 16. A survey made in 1959 of the rural population of Las Villas by the provincial university discovered that the average rural family still consisted of six members with a yearly income of 657 pesos or 30 cents per capita on a daily basis, that is, an improvement of 5 cents over the study made in 1956 by the Catholic University Association. However, 73% of the families had an average income of 715 pesos a year, while

The agricultural workers were supposed to consume at least 3,500 calories daily, but real caloric intake did not surpass 2,500. The principal source of energy was rice, constituting 24% of the total diet, followed by beans (23%) and root crops (22%).

Food Consumption of Agricultural Population[9]

Regular Diet Item	Percentage of Families Consuming Item
Meat	4.0
Fish	1.0
Eggs	2.2
Milk	11.2
Green Vegetables	0.0
Bread	3.3
Corn	7.0

The diet of most Cubans was extremely starchy, with few proteins, minerals, or vitamins and many carbohydrates. Close to 35% of the Cuban people suffered malnutrition, including six out of every ten rural residents.[10] Such a deficiency in nutrition was reflected in the general physical weakness, small bone structure, low resistance to diseases, and a high incidence of anemia.

Once, when speaking at the Ministry of Public Health, Ernesto Guevara referred to these children when he told his audience of physicians:

> You must have seen children [in the mountains] whose bodies appear to be eight or nine years old, yet most of whom are thirteen or fourteen. They are the authentic children of the Sierra Maestra, the authentic children of hunger and misery, creatures of malnutrition.[11]

27% earned less than 496 pesos annually. See Samuel Feijoó, "Abrumadoras razones del éxodo rural cubano," *Revolución* (Havana), November 2, 1959, p. 22.

[9] *Por qué Reforma Agraria, op. cit.*, pp. 20–24.

[10] Wyatt MacGaffey and Clifford R. Barnett, *Twentieth Century Cuba,* New York: Doubleday, 1965, p. 196.

[11] Rolando E. Bonachea and Nelson P. Valdés, ed., *Che: Selected Works of Ernesto Guevara,* Cambridge: MIT Press, 1969, p. 258.

A survey of the nutritional status of Cuban children was also made in 1956.[12] The sample[13] comprised children from the sixth grade ranging in age from eleven to thirteen. In terms of economic status the children represented the so-called middle class, since the survey excluded the wealthiest and the poorest sectors of the students. The data compiled disclosed the following dietary patterns:

Source of Calories	Percentage[14]
Rice	22.2
Sugar	17.5
Lards and Oils	13.7
Meat	11.5
Flour	8.8
Beans	5.6

The clinical data revealed that children in private schools were much better off than those going to public schools. This difference was reflected in the height and weight of students. Yet 10.4% of the children in private schools were underweight, although they had an adequate supply of food, which forces one to conclude that malnutrition must have been widespread among the poorer sectors.

Weight of School Children in Private and Public Schools, 1956[15]

Weight	Private Schools	Public Schools
Normal	70.6%	50.7%
Obese	19.0%	5.6%
Underweight	10.4%	43.7%

The frequency of underweight children, who also had the largest deficiencies in calcium, vitamin A, thiamine, and ri-

[12] "Nutritional Status of Cuban Children," *Nutrition Reviews,* Vol. 16, No. 9, September 1958, pp. 271–273.
[13] The sample had 2,171 subjects of a total sixth-grade population of 41,883 students from public and private schools. The urban population was represented by 1,016 students, the rural by 1,155.
[14] *Nutrition Reviews, op. cit.,* p. 272.
[15] *Ibid.,* p. 272.

boflavin, occurred in rural, rather than urban, areas, while the opposite was true with respect to the rate of obesity. Skeletal deformities were found in one out of every nine children due to the low consumption of calcium.[16]

Income distribution has been more evenly shared since 1958. However, the cities still receive a large proportion of the national wealth. On September 26, 1966, Fidel Castro acknowledged that, "There still remains a by-product of capitalist exploitation: the exploitation of the countryside by the city."[17] Is there still widespread poverty in the rural areas? Several revolutionary authorities say yes, although some outside observers disagree. In 1969 a former official of the United Nations Food and Agriculture Organization stated that 70% of the Cuban people since the Revolution "live better than they ever did before."[18] Nonetheless, the extent of betterment, due to the extreme austerity since 1962, still remains an open question.

No exact figures on food consumption have ever been given by the regime and a general idea can be gained only by considering the rationing system[19] begun in 1962. In principle, at least, rationing assures equality of consumption.[20] The system, it must be added, sets limits to the amount anyone can purchase of a given product but does not guarantee the availability of supplies. The table below presents a partial outline of the rationing system throughout the years and the situation in 1958.

[16] *Ibid.*, p. 273.

[17] *Radio Habana Cuba*, September 26, 1966.

[18] Erich H. Jacoby, "Cuba: the Real Winner is the Agricultural Worker," *CERES: FAO Review*, Vol. 2, No. 4, July–August 1969, p. 32.

[19] Rationing in the island cannot be compared to the seeming affluence of other underdeveloped countries. Other countries do not have their goods rationed because the purchasing power of a large segment of the population is extremely limited. In Cuba rationing is the consequence not only of low agricultural yields and a growing population, but also the by-product of the fact that most Cubans have money to buy what is on the market. In Cuba *goods* are rationed. In other countries *income* is rationed, hence a shortage of goods does not arise. The people simply cannot buy what is available.

[20] Preferential treatment in terms of food is accorded by the state to the military, police, scholarship students, and hospital personnel. High military officials have been reported to get more groceries than their ration cards state. See New York *Times*, December 11, 1970, p. 6.

Per Capita Food Availability, 1958–1969[21]

Item	Period	1958	1962	1963	1969
Rice	Monthly	10.2 lbs.	6 lbs.	6 lbs.	3 lbs.
Meat	Weekly	2.2 lbs.	0.75 lbs.	0.75 lbs.	0.75 lbs.
Grains	Monthly	2.4 lbs.	1.50 lbs.	1.50 lbs.	1.50 lbs.
Fats	Monthly	2.9 lbs.	2.00 lbs.	2.00 lbs.	2.00 lbs.
Eggs	Monthly	7 units	5 units	2 units	6 units (week)
Milk	Daily	0.45 liters	0.20 liters*	0.20 liters*	0.94 liters*
Fish	Biweekly	1.10 lbs.	0.50 lbs.	0.50 lbs.	1.0 lb.
Chicken	Monthly	3.20 lbs.	2.00 lbs.	1.01 lbs.	2.0 lbs.
Coffee	Monthly	19 ounces	19 ounces	12 ounces	12 ounces
Beans	Monthly	2.1 lbs.	1.5 lbs.	1.5 lbs.	1.5 lbs.
Bread	Daily	NI**	NI	NI	50 grams
Condensed milk	Monthly	NI	3 cans	3 cans	3 cans
Vegetables	Weekly	NI	3.5 lbs.	3.5 lbs.	3.5 lbs.
Sugar	Monthly	NI	NI	NI	6 lbs.

* Only for children under seven, aged, sick, or minors.
** NI = No information.

Thus, a decline in the availability of consumer goods, especially foodstuffs, has been experienced. The drop in percentages from 1958 to 1963 was marked, although it is possible that only those in the upper levels of the society really felt it, while the lower classes, despite the decrease, increased their consumption.[22]

In addition to their rations a large portion of the population is served free meals. In 1965 626,300 persons a day were

---

[21] *Source:* Rationing decrees of March 12, 1962, and October 8, 1963; United Nations Food and Agriculture Organization (FAO), *Agricultural Commodities Projections for 1975 and 1985*, Rome, 1967, 2 volumes; United Nations FAO, *National Rice Policies*, Rome, 1966, p. 99; Jacques Chonchol et al., *Proyecto de Plan Quinquenal para el Desarrollo de la Agricultura Cubana, 1961–1965*, Havana, 1961; *Informe sobre Cuba* (Miami), November 30, 1963; United States Department of Commerce, *Investment in Cuba*, Washington, July 1959; *Facts on File*, April 30–May 6, 1970, p. 313; *Keesing's Contemporary Archives* (London), June 7–14, 1969, p. 33395; *Revolución* (Havana), January 17, 1959, Instituto Nacional de Reforma Agraria, *Informe*, Havana, May 17, 1959.

[22] Several nutritional studies of various rural communities have been made on the island, but none, to our knowledge, were ever printed. See *Granma* (Havana), December 18, 1969, p. 5.

fed breakfast, lunch, or dinner without charge.[23] Five years later, two out of every eight Cubans (2.2 million) were being fed.[24] Also, there are restaurants and cafeterias selling food at moderate prices and many work centers have dining rooms where employees can eat lunch for 1 peso or less.[25]

But are Cubans better fed today? Estimates on the average daily per capita caloric intake indicate that it has declined.

Estimated Per Capita Calorie Availability Per Day[26]

Year	Calories (required = 2,460 daily)
1951–1957	2,740*
1958	2,870
1959–1961	2,730*
1962–1963	2,320
1965–1966	2,100–2,300

* yearly average

Yet, national averages are often misleading since they conceal disparities between regions. In the 1950's no rich man ever suffered from food shortage, but the poor were extremely lucky to escape it. Also, unquestionably, the rural people whose food consumption was much below the national average seem to have received a fairer share of calories and nutrients since 1959. This improvement, however, should not be construed as ideal. On September 17, 1966, Fidel Castro

[23] Mario Cerda Gutiérrez, "Cuba: alimentos para todos," *Punto Final* (Santiago, Chile), April 8, 1964, pp. 10–11.

[24] Fidel Castro, July 26, 1970, speech. In this volume.

[25] There are many high-priced restaurants too, quite out of reach of the budget of the average Cuban worker or peasant, which has aroused the anger of many people.

[26] The table has been prepared from the following publications: Wyatt MacGaffey and Clifford R. Barnett, *Twentieth Century Cuba*, New York: Doubleday, 1965, p. 196; Lester R. Brown, *Man, Land, and Food*, Washington: United States Department of Agriculture, 1965, p. 142; United Nations FAO, *Agricultural Commodities Projections for 1975 and 1985*, Rome, 1967, Vol. I, p. 36, Vol. II, p. 78; United States Department of Agriculture, *The Western Hemisphere Agricultural Situation*, Washington, 1966, p. 21.

recognized that there were still thousands of children not receiving all the nourishment they needed.[27]

Finally, it must be concluded that underconsumption still
exists in Cuba, despite the betterment of some rural areas.
Also, a dangerous trend has developed since 1961 in which
Cubans are eating less as the years pass by.[28]

2. Housing

Miserable housing conditions cannot foster the satisfactory
and healthy development of a people. In the 1950's Cuban
dwellings were far from adequate in meeting minimal requirements of hygiene. Many poor people, particularly children, were easy prey for a variety of diseases.

In 1953 63% of all dwellings were located in the urban
areas, where the population numbered 57% of the total.
Meanwhile rural people, constituting 43% of all Cubans,
lived in 37% of the total housing units.[29] Such a disproportionate concentration of urban homes meant an overcrowding of rural families. Moreover, while 15% of the homes
were in extremely bad condition, the rate was 25.9 in the
rural areas and only 8.6% in the cities.

A study in 1958 disclosed that 62.5% of all shelters had
thatched roofs and dirt floors, and 53% had no baths.[31] A
little over half the urban homes were built of masonry, but
the figure in the country was not even 3%. Palm and wood
thatch provided the building material for almost 70% of Cuban homes.

Seventy-one in every hundred homes in urban Havana
were made of masonry, but in the rainy countryside of
Oriente only ten in every thousand were fortunate enough to
have such shelter.

[27] *Granma* (Havana), September 25, 1966, pp. 4–5.
[28] Agricultural production grows at the rate of 0.1% annually while
the population grows at 2.1% since 1961. United Nations FAO, *The
State of Food and Agriculture,* Rome, 1968, p. 15.
[29] Marcia N. Koth, *Housing in Latin America,* Cambridge: MIT Press,
1965, p. 32; Unión Panamericana, *América en Cifras 1967,* Washington,
1969, Vol. I, p. 29.
[31] "Educación médica en América," *Universidad de La Habana,* July
1962, p. 93.

Housing Conditions, 1953 (in Percentages)[30]

National	Good	Fair	Bad
Cuba	43.4	41.6	15.0
urban	53.8	37.6	8.6
rural	25.7	48.4	25.9
By Province			
Pinar del Río	34.5	44.5	21.0
urban	48.9	38.4	12.7
rural	25.1	48.5	26.4
Havana	61.1	32.8	6.1
urban	62.9	31.8	5.3
rural	37.7	45.8	16.5
Matanzas	43.9	42.2	13.9
urban	51.2	38.3	10.5
rural	31.5	48.9	19.6
Las Villas	41.6	42.9	15.5
urban	50.5	39.1	10.4
rural	30.9	47.5	21.6
Camagüey	41.5	41.5	16.6
urban	55.0	36.4	8.6
rural	26.7	47.9	25.4
Oriente	25.9	50.3	23.8
urban	34.0	51.7	14.3
rural	19.9	49.2	30.9

Material Used in Building Dwellings, 1953 (in Percentages)[32]

Material	Urban	Rural	National
Masonry	51.8	2.7	33.5
Wood	34.6	16.4	27.7
Palm or wood thatch	9.7	75.4	34.3
Other	3.9	5.5	4.5

Floors were often dirty and muddy, homes infested with insects and rodents. The table below, although omitting the differences between provinces, demonstrates the unpleasant perspective.

[30] *Source:* República de Cuba, *Censos de Población, Viviendas y Electoral,* Havana, 1953, pp. 209–215.

[32] All figures and tables, unless otherwise noted, are derived from the 1953 census.

Material Used in Floors, 1953 (in Percentages)

Material	Urban	Rural	National
Tile	53.3	2.6	34.4
Cement	26.9	18.2	23.6
Wood	6.6	7.5	6.9
Earth	9.3	66.2	30.6
Other	3.9	5.5	4.5

Electric power was enjoyed in 58% of all homes. But once again such comfort was out of the reach of the poor people in the country and parts of the cities. Meager salaries could not afford such expensive luxuries. Small wonder then that eighty-seven urban families in every hundred had electric power at their fingertips, but the percentage in the interior was 9.1.

Electricity by Provinces, 1953 (in Percentages)

Province	Urban	Rural	Total
Pinar del Río	77.7	10.6	37.0
Havana	95.3	22.8	90.3
Matanzas	85.8	9.7	57.6
Las Villas	80.8	8.1	47.6
Camagüey	82.7	10.6	47.8
Oriente	74.8	6.4	35.6

What little food the poor managed to purchase could not be preserved if refrigeration were required. Mechanical refrigeration existed in 17% of all Cuban homes. As expected, for every refrigerator in the rural regions, there were thirteen in the cities. Ninety-six percent of country dwellings had no refrigeration whatsoever, whereas 62.5% in the urban areas did not.

The system for the disposal of human wastes was inadequate too. Twenty-eight percent of the entire number of homes had inside flush toilets, and 13.7% could be found outside of homes. Over one third of the families had latrines, and 23.2% of the dwellings (54.1% in the country) had absolutely no facilities whatsoever.

Good drinking water was not an inexpensive or easy item to come by. More than three fourths of all rural families obtained their water from rivers, wells, or springs, many of which were contaminated. Only 2% of the people in the interior enjoyed inside piped water, although the national average was 35%, climbing to 55% in the urban areas.

Has the housing problem found a solution at the hands of the revolutionary authorities? Definitely not. At first the Cubans discovered their needs, but only afterward did they come to the realization that the poverty of the country set tremendously high limitations to what they could possibly do. Cement and other resources were limited and what was at hand had to be used in the building of roads, port facilities, schools, dams, hospitals, and other structures. Consequently, housing was relegated to the back of the regime's priority list.

In 1964 15% of the dwellings, housing 18% of the population, were in extremely poor condition, and another 31% of the homes (with 36% of the people) were in poor condition. In other words, 655,000 homes were urgently needed to provide adequate housing to 54% of the Cubans.[33] In general, 1.2 million homes had to be improved or replaced.[34]

At the closing session of the National Builders Congress in October 1964, Fidel Castro dealt with the subject. He noted that to solve the deficit, a program of building 2 million homes by 1990 had to be introduced, producing 80,000 homes yearly.[35] The following year Castro noted the housing crisis again and proposed the building of 100,000 homes annually, adding then that it was impossible for the country to accomplish this because of lack of resources. He concluded with the pessimistic note that the housing problem was something "that the Revolution has not even begun to deal with seriously."[36]

On August 29, 1966, Castro returned to the same topic. He acknowledged that government officials were constantly be-

[33] Alberto Arrinda, "El problema de la vivienda en Cuba," *Cuba Socialista* (Havana), December 1964, p. 14.
[34] *Ibid.*
[35] *Radio Habana Cuba*, October 26, 1964.
[36] *Discursos de Fidel en los Aniversarios de los CDR, 1960–1967*, Havana: Instituto del Libro, 1968, p. 159.

sieged wherever they went by people in desperate need of housing. The need was genuine and widespread, but a solution in the immediate future, the Cuban leader noted, was absolutely impossible.

> The housing deficit in this country is approximately 1 million. A million new dwellings are required for those who have none, for those who live with relatives, those who are overcrowded in one room, live under a stairway or in thatched huts.[37]

And in late 1970 the Cuban Prime Minister reaffirmed that the housing shortage was a "terrible problem," adding, "This is a problem of which we are only too aware," since 90% of the people who approached the authorities always pointed out their tremendous need for a new shelter. According to Castro, "There is no way of solving that problem."[38] It is hardly a surprise, then, that the government has accepted overcrowding. One of the official organs of the regime puts it this way: "The scarcity of resources does not allow us to meet the great housing demand and forces us to adopt in these first years of the Revolution minimal norms of space per inhabitant."[39]

In 1964 the state repaired 13,502 dwellings and constructed 17,284,[40] according to a report given by the Cuban delegate to the World Health Organization. However, in early 1968 Fidel Castro reported that in the first nine years of the Revolution "we have not built more than 10,000 dwellings per year, whereas we need to build some 100,000 dwellings annually."[41] If that is really the case, then the figures mentioned before are exaggerated, or construction from 1965 to 1967 substantially declined to the yearly rate of 5,756. Moreover, a yearly deficit of 90,000 dwellings has been accumulating, creating an aggregate over the last twelve years of a little over 1 million homes required. Dwelling construc-

[37] *Política* (Mexico) September 15, 1966, pp. x–xi.
[38] *Granma* (Havana), December 20, 1970, p. 3.
[39] Alberto Arrinda, *op. cit.,* p. 20.
[40] WHO, Eighteenth World Health Assembly, *Official Records,* Geneva, 1965, p. 172.
[41] *Granma* (Havana), January 14, 1968, p. 2.

tion per capita seems to have declined from 1.5 per thousand
inhabitants in 1958 to 1.2 in 1967.[42]

In the first five years of the revolutionary regime an average of 11,089 homes were constructed annually. Forty-nine
percent of them were found in the countryside.

State Housing, 1959–1963[43]

Rural Homes	26,050
Urban Homes	29,397
Total	55,447

Meanwhile, a system of priorities has been drawn up for
the construction and delivery of new homes. The rural population has precedence over everyone else, followed by projects to eradicate urban slums and eventually run-down
tenements.

The need for rural housing is absolutely pressing. In 1960
a housing census in the countryside revealed that almost 2
million Cubans lived "in miserable huts, with the poorest of
sanitary conditions,"[44] requiring the prompt construction of
400,000 dwellings. Rural projects have been put into effect
and have delivered less than 10,000 new homes every year to
the rural population. The homes are simple, comfortable,
somewhat small, but equipped with furniture and sanitary
service and are free. Most slums have disappeared, and the
inhabitants have been placed in new housing units.[45]

Worthy of note is the thorough change in housing property relations brought about by the revolutionary regime. On

[42] Carmelo Mesa-Lago, "Availability and Reliability of Statistics in
Socialist Cuba," *Latin American Research Review*, Summer 1969, p. 72.
One Cuban publication states that from 1959 to 1969, 140,000 dwellings
were built. If this is true, then from 1967 to 1969 the yearly average was
16,600. The author, however, could have included the units built from
1959 to 1963 by the private sector, thus giving a false impression of the
real rate of growth. *Bohemia* (Havana), October 24, 1969, pp. 32–39.

[43] *Source:* Alberto Arrinda, *op. cit.,* p. 16.

[44] Arturo Acevedo, "¿Bohíos, para que?" *INRA* (Havana), December
1960, p. 46.

[45] A fairly useful summary of these programs can be found in Don
Burke, "Urban Renewal in Cuba," *Guardian* (New York), February 15,
1969, p. 18.

March 10, 1959, the revolutionary government enacted a law reducing the rent of housing units as shown below.

Rent Reduction, 1959[46]

Monthly Payments	Reduction (%)
Less than $100	50
From $100–200	40
More than $200	30

The Urban Reform Law, proclaimed on October 14, 1960, expropriated and placed under the state all urban flats. Rents were to be paid to the government and were considered as amortization payments which would allow a building's occupants to become its owners. Tenants have to pay rent on time and regularly, and maintain the building. And they can only change their homes for others through a state institution.[47]

Those living in homes built in (or before) 1940 were to cease payment in 1965 if rent had been paid punctually since 1959. And from May 1961 on all new and vacant units were distributed to families who had to pay rent equal to 10% of the family income. Moreover, in mid-1966 the right to live in their homes for the rest of their lives, without paying rent, was granted to all those residing in run-down tenements (if they had made at least, since 1959, sixty monthly payments).[48] A total of 268,089 families stopped paying rent in 1969.

Are sanitary conditions in Cuban homes better now? Information on the matter is somewhat sketchy. The most recent report on the disposal of sewage was made in 1964 by the Cuban government. That year it was disclosed that there were 4.1 million persons living in 276 communities with more than 1,000 inhabitants. Only 28 of the towns had organized

[46] *Source: Gaeceta Oficial* (Havana), May 3, 1959.

[47] Boris Goldenberg, *The Cuban Revolution and Latin America*, New York: Praeger, 1965, p. 195.

[48] *Urban Reform Law*, Havana, 1967, pp. 3–10. The Cubans announced in 1966 that four years later all rent would be abolished, but on December 7, 1970, Fidel Castro reversed that position.

arrangements for the disposal of human waste. Approximately 1.2 million persons were served by sewage systems, while 2.8 million had only septic tanks or latrines.[49] The water supply, on the other hand, has been markedly improved.

Percent of Population with Access to Inside Running Water[50]

Year	Urban	Rural	Total
1953	54.6	2.3	35.2
1966	90.0	60.0	75.0

An increment in the homes with electric power has taken place. In 1958 there were 732,000 homes with electricity;[51] twelve years later its comfort reached 988,000 families,[52] or a little over 50% of all homes.

In concluding this section it is clear that few positive achievements can be noted. There is still a housing crisis. Many people today, over 70% of the entire population, live in inadequate homes, dwellings that simply cannot facilitate the real sanitary environment indispensable for a healthy people.

The Health Sector

Health appears to have been "reasonably good"[53] in the years preceding the revolutionary takeover. Various authors have stressed the point that the rate of mortality was low and the number of physicians and hospital beds per capita high

[49] World Health Organization, *Third Report on the World Health Situation, 1961–1964*, Geneva, April 1967, p. 131.

[50] 1953 Cuban census and Ildeu Duarte Filho, "El financiamiento de proyectos de ingeniería sanitaria," *Boletín de la Oficina Sanitaria Panamericana* (Washington), January–June 1970, p. 65.

[51] Grupo Cubano de Investigaciones Económicas, *Un Estudio sobre Cuba*, Coral Gables: University of Miami Press, 1963, p. 169.

[52] *Bohemia* (Havana), October 9, 1970, pp. 30–35.

[53] José M. Illán, *Cuba, Datos sobre una Economía en Ruinas*, Miami: AIP, 1964, p. 26.

in Cuba.[54] Also, arguments have been put forth trying to prove that the health system of Cuba was efficient and progressive and needed little reform. Such assessments based on national averages, however, present a false impression. Any useful analysis of Cuban health hinges not on the question of figures for the whole nation, but on how health facilities and personnel were distributed.

1. Health Personnel and Facilities Before the Revolution

From 1899 to 1958 the Cuban people increased their numbers four times, while the number of physicians multiplied by five. In 1957 the doctor/population ratio was one physician for 998 persons, a figure surpassed by only one other Latin American country.[55]

Physicians, 1899–1958[56]

Year	Total
1899	1,223
1907	1,243
1919	1,771
1943	2,589
1953	6,201
1957	6,421
1958	6,286

These services, however, were relatively inaccessible to the inhabitants of the rural areas. Medical skills and facilities were concentrated in the large cities, while the countryfolk were disproportionately consumed by disease.

More than 60% of all physicians in 1958 lived and worked in Havana. Thus, Havana province had one physician for every 420 persons, but Pinar del Río's rural population had one for every 2,100. There was one doctor for every 2,550 persons living in Oriente province.[57] Needless to say, the

[54] *La Seguridad Social en Cuba,* Miami: FORDC, 1965, pp. 7–8.
[55] Theodore Draper, *Castroism, Theory and Practice,* New York: Praeger, 1965, p. 100.
[56] Censuses 1899–1953: *Granma* (Havana), February 12, 1967, p. 9.
[57] Robert Goldston, *The Cuban Revolution,* New York: Bobbs-Merrill, 1970, p. 58.

regions with the fewest physicians needed them the most.[58]

An idea of the unequal distribution of medical personnel can be gained by looking at the problem as it stood in 1958. That year the province of Havana, with less than one third of the total population, absorbed over two thirds of all the available physicians. Oriente province, with 3% more people than Havana, had, on the other hand, 50% fewer doctors.

Even when doctors practiced outside of Havana province they did so primarily in the provincial capitals. It remained palpably evident that the country people had little opportunity to see a professional for treatment. In 1962, after a revolutionary drive had begun to provide the interior with health services, the situation was still critical, which only shows how dismal the conditions must have been in the 1950's.

Distribution of Physicians by Provincial Capital, 1962[59]

Province	Pop. of Capital	Physicians in Capital
Pinar del Río	24%	35%
Havana	50	93
Matanzas	22	40
Las Villas	15	25
Camagüey	33	49
Oriente	10	27

What was the reason for such a concentration in the cities? Primarily it was the direct consequence of the medical profession's desire to do a good business. After all, in the cities, where the largest shares of the national income ended up, more people could afford to pay for treatment.[60] In other words, medical personnel congregated in the urban areas be-

[58] Noteworthy is the fact that 70% of the medical students graduating in 1955–1956 had to migrate because they could not find jobs in the capital. In 1956 the Cuban Medical Association held a symposium to discuss the problem.

[59] Carlos Font Pupo, "La salud del pueblo, preocupación básica de la revolución," *Cuba Socialista* (Havana), April 1963, p. 53.

[60] There are secondary causes, such as the facilities found in urban areas. For a thorough consideration of the issue, see "The Urban and Rural Distribution of Medical Manpower," *World Health Organization Chronicle* (Geneva), March 1968, pp. 100–105.

cause health was a commodity to be sold. Medical services, their scope and extent of coverage, were determined by a commitment to profits and not to serving the needs of the Cubans.[61]

The trend toward concentrating in the city of Havana is also visible among dentists. In 1899 49% of the total were in the capital. Fifty-eight years later it was 62%.[62] And the ratio of dentists per person, which in 1899 was one for every 3,000, in 1957 amounted to one per 2,224. Nurses also followed a similar pattern despite their increase in numbers.

Dental and Nursing Personnel, 1899–1957[63]

Year	Dentists	Nurses
1899	354	523
1907	390	822
1943	1018	921
1953	1934	1763
1957	2100	2876

In 1958 there were eighty-eight hospitals in the country. Cuba had one of the highest percentages of hospital beds in the Caribbean, with one bed for every three hundred persons. But the distribution was irregular and completely inadequate when the density and morbidity rates of the population were taken into account. The urban areas received preferential treatment. Eighty percent of all beds were in the city of Havana.[64] For the entire rural population there were only ten beds in one hospital. Moreover, with a few exceptions, the hospitals lacked internal organization.[65]

It was a distressing fact that the needs of the people received little consideration from those making decisions. The

[61] Charitable and mutual aid associations made a contribution to the health of the people in the cities, although often a fee was attached to it in one form or another.

[62] 1899 census and *Granma* (Havana), November 19, 1969, p. 4.

[63] 1899–1953 censuses and World Health Organization, *Second Report on the World Health Situation, 1957–1960*, Geneva, 1963, pp. 121–123.

[64] Carlos Font Pupo, "Hacia la salud pública socialista," *Cuba Socialista* (Havana), July 1965, p. 39.

[65] Raúl de Velasco, "Cuba," *World Medical Journal*, May 1959, p. 141.

Number of Hospitals, 1958

Hospital	Number
General Urban	41
General Rural	1
Industrial	22
Special	24
Total	88

Hospital Beds, 1958[66]

Hospital	Number
General*	15,013
Special	6,767
Others	3,965
Total	25,745[67]

* Includes mutual benefit clinics.

construction of hospitals and other health facilities then was "most often the result of political rather than technical decisions."[68] The health sector was a channel to distribute political patronage, a useful way of becoming rich. One study has stated on this aspect:

Often, access to a clinic or a hospital bed could be obtained only through the political organization of the town. Services were channeled to the rural population through leaders of the party in power. Those using the health services and facilities were strangely reminded of the source of the benefits, and many were required to vote accordingly. Public health positions, like other government jobs, also were subject to the patronage system.[69]

[66] Cuba, Ministerio de Salud Pública, *Salud Pública en Cifras,* Havana, 1963; *El Mundo* (Havana), December 3, 1967, pp. 1, 5.

[67] An official Cuban periodical gives the figure of 32,694 hospital beds for 1957, that is, almost 7,000 more units than the following year. *Bohemia* (Havana), January 2, 1969, p. 29.

[68] Wyatt MacGaffey and Clifford R. Barnett, *Twentieth Century Cuba,* New York: Doubleday, 1965, p. 201.

[69] *Ibid.,* p. 201.

Public officials were only concerned with the health of the people several weeks before elections, that is, every four years.

2. Radical Institutional Changes

The health system before the Revolution was plagued by a lack of coordination of private, charitable, and public institutions. In 1959 a series of administrative measures brought about a complete overturn of the institutional structure, and a more broadly based and comprehensive system of medical care was initiated. The Ministry of Public Health (MPH) acquired broad powers with which it introduced a unified health system under its control. This central authority, it must be noted, exercises a supervisory, coordinating, and financial, rather than executive, role.

Four years later the MPH established complete control over all health facilities as the result of the nationalization of private and charitable concerns. Reorganization became more thorough and planning more centralized. Uniform plans were drawn to assure maximum efficiency and to avoid duplication.

Presently the execution of health plans takes place at three different levels, all of which are directly supervised by the Ministry of Public Health. These levels are provincial, regional, and local.[70]

There are six provincial health divisions, corresponding to the six provinces of Cuba. Each represents the authority of the Ministry and is responsible for the implementation of policy. At this level the provincial hospitals give specialized service to the inhabitants of the area. There are eight provincial hospitals, each with six hundred beds.[71]

Each province is divided into regions. There are thirty-

---

[70] The Cubans have taken this model from the Soviet Union and the Eastern European nations. United Nations Department of Economic and Social Affairs, *Report on the World Social Situation*, New York, 1963, p. 37; Cuba, *Gaceta Oficial* (Havana), February 6, 1962, and November 29, 1962.

[71] The hospitals are distributed as follows: two in Havana, two in Oriente, and one in each of the other provinces. Edward Rice, "Cuba: Services for All," *World Health* (Geneva), December 1968, p. 15; *Granma* (Havana), February 12, 1967, p. 9.

eight health regions with urban hospitals doing general surgery. Each establishment has a capacity of about 350 patients. Then, the regions are comprised of health areas. Each health area has at least one polyclinic.[72] The polyclinic, an institution for outpatients with preventative and social functions, has a gynecologist, dentist, pediatrician, epidemiologist, nurses, and one intern on duty. There are also health workers who teach the surrounding communities basic principles and methods of hygiene. Each rural polyclinic has between twenty and thirty beds, and is equipped to deal with general medicine, obstetrics, and pediatrics. Surgical cases are sent to the regional hospitals. Furthermore, in the most remote rural areas, dispensaries have been built to provide primary medical assistance. Some have dentists, but are lacking beds. When necessary, patients are sent to the rural hospitals.

More important still was the extension of health and medical care as a biological right available to everyone at no direct cost.[73] Since the outset the revolutionary state has recognized the responsibility of assuring all of its citizens a healthy development. This is a radical break with the past. Health is no longer an instrument to assure the individual wealth of a few, but a way of creating the conditions for the wealth of the entire nation. The popularization of health, however, demanded an expansion of facilities and personnel.

3. Facilities and Personnel in the Revolution

The quantitative development of public medicine became a priority in the first five years of the revolutionary government. The Ministry of Public Health increased the capacity of the facilities at hand and built new units throughout the nation. From 1959 to 1964 66 new hospitals[74] were constructed, 38 of them in the countryside. This brought the

[72] World Health Organization, *Second Report on the World Health Situation, 1957–1960,* Geneva, 1963, pp. 121–123; *Third Report on the World Health Situation 1961–1964,* Geneva, 1967, pp. 129–130; *Cuba Internacional* (Havana), September 1970, p. 7.

[73] Health services are free for all inpatients. Outpatients, on the other hand, must pay for their medicine.

[74] Carlos Font Pupo, "Hacia la salud pública socialista," *Cuba Socialista* (Havana), July 1965, p. 39.

number of state hospitals to 120, which, added to 25 others that were nationalized by 1963, provided a total of 145 hospitals. Thereafter, the number of hospitals continually went up. In 1968 there were, according to one version, 180 public hospitals in the island. If the mutual benefit clinics are added, then 215 hospitals could be counted.[75]

Public Hospitals, 1959–1968[76]

Year	Number
1959	54
1960	61
1961	100
1962	135*
1963	148*
1964	145*
1965	155
1966	168
1967	177
1968	180

* Includes nationalized private institutions.

The quantitative growth of health facilities from 1959 to 1968 yielded the following: 92 new hospitals, 260 polyclinics, 56 rural dispensaries, 20 public health laboratories, 40 stomatological clinics, 8 dental surgery services, and 14 blood banks.[77] Moreover, 50% of all new hospitals have sprung up in the rural regions, thirty of them in Oriente province, the region that suffered the most from backwardness and the lack of facilities. The other seventeen are scattered throughout the country.

The rural hospitals are small, efficient, and simple. But more important, they have brought health to people who knew it only in their dreams. One observer notes:

[75] *Bohemia* (Havana), January 2, 1969, p. 29.
[76] *Granma* (Havana), April 3, 1968, p. 6; and *Bohemia* (Havana), January 2, 1969, p. 29; *OCLAE* (Havana), January 1969, p. 28.
[77] "Salud Pública," *Bohemia* (Havana), January 2, 1969, pp. 28–29; Francisco Rojas, "Revolución: Salud Pública, logros y perspectivas," *OCLAE* (Havana), January 1969, p. 28; K. S. Karol, *Guerrillas in Power,* New York: Hill & Wang, 1970, p. 597.

These units, built in the most remote areas, are bringing health care to thousands who previously had to wait on the coast to signal a passing ship to take them to the cities for treatment. All along the coast of the rural provinces are the graveyards of those who could wait no longer.[78]

The rural hospitals, however, have one major weakness: the scanty supply of beds.[79] In 1968 these hospitals comprised 22% of the total number of hospitals, but had only 3% of the beds, that is, 1,350.[80] Of course, these units have not been created for intensive treatment of patients, but to deliver general medical care.

The availability of hospital beds, by itself, is not a reliable indicator of the level of health. Nonetheless, from 1959 to 1968 public health beds almost tripled, the major increase taking place in the early 1960's due to the rapid construction of hospitals and the expropriation of the private sector.[81]

Public Health Beds[82]

Year	Number
1959	10,843
1960	16,913
1961	21,639
1962	32,707
1963	33,650
1964	35,310
1965	37,791
1966	37,427
1967	38,760

[78] Don Burke, "Cuba Makes Health Care Revolution," *Guardian* (New York), February 1, 1969, p. 16.

[79] The building of polyclinics started to receive preference after 1965, which could account for the low rate of beds in the countryside.

[80] Carlos Rafael Rodríguez, "Análisis para el primer decenio y perspectivas para el segundo," *Panorama Económico Latinoamericano* (Havana), September 1969, pp. 22–23.

[81] In 1959 estimates were that Cuba needed 40,000 new beds. If the estimate was correct a deficit of 18,000 beds still exists. See Raúl de Velasco, "Cuba," *World Medical Journal*, May 1959, p. 141.

[82] *Granma* (Havana), April 3, 1968, p. 6. Includes only budgeted beds, and not those in mutual benefit clinics.

Moreover, bed facilities at all levels almost doubled during the same period. The hospital bed/population ratio has thus changed considerably. In 1958 there were 3.9 beds for every 1,000 persons. Ten years later the ratio was 5.9 beds per 1,000 inhabitants.[83]

Total Number of Beds* in Health Sector[84]

Year	Number
1958	25,745
1960	30,000
1962	41,898
1963	45,671
1964	47,861
1965	49,949
1966	43,062 (42,221)
1968	47,660

* Includes public and mutual benefit clinics.

The expansion of services demanded a larger number of medical personnel. But here the government confronted a serious shortage, not only because of the growth of facilities, but also from the migration of physicians. From 1959 to 1964 the medical ranks declined by 1,445, which, if the rate of

[83] World Health Organization, Twenty-Second World Health Assembly, *Official Records,* Geneva, 1969, pp. 68–69. The hospital bed/population ratios supplied by Cuban officials for similar years often show great divergencies, as exemplified in the yearly reports presented by the Cuban delegation to the World Health Assembly.

[84] For 1958: *Bohemia* (Havana), January 5, 1964, pp. 25–31; 1960: World Health Organization (WHO), *Annual Epidemiological and Vital Statistics,* Geneva, 1964, pp. 702–703; 1962: WHO, *Third Report on the World Health Situation 1961–1964,* Geneva, 1967, p. 130; 1963: Cuba, Ministerio de Salud Pública, *Salud Pública en Cifras,* Havana, 1963, and *El Mundo* (Havana), 1964 (supplement); 1964: WHO, Eighteenth World Health Assembly, *Official Records,* Geneva, 1966, p. 171; 1965: WHO, Nineteenth World Health Assembly, *Official Records,* Geneva, 1966, pp. 172–175; 1966: the first figure from United Nations, *Statistical Yearbook,* New York, 1970, p. 674, the other from WHO, *World Health Statistics Annual,* Geneva, 1970, p. 77; 1968: *Bohemia* (Havana), January 2, 1969, p. 29, and *Granma* (Havana), January 19, 1969.

graduating medical students is considered, means that over 2,000 doctors fled the island.[85]

It was imperative to overcome such a serious problem by introducing a crash program that would make up the losses. The time of study was shortened and qualifications reduced. From 1964 on, this extensive and concentrated program began to pay off numerically as the number of doctors went up by almost 55%.

Medical Personnel[86]

Year	Number
1959	6,300
1960	6,609
1961	5,793
1962	5,841
1963	6,124
1964	4,855
1965	6,815
1966	6,862
1967	6,880
1968	7,148
1969	7,500

In 1969 there were 1,200 more doctors than ten years earlier, but despite this increment the ratio of physicians per person has not improved. In 1958 for every physician there were 1,000 inhabitants; it was one in 1,000 in 1969.[87]

[85] One author estimates that from 1959 to 1965 over 2,500 trained doctors left for the United States. See Willis P. Butler, "Cuba's Revolutionary Medicine," *Ramparts*, May 1969. A lower figure (1,275) appears in Organización Panamericana de la Salud, *Migration of Health Personnel, Scientists, and Engineers from Latin America*, Washington, 1966.

[86] For 1959: *Granma* (Havana), January 19, 1969, p. 2; 1960: World Health Organization (WHO), *Second Report of the World Situation, 1957–1960*, Geneva, 1963, pp. 121–123; 1961: United Nations, *Statistical Yearbook*, New York, 1970; 1962: WHO, *Third Report on the World Situation, 1961–1964*, Geneva, 1967, p. 130; 1963–1964: WHO, *World Health Annual Statistics, 1964–1970*; 1965: WHO, Nineteenth Health Assembly, *Official Records*, Geneva, 1966, pp. 172–175; 1966: *World Health Chronicle* (Geneva), January 1969, p. 31; 1967: *World Health Chronicle* (Geneva), August 1968, p. 374; 1968: *Radio Habana Cuba*, January 9, 1969; 1969: *Granma* (Havana), January 19, 1969, p. 2.

[87] *Boletín de la Oficina Sanitaria Panamericana* (Washington), January–June 1970, p. 33; and World Health Organization, Twenty-Second World Health Assembly, *Official Records*, Geneva, 1969, p. 382.

Distribution has improved, albeit slowly. In 1963 the national average was one physician for every 1,180 persons. But Havana province had 3,253 physicians, that is, one for every 320 persons, while the remainder of the country claimed only one physician for every 2,150 inhabitants.[88] In 1969 approximately 50% of the nation's doctors were still in the capital.[89] One physician out of every seven was practicing in the countryside that year.[90]

4. The Training of Medical Personnel

The Cubans believe that merely to produce qualified health personnel cannot solve the health problems of the country. The graduates must also be trained to face adverse conditions. Hence, the teaching of medicine has changed. Preventive medicine is taught as an integral part of clinical subjects, and from the outset the students are brought into contact with the socio-cultural and -economic peculiarities they will face while practicing.[91]

The biological foundations of medicine were combined with social and political studies, in the words of a government authority:

so that the students would not regard the sick person simply as a hospital patient, but see him in his totality, as a social being, since any other view leads to the dehumanization of man.[92]

Years earlier the Minister of Public Health made the same point in a different way.

Doctors should first understand the problems that affect our society and refrain from being individuals enclosed in ivory towers under the slogan of science for its own sake.

[88] World Health Organization, *World Health Statistics Annual,* Geneva, 1967, Vol. II.

[89] *Zdravookhraneniye Rossiyskoy Federatsii* (Moscow), February 1970, pp. 38–41.

[90] *Radio Habana Cuba,* January 9, 1969.

[91] Such measures have not been taken in most of Latin America. "Medical Education in Latin America," *World Health Organization Chronicle* (Geneva), October 1970, pp. 467–470.

[92] *Juventud Rebelde* (Havana), July 9, 1970, p. 2.

Rather, the watchword must be: science for the health of all our people.[93]

Government authorities link the problems in public health directly to the meaning, goals, and philosophy of the Revolution. Since the professional objective of physicians is man, this objective is identical with the aim of the revolutionary process. As a result, the Revolution wants the "best moral, intellectual, and physical conditions,"[94] allowing the full development of men and women. The President of Cuba stated on January 16, 1970:

The importance of the doctor in a revolutionary process, in the historic task of building a new society, is much greater and more important than his role in pre-revolutionary societies. It is not only a matter of humanitarian service. It is more; it is an attempt to create the physical and mental preconditions for everyone for his full development as a human being in a new social and historical situation.[95]

Those enrolling at the three medical schools[96] must be at least seventeen years of age and have a secondary school certificate. After passing competitive entry examinations the pupils study for six years. The first three years are devoted to the study of pre-medical sciences. In the second year historical and dialectical materialism, as well as political economy, philosophy, and foreign language courses must be taken. In the fourth and fifth years the curriculum includes therapy, psychiatry, surgery, pediatrics, obstetrics, and several other courses. Finally, in the sixth year time is devoted entirely to practice at hospitals and clinics. There are twenty-three health establishments where the interns practice therapy, surgery, obstetrics, gynecology, pediatrics, hygiene, and epidemiology.

[93] *Granma* (Havana), September 11, 1966, p. 4.
[94] *Granma* (Havana), January 19, 1970, p. 2.
[95] *Ibid.*
[96] Of the 158 senior professors teaching medicine at the University of Havana, all but 17 migrated after 1959. Leo Huberman and Paul Sweezy, *Socialism in Cuba*, New York: Monthly Review Press, 1969, pp. 56–57. In 1966 there were 207 professors at the Havana school.

The work of each sixth-year student is graded by his instructors for a whole month. The rating is based on the instructors' observations and not on the basis of tests. A Soviet observer has noted that "in rating a student's internship due consideration is given to his interest in the science, his reports on theoretical matters, practical or laboratory work, as well as his ideological level."[97]

After the sixth year an annual examination is taken, after which the student becomes a physician and is allowed to practice. However, each graduate must work two or three years in a rural area.[98] The number of graduating physicians since 1961 has been as follows:

Medical Graduates[99]

Year	Number
1961	335
1962	424
1963	334
1964	315
1965	322
1966	355
1967	400
1968	420
1969	923

Upon graduating, Cuban physicians pledge to renounce private practice and work only for the state.[100] The trend

[97] *Zdravookhraneniye, op. cit.*, pp. 39–40.
[98] Law Number 1141, January 11, 1964. See *Granma* (Havana), June 21, 1968, p. 2.
[99] *Granma* (Havana), January 25, 1970, p. 2.
[100] The pledge, begun in 1965, states: "We promise . . . to renounce private practice . . . and to make effective with our attitude the new proletarian philosophy of the medical sciences and . . . to maintain in ourselves the spirit of scientific and political improvement in order to reach the technical level necessary and to make ourselves true communists. . . . We state our readiness to give our help, scientific or otherwise, to the peoples that are fighting for their national liberation and their economic, political, and social independence. . . . We pledge to defend with our lives this heroic socialist and communist revolution. We make this pledge before our people and our Maximum Leader, Fidel Castro, Commander in Chief, whatever it may be, wherever it may be, whenever

has increasingly been toward that goal. In 1959 83% of all doctors (5,297) were in private practice while 17% (1,003) were employed by the state. Ten years later, 93% of the physicians (7,291) worked for the state while only 7% (709) were still in private practice. Some of these private practitioners were also employees of the Ministry of Public Health.[101]

To make up for the shortage of doctors, stress has been given to the development of medical assistants. These assistants, often young, are trained from two to seven months in hygiene and given the responsibility of looking after the health of ten to fifteen families in isolated areas. The auxiliaries also receive adequate supervision.[102]

The ranks of medical assistants have grown. From 1959–1969 over twenty thousand persons were trained as nurses, nurses' aides, or laboratory technicians.[103] Dental personnel does not appear to have increased in relation to the population. In 1960 there were 3.3 dentists for every 10,000 persons. Seven years later the ratio was 1.9 to 10,000.[104] Approximately 80% of the dentists worked for the state in 1968, 70% more than ten years earlier. Forty-five out of every hundred dentists worked in Havana province in 1967.[105]

Medical care is only for the people, and carried out with the direct participation of the people. From the very first years, the Revolution, realizing the urgency of the health problems, solicited the aid of the people. This is an exercise in social medicine. Citizens aid medical personnel in prevention, care, aftercare, sanitation, and mobilization. This participation is nationwide, and the fight against dis-

it may be, at your orders! Fatherland or Death. Venceremos." This pledge was read over *Radio Habana Cuba,* November 14, 1965.

[101] *Granma* (Havana), January 19, 1969, p. 2, and January 25, 1970, p. 2; Carlos Font Pupo, "Hacia la salud pública socialista," *Cuba Socialista* (Havana), July 1965, p. 4.

[102] Cuba, *Gaceta Oficial* (Havana), March 23, 1962, pp. 3592–3594.

[103] World Health Organization, Twenty-Second World Health Assembly, *Official Records,* Geneva, 1969, pp. 68–69.

[104] Organización Panamericana de la Salud, *Resumen de los Informes Cuadrienales sobre las Condiciones de la Salud en las Américas 1957–1960,* Washington, 1962, p. 96; and *Granma* (Havana), February 26, 1967, p. 6, January 19, 1969, p. 2.

[105] *Granma* (Havana), February 26, 1967, p. 6.

ease is enthusiastic.[106] Only such a break with tradition, despite criticisms to the contrary, has filled the vacuum of medical personnel. To have followed the old schemes would have meant not serving a portion of the people, something the Revolution refused to do. Service to all, even if quality suffered, took precedence.[107]

Government expenditure in health in 1968 was ten times higher than ten years earlier.[108] This figure, however, does not account for what was spent on private medicine, nor the change in the value of money. Nonetheless, from spending three pesos per person in 1959, the country invested twenty-three pesos in the health of each Cuban in 1968.

Public Health Budget[109]

Year	Total (In millions of pesos)*
1958	22
1959	25
1960	53
1961	82
1962	116
1963	118
1964	141
1965	148
1966	157
1967	204
1968	220
1969	236

* Includes running expenses and investments.

[106] Edward Rice, "Cuba: Services for All," *World Health* (Geneva), December 1968, pp. 14–16.

[107] This position has been supported by international health authorities. See Dr. Abraham Horwitz, "Agenda para la salud en las Américas," *Boletín de la Oficina Sanitaria Panamericana* (Washington), October 1970, p. 333.

[108] Divergent figures from those cited here appear in the various reports given by the Cuban delegation of the World Health Organization. Sometimes the figures are higher, sometimes lower than the ones appearing in our table.

[109] 1958: *Juventud Rebelde* (Havana), January 8, 1969, p. 2; 1959–1967: *Granma* (Havana), April 3, 1968, p. 6; 1968: *Bohemia* (Havana), January 2, 1969, p. 29; 1969: *Granma* (Havana), August 2, 1970, p. 2.

The Health of the Cuban People

The principal objectives of expanding the health sector under the revolutionary government have been to furnish medical services to all the people in order to improve their physical and mental well-being and prevent disease. In evaluating these efforts and the extent of any improvement, suitable indicators are called for. The most useful yardsticks are general and infant mortality, life expectancy, and the frequency of diseases.

1. General and Infant Mortality

On January 2, 1967, Fidel Castro stated that, "There are certain highly indicative figures showing what a revolution can mean to a country," adding that one of them is the annual death rate (the number of deaths per 1,000 persons). According to the Cuban official, "The annual death rate in our country was 13 in every 1,000 inhabitants" before the Revolution, and that figure had been reduced to 6.8. Castro challenged "any slanderer or smearer" of the Revolution to deny such progress.[110] The assertion, however, was misleading.

The crude annual death rate is a limited indicator of the level of health of a country, restricted by differences in the frequency of deaths in specific ages or sex of the population. Moreover, the Cuban Prime Minister was possibly using as a comparison of pre-revolutionary health an estimate made by the Economic Commission for Latin America for the years 1945 to 1954.[111] Yet it could be shown that the annual mortality rate[112] in the ten years before and after 1959 had

[110] Fidel Castro, "Aniversarios del triunfo de la revolución cubana." Havana: *Editora Política*, 1967, p. 239.

[111] The same report pointed out that from 1945 to 1960 the estimated yearly mortality rate was 12 for every 1,000 inhabitants, but Castro preferred to use the higher figure covering 1945–1954. See Comisión Económica para América Latina, *Boletín Estadístico de la América Latina*, Vol. VII, No. 1, October 1962 (supplement), Table IV.

[112] The *Population Index*, which obtains its figures from the United Nations, also presents divergencies with the Castro and CEPAL esti-

not changed at all, but remained 6.5 for every 1,000 inhabitants.

Mortality Rate Per 1,000 Population, 1949–1969[113]

Year	Rate
1949	7.5
1950	7.1
1951	7.3
1952	6.5
1953	6.3
1954	6.5
1955	6.1
1956	5.8
1957	6.3
1958	6.5
1959	6.6
1960	6.3
1961	6.6
1962	7.3
1963	6.8
1964	6.4
1965	6.5
1966	6.5
1967	6.4
1968	6.2
1969	6.8

The rates before 1959, however, should be taken with some reservation because less than 90% of all deaths were registered, and infants dying before registration of birth were not recorded. Since 1959 these shortcomings have been improved to a large degree. All infant deaths are noted, although it is possible that some people passing away in iso-

mates. The death rate given for 1950–1954 is 6.6/1,000 (in the July 1962, July 1966, and July 1969 issues). But the rate of 12 per 1,000 is also supplied (in the July 1964, July 1965 issues), and one version even offers a third figure, that is, 7 deaths per 1,000 inhabitants (July 1960). Similar contradictions appear for the period 1955–1959, all of which are also based on United Nations estimates.

[113] United Nations, *Demographic Yearbook*, New York, 1957–1969; Ministerio de Salud Pública, *Salud Pública en Cifras*, Havana, 1968; Cuba, Dirección General de Estadísticas, *Compendio Estadístico 1967*, Havana, undated; *Granma* (Havana), October 11, 1970, p. 11.

lated areas go unrecorded. Hence, it could be said that the death rate appears to have declined somewhat. But to pinpoint the extent, without making educated guesses, is simply impossible.

Cuba has one of the lowest mortality rates in Latin America. However, the number of total deaths has steadily increased, particularly after 1961, as the table below clearly indicates. This increment could possibly be the direct result of the upward trend in population growth.

Annual Number of Deaths[114]

Year	Total
1957	40,409
1958	42,508
1959	44,043
1960	43,164
1961	45,945
1962	51,579
1963	49,624
1964	47,922
1965	49,279
1966	50,472
1967	50,442

A more acceptable indicator of changes in the health of a people is the rate of infant mortality (deaths under one year of age per 1,000 live births). Underdeveloped nations show a high infant death rate due to the lack of services, low income, inadequate nutrition of parents, and bad hygiene. Whenever those conditions change, infant deaths decline.[115]

In comparing information on this important factor in Cuba, the analyst rapidly encounters several difficulties. First, as mentioned earlier, those children who died before they

[114] United Nations, *Demographic Yearbook,* New York, 1957–1969; Cuba, Dirección Central de Estadística, Junta Central de Planificación, *Compendio Estadístico de Cuba,* Havana, 1967; Lowry Nelson, "Cuban Population Estimates, 1953–1970," *Journal of Inter-American Studies and World Affairs,* July 1970, pp. 392–400.

[115] United Nations, *Report on the World Social Situation,* New York, 1969, pp. 23–24.

were registered as born do not appear in the records. Secondly, underregistration in the rural areas was previously widespread, presenting a lower infant mortality rate than actually existed.[116]

In the 1930's infant deaths comprised 18% of all deaths, and the rate per 1,000 live births was 76.[117] By 1958 it was reported that 33 in every 1,000 children died before reaching their first birthday.[118] Twelve years later the mortality rate of infants numbered 44.7 per 1,000, which is a significant increment.

Infant Mortality[119]

Year	Number	Rate (per 1,000 live births)
1958	5,906	33.0
1959	6,646	34.5
1960	7,604	35.4
1961	9,046	38.6
1962	10,389	39.8
1963	9,906	38.6
1964	10,136	38.4
1965	10,132	38.4
1966	9,597	37.6
1968	–	37.4
1969	–	44.7

How can this dramatic upward change be explained at the very moment when medical care seems more readily available? It is possible that registration has improved, giving the

[116] Oficina Sanitaria Panamericana, *Informe sobre el Progreso de la Investigación Interamericana de Mortalidad de la Niñez,* Washington, 1970, p. 2.

[117] O. Andrew Collver, *Birth Rates in Latin America: New Estimates of Historical Trends and Fluctuations,* Berkeley: University of California Press, 1965, p. 108.

[118] The rate of 125 deaths per 1,000 live births is given for 1950–1955 in Wyatt MacGaffey and Clifford R. Barnett, *Twentieth Century Cuba,* New York: Doubleday, 1965, p. 198, but such an estimate is too high.

[119] WHO, *World Health Statistics Annual,* Geneva, 1962–1970; WHO, *Third Report on the World Health Situation, 1961–1964,* Geneva, 1967, p. 129; United Nations, *Demographic Yearbook,* New York, 1969; *Granma* (Havana), November 23, 1969, p. 4.

appearance of more cases. It has often been pointed out that better statistics always follow better health services.[120] This explanation would mean that every year the statistical collection of the revolutionary regime has been greatly improved. Such a generalization, however, will not do. It appears that a deterioration in the health of children has taken place, primarily as the result of the scarcity of foodstuffs and medical products[121] (due to the blockade established by the United States and the inability of the Eastern European nations and the Soviet Union to supply enough). The quality of the medical personnel might also be another factor.

The children in the rural areas are still more prone to chronic and debilitating diseases. In 1969 the mortality rate of children under the age of one ranged from 34.3 per 1,000 in Havana province to 52.5 in Oriente.[122] A program of sanatoriums with intensive care and feeding units has begun to operate in the latter province. There are also nine thousand hospital beds in pediatric wards in the island.

In the 1960's 15% of Cuba's children were under five years of age, but the mortality rate in this group was still high, accounting for 23% of all deaths in 1963. Two years later the figure was lowered to 21%, but by 1969 had increased again to 24%.[123] The mortality rate of children between the ages of one and four has experienced little change.

To ascertain change by comparing the distribution of deaths by age in the 1950's and after is impossible. Accurate information for the years preceding 1959 is lacking. Suffice it to say, then, that infant mortality accounted for 19% of all deaths between 1959 and 1966. One quarter of all deaths in Cuba take place among those who are less than fifteen years old.

[120] George J. Stolnitz, "Recent Mortality Trends in Latin America, Asia and Africa," *Population Studies,* November 1965, p. 9.
[121] The lack of medicaments has been acute since 1961. *Granma* (Havana), November 27, 1966, p. 5.
[122] *Granma* (Havana), October 11, 1970, p. 11.
[123] WHO, *World Health Statistics Annual,* Geneva, 1966–1969; *World Health Organization Chronicle* (Geneva), January 1969, p. 31; *Boletín de la Oficina Sanitaria Panamericana* (Washington), January–June 1970, p. 33.

The distribution of deaths by age in the first seven years of revolutionary power has been the following:

Distribution of Deaths by Age, 1959–1966[124]

Age	Total Population (%)	Total Deaths (%)*
Less than 365 days	1.4	19.0
1 to 4 years	14.0	2.9
5–14	21.9	2.8
15–24	17.8	2.8
25–34	14.3	2.6
35–44	11.1	4.1
45–54	8.9	7.3
55–64	6.2	13.0
65–74	3.0	15.1
75+	1.4	28.0

* A difference of 2.4% due to deaths for which no age is specified does not appear.

When we turn to the main causes of death by disease, the picture for the 1950's showed that heart disease represented 19% of the total deaths, followed by gastrointestinal diseases (9%), tuberculosis (5.4%), arteriosclerotic diseases (5.4%), bronchitis (4.5%), vascular lesions affecting the central nervous system (4%), and diseases peculiar to early infancy (3%). All other illnesses accounted for the rest, but in percentages they were minor in importance.[125]

Infectious and parasitic diseases were the main illnesses affecting children. Deaths from these causes were tragic because they were preventable. Among them gastroenteritis was the most dread killer. In 1951 65 persons in every 100,000 died from it.[126] The rate was 43 per 100,000 in 1959, climbing to 51 in 1962.[127] Thereafter, the frequency has dimin-

[124] Unión Panamericana, *América en Cifras,* Washington, 1968; WHO, *World Health Statistics Annual,* Geneva, 1966–1969.
[125] Figures supplied represent only 1951.
[126] 1953 census.
[127] Organización Panamericana de la Salud, *Resumen de los Informes Cuadrienales sobre las Condiciones de Salud en las Américas 1957–1960,* Washington, 1962, p. 35.

ished for all ages, but whether caused by bacteria, viruses, or parasitic infestations, in 1964 these diseases were still the principal cause of morbidity in children, accounting for 80% of deaths under one year of age. Due to the high death rate a special program was instituted whereby the cases were taken, whenever possible, to special hospitals for rehydration. As a result of this program, in 1968 deaths from gastrointestinal diseases were 28.1 per 100,000 persons, or 16% of all infant deaths.[128] Moreover, while 7,000 persons died from diarrhea-related illness in 1958, ten years later the toll was 1,300,[129] that is, a decline of 64%. The rural areas, despite the improvement, are still the worst hit.[130]

Deaths from parasitism in 1965 accounted for 4.3% of the total, but the percentage was 22.8 for those under fifteen. Most of the deaths were children between one and four years old.[131]

Similarly, while deaths from respiratory diseases (influenza, pneumonia, bronchitis) had a rate of 44 per 100,000 persons, the rate among those who were less than one year was 546.3 deaths for every 100,000.[132]

It should be observed that more people over sixty years of age live today than before. In 1953 it was 6.9%. Eight years later the percentage was 7.2.[133] This slight betterment emerged from two factors. First, life expectancy, which had been fifty-seven years (1945–1960), jumped to sixty-seven years by 1969. Secondly, the increase in the number of people over sixty was the direct result of the baby boom in the early 1900's after the dramatic shrinkage of births between 1894 and 1898, during the war of independence against Spain.[134]

[128] WHO, Twenty-Second World Health Assembly, *Official Records,* Geneva, 1969, pp. 68–69; *Granma* (Havana), January 19, 1969, p. 2.
[129] *Granma* (Havana), January 19, 1969, p. 2.
[130] The infant mortality in Las Villas, for instance, in 1965 from gastroenteritis was 71.3% of all deaths. *Revista Cubana de Pediatría* (Havana), February 28, 1967, pp. 85–97.
[131] WHO, *World Health Statistics Annual,* Geneva, 1969, Vol. I, p. 584.
[132] *Boletín de la Oficina Sanitaria Panamericana* (Washington), November 1970, p. 402.
[133] *Radio Habana Cuba,* March 13, 1968.
[134] Carmen A. Miró, "The Population of Latin America," *Demography,* Vol. I, No. 1, 1964, p. 39.

2. Prevention and Treatment of Disease

The concept of health in the first five years of the Revolution was dominated by an emphasis on treatment and the availability of medical services to as many people as possible. In 1964 a shift took place from quantity and treatment to quality and prevention. Prevention and promotion of the people's health became the watchword. It was a natural second step after the material basis of health planning had been established through the expansion of facilities and personnel.

One of the main communicable diseases of Cuba has been intestinal parasitism. The International Bank for Reconstruction and Development reported in 1951 that between 80 and 90% of the children in rural areas suffered from the illness.[185] In 1956 a survey of rural families showed that at least 36% of them were aware they had parasites.[136] The following year a study of infants for whom medical aid was sought in public health centers revealed that 55% of those who were examined had parasites.[137] And in 1959 an exhaustive study made by public health authorities throughout the country discovered that 71.96% of all Cubans were afflicted with parasitism. In the rural zones the percentage was 86.54.[138]

Effective measures to curtail intestinal parasitism from 1959 to 1964 were few and minor.[139] Exact information on how many people have suffered from parasites since then is not available, but it appears that the frequency has declined dramatically.

Another preventable disease is tuberculosis, known as the "disease of the workers." Its principal cause, like parasitism, originates in miserable living conditions and lack of hygiene and medical care. In 1956 14% of the rural population suf-

---

[185] International Bank for Reconstruction and Development, *Report on Cuba*, Baltimore: Johns Hopkins Press, 1959, p. 441.

[136] *Por qué Reforma Agraria, op. cit.*, p. 28.

[137] *Boletín de la Oficina Sanitaria Panamericana* (Washington), September 1959, p. 259.

[138] Pedro M. Baeza, "Educación Médica en América," *Universidad de la Habana*, July–August 1962, p. 97.

[139] Carlos Font Pupo, "Hacia la salud pública socialista," *op. cit.*, p. 47.

fered or had suffered from tuberculosis.[140] Yet from 1954 to 1959 the average rate of vaccination was 43,245. Only about 10,000 children received the BCG immunization annually.[141]

With the Revolution, the reported cases of tuberculosis climbed, reaching in 1964 more than double the figure for 1958. That year a national tuberculosis control program was established. A massive campaign of vaccination and radiography was launched. Under the slogan "No truce against tuberculosis," anti-tuberculosis committees were formed in all neighborhoods, and extensive health education propagated. Over 90% of all children born in hospitals[142] are immunized, as well as all students in elementary schools, and close to 25% of the population over fifteen years of age. The number of deaths diminished from 1,402 in 1962 to 940 in 1967.

Malaria and poliomyelitis have been totally eradicated from Cuba.

Conclusion

It can be safely stated that health care in Cuba has undergone profound transformation. The government has taken the responsibility of promoting, protecting, and recovering the health of the people. Toward that end a quantitative growth in the personnel, facilities, and budget has occurred at the same time that the administration of health has been centralized and execution decentralized. Side by side with the free provision of medical care has been the active mobilization of the population to attain massive immunization, blood donations, the clearing of garbage dumps, and the cleaning up of large portions of the country. Rural medical services have dramatically improved the health of the country people. Yet nutrition and housing have undergone little change. Medical supplies are lacking, and the quality of the medical and para-

[140] *Por qué Reforma Agraria*, p. 28.
[141] *Pedro M. Baeza, op. cit.*, p. 97.
[142] Ninety-eight percent of all births took place in hospitals in 1969. It was 64% in 1962. *Granma* (Havana), October 11, 1970, p. 11.

medical personnel has been sacrificed for the sake of quantity. Infant mortality has increased while the crude death rate remains constant. The health of the Cuban people, then, in many respects, still awaits major improvements.

Part V

++

CULTURE AND REVOLUTIONARY IDEOLOGY

INTRODUCTION

Cuban intellectuals, from the outset, accepted and defended the Revolution. But they were fearful of witnessing in their country the tragic cultural policies imposed in the Soviet Union and Eastern Europe. Hence, their fundamental concern was not only to support the revolutionary experiment but to defend freedom of expression and creation. Aesthetic control by the state could not be allowed to establish its dogmatic roots in the fertile soil of literature and the arts.

At first the revolutionary authorities did not disagree with the views of the intellectuals. Artists and writers were considered revolutionary not because they wrote didactic works or painted pedagogical murals, but because they supported the Revolution and worked, as private citizens, in its behalf. Hence, a sort of peaceful coexistence bloomed between intellectuals and the state. Intellectuals were not immersed in political criticism, nor did the state enter the realms of making cultural policy. However, in 1961–1962 this state of affairs was shaken when the regime tried to impose socialist realism. After several skirmishes, an uneasy separation of politics and culture was preserved. The truce continued until 1968, when a change took place.

By 1966–1967 the revolutionary leadership had developed a system of well-defined goals and ideas. Economic development, already a passion, now was the ideological instrument for the total integration of the society. Strict discipline, hard work, and adherence to the new ideology became all-important. Under such conditions, questioning, criticism, and doubt were unthinkable. There had to be faith in the revolutionary leadership, and everyone had to subordinate to it. Intellectuals could be no exception.

The essay by Mario Benedetti discusses cultural developments until 1968, when the shift in the relations between the government and intellectual circles occurred. Since then an attack has been waged against the "anti-political" (i.e., critical) thought of writers and artists (see the Padilla poem).

In 1968, after receiving the Cuban Writers Union's annual prize, Heberto Padilla was subjected to criticism by *Verde Olivo* as well as by other colleagues. Since that time, his writings have been surrounded by controversy which culminated in his arrest on March 20, 1971, without charges and by personal order of Fidel Castro. His arrest brought an outcry from intellectuals around the world, including many who had been sympathetic to the Cuban Revolution.

On April 25, 1971, Padilla was released after agreeing to appear before UNEAC to read a self-critical statement in which he described himself with all of the adjectives utilized by his adversaries in the preceding years (counterrevolutionary, malignant, source of distorted information to foreign writers, and so forth).

In the context of Cuba's revolutionary process, Padilla is not the first intellectual to be gagged under charges of counterrevolution. In 1959–60, the usual explanation given by the revolutionary government was that "enemies" of the Revolution could not be allowed to undermine the regime, thus giving way to the right of criticism within the Revolution, a right which has now been denied to Padilla.

To be an intellectual, the Cubans argue, one must be a revolutionary. And to be a revolutionary one must not be concerned with aesthetic questions, or matters surrounding artistic freedom. The function of the intellectual is to contribute his work toward the development of the Revolution. Literature and art are the arms of combat against all weaknesses and problems that interfere in any way with revolutionary objectives. A revolutionary intellectual provides unconditional support to the men of power and aid in the mobilization of the masses, in transmitting objectives to them while exalting the accomplished achievements. The President of the Unión de Escritores y Artistas, the most powerful bureaucratic-cultural organization, has summarized the Revolution's views as follows:

> In a state of war everybody has to have a war mentality. We writers and artists cannot ignore such war. Just imagine a soldier in an invaded nation who in the midst of the battle decides to use his rifle to hunt ducks. He is an excellent marksman, his weapon is in perfect condition, he has enough ammunition, but he chooses the wrong target. Hence his effectiveness is nil, and because of his improper behavior he will end up before the firing squad. The Cuban writers and artists are no different from this soldier.[1]

At the root of this problem lies the conception of socialism and freedom of the revolutionary regime. These issues and their relationship are discussed by C. Ian Lumsden in his perceptive analysis of the ideology of the Cuban Revolution.

---

[1] *Granma* (Havana), December 2, 1969, p. 5.

21

PRESENT STATUS OF CUBAN CULTURE*

Mario Benedetti

Ten years have not gone by in vain, and during this period, which had its ups and downs, its mistakes, its success, its readjustments, and even an inevitable phase of sectarianism (luckily left behind around 1963), Cuban culture has produced its works and created its instruments, and the present article intends primarily to treat that inventory.

A small country, which annually publishes thirteen million copies of books, which has succeeded in shaping up a public who drains off in a few days, and sometimes in a few hours, issues of ten, fifteen or twenty thousand volumes (at the end of November, a printing of twenty thousand copies of *The Moonstone,* the classic by Collins, was sold out in less than one week), is obviously a country that has known how to create highly effective conditions and instruments. Let it suffice to recall that the first two hundred fifty thousand copies of the *Diary of Che in Bolivia* were out of stock in half a day (the total printing amounted to seven hundred thousand).

The literacy campaign carried out in 1961 and considered by the UNESCO technicians as an exceptional feat, forms not only the spectacular and almost incredible basis for those conditions and those instruments, but also it is the most amazing cultural achievement of the revolution. Suddenly, as if by magic, the Cuban writer (who, prior to 1959, had virtually no readers) is confronted with a public but also with prospects. Adults have been made literate and sometimes, although perhaps not to a considerable degree, they are up to the work

* Reprinted by permission from *Marcha* (Montevideo), December 27, 1968, pp. 16, 18–20, 32. Translation by Joint Publications Research Service, U. S. Department of Commerce.

of art; but there are especially the children who were approximately ten years old in 1961 and who now are already men and women eager for knowledge, the protagonists in a cultural escalation that, in addition to making them technicians and capable professional people, is turning them into the natural consumers of literature, drama, music, plastic arts, etc.

Education in Cuba is a simple, vital and impressive task. The big problem now confronting the Universities of Havana, Las Villas and Oriente is how to take adequate care of the avalanche of those who were children in 1959 and who today are filling their classrooms with a peremptory presence. On the primary, secondary and pre-university levels, the constantly serious problem of an insufficient number of teachers has been alleviated by making use of a means very little employed until now for educational purposes in Latin America: television. In the morning and first hours of the afternoon, Channel 6 televises class after class (all of a good pedagogical quality and with a superb technology adapted to the means of dissemination), and in this way instruction reaches the most remote places on the Island, since the appropriate television receivers were placed in advance in every center of population. And this is merely one more factor, an important one however, that is added to the groups of scholarship-holders disseminated over a large part of the nation's territory.

Education on so massive a scale (obligatory education will soon include the pre-university level) has created a craving for culture that cannot always be met by the present Cuban artists and intellectuals, and this is easy to understand: a culture is not improvised in a decade. Of course, there is always someone who demands great creations, legitimate masterpieces on the topics to which the revolution gives rise every day, and that, without doubt, is a demand that has not been fully met to date. And I am not referring only to meeting it ideally, the best way without doubt, which would be the work itself, but rather to meeting it with an explanation that will make impatient people realize that no great historic explosion has given rise simultaneously to pertinent masterpieces that concentrate on it at the precise moment of the outbreak. Several generations had to pass before the French Revolution, or the October Revolution, appeared reflected in artistic works of the highest quality. The newsman and the photographer are, in a certain sense, so fortunate as to be able to give their immediate testimony without hindrances or inhibitions, but the writer, and especially the novelist, usually need a distance in time that will provide them with sufficient perspective thus to convert the turbulent reality into a source of imagination, the status as a wound-torn protagonist into the status of a calm witness. There is a good reason that the best expression of the revolution appears in poetry, since poetry is a genre that usually thrives more on turbulence than on serenity.

Now then, perhaps it is true that Cuban culture has not produced, in these first ten years, the great revolutionary work to which so exceptional an experience and process have a right. However, there is an assemblage of creations, not exactly on revolutionary topics, that make up the artistic contribution of this critical decade. In 1966, on occasion of receiving the *Granma* Prize, the poet Luis Pavón (present editor of *Verde Olivo,* the magazine of the Revolutionary Armed Forces, which has been the focal point of a controversy in Cuban culture in 1968), said in a news interview: "I think that a poet expresses the revolution to the extent that he expresses his own life, in which he picks up in a poem the circumstances under which he is living, even though he does not intend to do that. The creator is a revolutionary. He works inside the revolution; he lives in it; he is not artificially encrusted in it; he is vitally identified with the revolutionary reality. I believe sincerely that a good book of poems, of short stories, a good work of drama or a novel are contributions to the building of socialism, even though they do not necessarily deal with the revolution as a topic in itself, although if they do treat it and do it well, the basis for our admiration is broader." There appears to be no justification for believing that this opinion has lost effectiveness.

For some creative artists, the revolution was an event that surprised them in full maturity but, at any rate, it meant a welcome and wonderful opportunity for revitalizing their art. Novelists like Alejo Carpentier; short story writers like Onelio Jorge Cardozo; poets like Nicolas Guillén, Lezama Lima, Eliseo Diego and Cintio Vitier; painters like Portocarrero, Amelia Pelaez and Mariano; musicians like José Ardevol, Carlos Fariñas, Juan Blanco, Harold Gramatges and Leo Brouwer; dancers like Alicia Alonso; scholars like Fernando Ortiz, who already had an established reputation in 1959, had the possibility, starting at that time, of reaching increasingly broader sectors of the public and most of them replied to that possibility with new creations. *El siglo de las luces* (The Century of Light), *Paradiso* (Paradise), *El gran zoo* (The Big Zoo), *El muestrario del mundo o libro de las maravillas de Bolona* (The Sample Book of the World or Book of the Wonders of Bolona), the poems assembled by Vitier under the subtitle of *Entrando en materia* (Getting into the Matter), the huge mural by Portocarrero in the Palace of the Revolution, the jovial *Serie de las frutas* (Series of the Fruit) by Mariano, as well as a large number of symphonic works with a revolutionary theme, have been appearing after 1959 and have been making up the culture of the revolution inexorably.

Perhaps where the process can be viewed most clearly is in painting (one of the two genres—the other is poetry—in which Cuba has always maintained a level of excellence). Of the artists who had a solid reputation in 1959, only one, Cándido Bermúdez, preferred exile, since Wilfredo Lam (who always has been on good terms with the revolution and who has visited Cuba on various occasions in these ten years) resided in Europe from the end of the decade of the forties. The others—Eduardo Abela, Victor Manuel, Portocarrero, Amelia Pelaez, Mariano, Martínez Pedro—remained in Cuba.

I have visited Portocarrero on more than one occasion in his sixth-floor apartment, from whose balcony it is possible to view the sea and also part of Havana, certainly less variegated and colorful than the Havana that appears in his painted cities. There, he has talked to me at length, with a retrospective humor, of his vicissitudes as a painter in various periods before the revolution; of his economic distress, of his haste to finish the job commissioned by some unscrupulous merchant, of the clutter in which it was necessary not only to live but also to paint. For anyone who believes that the artist has an obligatory need for poverty and anxiety as a nutrient medium for his creative work, there is Portocarrero to disprove that. From his present calm security, the painter has created new cathedrals, his women in blue, gray, green, his carnival figures, his various faces of Santa Barbara, his heads of Flora.

Perhaps Mariano Rodríguez, of that first group of painters, is the one who has best integrated himself with the revolution (and here I am not referring so much to the work as to the attitude toward life). I see him almost every day in the House of the Americas, where he directs the Department of Plastic Arts, so that it is easy to ascertain what he thinks about these topics. For example: what changes has the revolution brought in the work of the painters of his generation? "I do not believe that it is possible to speak of changes in the work. Perhaps a greater emphasis on what is Cuban, which already was the keynote that inspired us before the revolution. Note that among us there are none of those great universal themes that are shaking contemporary painting. For example, there is no distress. We can reflect the revolution in that way and in no other. The revolution enters our paintings with joy." I cannot refrain from recalling here an opinion expressed by Portocarrero: "The painter always knows what he has to do. Perhaps the hero does not trample on his own heart and go toward death in search of a total desire for perfection? Perhaps the painter also does not trample on his own heart and go toward joy—joy and death, in this case, are the same thing—in search of a total desire for perfection?" Why not ask Mariano about Portocarrero? "He is a baroque artist, of course. Before 1959, he had to his credit a series of searches (constructivism, surrealism, etc.) and he had even dealt with the topic of Havana, but he began to find the real city only when he reached the revolution." And what about Amelia Pelaez? "She sought for what is Cuban, but within the colonial element. She tackled the Cuban element with the solidness that the structure of the cubist pictures has. Do not forget that she spent seven years in Europe studying cubism." Lam? "Well, he is not a painter who is much a part of Cuba. There is no influence of Lam on Cuban painting. That is not the case with Carlos Enríquez. He really has had influence on it, since he made surrealism, but a Cuban surrealism. Lam, who is a noteworthy painter, incorporated in his work a Black theme (significantly voodoo and not Yoruba). Perhaps it may be said that he is Antillean, but not specifically Cuban." And what about your "Series of Fruits"? "That is the joy of which I was talking to you. In the revolution there is work (and how!) but also love and another series of factors. I relate fruit to work and to the figure. There is a sensual relation. In addition, I use space, enormous space. My enormous fruit is somewhat as if in the air, but always there is a small figure that supports it." Why do you not paint more roosters? "They bored me. Originally, that also was a sensual thing. I spent three years painting roosters. Everyone bought them from me. Then my roosters began to become commercialized, and it stopped. However, from time to time, I incorporate a rooster in some of my new themes."

Servando Cabrera and Carmelo González, who are of an intermediate group, work with topics of the revolution; González, with a certain surrealist spirit. Then comes the generation of Antonia Eiriz, Raúl Martínez, Antonio Vidal, Lesbia Vent Dumois, Corratge, etc. (There also is a dissident—Consuegra—presently in exile.) Some of them are trying to include the topics of the revolution in their painting. Raúl Martínez does so by utilizing pop; Antonia Eiriz, in expressionism; Vidal, in abstract expressionism; Corratge (like Martínez Pedro, mentioned above) works on bases of kinetics and constructivism. It may be said that they all work in accordance with the present trends. The youngest artists—Fernando Luis, Umberto Pena, Sosa Bravo, Acosta Leon and José Masiques (the last two prematurely deceased)—are enrolled in the most recent methods. The impact made by the visit to Cuba by the Argentine painter Antonio Seguí, who won the Grand Prize for Engraving in the 1966 Havana Exposition, is noted in some of them.

Teaching of painting has two outlets: the Cubanacan school, in which every trend of contemporary art is present, and the old Academy (known as San Alejandro), which has tried to rejuvenate itself but still retains the academic spirit. The influence of this second school on youth is considerably less than that of Cubanacan.

Anyone going through the Havana art galleries today does not have to ask the traditional questions on freedom of expression. Moreover, it seems impossible that Cuban painters have felt restricted at any time. "Nevertheless, that happened," Mariano told me, "and it was in 1963. It was not an official attitude, but rather of some civil servant who tried to set up interference to creative work, especially formal research. Fortunately, the revolutionary stand of artists and writers prevented that attitude from thriving."

Differently from painting, sculpture has a very limited development. There are barely two names to put down: José Antonio Pelaez and Tomás Oliva. Among the younger sculptors, there are Osneldo García and others coming from Cubanacan. In engraving they work especially in stone and somewhat less in wood. Most of the above-mentioned painters also devote themselves to xylography and lithography. It should be pointed out that the smaller degree of development (in comparison with painting) of sculpture and engraving is owing in part to the difficulty in obtaining materials.

It is evident that in the revolution there is a salutary intention to associate the people in some way with art and for that association to take place at a level of proven quality. That is not always achieved, but at least there are some aspects in which the miracle is taking place. Several months ago, an official of the House of the Americas was visiting a rural area with some foreign guests. A farmer heard them talking about art and artists and he ventured to say: "In my house I have a Mariano and a Portocarrero." And in its way, it was true: he had two boxes of crackers of a series that was designed by those and other Cuban painters. (The idea turned out to be so attractive that, a few days ago, a spontaneous design was received in Cuba sent by none other than Joan Miró, who, at the age of 75, also wants to reach the Cuban consumer on cracker boxes. Artists as famous as the Argentine Seguí, the Chilean Matta, the Spaniard Saura and the Peruvian Szyszlo had done so previously.)

But the two artistic products that have best been able to introduce themselves into the people's yearning are the poster and the motion-picture documentary. Both cultural posters as well as large signs and political propaganda murals (on topics like the sugarcane harvest, coffee planting, the Havana Greenbelt, etc.) are of an exceptional quality. Only Poland, among the socialist countries, can perhaps equal that level.

With regard to Cuban motion-picture documentaries, the spectator in Montevideo is very familiar with them, since films by Santiago Alvarez and other Cuban producers are usually the main course in the *Marcha* festivals. A week ago, the latest film by Santiago Alvarez—*LBJ*—opened in Havana. As is obvious, the title corresponds to the initials of Johnson, but also to the initials of Luther (Martin Luther King), Bob (Robert Kennedy) and Jack (John F. Kennedy), the three men killed who in some way mark the political career of the President. It should be added that the stories of the Vietnam aggressor and of the three assassinated men are suitably shuffled around by the producer. *Honni soit qui mal y pense.* Curiously, the film could not participate in the Leipzig Festival, because the admission board, in the German Democratic Republic no less, found political reasons to prevent its inclusion. At any rate, another Cuban, Octavio Cortazar, won the *Paloma de Oro* (Golden Dove) with a delightful short for the first time (it lasts only eight minutes), in which the reactions of children and adults are shown while viewing a Chaplin film, in a town in the middle of the mountains where no one had brought motion pictures up to that time. Needless to say, those virgin spectators went mad with amusement and one of them amused himself with his amusement.

But it is not worth entering upon a commentary on such-and-such a short. What I wanted to stress here was the remarkable communication with the spectator achieved by the producers of documentaries. As is well known, it is not always easy to grasp the style of the Cuban shorts. For example, the newsreels by Santiago Alvarez have a vigor, a subtlety, a

way of suggesting by the image more than by the word, and
require the spectator's entire attention and sensitivity. Very
well, the Cuban is so familiarized with this suggestive and
provocative style that by now he has no difficulty in assimilat-
ing any new nuance. Alvarez is truly popular. At any motion-
picture theater, when the running of the main film has
concluded, the people coming out are asked from the ticket-
window line: "Hey! Are they showing something of Santiago?" Because here the people sometimes go to the movies to
see the documentary or the newsreel by Santiago, and the
full-length feature only to fill in.

With regard to Cuban full-length films, until 1968 they
were much below the level of the shorts or of the newsreels.
La muerte de un burocrata (The Death of a Bureaucrat)
barely gave off its discreet sparks from the past. However,
ICAIC [*Instituto Cubano de Arte e Industria Cinematografica*
= Cuban Institute of Cinema Arts] has produced two first-
rate films: *Memorias del subdesarrollo* (Recollections of Underdevelopment), by Tomas Gutiérrez Alea, based on the
novel with the same title by Edmundo Desnoes, and *Lucia,* by
the young producer Humberto Solas. Another title could perhaps be added: *La ausencia* (Absence), by Alberto Roldán,
which, without attaining the level of the first two, demonstrates, however, the degree of technical and artistic self-
demanding attained by Cuban cinematography. The film by
Gutiérrez Alea undoubtedly deserves the various prizes that
it gathered at Karlovy Vary. Cuban cinema presents for the
first time a complex character, full of nuances and of likely
ambiguities.

The director obtained a first-rate performance from the
interpreters. Humor is introduced as a catalyzing and emphasizing factor, and in spite of the fact that the action frequently
takes place on a political plane (bear in mind that the de-
nouement occurs in the middle of the October Crisis), it does
not indoctrinate but rather suggests: the hidden power of the
omissions is almost as important as the common power of
what is in evidence. *Lucia,* which aims at being something
like the history of the Cuban woman, brings together three
portraits of three Lucias: one, in the height of the colonial

period during the period of the Mambis insurrection; another, at the time of Machado's fall; the third, during the year of literacy, 1961. Humberto Solas takes a revealing leap forward in comparison with his immediately preceding film, *Manuela,* which did not succeed in concealing a certain amount of professional inexperience, although it had a wholesome freshness. In *Lucia,* Solas has no inhibition about laying upon the table all his Fellini, his Bergman, his Glauber Rocha, his Antonioni, his Buñuel, his Resnais, but fortunately the film is much more than a confidence aloud about such sacred adorations. *Lucia* is still an uneven creation, which intelligent cutting (the film lasts almost three hours) might reduce to almost perfect dimensions, but in any event it includes definitely brilliant sequences, without doubt the best achieved up to now by Cuban motion-pictures. After this lesson in vitality and cinematographic culture (I explain that not even this second aspect has the appearance of pedantry but rather of youthful bewilderment), Solas virtually has available to him what perhaps is the most promising future in the talented team of the ICAIC. It is a question of a young man who is not yet thirty years old, but, at this stage in the game, who is amazed at what young people can do in Cuba?

The Cuban Institute of Cinema Arts has also become a center of great encouragement for musical creators. Most of the composers of serious music have collaborated with the ICAIC, especially with regard to matters concerning the documentaries. Electroacoustic experiments, both with regard to concrete music and to electronic music, have been started through the Institute's laboratories. Of course, this is only one of the cultural sectors that encourages the participation of music composers. At the same time as the composers work on the tasks of personal creation (symphonies, cantatas, etc.), and a good part of them make use of techniques belonging to dodecaphonic and serial music, they also perform a creative function that serves to put them in closer contact with the masses. Thus, they produce songs; they create music coming from folkloric sources (somewhat in the manner of Bartok); they work for the various ballet or modern dance groups; they turn out incidental music for the theater, the radio and television, replacing in that way the so-called made music, and they resort to the most advanced technique to do this. A symphonic composer told me: "I can just as well write a concerto as a *guajira.*" What matters is for the public to recognize the *guajira,* and that recognition probably serves to lay the bases for a subsequent enjoyment of more elaborate music.

A modern conception of music starts in Cuba with two names: Amadeo Roldán (1900–1939) and Alejandro García Caturla (1906–1940). Both died very young, barely a year apart, but their contribution was substantial. Actually, they belong to the generation that produced, in another field, a Carpentier, a Marinello, a Guillén; that is, they were part of the elite movement that occurred in the decade of the twenties. At the time of occurrence of this movement, this revision of values, the presence of Fernando Ortiz was in full force. The one who put things in their place with regard to the roots of the African trend when Roldán and Caturla died is José Ardevol (a Catalan, who became a Cuban immediately after his arrival). He picked up the legacy and became the center of a group that includes several of the most prominent composers in revolutionary Cuba: Edgardo Martin, Harold Gramatges, Hilario González, Argeliers León, Gisela Hernández. In the decade of the fifties, Nilo Rodríguez, Juan Blanco, Carlos Fariñas and (the youngest and one of the most talented) Leo Brower were added to that group. The most recent group includes Jorge Berroa, Carlos Malcom, Calixto Alvarez, Sergio Fernández, Roberto Valera, Antonio Balboa and Héctor Angulo. It is obvious that symphonic music does not have a large following in Cuba (in spite of the very low price of tickets to all cultural spectacles). It is hard to find the long lines seen for the movies, the ballet, the opera and at times the theater at the Amadeo Roldán, the hall in which the symphony orchestra appears traditionally. To what is that owing and how can it be remedied? The question was put to Harold Gramatges, one of the most active composers, technical music adviser to the National Culture Council and director of the Department of Music of the House of the Americas. "Up to 1959, there was a middle and upper bourgeoisie following, accustomed to symphony concerts. Starting with the triumph of the revolution, we have been trying to intensify the possibility of arranging concerts of a didactic nature and of turning the work of the musical organizations toward places where the masses are present. I am talking about places of agricultural, industrial and other work. New forms of promotion are being studied, and we have ascertained that the work of auditory education is being performed excellently by means of music in the motion-picture theater and on radio and television. I have had that experience personally in lectures and courses that I have given in various places. On talking about certain trends in contemporary music and on illustrating them with examples, I have found that in many cases that was not an unknown world to an audience that, nevertheless, was not specialized. Then I asked the audience and I was informed that they had already heard similar things in the movies, on radio or on television." What substantial difference has the revolution brought to music composers with regard to creative composition? "Before 1959, we were rarely called upon to participate in the cultural life; some rare occasion on which the symphony orchestra performed our works, some opportunity when we were asked to collaborate for the ballet, and no more. Now, on the other hand, there is real zeal on the part of the political leaders to have us contribute."

In speaking of other fields of art, I mentioned television. In Cuba, television still has much unutilized territory. However, if it is compared with television in Buenos Aires or Montevideo, the advantages are for Cuban television. And not only owing to a lack of commercial advertising (which already is a blessing). The teletheater frankly is good (a few nights ago I saw a very worthy version of *Barranca abajo* [Down Hill]); the news programs are always interspersed with prompt national and foreign takes; the shorts and documentaries are on so high a level that sometimes they can compete with the ones produced by ICAIC, and in general the cameras are handled with expertness and with a modern sense of framing. In addition, whenever an important foreign drama or ballet company comes, television sets up its cameras right in the hall and televises the spectacle to the whole island.

In the ballet, Alicia Alonso remains firm on her pedestal and on it, of course, she dances *Giselle*. A few weeks ago, she received in a full hall a monumental tribute in commemoration of the twenty-fifth anniversary of that creation. Alicia attended the apotheosis in full activity. She danced *Giselle* once more. To tell the truth, both she and Fernando and Alberto Alonso (director and choreographer, respectively) have been able to continue to train a new generation of dancers, which has already given four first magnitude names in the feminine sector: Josefina Méndez, Loipa Araujo, Mirta Plá and Aurora Bosch, each of whom already has her cohort of fans, who, although they admit Alicia's singular presence without discussion, dispute heatedly, on the other hand, concerning who follows her on the ladder of merits. Of course, they all forget their differences when it is necessary to express an opinion against the common enemy, the modern dance, a genre that has, however, good reasons to exist in the ensemble directed by Ramiro Guerra. The National Folkloric Ensemble is a chapter by itself. Smooth, well-conceived and well-dressed, it is an indispensable spectacle, and it signifies a good lesson in how to profit artistically from the rich Yoruba tradition. In addition, two schools are operating in Cubanacan: the school for classic ballet, headed by Ramona de Saa, and the school of modern dance, under the German Elfrida Mahler.

At this point, it is well to point out a factor that has been vitally important in the development and expansion of Cuban cultural life. I am referring to the congresses and cultural events that take place constantly on the Island. During this decade, the following have been held in Cuba: two international ballet festivals, one Latin American music festival, a protest song meeting on an international basis, six Latin American drama festivals, ten versions of the House of the Americas prize (without doubt the most famous literary contest in the Spanish-speaking world), seven events in the Havana Exposition (with prizes to which every Latin American engraver may aspire), the explosive May Salon brought from Paris with the widest variety of samples of the very latest trends in European painting, and especially the Havana Cultural Congress, which met early in 1968 and which was attended by five hundred intellectuals from all over the world and which can be criticized only because of the excessive number of Europeans.

More world-renowned cultural figures have passed through Havana in these ten years than in any other Latin American capital. I believe that it will suffice to mention a few names of the very first magnitude. In ballet: Mayya Plisetskaya, Patricio Bunster, Maurice Bejart. In music: Luigi Nono, Luis de Pablo, Peter Schat, Camargo Guarnieri. In painting: Siqueiros, Seguí, Matta, Saura. In the motion-picture: Godard, Joris Ivens, Zavattini, Agnes Varda, Tony Richardson, Francesco Rossi. Writers: Sartre, Leiris, Simone de Beauvoir, Regis Debray, Enzensberger, Graham Greene, Nathalie Sarraute, Semprun, Calvino, Marguerite Duras, Oscar Lewis, and among the Latin Americans, Cortazar, Aime Cesaire, Vargas Llosa, Fuentes, Neruda, Asturias, Parra, Martínez Estrada, Marechal, Arguedas, Manuel Rojas, Cardoza and Aragón. Drama: Weser, Gelber, Peter Weiss, Maria Casares, Alonso Sastre, and among the Latin Americans, Atahualpa del Cioppo, López Tarso, Antonio Larreta, Isidora Aguirre. For the most part, these creators stay at least several weeks in Cuba, during which time they grant interviews, give lectures or hold seminars. They live with the Cuban artists, are members of prize-juries, talk with the people, tour the Island, and as a logical result become familiar figures. In no other country in Latin America (and less so in Europe or the United States) can the people have important creators so much within reach. That closeness gives the people not only data for judgement but also confidence and the right to express an opinion when they hear that some of those names (for example, Neruda or Asturias) are not equal to their intellectual responsibility in their political attitudes.

Of all the cultural sectors in Cuba, perhaps the theater is the one experiencing a serious crisis at the present time. The first time that I came to Cuba, in 1966, there was sustained theatrical activity, with various good quality companies. On my second visit, in 1967, I saw a couple of high-level shows, like, for example, *Unos hombres y otros* (Some Men and Others), an adaptation of stories by Jesús Díaz, and *La noche de los asesinos* (The Night of the Assassins), by José Triana. An acceptable version of *Who's Afraid of Virginia Woolf?*, whose scenography is without doubt the best of the various versions with which I am familiar of the play by Albee, was still being billed at the beginning of 1968. But then came the collapse. Several of the groups divided and each of the sub-groups divided again. And it is well known what happens when a theatrical environment begins to disintegrate. Conflicts take on a hysterical tension, and there is not a Christian (or a Marxist) who is capable of righting the nuanced wrong. As a result, theatrical activity practically does not exist now in Havana, and this is all the more regrettable if it is realized that actually there are in Cuba directors, dramatists, interpreters and scenographers of an unmistakable professional quality. The only survivor of importance is the remarkable National Guignol Theater, an undertaking of a truly unaccustomed quality in Latin America. Under the increasingly more competent direction of Carucha and Pepe Camejo, the group continues to offer its good-humored spectacles in which imagination and lighting make the most of actors and puppets. With regard to dramatists, the following names should be indicated: Virgilio Piñera, Carlos Felipe, José Triana, Antón Arrufat, Héctor Quintero, José Ariza, Abelardo Estorino and José A. Brene.

In the specifically literary field, poetry is the genre in which most of the creative writers have been able to strike a better balance between their personal ambition and actual possibilities. From Nicolás Guillén (1902) to Nancy Morejón (1944), Cuban poets advanced in abundance toward a level of quality that will soon be, if it is not already so, the highest in Latin America. The vitality of the revolution is shaking not only the young writers but also the veterans. The situation in Cuba has taken a leap forward that was unforeseeable fifteen years ago, and the change in the environment has brought to the poet the felicitous consequence of a renovation of images. For example, in the poetry of Guillén, his last years of exile had turned rough joy into gray resentment. Now, inserted in his natural medium, comfortable in its color, installed in the revolution that always figured in his loves to be conquered, Guillén is rejuvenating; he is recovering a good-humored manner of creating images, and he has created that experimental prank: "the big zoo". The writers in the Origins Group (Lezama Lima, Eliseo Diego, Cintio Vitier), who have had a Catholic education that they have never reneged and surely will not renege, approach the revolution sometimes from the side, but one by one they are participating without violence, not in its ideology, it is true, but indeed in its work, in its style of justice. Lezama, in addition to bringing his poetry into an area of clarity (for example, in the clear ode to Julián del Casal) that he had frequented rarely before, has broken into Latin American narrative writing with so strange a novel as *Paradiso* (Paradise), and without going one millimeter away from his Havana and his asthma, he is settling himself and his 265 pounds in the boom. This is something that disconcerts many, but to Lezama himself it probably means nothing more than a subtle (and somewhat delayed) variant of social justice. Eliseo Diego, for his part, is choosing a succession of fixed topics (who could imagine that this acme of simplicity could become involved in an almost structuralist sense of literary creation?)—*Las viñetas de Bolona* (Vignettes of Bolona)—and on the basis of that intention he is opening up windows on the world. Cintio Vitier, finally, is right now at the culmination of a long process in his relations with the revolution. From mistrust he went to reticence, from reticence to anticipation, from anticipation to sympathy, from sympathy to participation. No one demanded that he hasten his pace. Cintio arrived by himself at poems so austere, honest and individual a commitment as "No me pidas" (Do Not Ask Me), "Estamos" (We Understand), "Clodomira", "La noticia" (The News), and others, from his most recent book: *Testimonios* (Testimonies).

The most active group is perhaps the group of those born around 1930—Roberto Fernández Retamar, Pablo Armando Fernández, Fayad Jamis, Heberto Padilla—and the younger ones—Cesar López and Luis Suardiaz. Of all of them, Retamar is the one who exercises a broader cultural action. Editor of the review *Casa de las Americas* (House of the Americas), university professor, essayist who moves ideas, he is above all a poet. Once I pointed out that the vital insertion of this writer into the contents (better still than in the forms) of the revolution makes his poetry come not from a monolithic man but rather from a complex being, not from an impoverished art of failures, but rather from someone enriched by a new, accessible aptitude for discussing problems of the situation. The fact that it has been realized in Cuba (much sooner than in most of the European socialist countries) that the two vanguards—the political vanguard and the esthetic vanguard—not only can but must "fertilize each other mutually" has contributed without doubt to an ennoblement of the artistic opportunity in that revolutionary environment, and also to a purification of Retamar's poetic task. Pablo Armando Fernández, with several books of poems published since 1959, curiously reaches his most fertile creative level, from a poetic point of view, with a voluminous novel, *Los niños se despiden* (The Children Take Their Leave), which won the 1968 House of the Americas prize. Fayad Jamis, a painter and poet with increasing influence among the young writers, edits the magazine *Unión* and from it he is cautiously delivering his new productions. With a surrealist past on which he has not entirely turned his back, Fayad is perhaps a romantic deep down, but a romantic who has gone through poverty, loneliness, hunger, various snows and various suns. Now, when his poetry is learning to smile, the reader cannot help feeling alluded to by that recently inaugurated joy. Heberto Padilla should also be discussed, but since various circumstances (Cuban and non-Cuban) have combined to turn him into the "Padilla case", he will be focused upon as such at the end of this article. The following are making themselves deserving of the greatest hope, in the most recent group: Miguel Barnet (with a streak of anthropologist, who so far has come up with an international best seller, *Biografía de un cimarron* (Biography of a Fugitive Slave), translated into several languages), Belkis, Cuza Male (not because of his published books, which are rather weak, but for his effective, latest poems, not yet gathered in a volume), Luis Rogelio Nogueras and the Negro writer Nancy Morejón, author of *Richard trajo su flauta y otros argumentos* (Richard Brought His Flute and Other Subjects), a delightful lyric report on the attractions and disappointments of a young (alas, temporarily) world.

As a sum total of works, narrative writing was, until very recently, far below poetry. (Today the distance has shortened considerably.) There was, of course, the masterly contribution of a Carpentier, *El Siglo de las Luces* (The Century of Light), and work without haste and without pause of an Onelio Jorge Cardozo. But the genre had had several deserters: Carlos Montenegro, Lino Novas Calvo, Calvert Casery, Severo Sarduy and (the most recent one) Guillermo Cabrera Infante. Not all display the same level, but at any rate some of those names had had a place in Cuban literature, and place also means surroundings. The surroundings (in which some excessively ingenuous people usually act) are precisely the ones that now are maladjusted. Fortunately, no maladjustment lasts a hundred years. Little by little, the naive people learn that a counterrevolutionary does not cease being one because of the mere fact that he is a writer.

A considerable rally has occurred in narrative writing in recent years. It is true that two of the novels (*Paradiso* and *Los niños se despiden*), which have best contributed to that recovery, are basically works of poets. It is also true that one of the most talented short story writers in pre-revolutionary Cuba, Enrique Labrador Ruiz, has remained in Cuba but has published virtually nothing in these ten years (his participation in the cultural life is limited to membership on some literary jury). However, a multifaceted veteran like Virgilio Piñera is continuing to produce short stories, novels and also drama at a good rate. In the group equivalent to the group of Fayad and Retamar are Edmundo Desnoes, José Lorenzo Fuentes, Lisandro Otero, Ambrosio Fornet, Francisco Chofre, Antonio Benítez, Humberto Arenal, Cesar Leante and the skillful, indefatigable David Buzzi, who submits in every literary contest at least a couple of works and who has just obtained the novel prize in the UNEAC [*Unión Nacional de*

Escritores y Artistas de Cuba = Cuban National Writers and Artists Union] contest. In the genre of the novel, so far the greatest credit should be given to writers like Lisandro Otero (from *La situación* [The Situation] to *Pasión de Urbino* [Urbino's Passion] there is a remarkable progression), Edmundo Desnoes, who is in a position to excel shortly over his widely read *Memorias del subdesarrollo* (actually the novel has already been excelled by the motion-picture scenario by Desnoes himself), a work in which, in spite of its undeniable merits, the author does not take every possible advantage of a character who, owing to the complexity of his nature, opens up a new vein to narrative writing under the revolution; and, finally, Francisco Chofre, author of *La Odilea* (The Odylley), in which an old myth (the Odyssey, of course) loaded with fascination and at the same time with the resultant rhetoric accumulated over the centuries, is revitalized in its passage through the humor and language of the people. The author's imagination, his epigrammatic conciseness, his verbal boldness (the wandering is constantly going over the imprecise border separating humor from blasphemy, devotion from disrespect) redeem the theme incessantly from the limitations of a mere parody to turn it into an amusing apotheosis of the best Cuban dialectal humor. The title of the tenth chapter is "About When Odylleus Continues to Unload." Perhaps it is possible to reach from that a more accurate definition of this singular work. Let us say that it is an epic turned into "Unloading."

In the short story, the author who is most gratifying and at the same time the most profound continues to be Antonio Benítez (two first prizes in less than two years: one from House of the Americas and the other from UNEAC). He is the author of a story that cannot be missing from any anthology, "Estatuas sepultadas" (Buried Statues), included in *Tute de reyes* (All Kings), and he has so imaginative an equipment that he takes his place at the head of the short story writers of his generation, with one single book published and another one to come out shortly. Benítez inserts the revolution in some of his stories in a fantastic manner. The mutual contamination enriches both elements and the result is unexpectedly attractive. Prominent among those born after 1940 is Reinaldo Arenas, author of *Celestino antes del Alba* (Celestino Before Dawn), a novel with a first half that is a lucid feat and a second part in which the initial freshness regrettably is lost and in which the author repeats himself. Of the younger short story writers, so far no one can snatch away the supremacy of Jesús Díaz, who came out of the unknown in 1966 with nothing less than the House of the Americas Prize, awarded to *Los años duros* (The Hard Years), which includes some stories (for example, the first three and the very short one entitled "With the Point of a Stone") that serve superbly to demonstrate how, when it is a question of an author with talent, the revolutionary point of view has no reason to be in contradiction with the highest degree of artistic strictness. Another House of the Americas prize-winner, Norberto Fuentes, has written, in *Condenados de condado* (The Condemned of Condado), some plain, very short, well-constructed stories in which he gives only one side, the antiheroic side, of the struggle against the counter-revolutionary gangs in El Escambray.

The most difficult genre is without doubt the essay. Some writers whose principal work is in narrative writing or in poetry occasionally tackle essay prose. That is the case with Fernández Retamar ("Papeleria" [Paper-work], "Ensayo de otro mundo" [Essay of Another World]), Edmundo Desnoes ("Punto de Vista" [Point of View]), Ambrosio Fornet ("En blanco y negro" [In White and Black]), Fina García Marruz. But there is no regular production of essays, similar to what happens, for example, in Mexico or on the Rio de la Plata. As a consequence of that scarcity, criticism (and not only literary criticism, but also drama criticism) has few followers, barely a book review section in magazines like *Unión, Casa de las Américas* or the *Gaceta de Cuba*. This is perhaps the only field of culture in which the revolution is at a manifest disadvantage in comparison with the period prior to 1959, since obviously the new Cuban essay has not succeeded in approaching the level of Fernando Ortiz, Medardo Vitier, Juan Marinello, Raul Roa, Jorge Mañach and Cintio Vitier. The latter is author of an exceptional work, *Lo cubano en la poesia* (The Cuban Element in Poetry), probably the most brilliant attempt at poetic interpretation to have been made in Latin America.

It is likely that precisely that weakness in criticism observed in Cuban culture after 1959 has something to do, at least as an indirect cause, with the recent tensions that have appeared in the literary environment. In the South Cone of Latin America, every creative writer is aware that at any time—justly or unjustly—he may be flogged by criticism, and any way this generates not exactly a custom (one never becomes accustomed to being flogged) but indeed a normality of clear accounts. In Cuba, the few times on which someone establishes his disagreement with any work, the circle is shocked, the archway of the group shivers. It is odd to observe that a country that has turned armed struggle into little less than a gospel should display, nevertheless, in cultural circles a complete lack of being accustomed to critical aggressiveness. Recently, there have been two occasions on which that aggressiveness has had public manifestation. Oddly, both occasions had as their protagonist the poet Heberto Padilla. On the first occasion, as an aggressor; on the second, as the one aggressed.

It is well to go into detail on the data of this story, since the present conflict has been picked up tendentiously by the news agencies and it has caused some alarm among the European intellectuals, or the Latin American ones residing in Europe. The recent data are the following: last October, the Cuban Writers and Artists Union convoked Cuban writers, as it does every year, to a literary contest in which prizes are awarded in poetry, the novel, the short story, the essay, drama and biography. The pertinent juries, which included several foreign members, issued their decisions. There were no problems in most of the genres; there were some in drama and poetry. In drama, the work by Antón Arrufat, *Los siete contra Tebas* (The Seven Against Thebes), obtained three of the five votes. In poetry, the work by Padilla, *Fuera del juego* (Out of the Game), achieved unanimity. It was a question of two works against which the executive board of UNEAC drew up serious ideological objections. Finally, it was determined to respect the decision of the juries and consequently to award the prizes and publish the books, but in the special case of the two questioned works, it was decided that they should be published with a double opinion attached: the favorable one and the one by UNEAC. That was not the end of the matter. A series of articles that no longer were unfavorable but rather frankly aggressive against Padilla and Arrufat began to be published in the magazine *Verde Olivo*, official organ of the Revolutionary Armed Forces (which has been including a book review section for some time now). Two later articles (signed, like the first ones, by Leopoldo Avila) draw away from the personal attack and refer rather to most general aspects of Cuba's literary activity, without abandoning the aggressive tone.

The news agencies immediately echoed the most forceful parts of Avila's articles. Since he suggested in them that Padilla was playing into the hands of the counter-revolution with his poems, the well-intentioned Associated Press immediately deduced that this could mean nothing less than the poet's execution by shooting. In Paris, *Le Monde* announced pompously: "Fidel breaks his truce with the intellectuals." In Europe, the not-too-distant Stalinist past has not been forgotten by writers and artists, and any news like this always makes them bristle, because it appears to them to be the announcement of a generalized persecution. Oddly, the Latin American intellectuals residing in Latin America were not alarmed as much: they still trust the Cuban Revolution more than the Associated Press or the Voice of America, the broadcasting station that rejoiced in announcing that Padilla and Arrufat were in prison. The truth is that both writers enjoy freedom, and any foreign visitor encounters no difficulty in interviewing them and in learning their opinions. For example, Padilla recently granted an interview to the Associated Press, in which he makes that evident and in which he clearly recognizes a newsman's right to express an opinion—even caustically—against the work of a writer. Moreover, the two books in question have already been turned over to the printshop and I understand that they will come out shortly.

I have not had access to Arrufat's text. On the other hand,
I am familiar with Padilla's poems. It is a question of a work
of undeniable literary quality, and besides I do not believe
that it can be described as counter-revolutionary. However
it is an ambiguous, conflicting and bitter book. After reading
it, one is left as after one of Bergman's films; that is to say,
with one's spirit in one's feet. In any event, what one regrets
is the fact that a poet with Padilla's obvious standing has not
achieved a better communication with so stirring a social and
political phenomenon as the Cuban Revolution. It is impossible to avoid a certain feeling of discouragement on seeing
that a young man, a talented and sensible intellectual, does
not have a more understanding attitude toward the revolution. And I say this without tarrying too long over Padilla's
protests to the effect that the poems interpreted as counter-
revolutionary or something like that do not refer to Cuba
but rather to the Soviet Union; and I do not tarry over it
precisely because it seems to me possible that those who see
in Cuba an unjustified recipient of those darts are not completely misguided. (Of course, in addition the generalized
warning attributes counter-revolutionary intentions to other
poems with innocent metaphors.)

Now then, is the fact that the book includes criticizing
poems sufficient reason to unleash those chain attacks against
Padilla? After all, Fidel himself, in his "Words to the Intellectuals," provided the rule, some years ago, that has governed since then in Cuba the limits of artistic freedom:
"Within the revolution, everything; against the revolution,
nothing." Just where does that border pass? Are Padilla and
Arrufat inside it or outside? In the now famous letter sent
to Quijano[1] ("Socialism and Man in Cuba"), Che tacitly
encouraged the function of the intellectual to criticize when
he pointed out the following in concrete reference to intellectuals and artists: "We must not create wage-earners docile
to official thinking." Recently, a high Cuban official stated
to several foreign juries these words, more or less: "We admit
criticism within the revolution perfectly, but to exercise that

---

[1] Editor of the Uruguayan weekly *Marcha*. (Eds.)

right it is first necessary to win it." Is it then possible that what really matters in the Padilla case is the writer's attitude and not so much the letter of his poems? Finally, what was that attitude?

I explain that I ask (and I ask myself) those questions so that the reader may become aware that the problem is not as simple as some intellectuals residing in Europe seem to have understood it through the news disseminated there. And it is not so simple, especially because the story does not begin with the UNEAC contest but rather several months before. At the end of 1967 and the beginning of 1968, a bitter polemic took place on the pages of *El Caimán Barbudo*. There, Padilla debated, on the one hand, with Lisandro Otero, the well-known novelist who holds the vice presidency of the National Culture Council, and, on the other hand, with the team of young intellectuals who were editing that publication at that time. It all started with an inquiry concerning *Pasión de Urbino*, a novel by Otero. In his replies, Padilla took advantage of the opportunity not only to attack that novel violently but also to attack Otero as an official and to defend with an ardor and brilliance worthy of a better cause the personality of Guillermo Cabrera Infante, an individual who at that time had not yet given out the ridiculous and not very proper opinions that he sent later to *Primera Plana*[2] but who already gave the appearance—in his procedure and his associations—of being a worm [counter-revolutionary], and not precisely a silkworm. Among other things, in defending Cabrera, Padilla attacked State Security, but that was not disseminated either by Associated Press or by *Le Monde* at that time. When the self-unmasking of the author of *Tres tristes tigres* (Three Sad Tigers) occurred, Padilla was left in a frankly unattractive position. His friend came from London and through Buenos Aires to prove that Lisandro Otero, the *El Caimán Barbudo* team and, of course, State Security were right.

It is impossible to know what would have happened if the book *Fuera del juego* had as its author any other poet who

---

[2] Argentinian weekly. (Eds.)

did not have that background. But it really is easy to imagine that a background like this had importance in the reaction caused by that book (a completely unaccustomed reaction to what had been the style of the revolution in this field).

I explain personally that I cannot agree with many of the terms and concepts handled by the writer of the articles in *Verde Olivo*. Likewise, I confirm that, in my opinion, the text of Padilla's book cannot be considered as counter-revolutionary. Nevertheless, I believe that an intellectual should be a realist and should judge events on the basis of that realism.

Let the reader give a moment's thought to the extraordinary effort involved in taking a small country out of underdevelopment. Such a feat depends not only on good intentions. In order to get out of underdevelopment, so huge an effort is needed that there is no material stimulus that can serve as an effective and adequate lever. The only formula must combine a maximum effort with minimum cost. How can this be achieved except by instilling in the masses the famous revolutionary mystique, the ethical quality of effort, the only stimulus capable of making the people work overtime voluntarily without extra pay or of making a very large number of Havana bureaucrats go to the countryside for short or long periods thus to help the country effectively to rise up and to become more and more independent? An extraordinary power of conviction is needed and, in addition, that power must be backed up every day by a constant example. Today, the Cuban people are highly politicized. The leaders have succeeded in transmitting to them their undeniable conviction and they have done so primarily through their behavior. But the truth is that this osmotic feat has required, as is logical, an extraordinary effort. Now then, Padilla's book, regardless of how limited the action range of a poet may be, enters into the events to break up—even extremely slightly (for these purposes it does not matter whether consciously or not)—that collective state of mind that it has taken so much hardship to create. Therefore, it is at least understandable that someone who causes that discouragement should not be viewed with sympathy precisely by those who have done everything possible, and everything impossible, to infuse a powerful social spirit, to infect the people with their own revolutionary tenacity.

The size of this domestic conflagration must not be exaggerated either. After all, Padilla is a mere episode in a greater tension. On an international scale, his name has been handled purposely as a "Cuban Pasternak" and an attempt has been made to stir up in the European and Latin American intellectuals in the boom (by chance they are all residing in Europe) an appropriate panic with regard to a possible restoration in Cuba of the socialist realism that had withered away, as the only official artistic trend. On a strictly national basis, the Padilla affair takes on more modest proportions, and at present the controversy seems to be approaching a more enlightening stage. I point out, however, that at this time any personal opinion, like the one that I am expressing here, can only be provisional, since new data and factors are appearing every day that are enriching the collation of versions and at the same time are making any prognosis difficult. What seems clear at any rate is that with regard to the admission and dissemination of various trends artistic freedom will suffer no restriction whatsoever. The latest fact in this regard appears precisely in the recent speech delivered by the Minister of Education, José Llanusa, in the first graduation ceremony of the National Art School: "It will be necessary to discuss with those who are concerned about freedom of expression and to ask them to what freedom they are referring. Our revolution defines a line. There is no discussion on esthetic expression, but rather on how art serves the people, their happiness, their cultural development. There is complete freedom to do this."

If some prognosis can be made at this stage, it is that from now on perhaps there will be a stronger social pressure on intellectuals to participate in the revolution. Many of them had already done so, and to a considerable extent, thanks to their effort, the activity of organizations like ICAIC, House of the Americas, the National Culture Council, the Institute of the Book and UNEAC itself takes place. For the most part they are artists who report voluntarily for agricultural work and who do their duty in the citizen militia. On the other hand, others defended virtually the right to contemplate the work of others and nevertheless to live on it. But a revolution has, in its turn, the right not to put up with that kind of contemplative people and even to be unjust toward them. A revolutionary event is no parlor game, but rather dilemma and tearing apart, breaking and impulse, but it is also the only opportunity (and watch out when it is lost!) that a human being has for participating in a collective assumption of dignity.

22

FUERA DEL JUEGO

Heberto Padilla

¡El poeta, despídanlo!
Ese no tiene aquí nada que hacer.
No entra en el juego.
No se entusiasma.
No pone en claro su mensaje.
No repara siquiera en los milagros.
Se pasa el día entero cavilando.
Encuentra siempre algo que objetar.
¡A ese tipo, despídanlo!
Echen a un lado al aguafiestas,
a ese malhumorado
del verano,
con gafas negras
bajo el sol que nace.
Siempre
le sedujeron las andanzas
y las bellas catastrofes
del tiempo sin Historia
Es
    incluso
        anticuado.
Sólo le gusta el viejo Armstrong.
Tararea, a lo sumo
una canción de Pete Seeger.
Canta,
    entre dientes,
        La Guantanamera
Pero no hay

quien le haga abrir la boca
pero no hay
quien le haga sonrier
cada vez que comienza el espectáculo.

OUT OF THE GAME

The poet, get rid of him
He has nothing to do around here
He does not play the game
Lacks enthusiasm
He does not make his message clear
does not even notice the miracles.
He spends the whole day thinking
Always finding something to object to
That fellow, get rid of him
Remove the party-pooper
the summer malcontent
who wears dark glasses in the new dawn
He always was seduced by adventures
and the beautiful catastrophes
of time without History
He is even out of date
He likes only the old Louis Armstrong
Humming, at most, a song of Pete Seeger.
He sings the "Guantanamera" through clenched teeth
But no one can make him talk
No one can make him smile
each time the spectacle begins.

23

THE IDEOLOGY OF THE REVOLUTION*

C. Ian Lumsden

Cuba's size and location have affected the course of its revolution from the outset. Its small population and scarce natural sources of power are major obstacles to the achievement of its ambitious economic goals. The impact of Soviet aid, of decisive importance in minimizing the hardships of the revolution, has been much greater than it would have been if Cuba had been a larger country. Cuba's position as an island isolated from the mainland of Latin America has also conferred mixed blessings. The Caribbean has impeded American attempts to overthrow the revolution, but it has also impeded Cuba's attempts to export it to neighbouring Latin American countries. Cuba's isolation has made it easier to consolidate the revolution; it also poses a claustrophobic threat to the humanism that differentiates its socialism from that of the Soviet Union and Eastern Europe.

Although reluctant to do so at first, Cuba now accepts that its limited resources prevent it from becoming economically self-sufficient in the foreseeable future, and that it must remain uncomfortably dependent upon Soviet aid.[1] It counterbalances this economic dependence by zealously upholding its right to political sovereignty and by propagating a distinctive revolutionary ideology.

Ideology, Fidel Castro insists, recognizes no national boundaries to its influence. Within Cuba it strengthens popular

* From C. Ian Lumsden, "The Future of Castroism," *International Journal*, Summer 1969, pp. 545–558. Reprinted by permission of the *International Journal* and the author.

[1] Castro acknowledged the "decisive" character of Soviet aid on 2 January 1969. *Granma Weekly Review* (*GWR*), 5 January 1969.

resistance to the political pressures that undoubtedly accompany aid from other members of the communist camp;[2] without, it is a means of combating Cuba's isolation in the western hemisphere. This policy has led to increasing friction with the Soviet Union and with those Communist parties that are associated with it.[3] In fact, Cuba's relations with the Soviet Union have deteriorated to the extent that speculation has been aroused with regard to the possibility of an open rupture between the two countries. The Tri-Continental Conference and the First Conference of the Organization of Latin American Solidarity (OLAS), which took place in Havana, have been interpreted by some observers as indications that Cuba is about to sponsor a third bloc within the international communist movement.[4] It seems unlikely, however, that Cuba would be willing in the final analysis, to endanger its economic development which will hinge upon continued Soviet aid and trade for the foreseeable future, merely because of ideological differences.

Cuba's ideology diverges most conspicuously from that of the Soviet Union with regard to the revolutionary strategy that should be pursued in underdeveloped countries, particularly those in Latin America. The strategies prescribed by the leaders of the Cuban revolution have attracted a number of adherents amongst Latin American revolutionaries but, in practice, have achieved few concrete gains so far. It is evident that their effect upon the vast majority of the Latin

[2] See Andrés Suárez, *Cuba: Castroism and Communism, 1959–1966* (Cambridge, Mass., 1967); evidence of the activities of a pro-Soviet "microfaction" was produced during the much publicized trial of Aníbal Escalante (*GWR,* 11 February 1968).

[3] Carlos Rafael Rodríguez, a member of the Communist party secretariat, asserted at the time of the Escalante trial that it was "impossible to neglect this situation any longer, one in which a whole series of functionaries and members of socialist organizations (and) socialist countries, work against the Cuban Revolution here and in their own countries" (*GWR,* 11 February 1968). See D. Bruce Jackson, *Castro, the Kremlin and Communism in Latin America* (Baltimore, 1969). At the same time the Central Committee announced Cuba's decision to boycott the 1968 Budapest conference of Communist parties.

[4] See John Gerassi, "Havana: A New International is Born," *Monthly Review,* XIX, 5 (October 1967), 22–35; Robert Alexander, " 'Third Force' in World Communism?" *New Politics,* VI (winter 1967), 72–9.

American people, and the conditions in which they live, has been negligible.

The insurrectionary strategy associated with Castroism has been most clearly articulated by 'Che' Guevara and Régis Debray.[5] It asserts that violent revolution is the only means left for underdeveloped countries to use in securing their national independence and economic development. In consequence, revolutionaries have an obligation to begin guerrilla warfare as the best means of initiating the armed struggle. All other revolutionary activity must be subordinate. Since the need for violent revolution, according to the Castroist analysis, has been dictated by the global character of American imperialism, the struggle must acquire a transnational dimension from the outset. A further assumption is that, since the present Communist parties in Latin America have virtually abdicated their vanguard roles, the leadership of the revolutionary struggle must fall to those revolutionaries who, in practice, actually begin to "make the revolution,"[6] that is, the guerrillas.

The attraction of the strategy advanced by the Castroists is that the Marxist concept of historical determinism is displaced by the idea of immediate revolutionary action. Orthodox Marxist-Leninist analysis, at least as portrayed by the existing Communist parties, appears to offer no ready solution to the desperate plight of the Latin American masses. The experiences of the Cuban revolution and the National Liberation Front in Vietnam, in contrast, suggest that revolutionary will may overcome insuperable odds. They provide a powerful argument for those impatient students and alienated intellectuals who reject the cautious behaviour of the local communists and the pragmatic foreign policy of the Soviet Union, and who claim the right to represent the real interests of the

[5] See, in particular, "Guerrilla Warfare: A Method" and "Vietnam and the World Struggle for Freedom" in George Lavan, ed., 'Che' Guevara Speaks: Selected Speeches and Writings (New York, 1967); Régis Debray, Revolution in the Revolution (New York, 1967); see also "O.L.A.S. General Declaration," International Socialist Review, XXVIII (November/December 1967), 50–60.

[6] One of the main slogans of the Cuban revolution is taken from the Second Declaration of Havana. "The duty of every revolutionary is to make revolution," Obra Revolucionaria, No. 5 (1962), p. 23.

masses. The greater the obstacles to change, the more strident become their demands for action rather than theory. The Castroists have yet to demonstrate, however, that their revolutionary zeal will be matched by practical results. In fact, their strategy may be based upon an incorrect premise, that is, that the Guevara model of guerrilla warfare is applicable elsewhere in Latin America at the present time. Guevara's three-point thesis stated that popular forces could defeat a standing army, that an insurrectionary focal centre could create the necessary revolutionary conditions where they were otherwise not fully present, and that the countryside must be the main terrain for armed struggle in Latin America.[7] Guerrillas have attempted to apply this model in various countries without much success. Their failure may be due to their having ignored the principal prerequisite for guerrilla warfare laid down by Guevara: guerrilla warfare can only be initiated after a régime has given up all pretence of "constitutional legality."[8] It is doubtful whether any of the countries (with the exception of Guatemala) that have witnessed significant guerrilla activity could be placed in this category. Yet such archaic dictatorships as those of Haiti, Paraguay, and Nicaragua have experienced little revolutionary violence. Brazil, too, is a strange exception.

Recent experience in Latin America suggests that Cuban conditions may have been quite exceptional and that alternative strategies will have to be developed for the rest of Latin America.[9] For example, the fantastic migration of peasants to the cities suggests that violent revolution may find its main focus in the urban slums rather than in underpopulated hinterlands. However, this possibility was deliberately ruled out by the Cuban delegation to the OLAS conference. It denied the relevance of the "classical model of European revolution" to Latin America and insisted that "the basic situation that can produce the vanguard in the revolutionary struggle is not the city but the country."[10]

---

[7] 'Che' Guevara, *Guerrilla Warfare* (New York, 1961), p. 15.

[8] *Ibid.*, p. 16.

[9] See *Régis Debray and the Latin American Revolution,* special issue of the *Monthly Review,* XX (July–August 1968).

[10] Cited by Sergio de Santis, "The O.L.A.S. Conference," *International Socialist Journal,* IV (1967), 714–15.

Ultimately, the prospects of specific revolutionary movements will hinge upon their ability to attract the support of the masses. In this respect, ideology becomes one of the key mobilizing factors. In contemporary Latin America it seems highly unlikely that a serious revolutionary movement could have other than an explicitly socialist ideology. Nationalism may provide an initial Sorelian myth that arouses popular passions,[11] but neither Latin America's parasitic bourgeoisie nor the United States (as was made clear by its intervention in the Dominican Republic in 1965) is prepared to allow it to acquire a truly revolutionary momentum. They recognize that nationalism, in current circumstances, has a natural tendency to merge with revolutionary socialism. Consequently, since the issue of socialism is raised willy-nilly by those committed to the maintenance of the status quo, a revolutionary movement has little alternative but to espouse it from the outset. Thus, there is one crucial difference between the Cuban revolution and prospective revolutions elsewhere in Latin America. In Cuba, mass support for a *socialist* revolution came after the seizure of power; elsewhere, it will have to come before the seizure of power. In this respect, the region's general image of the Cuban revolution, the only socialism directly experienced by it, will influence the possibility of forging a revolutionary consciousness amongst the masses.

The pro-Cuban demonstrations that occur from time to time should not blind one to the fact that the majority of Latin Americans are, at present, either indifferent or hostile to the Cuban revolution. Castroism has elicited a positive response from only a small minority of the population. The ruling classes have been successful in containing its appeal which is, essentially, restricted to student radicals, intellectuals, and some working-class elements. Their number reflects the traditional strength of the left and the prevailing ideological spectrum within each country rather than economic factors, for the so-called objective conditions for revolution clearly exist throughout Latin America. It is by now quite evident

[11] Donald J. MacRae, "Nkrumahism: Past and Future of an Ideology," *Government and Opposition,* I (October 1966), 537.

that the Cuban revolution has not succeeded in animating
Latin America's exploited peoples, the peasants and urban
masses to whom the Second Declaration of Havana was so
confidently addressed. Latin America's negative attitude towards Castroism is related to the success (even if temporary)
of the counter-revolutionary strategies devised by the United
States in response to the Cuban revolution; it is also based
upon ignorance of its achievements within Cuba, and upon
prejudices that have been diffused by the mass media. The
continuing emigration of large numbers of Cubans further
undermines the arguments of those who uphold the revolution as a model for the rest of the region.

The sociological character of the Cuban emigration reflects
the economic and political difficulties that the Cuban people
are now having to experience. At the outset, the overwhelming majority of the population supported the revolution,[12]
but this support has gradually waned as a result of the hardships imposed by the American economic boycott and the
increasing demands made of its people by the Castro régime.[13] The enormous investment in education, agriculture,
and in the infrastructure of rural Cuba, hopefully the basis
of a rapid expansion of the gross national product in the
1970s, has been made possible not only by Soviet aid, but
also by depressing material living standards in Havana. The
consumption of food and clothing, in particular, has been
restricted while increased effort is continually demanded of
the labour force.

Those Cubans who tend to feel most deprived by the régime's policies of economic austerity, that is, the better-off
urban inhabitants, also tend to be the most articulate critics
of the régime's political institutions. Their criticisms are not
without some foundation, for Cuba has yet to demonstrate
that it has developed democratic political procedures within

[12] See Robert Scheer and Maurice Zeitlin, *Cuba: An American Tragedy*
(London, 1964), pp. 171-2.
[13] The emigrants still under-represent the peasantry and the unskilled
working class but many more lower middle-class employees and skilled
workers are now among their number. See Richard R. Fagen *et al.*, *Cubans in Exile: Disaffection and the Revolution* (Stanford, 1969).

its revolutionary institutions.[14] In theory the Communist party is democratically organized and Cubans as a whole may participate in the nomination and selection of party members. In practice, however, only a fraction of the population relates to the party's activities in a meaningful way. Admittedly, many more people are active in such mass organizations as the Committees for the Defence of the Revolution (CDRS) and the Federation of Cuban Women. The CDRS, in particular, play an important role in involving the Cuban people at the grass-roots level in such community matters as education, health, and social services. On the other hand, it remains to be seen whether the régime will permit unions to become effective vehicles for expressing the felt needs of labour at the work site, and if it will be able to develop a viable form of local government that will lead to increased popular participation in its activities.

Until now Cuba has had little success in combating the autocratic tendencies that appear in the politics of virtually every communist country. Decisions continue to be made from above and implemented below. The revolutionary slogan "Comandante en Jefe, ordene" epitomizes Cuba's charismatic style of government. It is not surprising in the circumstances that many Cubans experience a sense of political constraint and alienation. Though Cubans are permitted to express criticism of the revolution, many do not feel free to do so in public. They fear that criticism, even if constructive, will be defined as counter-revolutionary in intent.[15] This is not an unreasonable belief in view of the fact that, particularly since the departure of Guevara in 1965, the mass media have ceased to articulate different points of view. As a result, no public dialogue involving coherent alternatives takes place with regard to governmental policies. The masses are expected to take their cues only from the person of Fidel Castro. The political cynicism that can ensue from this state of affairs

[14] An informative analysis of one institution, the Union of Writers and Artists (UNEAC), is offered by David Gallagher, "The Literary Life in Cuba," *New York Review of Books*, X (23 May 1968), 37–41.

[15] Castro's speech on 28 September 1968 (*GWR*, 29 September 1968), attacking liberalism and counter-revolutionary ideas in general, would not be likely to assuage such fears.

C. Ian Lumsden

is reflected, for example, in the attitudes of Catholics. The church enjoys considerable freedom, yet many Catholics feel that their religious beliefs are an impediment to their becoming fully integrated in the revolution.[16]

The Castro régime has been able to counterbalance these negative aspects of the revolution by stressing its immense achievements in the fields of education and public health and in the elimination of seasonal unemployment. Their impact upon the circumstances of the unskilled urban masses and the rural proletariat and peasantry, in themselves a majority of the labour force,[17] cannot be ignored even by those Cubans who have not received material benefits from the revolution. The régime's defence of Cuba's national sovereignty against external pressures emanating respectively from the United States, the Soviet Union, and China has also evoked a very popular response, particularly from Cuba's youth which comprises over 40 per cent of the population.[18]

Cuba has evidently been able to discard Latin America's traditional inferiority complex, still so evident in Mexico's chauvinistic brand of nationalism, for example, and replace it by a modern, yet autochthonous culture. Paradoxically, however, in vitalizing the Cuban people, the revolution has also made many of them aware of the price they are having to pay for the attempt to build socialism in one small island. In consequence, the exodus of disaffected Cubans is not likely to cease in the foreseeable future. Since the Castro régime cannot afford to ignore the impact these *émigrés* have upon Latin America's image of the revolution, it should re-examine the causes of their disaffection and soften the harsh conditions attached to their departure from Cuba. Permitting *émigrés* to return on visits to Cuba would be one way of tempering their bitterness towards the Castro régime and in time, perhaps, of conveying information about Cuba's progress to the rest of Latin America.

[16] See "Cuba: The Church Attempts a Rapprochement," *Latin America*, II (23 February 1968), 57–8.

[17] Maurice Zeitlin, *Revolutionary Politics and the Cuban Working Class* (Princeton, 1967), p. 277.

[18] It is estimated that 39 per cent of the population will be under 15 years of age in 1970 (*GWR*, 24 March 1968).

As it enters the second decade of its revolution Cuba finds itself in an uncertain position. In spite of Latin America's economic stagnation and the deteriorating living standards of large segments of its rural and urban populations, Cuba's prospects for breaking out of its regional isolation are not nearly as bright as they appeared in the early 1960s. In fact, the immediate prospects for revolutionary changes elsewhere, and for guerrilla warfare, in particular, look bleak everywhere in Latin America. The Soviet Union's policy of increasing its trade with Latin America by offering credits to such key states as Chile, Argentina, Brazil, Colombia, and Venezuela, and its increasing impatience with "ultra-leftist adventurist groups"[19] does not augur well for Castroist revolutionaries. The Paris peace talks and the Soviet reaction to Richard Nixon's victory in the American presidential election strengthen the impression that Moscow continues to be committed to its policy of peaceful coexistence with Washington. Accordingly, Cuba is unlikely to succeed in persuading the Soviet Union or those communist parties loyal to it in Latin America that the moment is at hand to pursue a revolutionary offensive in the western hemisphere. The crisis in Czechoslovakia, too, may lead the Soviet Union and its Eastern European allies to concentrate more on tending their own domestic affairs than on furthering revolutions in the underdeveloped world. There is no reason to suppose that they will share Fidel Castro's belief that the root causes of Czechoslovakia's "counter-revolutionary situation" were the very same quasi-bourgeois policies which are increasingly being pursued within their own countries.[20] For them to do so would imply reversing their present "revisionist" economic policies and attempting to instil in their people a genuine revolutionary consciousness.

The Cuban revolution may be the vanguard of the changes that will ultimately revolutionize Latin America. But now Cuba must pay the price for such a role. Politically isolated,

[19] *Globe and Mail*, 21 November 1968; see Jackson, *Castro, the Kremlin and Communism*, pp. 134–42.

[20] See speech of 23 August 1968 (*GWR*, 25 August 1968).

and economically handicapped by its dependence upon one distant trading partner, a great power whose intervention in Czechoslovakia bolstered its imperialist image, Cuba finds itself in circumstances that undermine its attempts to establish for the rest of Latin America that its future lies in Castroism. It is no longer a question of exporting its revolution, but of preserving its distinctive qualities for a decade, or perhaps longer, until its capital investments in agriculture and education really begin to pay off. Only then will Cuba have succeeded in demonstrating beyond doubt that its revolutionary socialism offers Latin America a viable and preferable alternative to capitalism under the hegemony of the United States.

In the meanwhile, the ideology of the Cuban revolution disseminated in the speeches of its leader, Fidel Castro, must continue to function as one of the principal means by which the loyalty of the Cuban masses can be retained despite the material hardships that they will undoubtedly continue to endure during the next decade. Cuba's ideology seeks to counterbalance the impact of the shortages of food and other products by stressing the greater importance of political consciousness; it accounts for the former by emphasizing the enormous obstacles that impede the development of the entire underdeveloped world, and it promises dramatic economic growth for Cuba once technology has been harnessed to the country's needs.[21]

It is not easy to define Castroism,[22] for its emphasis lies on action rather than theory. Admittedly, its underlying principles are purportedly Marxist-Leninist, but its distinctive character really stems from Castro's dictum that Marxism is above all else "revolutionary thinking and action," and from his insistence that socialism depends upon the development of "human awareness" as much as "material wealth."[23] This

[21] Castro's speech on 26 July 1968 (*ibid.*, 28 July 1968) contains a good synthesis of the political beliefs that are currently stressed in his speeches.

[22] Castro himself denies the relevance of the term. *Obra Revolucionaria*, No. 4 (1963), p. 21.

[23] Speech of 13 March 1967 (*GWR*, 19 March 1967); speech of 9 December 1967 (*GWR*, 17 December 1967). Castro contends that you cannot create "political awareness with money or with wealth." On the

latter belief, even more than the strategy of guerrilla warfare, symbolizes Che Guevara's contribution to Castroism. For Guevara, socialism entailed man's conscious decision to master his environment for the benefit of all humanity. He did not delude himself into believing that Cubans were naturally predisposed towards such altruism. On the contrary, he recognized that it would have to be deliberately nurtured by the revolution. Thus "to build Communism, you have to build new men as well as the new economic base."[24]

Every domestic policy implemented by the Castro régime is ideologically linked to the creation of this new socialist consciousness. This has led, with regard to the economy as a whole, to official stress upon moral incentives rather than material incentives, and to the rejection of the market as a planning device.[25] "Voluntary" labour campaigns at the height of the *zafra* and the involvement of much of the urban population, including women and children, in part-time agricultural work typify Cuba's approach to the economic development of its natural resources. Voluntary agricultural work is regarded as a means of combating the traditional urban disdain for rural life and as a means of inculcating a new social attitude to labour. The régime's determination to eliminate notions of profit and personal gain as social stimuli was dramatized by its decision to terminate the remaining private businesses in 1968, even though it must have been a very unpopular action.[26] Increasingly, moreover, the régime has attempted to combat the appeal of private property by adding to the range of the basic necessities, such as housing, public utilities, education, and medical care, which are provided free of charge.

Above all else, Castro is attempting to build a new generation of Cuban socialists that will identify itself with the plight

contrary, you create "wealth with political awareness." 26 July 1968 (*GWR*, 28 July 1968).

[24] "Notes on Man and Socialism in Cuba," in Lavan, ed., *Guevara Speaks*, p. 126.

[25] Edward Boorstein is particularly informative on the question of incentives. *The Economic Transformation of Cuba* (New York, 1968), pp. 252–89.

[26] See Castro's speech of 13 March 1968 (*GWR*, 24 March 1968).

of the underdeveloped world in general, and which will commit itself to a long and arduous revolutionary struggle as the only means of freeing the underdeveloped world from its present dependency upon the developed world (including Eastern Europe). Cubans are socialized from an early age, particularly in the schools, in preparation for a lifetime commitment to struggle and sacrifice. Their mettle is continually tested by involvement in ever more demanding tasks. One "revolutionary offensive" unremittingly follows another. The attempt to make Havana agriculturally self-sufficient by creating a green belt around it is the most recent example of the régime's dramatic mass mobilization campaigns. Another example is the former Isle of Pines, renamed the Isle of Youth, where tens of thousands of Cuba's youth have been set the task of remaking the agricultural landscape and of creating a model communist community in which, from the outset, there will be no place for money as a basis for human relations.

The Cuban response to the predicament of underdevelopment has so far been both revolutionary and pragmatic. It has sought and accepted technical assistance and economic credits from many countries including Britain, France, and Spain, while refusing to admit the possibility of restoring normal relations with the United States, which it considers the bastion of imperialism. Although Cuba formally addresses itself to concrete domestic problems in terms of Marxism-Leninism akin to the official ideology of the Eastern European countries, in practice it has shown itself to be non-dogmatic and innovative in its capacity to apply this type of analysis to the exigencies confronting the revolution.

Castro contends that communists are distinguished by how they actually behave in "action and struggle" and not by their adherence to specific revolutionary theories. He has increasingly stressed, in this respect, that Marxism must rid itself of its old dogmas and even of some "falsehoods." "Marxism needs to develop, to break away from a certain rigidity, to interpret today's reality from an objective, scientific viewpoint, to conduct itself as a revolutionary force and not as a pseudo-revolutionary church."[27] This attitude may account for Cuba's seeming reluctance to draft a new constitution, to hold its first Communist party congress, or even to publish an official Marxist-Leninist manual. Castro continues to believe that the "best textbook in matters of revolution will be the revolutionary process itself."[28] One student of the Cuban revolution has suggested that its Marxism has become no more than "the heuristic principle for making revolution."[29] In fact, Castro is alleged to have admitted on one occasion that the Cubans "don't talk very much of Marxism any more."[30] This has important implications, since the future of Castroism in Latin America may well be linked to Cuba's willingness to break completely free from any formal association with the ideological straightjacket that has imprisoned many other communist countries.

Cuba's problem is that it must retain the libertarian humanistic character of its revolutionary socialism in circumstances that increasingly militate against it. Even if Cuba's economy expands rapidly in the next decade,[31] it must still contend with the enormous political pressures that ensue from its small size and geographic isolation. Since Cuba is unlikely to win many converts to its ideological position within the Eastern European countries, it becomes even more important that it succeed in breaking down its regional isolation within Latin America. A starting point, in this respect, would be to recognize that the image that Castro had of communism in 1959 is precisely the one that is held by the rest of Latin America today: that "capitalism starves people to death, [while] Communism . . . resolves the economic problem, but

[27] Speech of 13 March 1967 (*ibid.*, 19 March 1967); speech of 13 March 1968 (*ibid.*, 24 March 1968); speech of 12 January 1968 (*ibid.*, 21 January 1968).

[28] Speech of 28 September 1967 (*ibid.*, 8 October 1967).

[29] Irving Louis Horowitz, "Cuban Communism," *Trans-Action*, IV (October 1967), 9.

[30] John Gerassi, "The Spectre of 'Che' Guevara," *Ramparts*, VI (October 1967), 30.

[31] 1969 has been named the "year of decisive endeavour," but everything suggests that Cuba will have to face at least a twelve-year period of decisive endeavour. See Castro's speech of 2 January 1969 (*GWR*, 5 January 1969).

suppresses the liberties which are so dear to man."[32] The
recent domestic and external behaviour of the Soviet Union
buttresses these Latin American prejudices against communism. Cuban socialism is quite different to Soviet communism;
nevertheless, it is far from persuading Latin America that
this is the case.

One possibility that Cuba might consider would be to
identify its official ideology so as to differentiate it explicitly
from Soviet communism (perhaps by adopting some name
such as revolutionary socialist humanism[33]) and to permit it
to discard some of the more inane and self-defeating dogmas
of communist orthodoxy. An obvious example is the belief
that, since the ruling Communist party represents the proletariat, any dissent must be bourgeois or counter-revolutionary
in origin. It is this myth that prevents Castro from truly coming to terms with the continued heavy migration from Cuba
—a migration which has much to do with Cuba's external
image.

Cuba's explicit liberation from the mythology of communism might lead it to re-examine the whole concept of the
vanguard party and the political institutions that are associated with the European communist countries. For example,
Cuba has yet to develop institutions which permit popular
participation in decision-making, and which encourage a political dialogue amongst the masses. Mass mobilization campaigns are not the same as political participation. What is
disturbing is Cuba's unwillingness to encourage reasoned
public discussion with regard to the political experiments that
have taken place in other socialist countries, ranging from
Yugoslavia to China. In the final analysis, the libertarian
character of the revolution depends upon democratizing its
political institutions and permitting conflicting points of view
to be represented in its presently simplistic, propaganda-laden
communications media.[34] Cuba could also profitably reex-

[32] *Revolución*, 22 May 1959.

[33] Such a name would be more compatible with the Latin American
political tradition, and yet, in all probability, not so offensive to the
Soviet Union that it would terminate its economic aid.

[34] This possibility seems remote at present. See Castro's speech of 28
September 1968 (*GWR*, 29 September 1968). The extinction of *El Mundo*

amine the relationship of Catholicism to a professed communist ideology. The failure to do so makes nonsense of Castro's references to an alliance between Marxists and honest Christians[35] and ignores the implications of the deep-rooted appeal of Catholicism to the vast majority of Latin Americans, as well as the widespread debate that is taking place within the church with regard to its attitude to revolutionary changes in the western hemisphere.[36]

It is not easy to be sanguine about the future of Castroism in Latin America. However much one may empathize with the overall objectives of the Cuban revolution, the fact remains that their realization ultimately depends upon a vast increase in Cuba's productivity and the revolution's extension to adjoining Latin American countries. The achievement of its economic goals remains problematic;[37] likewise, the possibility of Cuba succeeding in exporting its revolution appears uncertain. In contrast to the United States which seeks to enforce the status quo, and the Soviet Union which accommodates itself to it, Cuba can offer those who seek to overthrow the existing régimes nothing beyond its example and an insurrectionary strategy—and at that, one that has yet to demonstrate its viability.

From the outset, Castroism has contained an irrational, romantic element within it. There is a real danger that this element may be the undoing of the humanistic qualities that presently differentiate it from Soviet communism. Cuba persists in an unequal struggle against the world's two great powers and most of their respective allies and dependencies; the pursuit of this ultra-revolutionary strategy may lead the

---

in April 1969 means that Havana is now served by only two party newspapers, *Granma* and *Juventud Rebelde*, the organ of the Young Communists (UJC).

[35] Speech of 5 January 1969 (*ibid.*, 12 January 1969).

[36] See "Colombia: Communists among the Bishops?" *Latin America*, III (7 February 1969), 46–7; "Brazil: Is the Church a Subversive Organization?" *Latin America*, I (24 November 1967), 244–5.

[37] Cuba is committed to achieving a 10-million-ton sugar harvest in 1970. This is twice as large as its 1968 harvest, and Castro has implied that the 1969 harvest may fall short of expectations. See speeches of 30 January 1969 (*GWR*, 2 February 1969) and 13 March 1969 (*GWR*, 16 March 1969).

régime to become increasingly self-righteous and to demand even more revolutionary commitment and material sacrifices from the Cuban masses.[38] Such a policy could yet result, paradoxically, in Castroism acquiring a repressive character. It therefore becomes all the more urgent for Cuba to proceed with the democratization of its institutions and the liberalization of its political climate.

[38] See Charles Bettelheim, "On the Transition between Capitalism and Socialism," *Monthly Review*, XX (March 1969), 8–10.